New Zealand

WORLD BIBLIOGRAPHICAL SERIES

General Editors:
Robert G. Neville (Executive Editor)
John J. Horton

Robert A. Myers   Hans H. Wellisch
Ian Wallace   Ralph Lee Woodward, Jr.

John J. Horton is Deputy Librarian of the University of Bradford and was formerly Chairman of its Academic Board of Studies in Social Sciences. He has maintained a longstanding interest in the discipline of area studies and its associated bibliographical problems, with special reference to European Studies. In particular he has published in the field of Icelandic and of Yugoslav studies, including the two relevant volumes in the World Bibliographical Series.

Robert A. Myers is Associate Professor of Anthropology in the Division of Social Sciences and Director of Study Abroad Programs at Alfred University, Alfred, New York. He has studied post-colonial island nations of the Caribbean and has spent two years in Nigeria on a Fulbright Lectureship. His interests include international public health, historical anthropology and developing societies. In addition to *Amerindians of the Lesser Antilles: a bibliography* (1981), *A Resource Guide to Dominica, 1493-1986* (1987) and numerous articles, he has compiled the World Bibliographical Series volumes on *Dominica* (1987), *Nigeria* (1989) and *Ghana* (1991).

Ian Wallace is Professor of German at the University of Bath. A graduate of Oxford in French and German, he also studied in Tübingen, Heidelberg and Lausanne before taking teaching posts at universities in the USA, Scotland and England. He specializes in contemporary German affairs, especially literature and culture, on which he has published numerous articles and books. In 1979 he founded the journal *GDR Monitor*, which he continues to edit under its new title *German Monitor*.

Hans H. Wellisch is Professor emeritus at the College of Library and Information Services, University of Maryland. He was President of the American Society of Indexers and was a member of the International Federation for Documentation. He is the author of numerous articles and several books on indexing and abstracting, and has published *The Conversion of Scripts and Indexing and Abstracting: an International Bibliography*, and *Indexing from A to Z*. He also contributes frequently to *Journal of the American Society for Information Science*, *The Indexer* and other professional journals.

Ralph Lee Woodward, Jr. is Professor of History at Tulane University, New Orleans. He is the author of *Central America, a Nation Divided*, 2nd ed. (1985), as well as several monographs and more than seventy scholarly articles on modern Latin America. He has also compiled volumes in the World Bibliographical Series on *Belize* (1980), *El Salvador* (1988), *Guatemala* (Rev. Ed.) (1992) and *Nicaragua* (Rev. Ed.) (1994). Dr. Woodward edited the Central American section of the *Research Guide to Central America and the Caribbean* (1985) and is currently associate editor of Scribner's *Encyclopedia of Latin American History*.

VOLUME 18

New Zealand

Brad Patterson
and
Kathryn Patterson

Compilers

CLIO PRESS

OXFORD, ENGLAND · SANTA BARBARA, CALIFORNIA

DENVER, COLORADO

British Library Cataloguing in Publication Data

Patterson, Brad
New Zealand – Rev. ed. – (World bibliographical series; v. 18)
1. New Zealand – Bibliography
I. Title   II. Patterson, Kathryn
016.9'93

ISBN 1–85109–279–X

ABC-CLIO Ltd.,
Old Clarendon Ironworks,
35A Great Clarendon Street,
Oxford OX2 6AT, England.

ABC-CLIO Inc.,
130 Cremona Drive,
Santa Barbara,
CA 93117, USA.

Designed by Bernard Crossland.
Typeset by Columns Design Ltd., Reading, England.
Printed in Great Britain by print in black, Midsomer Norton.

THE WORLD BIBLIOGRAPHICAL SERIES

This series, which is principally designed for the English speaker, will eventually cover every country (and some of the world's principal regions and cities), each in a separate volume comprising annotated entries on works dealing with its history, geography, economy and politics; and with its people, their culture, customs, religion and social organization. Attention will also be paid to current living conditions – housing, education, newspapers, clothing, etc. – that are all too often ignored in standard bibliographies; and to those particular aspects relevant to individual countries. Each volume seeks to achieve, by use of careful selectivity and critical assessment of the literature, an expression of the country and an appreciation of its nature and national aspirations, to guide the reader towards an understanding of its importance. The keynote of the series is to provide, in a uniform format, an interpretation of each country that will express its culture, its place in the world, and the qualities and background that make it unique. The views expressed in individual volumes, however, are not necessarily those of the publisher.

VOLUMES IN THE SERIES

For Richard, who waited patiently while his parents were distracted.

Contents

Contents

Contents

Contents

Contents

Contents

Introduction

For the greater part of the present century New Zealand, most distant of English-speaking countries, has presented itself as a somewhat staid, albeit green, outpost of Europe. Stereotyped as a supplier of food and raw materials to more industrialized countries, it has been better known internationally for its millions of sheep than for the activities of its people. Though sometimes hailed as a 'social laboratory', a country where developed welfareism assured citizens of lifelong personal security, it has also been depicted as a country strangled by regulation and red tape. An inherent conservatism in outlook has been discerned, encompassed in the standing joke of the overseas visitor who arrived at a weekend and found the country closed. While the uniqueness of Maori culture has been recognized, some quaint semblance being carried to the world through postcards, calendars and posed tourist photographs, the derivative cultures of the country's European peoples have received scant attention. The All Blacks, the national rugby team, have provided probably the nearest approach to a global cultural icon. In the words of current British MP, and former New Zealand university lecturer, Austin Mitchell, writing in 1972, New Zealand was the 'half-gallon quarter-acre pavlova paradise'.

From the early 1980s all this changed, there being strenuous attempts to project a very different image to the world. While the immediate catalysts for change were successive post-1984 political administrations – of nominally different hue but ultimately of the same New Right ideological stamp – backed by a nascent business elite and reforming technocrats, all largely drawn from the post-war 'baby boom' generation, the transformation proceeded with the enthusiastic support of international commentators. As early as 1985 an *Economist* correspondent was enthralled by New Zealand's 'exhilarating dash for economic freedom'. The early structural reforms, initiated by a Labour government, were described as 'a free-market experiment in socialist sheep's clothing'. He could remember no economic experiment he had been more eager to see succeed. These paeans were echoed in subsequent years by the World Bank, the OECD (Organization for Economic Co-operation and Development) and other like-minded guardians of the global economy. Though the reforming text borrowed both from Thatcher's Britain and Reagan's America, and bore a startling resemblance to structural adjustments imposed on Third World governments, new twists were added in the Antipodes. There was a breathless desire to be 'world leading'. Moreover, while the initial emphasis was on economic reform, reforming zeal eventually extended to all facets of New Zealand life. No field of endeavour was considered exempt; no institution sacred. New Zealand, the country, became New Zealand Incorporated. By 1996 the 'half-gallon quarter-acre pavlova paradise' had become, at least to the mind of expatriate journalist John Ruck, 'the cross-leased chardonnay cell-phone paradise', although strong doubts were harboured as to whether these manifestations were widely shared, and consequently whether the appellation 'paradise' still held much meaning.

This bibliography, while attempting to capture the flavour of traditional New Zealand – New Zealand as it was as distinct from as it is now – places particular emphasis on the documentation of recent changes. Hence it may be regarded as updating, rather than completely superseding, Ray Grover's first edition in this series (1980). In many respects the two bibliographies should be used in conjunction. Only a few entries from the earlier volume – acknowledged classics, or those works providing pertinent background information not elsewhere available – have been retained. The recent emphasis has also been dictated by the effusion of New Zealand publishing since 1980. In 1981 books and monographs published in New Zealand, or relating to New Zealand, totalled 1,588. By 1990 the tally was 5,237. In subsequent years this figure has continued to climb steeply. A rough calculation indicates that over 77,000 titles have been produced since the appearance of the first edition of this bibliography. To place this output in perspective, A. G. Bagnall's five-volume *New Zealand National Bibliography to the year 1960* (this, and other works mentioned below, are listed in the main body of the current bibliography) contains around 33,000 entries, less than half the output of the past 17 years. Coverage in this edition extends to June 1997.

The torrent of New Zealand publications since 1980 clearly poses logistical problems for the bibliographer. Even if the availability of modern finding aids, for example the *New Zealand National*

Bibliography (published monthly since 1967), facilitates the identification of potential individual entries, the necessity to examine and evaluate each against other possible titles remains. When, through the publishers' understandable strictures, the total number of entries is severely constrained, the bibliographers' predicament becomes the more acute. On many occasions in the selection process there has been little to differentiate between several, often more, closely related titles. In such cases there is inevitably an element of subjectivity in choice, the ultimate selections being determined by the bibliographers' personal knowledge of the field, by the advice of specialists, in the most difficult instances by close comparisons. What is certain is that many titles omitted, perhaps twice as many as those in the final selection or more, could appropriately have been included. That they have not, is due rather more to an embarrassment of riches than to deficiencies of quality. Care has also been taken to ensure as wide and as representative a coverage of views as possible. This accounts for the inclusion of a number of titles which might under different circumstances have been omitted.

Why more New Zealand books have been published in the past two decades than ever before is a nice question. It might be speculated that New Zealanders have been more impelled to comment on their changing country, whether in praise or derogation of the changes, perhaps through nostalgia for days past; but in the absence of research this must remain speculation. Perhaps more importantly, technological advances have made the writing and production of books easier and cheaper. The advent of the word-processor, later the personal computer, appears to have encouraged budding authors. More than 100 specialist book publishers now provide outlets for a range of local markets. There has been a tendency towards shorter runs of more titles. The 1996 *New Zealand official yearbook* reports that New Zealand titles by commercial and university publishers have increased by more than 100 per cent in the last 10 years. Self publishing has become more possible and more respectable. Whatever the source, a strong demand for New Zealand books clearly exists. The Commerce Commission has estimated that around NZ$160 million worth of books was sold by retail booksellers in 1993. Books published in New Zealand comprised approximately 35 per cent of that total. New Zealanders' interest in books compares more than favourably with other English-speaking nations.

Analysis of the annual *New Zealand National Bibliography* cumulations suggests some changing preoccupations for New Zealand publishers. New subject areas of wide public interest have arisen, and these are reflected in the layout of the present bibliography. In several cases the volume of works published on particular topics has necessitated the creation of quite new sections. Two stand out. The first covers publications focusing on the Treaty of Waitangi (signed between Maori tribes and the British Crown in 1840), Maori claims for redress of past grievances, and the implications for future Maori-European relations. Though the Treaty has always been recognized within Maori society as an affirmation of rights, it was not until the mid-1980s that this began to be formally acknowledged by New Zealand governments. Hence there was not a single related entry in the 1980 edition. The titles here listed indicate that the lacuna is beginning to be filled. A second completely new section sets out publications relating to women's issues and rights. While women comprise, and have long comprised, the majority of the New Zealand population, a feminine viewpoint has often been lacking from public debate. In 1980 the women's movement in New Zealand, certainly as a mass movement, was still young. Basic organization took precedence over printed advocacy. That gap, too, has been made good. Women's publishing is now a major growth area.

Other sections, while retaining their broad form, have changed significantly in terms of incorporated content. Further, there have been internal rearrangements, within and between sections, to, as far as possible, place 'like with like'. Undoubtedly placement anomalies remain, but it is hoped that these are offset by selective cross-referencing. Nowhere is changing emphasis in content more apparent than in the sections relating to the structure and sectors of the New Zealand economy. On the evidence of the first edition, New Zealand writing on economics was thin prior to 1980. Few substantial titles were listed in the 'General Economics' section, the compiler of the first edition being compelled to bulk his listings with periodical articles and short discussion papers. There was no such shortage in 1997. In response to the new national ethos, there has been an outpouring of texts, scholarly treatises and guides for the intelligent layperson – to the point of saturation. Related titles have also mushroomed. In addition to the more than fifty titles listed under 'Economics' in the 1994 *National Bibliography*, the enquirer is directed to further titles under eleven separate headings. Publications on business management, for example, have almost assumed industry proportions. With most recycling overseas concepts, only those with a distinctively New Zealand bias are listed there.

Understandably, a number of sections have changed little in form or in nature of content from the first edition. Notwithstanding the ongoing resculpting of New Zealand's human and cultural landscapes, the build of the country remains largely unchanging. Its geology, soils and topography are constant. Despite heightening concern about ozone depletion and unseasonal weather patterns, so too is its climate. Similarly, the indigenous flora and fauna. The concentration in these sections has been on providing references to the most up-to-date surveys. In the sections entitled 'Landforms, Geology and Climate', all entries are post-1980. In that relating to 'Fauna and Flora', several earlier distinguished works are retained but the majority of the entries are new.

In 1980, Grover argued that the enquirer curious about New Zealand and New Zealanders might well commence with a dip into the country's creative literature. This probably remains a truism but, as in the first edition, individual novels, short stories, poems and plays are not listed in the bibliography. Signposts are provided, however, in the subsection on 'Literary history and criticism', while the listed anthologies provide at least a taste of what is available. Grover rightly considered that fictional works, for example Maurice Gee's *Plumb trilogy: Plumb, Meg, Sole survivor* (1995) or Frank S. Anthony's Gus Tomlins books (*The complete me and Gus*, 1963), can provide a more accurate evocation of New Zealand life than most non-fiction discussions. Arguably, however, the time is still too soon for the post-1980 upheavals to be depicted to any great extent in New Zealand literature. Yet there are already hints of what may be to come, for instance in Maurice Gee's *Crime story* (1994), or Karl Stead's *The end of the century at the end of the world* (1992). Immediately disturbing are Maori writer Alan Duff's *Once were warriors* (1990), and *One night out stealing* (1992), harrowing tales of a frustrated and resentful underclass. It is no coincidence that some of the most starkly realistic current New Zealand writing is by Maori – by writers such as Keri Hulme and Witi Ihimaera, as well as Duff – for in the past two decades Maori voices have demonstrated a new assertiveness. The literary landmark of the period, albeit necessarily looking backwards rather than at the contemporary scene, has been Terry Sturm's *Oxford history of New Zealand literature in English*. While major authors figure prominently, this history contains more comprehensive information about New Zealand literature than has appeared before in a single volume. The period also witnessed the first serious reviews of regional literatures, and of masculinity and femininity in New Zealand writing.

By design, then, the primary focus of the present bibliography is non-fiction works. Beyond blanket and often facile descriptions of the country, 'coffee-table' editions lavishly illustrated but short on commentary, selected examples of which are nevertheless listed, there have been a number of works evaluating what has been termed 'the New Zealand experiment' and its impact on the country's people.

They range from the heavily academic, through works for the intelligent layperson, to the superficial and impressionistic. Perhaps most trenchantly critical is Auckland academic lawyer Jane Kelsey's *The New Zealand experiment*, caustically subtitled 'A world model for structural adjustment?'. Kelsey attacks the disparate outcomes from the near pure doses of neo-liberal economic theory applied to New Zealand since 1984, raising important questions about the effect of the regime on individuals' lives, communities and the nation. In similar vein, though more soberly expressed, are a series of books by economist and social commentator Brian Easton, the most recent being *The commercialisation of New Zealand*. Easton probes the origins, theory and history of the recent dramatic changes, illustrating through case-studies just how pervasive the 'more market' ethos has been. Both of these critiques may be regarded as being written from a broadly anti-New Right perspective. Polemics apart, and there have been many, often sponsored by organizations such as the Business Roundtable, the reformers have lacked comparable champions. For a time it appeared that business journalist Colin James might assume the mantle, his writings of the 1980s being supportive of the new thrust, but by the 1992 publication of *New territory* he was expressing second thoughts. At a more popular level, Marcia Russell's *Revolution*, offshoot of a television series, expresses breathless awe for a decade's restructuring achievements, but more typical of broad commentary is Gordon McLauchlan's *The big con*. The one-time scourge of 'the passionless people' had discovered there were alternatives he found even less palatable.

It was a throwaway line of former Prime Minister Sir Robert Muldoon that the average New Zealander would not recognize the national deficit if he or she fell over it in the street. His point was that citizens were largely ignorant of basic economic principles. This is no longer the case. As noted earlier, publications on the economy have proliferated in New Zealand bookshops. Press business pages have expanded greatly. Even the passive television watcher is nightly presented with commentary and share market indexes. While how much is actually absorbed by a still largely untutored public remains questionable, there can be little doubt that greater awareness has been stimulated. Although distinguished economic historian John Gould, in *The Muldoon years,* has cogently defended pre-1984 economic policies, and Sir Robert Muldoon has entered his personal plea (*The New Zealand economy: a personal view*), there is now general agreement that New Zealand was at an economic turning-point in the early 1980s. The economy was over protected and over regulated; it was largely unresponsive to external stimuli. That ameliorative actions were required is generally accepted. What has increasingly vigorously been debated is whether the most appropriate strategies were then embraced, or even explored. That the agenda was dictated by an ideologically captured New Zealand Treasury has become a popular view. Such a case is advanced by Wolfgang Rosenberg in his *New Zealand can be different and better*. Whatever the policy origins, the fourth Labour Government came to power in mid-1984 with three overriding economic objectives: rapid market liberalization, disinflation, and economic growth. Without question the first objective was soon achieved, if at considerable cost. The second, despite early stumbles, has also been largely achieved, and also at cost. The third remains problematical. All three objectives involved major structural reforms. The most comprehensive overview of the reforms is Brian Silverstone, Allan Bollard and Ralph Lattimore's *A study of economic reform*. Significantly, this book was published in Holland, presumably to access a wider overseas readership. While most of the authors are supportive of the reforms, their comments are measured. Bollard, chair of the Commerce Commission and a former Director of the New Zealand Institute for Economic Research, has been probably New Zealand's most prolific writer on the reforms. His publications extend across several sections in the bibliography. His views, however, are far from uncontested. Brian Easton's *In stormy seas* (in press at the time of writing[1]), places the reforms in the context of New Zealand's post-Second World War economic history. A recent interesting publication is Paul Dalziel and Ralph Lattimore's *The New Zealand macroeconomy*. With the former a critic of the reforms, and the latter a supporter, they identify where they find common ground.

The freeing up of the financial sector was the first step in the structural adjustment programme. Almost overnight it was transformed from one of the most regulated in OECD countries to probably the least regulated. Faced with an exchange crisis upon taking office, the fourth Labour Government first devalued the currency, then in rapid succession deregulated the financial markets, abolished interest rate controls, removed exchange controls and put the New Zealand dollar on a free float. Henceforth transaction rates were to be determined by the market forces of supply and demand. Foreign investment was viewed as a key to economic growth, and all possible impediments to such investment were to be dispensed with. Edna Carew's *New Zealand's money revolution* is an early evaluation of the changes, while the mechanics of the change process are discussed in more detail in Reserve Bank monographs. The immediate consequences were not entirely as predicted. Foreign investment was certainly attracted, and as writers such as Girol Karacaoglu and Brent Layton point out, new financial institutions and markets appeared, but the net impact in the overheated conditions was that spending was redirected from productive, to speculative, investment. Policies intended to curb inflation instead, at least in the short term, fuelled it. For a short period the country had the highest real interest rates in the Western world. The outcome was a boom, followed by the sharemarket crash of October 1987, outlined in David Grant's *Bulls, bears and elephants: a history of the New Zealand stock exchange*. Thereafter greater sobriety prevailed. A New Zealand Institute for Economic Research report, *Financial deregulation and disinflation in a small open economy*, reviews progress to 1989, while Roger Bowden's *Kiwicap: an introduction to New Zealand capital markets* addresses the current situation.

As part of the overhaul of the financial sector, the New Zealand banking system was transformed. Prior to 1984 the provision of full banking services was restricted to four commercial or trading banks, although there were also trustee savings banks and other institutions with quasi-banking functions. The major player was the wholly state-owned Bank of New Zealand. In mid-1986, in the interests of competition, the field was opened to all-comers, whether local or from overseas. By late 1991, twenty-two banks had been registered. In the following year the Bank of New Zealand, which in quest for market share had underwritten much of the speculation prior to the 1987 crash, which had had to be bailed out through an infusion of state funds, and which had then been part sold to merchant bankers Fay Richwhite in 1989, was completely sold off to Australian interests. Further rationalization continued through the 1990s, mergers and withdrawals reducing the number of registered banks to fifteen, and their control effectively passing completely from New Zealand hands. While a specialist study of modern New Zealand banking has yet to be written, the operations of the country's central bank, the Reserve Bank of New Zealand, are better recorded. As G. R. Hawke's 1973 study shows, in earlier years the Reserve Bank firmly supervised New Zealand banking activity. In the new era its role changed from direct control to one of surveillance. Under the Reserve Bank Act 1989 the institution was quarantined from direct political influence, and was charged to control the money supply, maintaining price stability becoming its sole objective. Differing views on how effectively it has met its new obligations are provided by economist Sir Frank Holmes and millionaire businessman Sir Robert (Bob) Jones.

In conjunction with reform of the financial sector, the productive sectors were also subjected to stringent scrutiny. Industry assistance was blamed for producing a lower level of national income than if prices were solely determined by the market. While it was acknowledged that withdrawing subsidies would create hardship as resources shifted from previously protected activities to notionally more efficient ones, this was a price the reformers were more than prepared to pay. The message to be sent was that only the most internationally competitive enterprises should survive. Agriculture, long New Zealand's economic mainstay, was the first target. In 1984 grass was still the country's main crop. It was exported to the world, processed, principally in the form of meat, wool and dairy produce. In that year agriculture still contributed more than sixty per cent of exports and accounted for seven per cent of GDP. Rural New Zealand remained a green, and largely pleasant, land. By 1990, however, life on the farm had become considerably less pleasant, pastures were assuming a browner tinge in the absence of fertilizers, plant was deteriorating, and stock numbers were being cut to service increasing debt levels. This decline was directly attributable to a raft of restructuring measures, outlined in Ron Sandrey and Russell Reynolds' *Farming without subsidies: New Zealand's recent experience*. Between 1984 and 1987 virtually all subsidies were withdrawn. As a result of the financial reforms, interest rates rose. User charges were imposed for services previously provided by the government free of charge or at minimal cost. It was symbolic that in 1989 the government-owned Rural Bank should be sold into private ownership. Both farm incomes and rural land values plummeted, ripple effects being felt throughout the country districts. Some came to the conclusion that farming was a 'sunset industry'. This was always too pessimistic a view, but as agricultural economist John Fairweather notes in a 1992 Lincoln University research paper, several important trends were set in motion. Sheep numbers declined, but dairy stock, deer and goats increased. Field cropping also declined, but specialist horticulture made strides. Farm employment stagnated, many being compelled to seek supplementary work. Fairweather also discerned a reduction in the overall number of farms, commenting on what he terms 'the disappearing middle'. While Fairweather argues strongly that the 'family character' of New Zealand farming has been reinforced, other commentators interpret the situation differently. They detect the accelerated emergence of agribusinesses, often operated on amalgamated farmlands bought cheaply in the late 1980s, run increasingly by entrepreneurial businessmen. Ironically, while attempts to push deregulation of the sector to a conclusion continue, most recently through assaults on the remaining producer boards, there can be little doubt New Zealand's farmers are already amongst the most exposed to market forces in the developed world.

Restructuring of forestry, New Zealand's second and oldest land-based industry, went even further. While the industry was sustained through most of the 19th century by indigenous forest cutting, recognition that there would soon be timber shortages motivated extensive planting of exotic plantations (particularly *pinus radiata*) from around the turn of the century. It was on the foundation of these plantings that a revived forest products export trade burgeoned in the post-Second World War years. While the processing of trees into lumber, pulp and paper, latterly woodchips, was largely left to private enterprise, though with significant government involvement and support, the state's principal role was as a guarantor of wood supply to the industry. Management of the exotic forests, as well as the remnants of the original bush cover, was entrusted to the New Zealand Forest Service, the origins of which are discussed in Michael Roche's *History of New Zealand forestry*. By 1984, despite private afforestation programmes, the state still owned more than half the country's cuttable timber. Less than twelve months after taking office the fourth Labour Government outlined an agenda which was to lead to the transfer of responsibility for exploitation of this resource wholly to the private sector. The Forest Service was dismantled, preservation functions being transferred to a newly created Department of Conservation and production forestry to a commercial New Zealand Forestry Corporation, one of the first state-owned enterprises. In the process of corporatization, outlined in Reg Birchfield and Ian Grant's *Out of the woods: the restructuring and sale of New Zealand's state forests*, more than two-thirds of the Forest Service's staff was shed, contracting out was initiated, and many milling settlements virtually closed down. It was a small step from corporatization of the state's forestry interests to privatization of the wood supply. When proposals to sell the forests outright were thwarted by Maori opposition to the sale of Crown lands in the late 1980s, the stratagem of instead selling off long-term cutting rights was settled upon. In 1990-91 the new National government put 344,000 hectares to tender, few restrictions or local processing requirements being imposed on bidders. A number of foreign investment companies, both Asian and American, made substantial purchases, but also sharing in the bounty were several of New Zealand's largest established wood processors. The ironic twist was that by this stage the latter could scarcely be described as New Zealand enterprises. Deregulation of the financial sector had accelerated their internationalization, their New Zealand holdings being but one part of worldwide operations. It was in this context that further retrenchments commenced. The story of New Zealand forestry may well be one of *A century of state-honed enterprise*, but as forestry historian Michael Roche has recently observed, it is no longer appropriate to write of 'New Zealand's forest resources'. In reality, the preponderance of New Zealand's productive trees are now globally owned, globally processed, and globally consumed.

That the open slather philosophy should be extended to other facets of New Zealand primary industry was inevitable, even if as yet commentators have contributed little substantial on the implications. Perhaps, because a generally permissive approach had been traditionally adopted to activities such as mining and exploitation of the nation's fisheries, it took longer for public disquiet to be expressed. Mining for precious metals, particularly gold, has a long history in New Zealand. While the gold-mining peak was in the 19th and early 20th centuries, rising world prices in the 1970s stimulated a new exploration round. In the 1980s the focus shifted from prospecting to extraction. The reformers' contribution, as evidenced by Valerie Jacobsen's *The evolution of institutional arrangements for gold mining*, was to legislatively ease the way. Today, more than eighty per cent of New Zealand's gold production is from three heavily capital-intensive open pit hard rock mines: Martha Hill at Waihi; Golden Cross, in the Coromandel; and Macraes Flat, in Otago. Significantly, all three are foreign owned, with profits being remitted offshore. Equally significantly, all three have also sparked environmental degradation concerns. Recent approval for a new mine in a national park indicates that politicians and bureaucrats continue to place private profits above such concerns. Heavy foreign investment has also been a feature of New Zealand fishing, a minor boom industry in the past two decades. Exports averaged over NZ$1 billion per annum through the early 1990s. That the potential had been previously recognized is demonstrated by the 1978 declaration of a New Zealand Exclusive Economic Zone covering 1.2 million square nautical miles, an area fifteen times the country's land mass. The trading of access to the Zone by foreign vessels for entry of other New Zealand exports to overseas markets set the scene for later developments. While a commercial deep sea Quota Management System was actually introduced in 1983, in the name of catch sustainability, it was a regime which presaged the new liberalizing ethos. Annual catch limits are now set for each fish stock, and tradable rights to harvest are put to tender. Such a system naturally favours the larger players and the result has been the squeezing out of many smaller local operators. International companies, a number of them also involved in forestry and other natural resource exploitation, have become dominant. The only break in the pattern has been the 'Sealords deal', the state being required to transfer fisheries assets and rights to Maori interests in settlement of a Treaty of Waitangi claim to seafisheries. Direct foreign involvement in the industry – by Russian, Japanese and Korean vessels – continues through charter arrangements and joint ventures.

Agriculture may have been the reformers' first target, but it was not necessarily the prime target. That doubtful honour rests with the manufacturing sector. Industrialization had been fostered as a key plank of development models from 1945. Although the resultant manufacturing base, catering primarily for the domestic market, had been propped up by tariff barriers and import licensing, the need to generate foreign exchange had seen successive governments offer export incentives to further boost production. Such protection was anathema post-1984. By late 1986 the removal of import licensing had been announced and a programme of progressive tariff reductions had been imposed. Export incentives were to go by 1990. While economists Alan Bollard and John Savage write approvingly of the measures in their study *Turning it round*, there can be few doubts that New Zealand manufacturing was in crisis for the remainder of the 1980s. Geographer Richard Willis, in his *New Zealand manufacturing: a study of change*, estimates that in these years some eighty per cent of unemployment could be attributed to manufacturing job losses. Other commentators note the decline in manufacturing's capital stock, due to liquidations and withdrawal of investment. Some manufacturers, particularly small manufacturers, simply closed their factory doors. It was considered more economic to either import foodstuff lines from Australia, or footwear from Asia or Brazil. Others downsized, closing decentralized plants and concentrating their activities closer to the major domestic market. The impact was catastrophic for many small towns south of Auckland. Yet others again relocated their production overseas. Apparel manufacturers, for example, opened joint-venture factories in Fiji, where labour costs are low, or subcontracted to Chinese or Indian manufacturers. A number of larger, heavily capital-intensive industries radically revised their supply strategies. The motor vehicle assembly industry had developed from the 1930s under franchise arrangements, but by 1990 ownership had passed back to the overseas parent companies. It was logical for such companies to plan on a regional or global basis, cutting back New Zealand production and importing built-up models. Any shortfall could be met through the importation of cheap used cars, principally from Japan. Virtually the only enterprises unaffected by the upheaval were operations such as the Tiwai Point aluminium smelter, already overseas owned, guaranteed cheap power, and in a privileged position. While there has been some revival from the early 1990s, stimulated mainly by labour market deregulation, that revival has tended to be confined to relatively large companies exporting niche products to targeted overseas markets. Despite media attention, small businesses have been of minor importance.

New Zealand's traditional industries, those processing farm produce, also experienced stress from the mid-1980s. Again, published studies of recent trends are surprisingly scant, but some features can be identified. The meat freezing industry was hard hit in the 1980s: by falling international meat prices, by the removal of farm subsidies, and by the resulting decline in stock numbers. With forecasts having been based on rising livestock numbers in the 1960s and 1970s, the product of price support schemes, the industry was faced with excess production capacity. An early reaction was the closure of older plants. In less than six years the meat freezing industry was recast, with many job losses along the way. The plant of the future, or so it was decided, was relatively small, specialized, utilizing up-to-date technology, with staff working shifts all year round. While most of the older plants were steadily phased out, new ones were constructed in their place. Between 1986 and 1994 the number operating increased by nearly fifty per cent. Curiously, perhaps because of lower profit margins, the industry largely reverted to New Zealand ownership, previously involved overseas companies relinquishing their interests. The dairy processing industry had, of course, always been in New Zealand hands, and that hold was retained. But a very different rationalization strategy was adopted. There was an opting for economies of scale, and by 1994 just three companies processed nearly three-quarters of New Zealand's milk fat. In the preceding ten years around half of the country's dairy factories had been closed. Foreign penetration was more evident in other food processing enterprises. By the mid-1980s Wattie Industries Ltd. was New Zealand's main processor of fruit and vegetables. In 1986, however, in response to the new conditions, the company merged with Goodman Feilder, an Australian-based corporation, though one already with strong New Zealand links. Despite drastic reorganization, the marriage was short-lived. In 1992 Wattie Industries Ltd. was divested to the American corporate giant H. J. Heinz, making it by proxy the dominant force in New Zealand horticultural processing. Likewise, the New Zealand wine industry was reorganized. By the mid-1990s, while many small boutique vineyards remained, just three companies accounted for over eighty per cent of wine production by volume. Overseas involvement in the industry was increasing.

The dismantling of domestic protections was driven by a vision of an internationally competitive New Zealand economy, one at least keeping up with, sometimes leading, the world's major trading nations. There was also probably a desire beneath the surface to throw off the past. New Zealand had developed as a colony supplying food and fibre to Britain, and as a captive consumer market for British goods. Until Britain entered the European Economic Community it remained New Zealand's largest export market. The urge to complete the disengagement and reposition New Zealand in world markets had become strong, as Ian Duncan, Ralph Lattimore and Alan Bollard demonstrate in their study of the tariff reforms. Protests that unilateral trade liberalization would place New Zealand producers at a disadvantage with those in other countries were ignored. The initial focus was on liberalizing trade between Australia and New Zealand. The Australia-New Zealand Closer Economic Relations Trade Agreement (CER) had nominally been already in place for nearly two decades, but until the mid-1980s it was honoured more in breach than by observance. Thereafter the agreement was viewed by New Zealand as a prime vehicle for informal integration of the two markets. In the course of the later 1980s trans-Tasman trade nearly trebled, but there was only a slow realization that CER was more important to New Zealand than Australia, matters considered by Stephen Hoadley in *New Zealand and Australia: closer economic relations*. In common with Australia, New Zealand strenuously sought to develop trading links with Asia. Successive governments actively supported the development of the Asia-Pacific region, even if rhetoric ignored the fact that the aggressive trade liberalization being pursued was at odds with the more pragmatic approaches adopted by most Asian nations. Through the General Agreement on Tariffs and Trade (GATT), New Zealand also endeavoured to take its free-trade message to the wider world. In negotiation rounds, in return for vague promises that agricultural protection would be reduced, firm undertakings were given that tariff reductions would continue and foreign access to New Zealand markets would be guaranteed. The results of these trade strategies were mixed. Trade with Britain, already falling in 1984, continued to slide. Not unexpectedly, Australia emerged as New Zealand's major trading partner, both in terms of exports and imports. Japan remained the country's foremost Asian trading partner, although business with South Korea and the two Chinas increased. Although exports to the United States dropped, imports from that same source increased. What was increasingly evident by the mid-1990s was that, while a free trade government could set the general terms under which trade was conducted, the form, volume, and participants were effectively decided elsewhere.

In the post-1984 free trade environment, as Malcolm McKinnon's *Independence and foreign policy: New Zealand in the world since 1935* demonstrates, economic imperatives have played a central part in shaping New Zealand's foreign relations. While sentiment has dictated that, as far as possible, traditional ties should be maintained, and New Zealand continues to be represented in the capitals of Europe and North America, the rapid erosion of trading links with Britain from the 1960s nevertheless left New Zealand feeling deserted and exposed. These feelings fostered a determination to promote friendly relations with other countries, and markets, not just the previous few. This determination has been manifested in a new activism in international affairs and by diligent diplomatic bridge building. As 'an international citizen', New Zealand has endeavoured to exert an influence disproportionate to its size; through vigorous support for United Nations' initiatives, through enthusiastic participation in other international forums, and through the country's willingness to take a lead in such matters as global environmental protection and disarmament. The more materialistic business of developing bilateral trading relationships was for the most part facilitated by the nation's career diplomatic service, the department concerned being now appropriately entitled the Ministry of Foreign Affairs and Trade. Then Prime Minister Muldoon's 1980 enjoinder that 'New Zealand's foreign policy *is* trade' aptly captures today's official mood.

In recent decades many of New Zealand's diplomatic preoccupations have been relatively close to home. The strong desire to cement a closer relationship with the country's largest neighbour, Australia, has already been alluded to. While the prospective eventual integration of the two markets has provided the strongest incentive, underpinning has been afforded by historic ties of long duration. Though New Zealand rejected federation with the Australian states in 1901, and it is likely that popular opinion would preclude full political integration in the foreseeable future, near open borders already exist. The implications are examined in Frank Holmes' *The trans-Tasman relationship*. Alongside, New Zealand has also sought to position itself as a Pacific leader, relationships long taken for granted being worked on. In respect of a number of island groups, in the second half of the century, New Zealand has moved from the status of administering colonial power to that of a freely associated polity. How the transition was managed is addressed in a number of works in the 'New Zealand and the Pacific' section, but an impression remains that New Zealand continues to regard many of the new micro-states as part of a sphere of influence. Missions are maintained in most South Pacific countries, special trade and investment incentives have been created, and over sixty per cent of New Zealand's overseas aid is directed to the region. Ron Crocombe's *Pacific neighbours* critically distinguishes the current links. New Zealand's awakened interest in Asia is reflected in the recent opening of new diplomatic posts, the total of which now exceeds those established in Britain and Europe. The new preoccupation with a region that provides a market for more than a third of New Zealand's exports and is a source of almost a third of imports is understandable, even if repeated claims that New Zealand should be regarded as an Asian nation remain somewhat overblown. New Zealand is one of the original dialogue partners of the Association of South East Asian Nations (ASEAN) and a founding member of the Asia-Pacific Economic Co-operation Forum (APEC). In *New Zealand and ASEAN*, Raj Vasil critically explores New Zealand's relationships with member countries. New Zealand's ties with the more distant Middle East also have a strong economic foundation. While exports to the region are currently less than those to Pacific countries, the Middle East has been, and remains, a principal source of New Zealand petroleum imports. The dearth of New Zealand diplomatic representation in other parts of the world is indicative of the presently underdeveloped nature of trading relationships with the countries of those regions.

With the heightened emphasis on economic diplomacy, New Zealand's longstanding defence arrangements have become more problematical. In the aftermath of the Second World War it was clear that it was the United States, rather than Britain, that emerged as the country's major ally; hence the tripartite ANZUS pact – between Australia, New Zealand and the United States – signed in 1952. For over three decades this agreement set the broad terms for New Zealand's security, the closeness of the relationship being evidenced by willingness to despatch troops in support of American forces in several theatres. The pact, however, came under severe stress in the 1980s. As Elsie Locke records in *Peace people*, strong public opposition to nuclear weapons built up in New Zealand in the 1960s and 1970s, first focusing on French nuclear testing in the Pacific, but later extending to the arsenals of the country's allies. Significantly, many of the most vociferous opponents were also Labour voters. Seeking to indirectly secure support for its economic reforms, the fourth Labour Government fastened on a symbolic gesture. While seeking to remain in ANZUS, it banned nuclear armed and/or propelled vessels from New Zealand's ports. The sharp reaction from the country's former principal ally is outlined in Paul Landais-Sharp and Paul Rogers' *Rocking the boat*, and in a clutch of related volumes, while the New Zealand government's perspective is put in David Lange's *Nuclear free – New Zealand way*. The United States immediately severed all intelligence and military contact and, through third countries, particularly Australia, sought to have the ban lifted. While New Zealand's unilateral action dismayed the services chiefs and many diplomats, it struck a chord with the voting public, not least because of the David and Goliath mien of the confrontation. The resulting support was sufficient to contribute significantly to Labour's victory in the 1987 election, and to impel the previously critical National Party to adopt a similar policy stance. In the mid-1990s, if not dismantled, the ANZUS pact remains in abeyance, even if relations with the United States have otherwise thawed. Though New Zealand has sought to compensate for the rupture by establishing a closer defence relationship with Australia, it has not been prepared to commit to the expenditure necessary to realistically contribute to an independent Pacific defence force. Recent defence policy is analysed in James Rolfe's *Defending New Zealand*. With commercial disciplines being applied to defence organization, and with defence spending as a percentage of GDP falling sharply in the 1990s, New Zealand's ability even to participate credibly in international peace-keeping missions, an important role in recent years, has come into question.

New Zealand's remoteness from its trading partners, together with its small population spread over two elongated islands, has dictated that effective transportation services have been vital to the country's development, a topic explored by James Watson in his historical overview of the sector, *Links*. For most of the 19th century the emphasis was on sea transport, but from the 1870s internal overland movements were facilitated by the construction of roads and railways. The advent of the motor vehicle in the early 20th century, soon followed by air carriage, further helped break down isolation. A number of listed titles detail the evolution of the various transport modes. A common feature, however, was that the state was heavily involved from the beginning, both in the provision of the necessary infrastructure, which was heavily capital intensive, and in the operation of internal services. The central government owned and operated New Zealand's railways. It built and maintained the nation's arterial roads, even if service provision was left to private operators. It also assumed control of air services, the national airline, Air New

Zealand, by the 1980s providing both internal and international flights. Local authorities operated ports and aerodromes, administered local roads and were largely responsible for local passenger services. Only overseas shipping was continuously in overseas hands, although the 1973 formation of the Shipping Corporation of New Zealand indicated a desire to break the grip. Unquestionably, future transport strategies were under review throughout the 1970s, but the 1980s brought a complete change of tack. The determination after 1984 was that New Zealand should become a transport-using, but not necessarily a transport-owning and operating, nation. With the 1989 sale of the Shipping Corporation (renamed the New Zealand Line), overseas shipping was returned entirely to foreign hands. Later, trans-Tasman shipping was opened to international competition, and in 1995 even the coastal trade was thrown open. In concert, New Zealand's main ports were placed under the management of companies, full privatization being a future objective. Changes were no less dramatic in civil aviation. New Zealand's domestic skies were opened to competition, and in 1987 Australian-owned Ansett New Zealand went head-to-head with the national carrier. With external links being also deregulated, fifteen foreign airlines commenced scheduled services to and from New Zealand in the ten years after 1985. In 1989, Air New Zealand itself was packaged and sold to a consortium of New Zealand and overseas interests. Airports were also corporatized. In this environment the outcome for New Zealand Railways was inevitable. In 1986 the then Railways Corporation became a state-owned enterprise, paving the way for its eventual privatization in 1994, the principal purchaser being the American Wisconsin Central Transportation Corporation. While the road transport industry was also drastically remodelled, commercial road services being largely deregulated, maintenance of the nation's 92,300 kilometres of formed roads and streets remained a joint central-local government responsibility. In 1989 policy development became the core business of a Ministry of Transport, while oversight of funding was delegated to a new corporation, Transit New Zealand. More recently the transfer of authority to a group of regionally based roading companies has been mooted, together with higher direct user charges.

In what has been termed 'the information age', in New Zealand, as elsewhere, sophisticated communication systems play an ever increasing part. The past decade has witnessed dramatic changes to the facilitatory infrastructure. From the beginnings of European settlement until the mid-1980s the provision of such services was almost exclusively the preserve of the New Zealand Post Office.

Public servants received and delivered the mails, installed telephones, and handled messages by cable, radio and latterly satellite. The Post Office was an archetypal all-purpose communications organization. In a process a commissioned writer has eulogistically termed *Reining in the dinosaur*, dismantlement of the all-purpose organization on functional lines commenced in 1987. Traditional postal services were transferred to a new state-owned enterprise, New Zealand Post Ltd. While the carriage of standard letters was afforded interim protection, much of the remainder of its business was thrown open to private sector competition. Ten years later full deregulation of postal services was announced. Telecommunication services passed to a second new state business, the Telecom Corporation of New Zealand Ltd., with an extensive modernization programme being initiated. Predictably, these services too were thrown open to competition. As A. C. Wilson notes in his *Wire and wireless: a history of telecommunications in New Zealand*, there was considerable official concern that escalating demand for telecommunications services would entail heavy ongoing investment. This led, in 1990, to the sale of Telecom to a North American-New Zealand consortium, the principal new shareholders being Bell Atlantic and Ameritech. While competition in the provision of services had until that point been muted, the sale was almost immediately followed by entry into the New Zealand market of two major rivals: Clear Communications Ltd., another North American-New Zealand consortium; and Bell South New Zealand, wholly overseas owned. By the mid-1990s the battle for business had become intense, even if this was scarcely reflected in the bills of residential subscribers for core services.

Like most developed countries, New Zealand has depended heavily on sustained energy supplies to ensure the effective operation of the economy and the well-being of its citizens. In the early 20th century the principal source was coal, and this remains the country's largest latent energy resource, but the advent of the combustion engine brought oil and petroleum products to the fore. Until the oil shocks of the 1970s New Zealand's oil supplies were almost entirely sourced overseas, but by the early 1980s there was a drive for greater self-sufficiency, both indigenous deposits and alternative energy sources being sought. As Mike Paterson details in *The point at issue: petroleum energy politics in New Zealand*, the state was heavily involved, underwriting the development of Taranaki's oil and gas fields and encouraging the expansion of the country's sole oil refinery. Yet, while by the mid-1990s around a third of New Zealand refined crude oil was of local origin, and synthetic petrol was being produced from natural gas, direct government involvement in the industry had effectively ceased, the Crown having sold its interests to multinational Fletcher Challenge Ltd. in 1987. It was the private sector that was profiting from earlier public investment. While the second major source of late-20th-century New Zealand energy, hydro-electricity, remained at least nominally in public ownership, generation and supply assumed commercialist trappings. From the early 1900s the country's many lakes and fast-flowing rivers had ensured the constant availability of this relatively cheap and continually replenished power source. John Martin's *People, power and politics in New Zealand* records how until the mid-1980s state departments assumed responsibility for the planning and construction of power stations in both main islands, and for the wholesale distribution of electricity, retail supply being allocated to local power boards and supply authorities. This perceived power monopoly was an obvious target for the commercializers. The 1989 conversion of the Electricity Division of the Ministry of Energy into the Electricity Corporation of New Zealand Ltd. (Electricorp) was the first step. In 1994 the Corporation's generation and transmission functions were split, the latter being allocated to a new entity, Transpower New Zealand Ltd. By this point retail supply had already been restructured, the elected authorities having been compulsorily transformed into competing companies in 1992. In the aftermath, overseas utilities acquired substantial New Zealand holdings. Reform of the electricity system is still not complete. Further splits of Electricorp are planned in the name of competition and, while continued public ownership of existing generation capacity is pledged, full divestment in the future cannot be ruled out. Commentators such as Barry Spicer et al. (*The power to manage: restructuring the New Zealand Electricity Department as a state-owned enterprise*) argue that the changes have delivered improved performance, certainly higher levels of profit-ability, but an image that endures in the public mind is the conspicuous consumption of those 'freed to manage'.

Increased consumption became a feature of New Zealand life in the 1980s. Clearly some New Zealanders enjoyed greater spending power as a result of the post-1984 reform programmes. All citizens, however, were presented with greater consumer choice, the rules and norms governing distribution and sale being legislatively loosened. The greater range of services available has already been alluded to, but by the 1990s New Zealand was also experiencing a retailing revolution. A new urban landscape of shopping malls, recreation centres, bistros and multiplexes began to materialize. Correspondingly, traditional icons of suburbia – the post office, corner dairy, owner-operated butchery and drapery – were disappearing. City centres became the preserve of boutique shoppers, mass consumption becoming centred on a plethora of new planned suburban shopping centres, many owned by property developers and finance companies. While the phenomenon has as yet attracted little serious study, Steve Britton et al., in their *Changing places in New Zealand*, note that 'large new malls have opened in competition with each other and older, less glamorous facilities. Each usually has a major food retailer (Foodtown, Countdown, Pak'N'Save) and a general merchandising store (K-mart, Deka, Farmers) around which is a collection of speciality stores, often outlets for overseas, national or regional chains'. They further note: 'The architecture of the malls is standardised and their content is so similar that anyone could be anywhere'. The blandness beneath the advertising froth, beneath the constant round of store openings and closures, of refurbishments and extensions, tended to mask several significant retailing trends. One was the penetration of the New Zealand retail market by overseas, particularly Australian, firms. By 1994, for example, around seventy per cent of food retailing was in the hands of just five trans-Tasman companies. This industry concentration gave the retail leaders more power, both in dictating supply arrangements and influencing the environment in which retailing was conducted. It was no coincidence that restrictions on trading hours should be largely abandoned, the hitherto sacrosanct New Zealand 'weekend' being eroded. Increasingly, shopping was depicted as a pleasurable leisure activity, for individuals and families, at least for those not required to staff checkouts or replenish shelves. The pressure to shop was intense, fostered by vigorous advertising and marketing campaigns. Predictably, the largest agencies, those engineering the media blitz, were all local subsidiaries of multinational players (Saatchi & Saatchi, Colenso, Ogilvy & Mather).

Undoubtedly the favourable conditions engendered by the new economic policies and the market-driven commercial environment encouraged a flowering of the entrepreneurial spirit. The businessman (rarely woman) was held up by politicians and community leaders as the new society hero, and the firm was celebrated as the preferred form of social organization. As Alan Bollard has suggested, the greatest stimulus was the Commerce Act 1986, designed to promote competition, not only as an end in itself but as a means of promoting both consumer welfare and efficiency. While the expressed concern for consumer welfare may have been illusory, this legislation, with amendments, effectively removed most remaining impediments to the freedom of large corporations to act much as they liked. Fuelled by financial deregulation, there was a wave of mergers and take-overs in the mid-1980s. In the process the New Zealand business world was turned on its head. Previously business leadership had been an exclusive and comfortable club, with membership often being hereditary. Many once familiar names, individual and corporate, were swept away as conglomerate, horizontal and vertical mergers were effected. While new names blossomed, there were nevertheless distinguished survivors who seized this opportunity to become even more distinguished. Foremost amongst them was Fletcher Challenge, already the largest New Zealand-based corporate in 1984, and soon destined to become the country's first true multinational. After 1984, Fletcher Challenge extended its tentacles over most sectors of the New Zealand economy, being one of the principal beneficiaries of the privatization of state assets. The rise of Fletcher Challenge is partially recounted in Selwyn Parker's *Made in New Zealand*, but this largely hagiographic account is offset by Bruce Jesson's *The Fletcher Challenge*. The rise of other, if smaller, corporate firms is recorded in *New Zealand's top 200 companies*. Yet, whereas there was initial enthusiasm for diversification of holdings amongst such enterprises, by the 1990s there was a trend back towards focus on core businesses. Another trend discernible by the 1990s, one signposted earlier, was the incursion of foreign companies. By 1994 over 40 per cent of the top 200 New Zealand-based corporations were foreign owned or controlled. And even this was not the full story. Other large New Zealand businesses – Watties, the Bank of New Zealand – became subsidiaries of overseas companies, thus disappearing from the New Zealand corporate league table. In some instances the tactics adopted by the new business leaders stretched, often breached, accepted canons of corporate behaviour. In the mid- and late 1980s a rash of corporate predators emerged, generally more intent on assets-stripping than on true productive investment. The way had been shown in New Zealand in earlier decades by Brierley Investments (Yvonne van Dongen, *Brierley: the man behind the corporate legend*), but post-1984 there were many emulators. High flyers such as Alan Hawkins (Equiticorp) and Bruce Judge (Ariadne) created business empires almost overnight, but as the October 1987 stockmarket crash demonstrated, a number of the new conglomerates had insecure foundations. The resulting bankruptcies and prosecutions reinforced a growing view that New Zealand was some kind of corporate 'wild west', and the activities of some of the country's leading merchant bankers, revealed in Ian Wishart's *The paradise conspiracy*, did little to dispel the impression. That by 1990 New Zealand wealth and power had become inordinately concentrated in the business sector is cogently argued by Bruce Jesson in *Behind the mirror glass*. The crass displays of new opulence in the 1980s may have been resented by the wider populace, but of more concern was the influence apparently wielded by the new business elite. Bound together by interlocking directorates and interests, given further power through appointment to SOE (State-Owned Enterprise) boards, divorced not only from ordinary citizens but also lesser members of the business sector, they seemingly had the power to take the country in whatever direction they determined. The most obvious manifestation was the Business Roundtable, made up exclusively of top corporate chief executives, which became New Zealand's most effective pressure group.

The Business Roundtable's most strident campaign entering the 1990s was for complete deregulation of the labour market. This was depicted as the crucial missing element of the structural reforms. The principal supporting arguments are advanced in Penelope Brook's *Freedom and work*. Yet, despite the fourth Labour Government's enthusiasm for restructuring, it was less keen to impose its philosophies in the labour sphere, this reluctance being related to the nature of its traditional constituency. The National administration elected in late 1990 had no such inhibitions. Within twelve months it had revolutionized New Zealand labour relations through enactment of the Employment Contracts Act 1991. The changes effected through this measure, however, have to be viewed against underlying changes in the nature of the New Zealand labour force, and in particular the degree of workforce participation. After the Second World War, New Zealand had embraced, and largely achieved, the social goal of full employment, described by Wolfgang Rosenberg as 'the fulcrum of the welfare state'. This had been inextricably linked to the concept of the single-income family, with a generally male breadwinner. From the 1960s, with greater emphasis on the services sector of the economy, this pattern began to change. The transition to a 'service society' encouraged increasing 'feminization' of the labour force. As Lisa Davies points out in her survey of female labour force participation, more jobs for women opened up. Conversely, job opportunities in traditional male occupations were reduced. Labour supply began to exceed demand for the first time since the 1920s. The post-1984 structural reforms greatly exacerbated these underlying problems. Economists Richard Harris and Bridget Daldy consider that the costs of restructuring were largely borne in the labour market. In their *Labour market adjustment in New Zealand* they conclude that the relatively high levels of unemployment, underemployment and casual work were mainly attributable to the reorganization of firms and rapid technological change. The net effect was to place much greater power in the hands of employers, which was manifested in intense pressure for greater flexibility in individually determining wage rates, hours of work and conditions. Labour should be viewed as simply a production input, the cost of which had to be adjusted in comparison with costs in other countries. Their wishes were acceded to, as described in Ellen Dannin's *Working free: the origins and impact of New Zealand's Employment Contract Act*, labour force rules, norms and expectations being radically redefined. In earlier decades the labour relations system had been held together by compulsory unionism, collective bargaining agreements, annual wage awards, negotiated relativities and an emphasis on improved employment conditions. These provisions were swept away as archaic. In their place were substituted new guidelines embodying voluntary unionism, contract bargaining, a switch to individual and enterprise agreements, strike bans and a clear movement towards placing employment relations on a wholly legalistic basis. At the same time, work conditions were rolled back. While there is still disagreement as to the overall effectiveness of the legislation, there is evidence that it was widely used by the business community to lower labour costs, and there can be little doubt that the consequence of labour market flexibility for most workers was a higher level of insecurity, the spectre of unemployment continuing.

Labour market reform dealt a severe blow to organized labour. Strong trade unions had been a feature of the New Zealand scene, and from the 1890s the country's industrial arbitration machinery had been held up to the world as an example of enlightened labour legislation. Even in 1990 over sixty per cent of the New Zealand workforce was unionized. Historian John Martin discusses the incremental assembly of this machinery in his study of New Zealand's Labour Department, *Holding the balance*. For much of the 20th century this machinery served the country reasonably well, notwithstanding the occasional outbursts of conflict recounted in histories of individual unions. But from the mid-1980s, with organizational rigidities being perceived, unions were strongly encouraged to reform themselves. While the fourth Labour Government had no strong inclination to do away with unions, it did wish to see a transfer towards industry- or enterprise-based bargaining. This could be best achieved, or so it was believed, through encouragement of the formation of fewer but stronger unions, and the Labour Relations Act 1987 addressed this objective. The move was sold to unionists on the grounds that mega-unions could act as a countervailing force against growing employer power. With a much higher minimum threshold (999) for official recognition being set, there were over 80 union amalgamations in the next 4 years. It was symptomatic of the proposed new order that 1987 saw the formation of the New Zealand Council of Trade Unions, an umbrella organization combining both public and private sector unions. The Employment Contracts Act, with its removal of compulsory union coverage, brought an entirely new complexion to the New Zealand labour scene. With unemployment high, and with traditional union bargaining weapons blunted, total membership dropped. To ensure survival, unions began to fight amongst themselves for the same groups of workers. Reviewing the preceding decade in 1994, Raymond Harbridge and Kevin Hince noted in their *A sourcebook of New Zealand trade unions* that a number of longstanding unions had already folded or been absorbed by other unions. The 248 unions of 1983 had reduced to around 60 and total membership was continuing to fall. The likelihood was that, while the more militant unions would retain much of their strength, workers in poorly organized or depressed industries, and those always likely to be exploited (women, youth, ethnic minorities, part-time workers and the unskilled) would suffer further declines in their working conditions and rates of pay. Pioneer labour historian Bert Roth has already detailed in *Remedy for present evils* how the new regime, coupled with restructuring of the public sector, has adversely impacted on one of New Zealand's foremost white-collar unions, the Public Service Association.

It was axiomatic that 'more market' would be synonymous with 'less government'. Beyond the corporatization and later privatization of many state trading enterprises, the core public service also came under the reformers' microscope. Without question, the state sector had become disproportionately large by the 1980s. By 1984 government spending constituted over forty per cent of GDP, and state organs were strongly represented in the landscapes of almost every community. Yet, while there were strong arguments for reviewing the state's overtly commercial activities, the case for radically restructuring the standard service departments and agencies was less clear cut. The core public service had many admirable features. Alan Henderson's *The quest for efficiency: the origins of the State Services Commission* recounts the post-1912 creation of an apolitical public service and the rationale for ensuring that public service efficiency was placed in the hands of a semi-autonomous agency. These remained guiding principles until the State Sector Act 1988 and the Public Finance Act of the following year. Taken together, these measures initiated what Jonathan Boston, probably the most prolific writer on the reforms, has termed 'the New Zealand model' of public sector management. Though justified on fiscal grounds, the resulting changes owed rather more to a deep-seated belief in the greater efficiency of the market in determining resource allocation. Under the new model, the power of the central agencies was reduced, managerial decision-making responsibilities being devolved to individual departments. In the place of permanent heads, new chief executives, where possible from the private sector, were appointed on performance-based contracts. From this point departments were required to embrace private sector management principles, many of their functions being placed on a cost recovery basis. To reinforce the new regime, policy, funding and delivery functions were separated. The thirty-nine government departments of 1984 by the mid-1990s were recast into three central (formerly control) agencies, ten policy agencies, nineteen delivery or transfer agencies and two with taxing functions. In addition, other functions had been assumed by 'crown entities', hybrids, not departments but not fully fledged state-owned enterprises either. The stated intentions of the upheaval had been the embedding of greater transparency in government transactions and the promotion of greater accountability on the part of public servants. Neither fully eventuated. Instead, new contractual fiefdoms developed, often more secretive and unaccountable than those they succeeded. The most dramatic manifestation of the new order was the shrinkage in the size of the core public service. In the decade after 1984 the number of public servants in the workforce more than halved. Paradoxically, however, there was no corresponding shrinkage in the scale of public expenditure. Indeed, as a result of the rising social costs of restructuring, in some areas it increased.

Reform of the public sector has not been without its critics. Jane Kelsey, for example, in *Rolling back the state*, deplores the relinquishment of much state power into the hands of the unelected. More measured is American public policy analyst Alan Schick's *The spirit of reform*, which acknowledges benefits of the upheaval while pointing out that major new problems were created. Many New Zealanders continue to harbour strong suspicion of the state sector reforms. Contributors to Andrew Sharp's *Leap into the dark: the changing role of the state in New Zealand since 1984* argue that politicians and their advisers have failed to carry the electorate with them, and that the reforms have been characterized by clumsiness and ineptitude.

That the push for reform of governmental administrative structures and procedures would spill over into local government was equally axiomatic. Claudia Scott's *Local and regional government in New Zealand* reviews the nature of local government prior to the 1980s. Since 1876 New Zealand had been characterized by a myriad of territorial local authorities – counties, boroughs and town districts – and a further structure of *ad hoc* authorities, such as harbour boards, pest destruction boards and electric power boards. While the numbers fluctuated, by 1984 there were over 230 territorial authorities and nearly twice that number had been established for special purposes. What was seen as the excessive fragmentation of local government had long been a target for potential reformers, but until the 1980s community resistance to rationalization had effectively stifled all attempts. Under the Local Government Amendment Act 1988, the Local Government Commission was empowered to unilaterally redraw the New Zealand local government map. It did so in little more than twelve months. While the wholesale amalgamation of territorial authorities was bitterly resented in many places, the resistance was to little avail. By 1990 the number of territorial local authorities had been compulsorily reduced to seventy-three, while all but a handful of the *ad hoc* local authorities had been abolished. Henceforth only two types of territorial local authorities – cities and districts – were to be permitted, with the respective functions of each more closely defined. To this structure was grafted a largely new tier of local government, regional councils, which would assume authority for those functions where there were wider communities of interest, involving perhaps several territorial local authorities. Many of the mandatory responsibilities previously assumed by the *ad hoc* authorities were transferred to the new regional councils, with, as in central government, commercial activities being corporatized. Local authority trading enterprises (LATEs) became a feature of the post-1989 New Zealand local government scene. The sweeping changes were justified by the Local Government Commission on the grounds of greater effectiveness and efficiency, all local authorities being required to conduct their business on corporate management principles. The process of reform is reviewed and assessed in Graham Bush's *Local government and politics in New Zealand.* That what was attempted was wholly in accord with the strictures of big business is further demonstrated in a research paper by Paul Harris, *Reforming local government?: a critical analysis of the views of the Business Roundtable.* There is also evidence that the reforms were not completely to the liking of the incoming 1990 National adminis-tration. Yet, while the idea of eliminating regional government, certainly of reducing the power of regional councils, was floated, few real changes have as yet been effected. Local authorities continue to follow a faltering path, uncertain as to just which of their remaining functions may be designated 'public good', and may therefore be financed from ratepayer funds, and which 'private good', subject to full user charges. Greater efficiency may have been delivered by the new structures, although this is a moot point, but there is growing citizen resentment at the corporate trappings now adopted by many local authority leaders, elected and managerial, and there is a mounting conviction that local authorities are much less democratic institutions than hitherto.

Redrawn local government boundaries are but one of many recent examples of spatial reorganization recorded in the second edition of Jan Kelly and Brian Marshall's *Atlas of New Zealand boundaries*. The compilers meticulously demonstrate the intricacy of New Zealand's division for administrative purposes. Less readily obvious is another spatial phenomenon, the emergence of a human landscape more closely resembling the physiographic, with figurative peaks and valleys, with areas teeming with activity and others near deserted. The territorial expression of change is much more complex than ten years ago. Spatial disparities are now more accentuated than at any time since the early colonizing period. The historical forces shaping New Zealand's human landscape were surveyed in pioneering volumes by A. H. Clark and Kenneth Cumberland, and an up-to-date survey, placing the New Zealand experience in international context, is Alan Grey's *Aotearoa and New Zealand: an historical geography*. But, as contributors to P. G. Holland and W. B. Johnston's *Southern approaches: geography in New Zealand* indicate, geography as a discipline has itself changed greatly over the past fifty years. The incorporated essays review past achievements, then identify, challenge and evaluate ways ahead for the subject. The editors enjoin practitioners to apply 'traditional concepts and new ways of thinking' to problem solving and the formulation of public policy. Two volumes co-operatively produced in the 1990s seek to take up the challenge. In 1992 fifty geographers combined to produce *Changing places in New Zealand: a geography of restructuring*, a contribution to discourse previously dominated by economists and political scientists. The underlying theme is that restructuring changes places, and the objective is to analyse 'new activity patterns, evolving organisations, altered personal and household circumstances – all outcomes of restructuring'. A sequel, *Changing places: New Zealand in the nineties*, published four years later, considers more recent change issues, assessing how they are affecting people's sense of place.

An accentuated redistribution of New Zealand's population has been one of the more obvious spatial outcomes of restructuring. Two established trends, a drift of people from south to north and an increasingly urbanized population, were already apparent prior to 1984, but they were lent impetus in subsequent years. The background to these developments is explored in the United Nations' publication *Population of New Zealand*. By the early 1990s nearly seventy-five per cent of the country's population was resident in the North Island, over half in the north of the North Island. Partially this reflected higher rates of natural increase in the north and overseas migrant location preferences, but between 1986 and 1991, while the Auckland, Waikato and Bay of Plenty regions all experienced substantial net internal migration gains, all other New Zealand regions, with the exception of Northland and Canterbury, recorded net losses. By 1991 some 85 per cent of New Zealanders lived in urban areas, 68 per cent in cities with populations of at least 30,000. Some 26 per cent of the country's population lived in the Auckland metropolitan area alone. New Zealand's population growth rate, however, was relatively static, the average annual rates of increase being significantly less than one per cent from the early 1980s. Further, with the post-Second World War 'baby boom' bulge moving through the age cohorts, and with fertility rates declining, the New Zealand population was an ageing population. As Natalie Jackson and Ian Pool demonstrate in *Fertility and family formation in the second demographic transition*, the dynamics of the current low fertility levels are complex. Increased use of contraception, greater participation of women in the labour force, rising divorce rates and the general economic conditions have all contributed, directly or indirectly. Patterns of marriage and family formation have also changed radically, as Jan Cameron argues in several publications, with pronounced shifts away from early marriage and childbearing towards later marriage and later childbearing, in some instances to decisions to forego children completely. An intriguing countervailing sub-trend has been the rapid recent growth of *de facto* relationships and ex-nuptial births. By the mid-1990s around forty per cent of all New Zealand births were ex-nuptial, almost certainly reflecting pressures on the family as a social unit, but the total birth rate was barely sufficient to ensure the population would replace itself. To offset projected future 'human resource' problems, immigration flows have been enthusiastically fostered in the 1990s, albeit with strict means tests for migrants from non-traditional supply areas being introduced. New Zealand has been a country built on immigration, but in the post-Second World War years, flows have fluctuated widely. In contrast to the 1950s and 1960s, net immigration losses typified the 1980s. Contributors to Gordon Carmichael's *Trans-Tasman migration* show that both traditionally and in recent years the greatest population movements have been to and from Australia, but the major sources of permanent migrants in earlier decades remained Britain and Europe. In the 1990s this changed. British and European migration declined, inflows from the Pacific Islands were small but steady, and, in response to positive incentives, Asian immigration increased significantly. The new immigration policies have been controversial. Some of the implications, most pertinently whether New Zealand should be a monocultural, bicultural or multicultural society, are examined in Stuart Greif's *Immigration and national identity in New Zealand.*

Despite the existence of a multiplicity of ethnic – and cultural – minorities in New Zealand, many of whose adaptive experiences have been recorded in print, New Zealand remains ethnically a relatively homogeneous society. At the 1991 census nearly eighty per cent of New Zealand's population was of European origin, predominantly from the British Isles, but with a leavening from mainland Europe. The indigenous Maori population made up the next largest grouping, around thirteen per cent, while Pacific Islanders accounted for five per cent of the population. Chinese and Indians constituted the most significant Asian minorities, but together still accounted for less than two per cent of the population. In other respects, however, New Zealand society was less than homogeneous, and rapidly becoming more so. A widely perpetuated myth about New Zealand is that it is a classless society. This is unlikely to have ever been true, as essays in David Pitt's *Social class in New Zealand* indicate, but post-1984 differences between social groups became accentuated. Contributors to Paul Spoonley et al., *New Zealand society: a sociological introduction* highlight the increasing inequalities arising not only from class, but also from racism, ethnicity and gender. Perhaps the most striking inequality, however, has been the widening gap between rich and poor. A 1990 New Zealand Planning Council report, *Who gets what?: the distribution of income and wealth in New Zealand,* concluded that income became far less equally distributed among New Zealand households during the late 1980s, and that the trend was likely to continue in the 1990s. While the position of the rich, particularly the business elite, has been impressionistically surveyed by Stevan Eldred-Grigg, serious analysis is awaited. Arguably the plight of the poor has attracted greater, if still slight, attention. Economist Brian Easton has contributed significantly to the debate, pointing out that the traditionally marginalized have been joined by growing numbers of new poor. His *Wages and the poor* advances the proposition that many wage earners and their families now fall below a notional poverty line. Charles Waldegrave and Rosalynn Coventry's 1987 polemic *Poor New Zealand* successfully, if transiently, drew public attention to the problem, attracting both praise for the authors' attempt to bring it into the open, and derision for what for many were unpalatable findings.

It was essentially to assist the poor and disadvantaged that earlier social reformers had conceived and promoted New Zealand's version of the welfare state, the foundations being laid in the late 19th century and the structure being capped off in the mid- and late 1930s. Thus, even before the Second World War, the concept of collective responsibility for ensuring individual and societal well-being had become commonly accepted. While the initial emphasis was on income maintenance, the reduction of social inequalities, and the provision of high standard social services, in the immediate post-Second World War decades the welfare state assumed wider and more pervasive forms. The achievements to the mid-1970s are summarized by contributors to Andrew Trlin's *Social welfare and New Zealand society*. The reality was that by that point few New Zealanders under the age of twenty-five had personally experienced severe economic insecurity. They were cared for, in a well-worn phrase, 'from the cradle to the grave'. By the early 1980s, however, as Brian Easton demonstrates in *Social policy and the welfare state*, the New Zealand welfare state was under stress. Full employment, one of the bases for the social contract which had fuelled its post-war expansion, was itself under threat. Declining real incomes were matched by rising real costs. As the state struggled to continue to deliver, feelings developed that the policies intended to ensure security of employment were failing, that despite heavy direct and indirect taxation the provision of quality social services was falling short of public expectations, and that inequalities, rather than reducing, were in fact increasing. The way was therefore made easier for the new, more individualistic, generation of political and bureaucratic reformers, ironically the very generation which had most benefited from the operation of the welfare state. From 1984 the watchwords became increased targeting and market competition. Individuals were to be assisted by the state only when in dire need. What since the 1930s had been viewed as collective goods – health, education and to a lesser extent housing – became redefined as individual goods, with the individual being charged for a proportion, if not the full cost, of the service. The implications of the change of thinking under Labour are examined in Mike O'Brien and Chris Wilkes' *The tragedy of the market*. Yet, while the enthusiasm for restructuring in the social arena was driven by budgetary problems, between 1984 and 1990 social spending actually increased, the consequence of escalating unemployment and adverse economic conditions. The perceived need for further expenditure cuts, as much as ideological commitment, underpinned the even more draconian social services restructuring under National after 1990. Recourse to the market in service provision became even more extreme, while the benefits system (income support), previously relatively inviolate, came under outright attack. It was a short step from highlighting the inadequacies of the welfare state to attributing to it direct responsibility for most of the country's social ills. Brandishing moral banners, polemicists such as David Green have argued strongly that 'individuals should accept responsibility for their own upkeep, wherever possible'. Their arguments have fallen upon receptive ears. There is now widespread agreement amongst government decision-makers that only 'a modest safety net' can be justified.

Changing attitudes to the state's social responsibilities are perhaps most glaringly evident in the restructuring of the public health system. From the 1930s universal services had been organized in three discrete sectors: primary health care, generally delivered by private practitioners under subsidy; secondary care, provided regionally through block grants to elected hospital boards; and public health services delivered via the Department of Health. The system is overviewed by Derek Dow in *Safeguarding the public health*. Though undeniably costly, the system nevertheless served New Zealand well. Just how well is indicated by the ageing population, an index of falling mortality rates. Concerned at the costs, however, the 1984-90 Labour Government commissioned a prominent businessman to prepare a report recommending public hospital reforms. The Gibbs Report, delivered in 1988, advocated the separation of health 'funders' and 'providers', and the creation of competition between the latter. This, it was agreed, would improve efficiency and give better value for the 'taxpayers' health dollar'. Though shrinking from this panacea, the commissioners nevertheless initiated a partial restructure in 1989, existing hospital boards being reorganized into fourteen area health boards to increase the potential for tighter management. The National government elected in 1990 early signalled it intended to go much further, reviving the 1988 report and adding embellishments. The objective of a fully competitive 'health market' would be achieved through the establishment of four regional health authorities (RHAs), which would act as purchasers for all health services for their populations. Labour's fourteen area health boards were to be abolished overnight and reconstituted as twenty-three commercially oriented crown health enterprises (CHEs), which would be required to compete for funding with private and voluntary providers. A rigorous user charges regime was to be instituted. The Department of Health was to be transformed into the Ministry of Health, a policy agency.

The purported aim was to increase efficiency while simultaneously containing spending. Predictably, responsibility for implementing the new structure was delegated to a group drawn from the business sector. The nature of the experiment is comparatively assessed in Robert Blank's *New Zealand health policy: a comparative study*, and in literature prepared by the opposition, particularly the Public Health Coalition. The proposals met considerable community resistance, both on the grounds of their general unmarketability and suspected deeper intents. The longer-term aim was considered to be privatization, while in the shorter term 'rationalization' of health services was likely to entail the closure of facilities. Protesters took to the streets. Within two years of the launching of the scheme the government was in partial, if by no means complete, retreat. The reformers were not helped by the inability of CHEs to meet financial targets, by the emergence of a burgeoning health bureaucracy, and by the failure of touted better services to materialize. In the run-up to the 1996 election the New Zealand health system was depicted as in crisis, and all contenders promised ameliorative action. The post-election changes, however, have been largely cosmetic, and the ruling coalition continues to cling tenaciously to its now much amended commercial model.

A bulwark of New Zealand's welfare state from the 1930s has been the provision of income support for the aged, the unemployed and those otherwise in need. If the curtailment of publicly funded health services has probably occasioned the greatest public protest, the recent slashing of benefits has given rise to at least equal bitterness. Again, rising costs provided the immediate rationale. To be sure, in the twenty years to 1990 annual expenditure had risen from just over a quarter of a billion (New Zealand) dollars to nearly ten billion dollars, and by the latter year there were three beneficiaries for every four individuals in paid employment, but what critics tended to ignore was that the most rapid increases had been from the mid-1980s, reflecting the social dislocations of the first phase of restructuring. Treasury's briefing to the incoming 1990 National government provided the underlying justification: the need to offset 'the negative social consequences . . . of welfare dependency'. Within months the new administration indicated its intention to 'redesign' the benefits system, announcing, in addition to major cuts to all benefits and much stricter eligibility criteria, the abolition of the universal family benefit and new rules enforcing prolonged stand-downs before the unemployed became eligible for state assistance. Universal superannuation, long considered a citizen's right, was radically modified to become a tightly tested welfare benefit. These measures effectively reduced the disposable incomes of virtually all beneficiaries, in some cases by more than a third. That there would be ongoing attempts to shift some of the state's responsibilities for providing support to those in need on to families and voluntary agencies was made clear. As Jonathan Boston and Paul Dalziel (*The decent society?*) observe: 'rather than encouraging a sense of security and safe prospect, National . . . created greater insecurity'. In subsequent years that insecurity has been little allayed. While forced to retract some policy details, and tinkering has been constant, the government has retained its broad thrust. Despite attempts to broker an all-party superannuation accord in the mid-1990s, the goal remains greater individual responsibility for maintenance in old age. A recent abortive referendum sought to impose a compulsory savings scheme. A punitive approach to the unemployed has also become entrenched, work for benefits schemes being mooted. The attitude to beneficiaries has been characterized by 'dob in a dole bludger' campaigns. Inevitably, the statutory social service agencies have also been restructured in line with the favoured public sector model, and the tasks and goals of those agencies have been redefined. As contributors to Robyn Munford and Mary Nash's *Social work in action* explain, this has vitally affected the ability of state social workers to adequately fulfil their professional obligations. Even agencies such as New Zealand's Accident Compensation Commission (ACC), a world pioneer in its field, have had their roles redefined. While the conversion of the ACC into a fully commercialized insurance company is not yet complete, the arraignment of successive chief executives on misappropriation charges suggests that the credo of individualism has had unexpected repercussions.

The early 1990s also witnessed radical changes to the ways in which the state provides housing assistance, especially to low-income families. As Gael Ferguson has shown in *Building the New Zealand dream*, state support for housing has been an intrinsic part of New Zealand life from the late 19th century, when cheap loan finance was first provided. The widespread state provision of rental housing, at modest cost, dates from 1936. By the 1960s the state was financing more than half of the houses built in New Zealand annually. While this represented a peak, when the Housing Corporation of New Zealand (HCNZ) became the principal delivery agency in the mid-1970s the rental stock stood at nearly 53,000 units, while in the financial year ending 31 March 1976, over 19,000 home loans were authorized. It was business as usual throughout the 1980s. By 1990 the rental stock had risen to nearly 68,000 units and, while the Corporation had become but one source of finance, over 25,000 loans were approved. The major changes after 1984 were reductions in the level of subsidies for state tenants and a general move to raise rents and interest rates nearer to market trends. In its 1991 budget the National government heralded major departures from established policy. The Housing Corporation was restructured and, in its place, a new commercial enterprise, Housing New Zealand, was charged with administration of the state's rental stock. What was in store was indicated by an announcement that full market rentals for these properties would be phased in. The government's intention to exit from the housing finance market was also announced. The Housing Corporation's mortgage portfolio was to be sold to the private sector. An accommodation supplement, payable by the Department of Social Welfare, would enable tenants unable to meet the new rentals to secure appropriate accommodation, whether provided by the public or private sectors. To complete the commercialization of state housing, policy was transferred to a new Housing Ministry. Implementation of the reforms began almost immediately. The introduction of market rents commenced in 1991, while the first batch of HCNZ mortgages was sold in 1993, to a consortium organized and controlled by merchant bankers Fay Richwhite. With the differentials between public and private provision being thus largely eliminated, the principal beneficiaries were landlords and finance houses. After six years the postulated gains for consumers have proven largely illusory. Renters continue to struggle, an increasing number of state properties being untenanted, while a further refinement, the sale of properties in high-value locations and their replacement in lower-status areas, has heightened the prospect of ghettoization. Former state mortgagees, their mortgages transferred to the private sector, have not uncommonly found their interest rates lifted to above current market levels. The original purpose of state housing was to enable low-income working families to share in the high-quality accommodation deemed to be a foundation of family life. In the absence of significant increases in income, the business approach seems unlikely to be able to deliver.

Business nostrums have also underpinned the restructuring of New Zealand's traditionally state-provided education services. Whereas from the 1930s equality of educational opportunity, at all levels, had been the overriding objective, the contestable provision of skills considered appropriate to the country's new enterprise culture became paramount from the late 1980s. As Alison Jones et al. have observed (*Myths and realities: schooling in New Zealand*) education has come to be officially regarded as 'just another commodity to be purchased . . . . utilised and consumed'. In 1989 Labour initiated the first experiments in respect of the state's primary and secondary schools. Although a new Ministry of Education retained the right to set broad policy parameters, substantial administrative and financial responsibilities were transferred from the centre, and from abolished regional education boards, to staff and locally elected boards of trustees at individual schools, the intention being that each school be managed as a semi-autonomous business unit. To monitor this performance a new supervisory agency, the Education Review Office (ERO), was set up. Two years later, to enhance competition between the 'provider units' (schools), enrolment procedures were deregulated, zoned catchment areas being abolished. By the mid-1990s, despite resistance, school boards were under pressure to accept a bulk funding formula, and consequent further responsibilities. What had at first been portrayed as a laudable attempt to more closely involve parents in their children's education in fact greatly exacerbated existing inequalities between schools. Those benefiting from the new approach were almost invariably located in middle- to high-income areas. Conversely, schools in lower socio-economic catchments tended to lose pupils, and with them funding. A further disturbing trend was that schools with falling rolls tended to have a higher percentage of Maori and Pacific Island enrolments. As several studies, in particular Cathy Wylie's *Self managing schools in New Zealand*, indicate, in many schools parental enthusiasm soon ebbed, with obligations to raise supplementary local funding to maintain services rancouring. The pressures of the marketplace were also transmitted to the tertiary, or post-compulsory, education sector. While no compelling case for reform was advanced, as Ruth Butterworth and Nicholas Tarling note, successive governments resolved on *A shakeup anyway*. The shake-up started from the top. Under the purview of the Ministry of Education, the councils of universities and polytechnics were directly bulk funded and required to operate as business boards. Perversely, while tertiary enrolments increased, partially through lack of job opportunities, funding per student dropped. As part of the new ethos, universal free entry to tertiary institutions was scrapped, students being required to pay increasing proportions of their course fees. Though targeted assistance for some groups remained available, the needs of the majority were to be met through an interest-bearing student loans scheme. Necessarily, institutions had to compete for students and fee income, and to meet funding shortfalls full-fee-paying overseas students were actively sought. The established tertiary 'providers' increasingly were also required to compete with private training establishments (PTEs), which also attracted government funding. It was symptomatic of official anxiety to fashion a seamless, skills-based education system that there should be vigorous attempts to integrate secondary education, trades training and tertiary education into a single co-ordinated qualifications framework, administered by a new body, the New Zealand Qualifications Authority (NZQA). That this approach has not enjoyed unqualified support is suggested by Roger Peddie and Bryan Tuck's *Setting the standards: the assessment of competence in national qualifications.*

Despite the heightened efficiency and greater fiscal responsibility justifications advanced for many of New Zealand's recent structural reforms, a range of indicators suggest that attempted achievement has been at considerable social cost. Paul Green's introductory *Studies in New Zealand social problems* sets out a formidable catalogue of issues currently negatively affecting most members of society – sexism, racism, violence, deviance and escalating substance abuse are but random examples – and seeks to predict where future problems may be anticipated. In almost all instances, problems of economic origin have been exacerbated by the retreat from welfare assistance. Probably the single greatest contributor to social dislocation has been the rising incidence of unemployment, the implications of which are discussed in Ian Shirley et al.'s *Unemployment in New Zealand.* Unemployment began to rise in the later 1970s, climbed steeply from the mid-1980s, then peaked in the early 1990s. By 1991 registered unemployed accounted for around 10.2 per cent of the workforce. Not unexpectedly, the unemployment rate was higher for males than females, youth unemployment was particularly heavy, those without qualifications fared worst, and Maori and Pacific Island people were three times more likely to be unemployed than Europeans. Even so, these trends were only part of the story. As corporations and state agencies were recast, redundancy also became a spectre for the middle class, the middle aged and the middle incomed. Few New Zealand families were completely unaffected. Inevitably, the resulting insecurity took its toll on this fundamental unit of social organization. Peggy Koopman-Boyden's collection, *Families in New Zealand society,* outlines traditional stereotypes and values, but by the mid-1990s the study had assumed a distinctly historical aspect. With marriages, and traditional gender roles, under intense pressure, the divorce rate rose sharply and single-parent families became increasingly commonplace. As the numbers of long-term unemployed (those unemployed for more than twenty-six weeks) swelled, feelings of hopelessness developed, especially among the young. Unsurprisingly, this was manifested in anti-social behaviour. Both property crimes and crimes of violence increased significantly, and by the mid-1990s nearly half of all apprehended offenders were under twenty-one years of age. The background to these patterns is examined by sociologist Greg Newbold in *Crime and deviance*. Between 1985 and 1995 convictions for violent sex offences more than tripled and, even more disturbing, the majority of the victims were aged sixteen or less. A disproportionate amount of the offending was by gang members, such groups providing alternative social bonding for young members of the new underclass. While Bill Payne (*Staunch*) argues that the gang phenomenon was not entirely adverse, their menacing public image further played on troubled minds. There is also evidence that gangs were heavily involved, both as suppliers and users, in New Zealand's proliferating drug culture. Though older New Zealanders continued to prefer alcohol as the means to temporary oblivion, the young were more catholic in their substance-abuse tastes. By the mid-1990s police were stretched to respond and prison populations had reached unprecedented levels. The official response, rather than appropriately addressing the problems at root, was to ponder the privatization of some police functions and to embrace the concept of privately run prisons. Social conservatives clucked disapprovingly at the decline in traditional values, but failed to see the correlation with the structural reforms that many of their number supported.

A particularly unfortunate by-product of the recent induced social stress has been a deterioration in race relations, between Maori and European, and between both of these groups and migrant communities. While New Zealand has long claimed to have model race relations, writers such as Angela Ballara (*Proud to be white?*) and David Pearson (*A dream deferred*) suggest that ethnocentric prejudice has been long term and deep seated. As long as prosperous conditions prevailed, however, overt demonstrations were muted. The onset of tougher times removed the lid from a pot of underlying resentments and misunderstandings, revealing that for generations New Zealand's major racial groups had been 'talking past each other'. Probably the most prolific writer on the subject has been Massey University sociologist Paul Spoonley who, most notably in the *Nga Patai* series, has sought to promote greater understanding of the dynamics of New Zealand ethnic relations. While in his most recent work Spoonley pays especial attention to attitudes to the new wave of East Asian migrants, there can be little doubt that resolution of Maori-European differences poses a greater challenge. The historical foundations of longstanding Maori resentments have been well documented: loss of sovereignty; loss of land; and, to a degree, loss of culture. All reinforce a conviction amongst many Maori that the terms of the Treaty of Waitangi have not been fulfilled, and that Maori have been permanently subordinated within their own country in terms of power relations. Attempts to redress past grievances through the Treaty claims process have had mixed results. For some Maori activists, as evidenced by several contributors to *Maori sovereignty*, too little has been offered, and possibly too late. Conversely, for some Europeans far too much has already been conceded. The late Stuart Scott's polemic *The travesty of Waitangi* captures the chagrined bewilderment of many Europeans who formerly subscribed to the racial harmony myth. An even more ugly reaction has been the emergence of 'white power' groups, purportedly to offset Maori counterparts. Howsoever these tensions are to be eventually resolved, as they must, there is irrefutable evidence that Maori were particularly disadvantaged by the post-1984 restructuring. It was in peripheral districts with heavy Maori populations, and in urban occupations with heavy Maori concentrations, that the adverse consequences were most acutely felt. A Maori unemployment rate several times higher than that for Europeans only compounded existing social disadvantages. Maori health problems, for example, continue to be of concern. Despite significant improvements since the 1950s, Maori life expectancy still falls some six years short of European rates. The Maori infant mortality rate remains twice that of Europeans. Maori continue to be particularly susceptible to a range of lifestyle-oriented illnesses. By the early 1990s the figure for Maori first admissions to mental hospitals was nearly twice that for Europeans. Also, despite a number of ameliorative initiatives, including Maori-language instruction, Maori educational achievement still lags behind that of other groups. Beginning with the establishment of *kohanga reo* (Maori-language early childhood centres), the stimulation of Maori education has extended into the compulsory schooling system, but Maori continue to be underrepresented in tertiary education. Many of these issues are addressed by Maori academic Ranginui Walker in collections of media columns published in the past decade. Walker provides insights into the new wave of Maori assertiveness which first appeared in the 1960s, gathered momentum in the 1970s, then broke in the 1980s. At one extreme this led to demonstrations and physical confrontations – the disruption of Waitangi Day commemorations, occupations of disputed lands – but at the other it fostered a determination to use the existing political machinery for Maori advantage. Lindsay Cox's *Kotahitanga* shows that since the beginnings of colonization there has been a continuing search for Maori unity, for the ability to speak with a distinct political voice. While this objective has still to be achieved fully, Maori politicians, whatever their party affiliations, now seemingly share a near-common view of Maori aspirations. More significantly, the 1996 election saw a record number of Maori members returned to the New Zealand Parliament.

The emergence of a new cadre of Maori politicians has been but one ingredient in an increasingly volatile New Zealand political mix. General vexation on the part of voters at the apparent powerlessness of the average citizen to influence national directions has pervaded New Zealand politics for much of the past two decades. It was disgruntlement over Sir Robert Muldoon's autocratic leadership of his 1975-84 National administration that paved the way for David Lange's Labour victory in 1984. While Labour's reforming intentions were unrevealed prior to the election, rightwing politics had already received a fillip through the short-lived emergence of the New Zealand Party, the creation of millionaire businessman Bob Jones. The election provided a platform for the individualistic free-market policies advocated by Jones in his earlier *New Zealand the way I want it*. He was to get his wish, but from an unexpected quarter. As Labour Finance Minister Roger Douglas subsequently confided in *Towards prosperity*, his personal agenda differed markedly from established Labour policy positions. Many traditional supporters watched stunned as their electoral representatives slashed and burned. While Labour's independent foreign policy stance, and a promise of enlightened social policies in the future, together with the support of a large but fickle swinging vote, held sufficient of the party's support base to ensure a second three-year term in 1987, notice was nevertheless served. It went unheeded. When Labour's 'drys' immediately endeavoured to jettison their social policy commitments, then to push for even more extreme restructuring measures, the party lapsed into internecine warfare. In the eighteen months leading to the 1990 election there was the curious spectacle of three different Labour prime ministers. Promising to deliver New Zealanders 'the decent society', Jim Bolger's National Party took the country in a landslide. What voters soon discovered, however, was that they had figuratively exchanged Tweedledum for Tweedledee. National's prescription was more of the same, but with even less concern for the social implications. In particular, Bolger's equally doctrinaire Finance Minister, Ruth Richardson (*Making a difference*), further fanned public disillusionment with the political process, and that disillusionment deepened as National turned its attention to reconstruction of the welfare state. For most of the post-Second World War period New Zealand politics had been a two-horse race between Labour and National, third parties only occasionally making respectable showings, but in the lead-up to the 1993 election two new forces emerged. Both new parties were political expressions of discontent. The New Zealand Alliance was a coalition of five established minority parties, led by exiled former Labour president, Jim Anderton. New Zealand First was a populist vehicle for sacked National cabinet minister Winston Peters. While the new parties made inroads, and Labour rallied in the 1993 polls, National just held on, the beneficiary of New Zealand's 'first past the post' electoral system. But it was highly likely this would be the last time any party would enjoy an absolute majority. A poll on electoral reform, held concurrently with the election, narrowly endorsed an earlier referendum approving a switch to a mixed member proportional representation system (MMP). While there must be suspicion that the endorsement owed rather more to a widespread desire to punish politicians for their broken promises than to careful consideration of what was proposed, between 1993 and 1996 there were nevertheless expectations that more democratic governments would result. All parties concentrated on positioning themselves for the new political order. As the first MMP elections loomed in 1996, the situation was complicated by the appearance of yet another party, the Association of Consumers and Taxpayers (ACT), led by several of the more extreme reformers of the preceding decade. As predicted, no clear winner emerged. After months of uncertainty, a coalition of National and its previously most virulent critic, New Zealand First, took office. With business as usual resuming, voter anger turned against the system which had delivered this incongruous pairing. Contributors to Raymond Miller's *New Zealand politics in transition* consider the implications for political institutions and parties.

Popular resentment has centred on the seeming omnipotence of ruling parties. With no chamber of review, and with statute law overriding common law, there have been few curbs on the actions of political executives, once elected. This theme is explored in Elizabeth McLeay's *The cabinet and political power in New Zealand*. But the dangers of New Zealand's unicameral legislature, and of the lack of a formal constitution, had long been noted. In the 1970s academic lawyer Geoffrey Palmer had written extensively on the perils of what he termed 'unbridled power'. In the 1980s it fell to Palmer, recast as a senior member of Labour governments, to effect some of the constitutional reforms he had preached. His foundation was the Constitution Act 1986. Until that time the country's constitution was a miscellany of statutory and customary law, welded together by a number of unwritten conventions. These were incorporated in a single piece of legislation. Passage of the Constitution Act initiated a short period of constitutional activism. While the power of the executive, in reality, was little diluted, there were strenuous efforts to establish counterbalancing rights. The culmination was the Bill of Rights Act 1990, which required legislators and the judiciary to take rights issues into account in conducting the business of the nation. Maori rights, including clarification of the status of the Treaty of Waitangi, also received close attention in these years, as did citizen safeguards offered by the Ombudsmen's Office and Freedom of Information legislation. Many of these matters are canvassed in Philip Joseph's *Essays on the constitution*. While the reforming impetus perceptibly slackened after 1990, and the withdrawal of Palmer from politics, constitutional questions continued to be debated, if less vigorously. The idea of restoring a second legislative chamber was floated as an alternative to reform of the electoral system, while the possibility of New Zealand becoming a republic was broached. Neither proposal, however, greatly captured the public imagination.

Palmer's second broad thrust in the 1980s was an attempt to reform Parliament itself, to make it a more streamlined legislating body. There were longstanding complaints that the lawmaking process had become sclerotic, that enactments were too frequently deficient or ill considered. The resulting procedural changes are summarized in the second edition of David McGee's *Parliamentary practice in New Zealand*. Yet, while the quality of legislation may have improved following these changes, although this would be challenged by many, there was no slackening in the volume emerging. Wholesale restructuring necessitated both a welter of amendments to existing legislation and new measures. Notwithstanding the creation of a Law Commission in 1985, charged to undertake 'the systematic review, reform and development of the law in New Zealand', the statute books continued to grow in size and complexity. Several studies consider the evolution of a unique body of New Zealand law, but the most recent is Peter Spiller et al.'s *A New Zealand legal history*. This places particular emphasis on the background to a number of major legal questions of contemporary concern. The most widely used general introduction to the New Zealand legal system is R. D. Mulholland's text, *Introduction to the legal system*, which is regularly updated. To date, apart from the establishment of several specialist courts and tribunals, reform of the courts has been largely cosmetic, judicial independence being enshrined in the Constitution Act. But there are nevertheless indicators that further changes may be in store, these including the replacement of career court registrars by business managers, and serious proposals that rights of appeal to the nation's highest court, the London-based Judicial Committee of the Privy Council, be abolished.

Resource management law was another area selected for major overhaul. Notwithstanding a longstanding tradition of development considerations overriding conservation values, New Zealand has enjoyed a reputation for environmental consciousness. In the eyes of many observers this 'clean green' image was enhanced in the 1980s through Labour's adoption of a nuclear-free policy and the involvement of some of its senior politicians in international environmental issues. Labour's decision to espouse these issues was electorally driven. From the 1960s a strong green movement, probed by Scott McVarish in *The greening of New Zealand*, had emerged. Fighting pitched battles over the future of indigenous lowland forests and the perceived misuse of lakes and rivers, adherents appeared to offer a promising constituency. To the 1980s, while a Commission for the Environment existed, environmental administration was largely entrusted to several multipurpose state agencies – in particular, the Department of Lands and Survey and the New Zealand Forest Service – with the greatest emphasis being on water and soil conservation, and on the preservation of national parks and other scenic areas. Lance McCaskill's *Hold this land* explains the origin of the country's soil erosion and flooding problems, while Michael Roche's *Land and water* describes a half-century of official attempts to offset them. David Thom, in *Heritage: the parks of the people*, outlines the creation of a national parks system, noting a bias towards mountain and other non-productive lands. Wider environmental planning issues were handled by the Town and Country Planning Division of the Ministry of Works. By the early 1980s this bureaucratic machinery was under heavy attack by environmentalists, conflicts of interest between the administering agencies' developmental and conservational functions being pointed out. While environmentalists were quick to claim responsibility for the comprehensive restructuring of environmental administration initiated by Labour in the late 1980s, many missed the point that the views of the Treasury and of the business community were as important, and that market liberals welcomed the opportunity to divorce resource development and conservation. In 1987 the multipurpose agencies were swept away, being replaced by new policy ministries (most significantly the Ministry for the Environment), two commercial corporations (Landcorp, Forest Corp), a Department of Conservation and a residual Department of Survey and Land Information. As Tom Buhrs and Robert Bartlett indicate in *Environmental policy in New Zealand*, what was conceived as a victory by environmentalists all too soon proved to be a pyrrhic victory. Despite their bad press, the multipurpose agencies had previously been able to fund conservation activities through cross-subsidization. Under the new regime the Department of Conservation was heavily dependent on voted funds, and from the very beginning it was on short commons. Chronic underfunding was to lead to tragedies in the 1990s. It was also to lead to increasing pressure for commercialization of the public domain. Reforming the administrative machinery, however, was but one aspect of the restructuring programme. At the urging of developers and their bureaucratic allies, it was also deemed necessary to alter fundamentally environmental and planning law. Conceived under Labour, but finally enacted by National, the Resource Management Act 1991 replaced fifty-nine separate statutes and various regulations and orders. Trumpeted by the Ministry for the Environment as 'world leading', it introduced to New Zealanders the new doctrine of 'sustainable management', which was freely interpreted by many supporters as 'sustainable development' in a more liberal administrative context. Behind a facade of concern, the measure incorporated many market-based mechanisms: tradable permits, user charges and performance bonds. The message was that direct environmental regulation should be a last resort, used only where economic instruments and voluntary measures were ineffective or too costly.

One of New Zealand's recent conservation success stories, attributable to small teams of dedicated scientists, has been the launching of programmes aimed at saving several endangered bird species. For a small country, New Zealand has had a proud record in scientific research. Moreover, while there has been an understandable preoccupation with primary production-oriented research, with improving grasslands and dairy technology, pure research has not been neglected. The Rutherford tradition has remained strong. From the 1920s, however, organized New Zealand scientific research was dominated by a small group of government departments. Foremost amongst these was the omnibus Department of Scientific and Industrial Research, the evolution of which has been recorded by J. D. Atkinson, but other Crown science agencies included the New Zealand Meteorological Service, the Forestry Research Institute, and specialist units attached to mainline government departments (e.g. Agriculture, Health). Whether or not this model afforded a viable framework for future scientific activity came to be questioned in the 1980s. Several commissioned reports offered views that science should 'play a fuller role in national development', this prompting decision-makers to conclude that a dose of market discipline might be beneficial. How the dose was administered is described in Chris Palmer's *The reform of the public science system in New Zealand*. In

1992 the development of science policy, provision of science funding and the actual conduct of research were separated 'to enable much clearer objectives to be established'. At the top of the new hierarchy, with existing agencies phased out, was the Ministry of Research, Science and Technology (MORST), charged to formulate government's overall science policy framework and to devise priorities and guidelines for future research funding. Assessment of funding applications was delegated to another new body, the Foundation for Research, Science and Technology (FORST), basically set up to administer a contestable 'Public Good Science Fund'. Researchers and research agencies, including the nation's universities, were now to be required to bid for funding, their likely success being determined by how they fitted in with an official statement of strategies prepared by MORST, and by the extent to which particular research projects would deliver realizable outputs. Perhaps not surprisingly, the major recipients of funding to date have been nine Crown Research Institutes (CRIs), many formerly parts of earlier public science agencies but now re-engineered as companies and expected to yield monetary as well as scientific dividends. Though the full impact of the science reforms still has to be assessed, early signs are that major· scientific programmes, a number of long duration, have been disrupted, in some instances completely jettisoned. Surveys of the official scientific community suggest low morale. In particular, pure science has been hard hit, measuring poorly against the commercial yardstick. It was partially to offset this difficulty that in 1996 the country's oldest scientific organization, the Royal Society of New Zealand, was allotted new functions. As Charles Fleming has demonstrated in his history of the Royal Society, *Science, settlers and scholars*, for over a century the organization has been an exclusive club for the country's senior scientists, but it is now proposed it be more inclusive and proactive. While it will continue to represent the interests of individual scientists and professional societies, it will also administer the Marsden Fund, set up to foster 'curiosity driven research'.

While public concern for New Zealand's physical environment has been marked in recent decades, and there have been some notable successes in protecting natural sites, protection of the nation's built environment, its historic sites, buildings and precincts, has been less than totally successful. Indeed, in the turbulent 1980s, at least until the 1987 stockmarket crash, demolition balls swung relentlessly in New Zealand's towns and cities, clearing sections for property developers. In the major centres much loved buildings, whole townscapes, were obliterated. Moreover, the destruction was not just confined to the urban environment. Beyond town boundaries the needs of enterprise were accorded primacy, even when the sites in question were ancient Maori sites. The New Zealand Historic Places Trust, the country's leading heritage agency, relatively toothless and chronically underfunded, was powerless to intervene. In view of the damage then wreaked, what is left is therefore the more precious. Several studies catalogue New Zealand's major historic sites, while there has been a profusion of books on New Zealand's architecture. A useful introduction to the built environment is Peter Shaw's *New Zealand architecture*, which examines 'the full diversity of architectural styles . . . from early Maori functional simplicity . . . to the post-modernism of the 1980s'. Frances Porter's *Historic buildings of New Zealand*, published under Historic Places Trust aegis, highlights some particular architectural treasures. Residential architecture is comprehensively surveyed in Jeremy Salmond's *Old houses, 1800-1940*, although particular styles are treated in greater detail in a number of specialist works. New Zealand's industrial and commercial buildings are less well served, but a trio of books by former Deputy Government Architect Geoffrey Thornton merit honourable mention. They cover business houses and factories, farm buildings and a wide range of structures made of concrete. That many of the buildings and structures described in these books remain under threat is suggested by contemporary editorials in the Trust's journal, officials and supporters noting that reformed local authorities have been reluctant to pick up heritage responsibilities and that government grants have been slashed rather than augmented. In 1996 the Parliamentary Commissioner for the Environment warned that 'the system for protection of historic and cultural heritage as a whole is performing poorly, is very reactive, and at present is characterised by poor resourcing and a lack of vision and integrated strategic planning'. The most encouraging sign was that in that same year some 33,000 New Zealanders still considered it worthwhile to be subscribing members of the Historic Places Trust.

It is probable that those subscribers also numbered heavily amongst the purchasers of the many new books on New Zealand's history to be published in the past two decades. As has been noted in other settings, in times of national stress there is often a deep-seated desire to align with forebears, to vicariously embrace their virtues, even if their vices tend to remain camouflaged. This wakening of interest in roots coincided with a coming of age of New Zealand history as a discipline. Earlier, New Zealand history had been dismissed by many as 'not real history', but from the 1970s university history departments grew in size, more postgraduate students opted to further their studies at home, and an increasing number of their teachers turned to New Zealand topics. With the number of non-university-based scholars also increasing, old problems were reworked and fresh ones discovered. Nowhere was the new vigour more apparent than in the related field of prehistory. The early human occupancy of the islands has been reinterpreted, utilizing both the findings of archaeological investigation and more sophisticated analysis of oral tradition. Janet Davidson's *The prehistory of New Zealand* skilfully presents in easily accessible form information previously only available in specialist journals. Of particular interest are two books by Geoffrey Irwin and Douglas Sutton, which further probe Maori migration myths and the features of Polynesian voyaging. Revisionism has also characterized what might be termed New Zealand's European settlement history, the history of the 150 years post-1840. The 1990s have drawn a rash of synoptic histories, single- and multi-authored, illustrated and otherwise, the most promoted being the first volume of James Belich's *Making peoples*. These works have a freshness about them, but the classic single-volume history of New Zealand rightly remains Keith Sinclair's *History of New Zealand*, first published in 1959. Thematic monographs have also proliferated, many the products of earlier thesis research. Trends in several fields are identified by contributors to *The future and the past: themes in New Zealand history*, edited by Colin Davis and Peter Lineham. There has been an obvious shift in interest from constitutional and political history, now considered *passé*, to what has been termed the 'new social history': urban history, rural history, society and social welfare. Linked events have also played their part in promoting interest in such topics. Celebration of New Zealand's sesquicentenary greatly extended publishers' lists. Distinguished productions included a new multi-volume *Dictionary of New Zealand biography*, while a recent by-product has been the publication of New Zealand's first *Historical atlas*. Women's history, already a growth node in the 1980s, was given an additional fillip by the 1993 centenary of female suffrage. Perhaps most significantly of all, the sifting of evidence for Treaty of Waitangi claims hearings has spurred a massive historical re-examination of past Maori and European relations, the enterprise being dubbed in some quarters 'the Treaty industry'. A new rigour has also been imparted to better examples of the near flood of regional, district and local histories, such works as W. J. Gardner's *A pastoral kingdom divided* or Jim McAloon's *Nelson: a regional history*. A field formerly reserved for antiquarians – and many productions admittedly retain this flavour – local history has now well and truly been infiltrated by professional historians.

Biography, too, has matured as a genre. A number of recent
outstanding examples are cited in the bibliography. At another level,
genealogy, previously confined to hobbyists compiling family trees,
has been transformed into family history. The high standards being
achieved are exhibited in essays in Colleen Main's *Our lesser stars*.
Possibly the most encouraging feature of recent New Zealand
historiography has been the first indications of a written Maori
history, by Maori, for Maori, often employing Maori sources. Until
the 1980s most Maori history, including tribal history, had been
authored by Europeans. Ironically, the most prolific writer on Maori
matters over the past two decades has been European historian
Michael King. Ranginui Walker's *Struggles without an end = Ka
whawhai tonu matou*, a general history of New Zealand written from
a Maori perspective, therefore constitutes a landmark.

The upsurge in interest in New Zealand's past has also been
reflected in much wider public support than hitherto for related
cultural institutions (libraries, art galleries, museums, archives),
though popular support has been no guarantee of enhanced official
funding. Indeed, since the late 1980s, while clienteles have increased
almost exponentially, these institutions have been generally
compelled to cope with shrinking budgets and, where possible, have
been required to turn themselves into business units. In the new
world, access to collections is increasingly equated with ability to
pay. The trend first became apparent in the nation's library system,
which is overviewed in Alan Richardson's *Library services in New
Zealand*. In the immediate post-Second World War years the number
of New Zealand libraries, public and specialist, had grown
spectacularly, and by 1980 over 2,000 were operating. At the apex,
from 1966, was the National Library of New Zealand, under the
umbrella of the Department of Education, maintaining a central
reference collection as a national resource and servicing the special
needs of schools, local libraries and rural dwellers. Its watchwords
were *Books to the people*. Reform of the National Library, abetted by
library bureaucrats, amounted to separation as a department, a drastic
and ongoing slashing of public services, the substitution of charged
services to the business and professional communities, and a
determined attempt to recast the institution as a policy ministry, 'the
principal adviser to government on information issues'. By the 1990s
the Library's mission statement had been altered to place emphasis on
its contribution to 'the building of a learning society and an enterprise
economy'. The extent to which priorities had changed was
demonstrated in 1995 by Treasury-inspired proposals, fortunately
soon quashed, to sell off parts of the collections of the internationally

celebrated Alexander Turnbull Library. Rachel Barrowman's *The Turnbull: a library and its world* explores the history of this research library, now part of the National Library. Public libraries, supported by most local authorities, fared little better in this climate. Over many years public libraries had fought, largely successfully, to provide free services to citizens. This ethos again came into question. Some controlling authorities responded by downsizing their library operations and reintroducing charges. Others have been even more radical. In Wellington, New Zealand's capital, the possibility of contracting out the provision of public library services to the private sector is being investigated. Perhaps the greatest damage has been to New Zealand's special libraries. Tertiary education providers have been forced to retrench. The libraries of restructured state agencies, many with unique holdings, have been broken up and dispersed, the most notable example being that of the former Department of Scientific and Industrial Research. Art galleries and museums have also felt the pinch. By the late 1980s there were approximately 600 public museums and art galleries in New Zealand, but many were relatively small, their collections oriented towards the history or fabric of a particular region or locality. Their specific features are catalogued in Keith Thomson's *A guide to the art galleries and museums of New Zealand*. Traditionally, however, the major players have been a clutch of institutions in the main centres, and since the early 1990s the greatest player of all has been the Museum of New Zealand (Te Papa), its new premises on Wellington's waterfront, scheduled for opening in February 1998. Already dominant in the museums' world, the concept of this new Museum of New Zealand has been controversial from its beginnings. While government has been an uncharacteristically generous funder, critics have castigated the project as an endeavour to create a local Disneyland, a lure for tourists, rather than providing an appropriate storehouse and study centre for New Zealand's material culture. Similar criticisms have been drawn by government proposals to reorient the nation's foremost archival repository, the National Archives of New Zealand. While but one of the 180 repositories holding collections of archives identified by Frank Rogers in a 1992 survey, National Archives' dominance of its field is even more absolute than that of the Museum of New Zealand. Following an abortive 1995 attempt to impose the health services policy-funder-provider split on the organization (one with less than eighty staff!) it is now proposed to subsume it as a branch within a new revenue-generating heritage 'business'. Reactions to these proposals have been strong, as evidenced by contributors to *New Zealand archives futures*.

Introduction

Predictably, there have been strenuous efforts to place the arts, too, on at least a quasi-commercial footing. For many years the state has been the principal patron of the arts in New Zealand and this situation seems likely to continue, but the limited availability of alternative funding has been viewed by politicians and officials as no good reason to preclude the imposition of market disciplines. The new approach was signalled by the creation in 1991 of a Ministry of Cultural Affairs, charged to provide policy advice and to administer payments on behalf of the Crown to a number of identified cultural sector organizations. Prospective beneficiaries included the New Zealand Film Commission, the Symphony Orchestra, the Museum of New Zealand and the Arts Council. In 1995, the Arts Council, itself an umbrella organization covering not only the visual and performing arts but also creative writing, was translated into a new entity, Creative New Zealand. The message to both new organizations was greater targeting of grants to ensure the best return on taxpayer dollars, and to ensure the message was heard that the controlling boards were infused with business talent. This more rigorous regime suggests that the futures of several long-established cultural institutions, the New Zealand Symphony Orchestra and the Royal New Zealand Ballet, have become the more precarious, especially given requirements that greater funding be devoted to Maori and Pacific arts. The inherent tensions, as well as other current issues, are examined in Peter and Dianne Beatson's *The arts in Aotearoa/New Zealand*.

The visual arts, which continue to flourish, have a long tradition in New Zealand, one dating back to the early explorers and settlers. The most respected general introduction to the tradition continues to be Gil Docking's *Two hundred years of New Zealand painting*, but Michael Dunn's *Concise history of New Zealand painting* presents a different perspective. Francis Pound's *Frames on the land* is a controversial introduction to early landscape painting. There have been few studies of individual artists to equal Gordon Brown's *Colin McCahon, artist*, but the work of contemporary artists is well covered in two volumes compiled by Warwick Brown. Much less has been written on the three-dimensional arts, and little in the 1990s apart from Winsome Shepherd's study of gold and silversmithing, but Richard Wolfe's *All our own work* takes a whimsical look at distinctively New Zealand folk art. Sydney Mead's *Maori art on the world scene* provides insights into Maori art and raises issues relating to how it should be preserved, while *Mataora: the living face* brings together the works of more than forty modern Maori artists. Mead has also written extensively on Maori crafts.

Music remains almost certainly the most popular of the performing arts in New Zealand, even if most aficionados prefer to listen to, rather than to read, much less write about, performances. The fostering of so-called serious music in New Zealand is surveyed in several publications by John Mansfield Thomson, most comprehensively in his *Oxford history of New Zealand music*. The post-1946 fortunes of the New Zealand Symphony Orchestra are charted in two books by Joy Tonks. New Zealand remains better known internationally as a producer of opera singers (Kiri Te Kanawa, Donald McIntyre, Keith Lewis) than as a producer of operas, but as music historian Adrienne Simpson reveals in *Opera's furthest frontier*, productions have been mounted in this country since the 1860s. The book also presents valuable insights into the entertainment world as a whole. As in other parts of the world, pop music continues to command a mass following, particularly amongst youth. John Dix's *Stranded in paradise* is an evocation of kiwi rock music, the highs and lows to the late 1980s. Ethnomusicologist Mervyn McLean's *Maori music* is the most authoritative guide to traditional Maori song and dance forms, also examining European influences on modern genres. Jennifer Shennan has also written on Maori dance, but curiously little has so far been compiled on European dance. The development of New Zealand theatre, particularly from the 1920s, is better documented, in memories and anecdotes by actor-producer Peter Harcourt and in more academic fashion by Howard McNaughton and J. E. P. Thomson. Outstanding playwright Bruce Mason's *Every kind of weather* incorporates comment on New Zealand drama in its cultural context. Jonathan Dennis and Jan Bieringa's *Film in Aotearoa New Zealand* is an introduction to New Zealand film-making, covering documentaries and short and experimental films as well as full-length features.

Both music and theatre had long been sustained by the state broadcasting system, the framework for radio having been forged in the 1930s, with television an introduction of the 1960s. By the early 1980s, with the exception of roughly a dozen licensed private radio stations, both radio and television were still firmly in public ownership. From 1977 both mediums had been under the overall supervision of the Broadcasting Corporation of New Zealand, that body's brief being to carry on public broadcasting services, and 'to promote and encourage artistic, cultural and educational development in the community'. In the case of radio, from the outset there had been a clear dichotomy between public radio, modelled on the BBC, and commercial radio, the reasons being explored in Patrick Day's *The radio years*. A longstanding criticism of both arms was that they lacked independence, were subject to political pressure, and consequently exhibited timidity in the presentation of news and current affairs. The criticism was not wholly just, but a prejudice was created which was employed when reform was mooted for quite different reasons. Few of state radio's harshest critics could have anticipated the wide-ranging changes wrought by Labour in 1989 in the name of improved efficiency: the separation of commercial and non-commercial functions; the removal of restrictions on ownership; and a commitment to promote competition through the encouragement of private sector broadcasters. The introduction and impact of these reforms are examined in John Yeabsley et al.'s *Broadcasting in New Zealand: waves of change*. With responsibility for promoting broadcasting's social objectives transferred to a new entity, New Zealand On Air, which was to collect the public broadcasting fee and from it fund approved programmes, transmissions became the core business of a state-owned enterprise, Radio New Zealand Ltd. Radio New Zealand was required to compete with all-comers. To cope with the anticipated increased demand for frequencies a market-based tradable rights system was introduced, broadcasting rights being put up to tender. That many tendered successfully is suggested by the annual statistics: in 1988 81 AM and 76 FM frequencies were in use; by 1995 160 AM and 437 FM frequencies had been taken up. The vast majority of new stations were operated by profit-driven private-sector broadcasters. This surge of new stations undoubtedly cut savagely into Radio New Zealand's share of the advertising dollar, and it was perversely logical that by the mid-1990s reform advocates should be arguing that continued ownership constituted an unacceptable risk for government. Commercial and non-commercial services had already been split in 1992, and in late 1995 all commercial Radio New Zealand activities were vested in a stand-alone company, Radio New Zealand Commercial, then offered for sale. The net impact is that while listeners certainly have greater choice on their tuners, the content, with the exception of that offered by the public radio rump, is arguably more bland than ever before. The principal alternatives are classic hits, easy listening, or interminable talk-back, all punctuated by extended advertising slots. As Paul Smith recounts in *Revolution in the air*, New Zealand television experienced similar upheavals. Until 1989 state-owned Television New Zealand, operating two channels, enjoyed a monopoly, but in that year the award of a transmission license to a private consortium, T. V. Network Ltd., emphasized the government's intention that the monopoly be broken. The part-purchase of financially embarrassed TV3 by Canadian broadcaster CanWest in 1991 stirred few misgivings. By that point New Zealand's first entry into direct-pay television had already come, the international company Sky Entertainment beginning broadcasts in mid-1990. That the state company had itself invested heavily in the local Sky subsidiary did not escape notice. In 1993 cable television, American-owned, made its first appearance. For those committed to 'free to air' television, still the majority of New Zealanders, there has been a perceptible drop in the quality of programming. Complementary programming has been eroded in the battle for ratings, and the advertising dollar, in the process New Zealand acquiring some of the most advertising-saturated viewing in the world. An attempt to establish a network of regional channels, concentrating on quality programmes, has been short-lived. Independently launched, the channels were subsequently acquired by Television New Zealand, which has now converted them to broadcast youth-targeted pop music. Calls to sell off state television have again arisen, further restructuring of Television New Zealand suggesting they are being heard. The concept of a BBC 1 channel, free of advertising, has found little favour with ruling politicians or Treasury mandarins.

In contrast to broadcasting, New Zealand's printed media has always been predominantly in private hands. Nevertheless, whereas in earlier years those hands tended to be local hands, often those of family companies, over the past two decades there has been a distinct trend towards ownership or control by overseas corporations. Despite competition from broadcasting, and recently telecommunications, the daily newspaper continues to be the principal source of information for many. It has been estimated that on a typical day more than 1.7 million New Zealanders over the age of 10 will at least glance at a newspaper. Even so, there are now significantly fewer 'dailies' than just twenty years ago, and the majority of those remaining are owned by just two publishing groups, both with substantial shareholdings by overseas media conglomerates. Given this concentration of ownership it is scarcely surprising that, local news apart, there is a remarkable sameness about New Zealand newspapers. The content is largely drawn from identical sources – international news agencies, and, in the case of national stories, the New Zealand Press Association. To a degree, therefore, the studies by Karl du Fresne and Judy McGregor on press freedom have a slightly hollow ring. A feature of the past twenty years has been the growth of community newspapers, delivered free to householders within defined circulation areas. These throwaways, however, are usually less indications of community initiative, rather more supplementary advertising vehicles, most being owned by the two big newspaper publishing groups. New Zealanders are also voracious consumers of magazines, over 2,300 titles being available in the country on a regular basis. A perusal of newsagents' stands indicates the wide variety of subject and format. Yet, of this number, no more than 129 are listed with the New Zealand Audit Bureau of Circulation as being published in New Zealand or in New Zealand editions. Hence the preponderance of New Zealanders' magazine reading is overseas sourced. A sign of the times is the popularity of New Zealand's principal 'lifestyle' magazine, *North and South*, while the growing Auckland population concentration is evidenced by support for the more parochial sister journal, *Metro*. A number of specialist limited circulation journals are available only by subscription, and thus do not figure in the circulation ratings, but paradoxically are stronger in their specifically New Zealand content. Consequently they loom disproportionately in the periodical titles cited.

As earlier noted, there has been a massive upsurge in New Zealand book publishing over the past two decades but, as with magazines, locally produced titles are still far outdistanced by titles brought in from overseas. Many local publishing houses actually import more than they publish, not surprisingly in view of the fact that most are now closely linked to, or are wholly owned subsidiaries of, overseas houses. University presses apart, the indigenous book publisher has become an endangered species. There has been a linked tendency to concentrate on commercial titles, those by proven authors or on popular subjects, in compiling lists. For many years the Government Printing Office published scientific, historical and other books containing information on New Zealand, but which were unlikely to make a profit. However, this outlet was closed with the sale of the Office to the private sector in 1989. Even fewer books are actually being printed in New Zealand, the prices offered by overseas presses, particularly Asian presses, proving attractive. Ironically, the underpriced assets of the Government Printing Office also enabled the lucky purchaser, previously a purveyor of firefighting equipment, to diversify horizontally, he soon securing near dominance of the New Zealand bookselling trade. With a few notable exceptions, specialist booksellers were dislodged, or had their businesses drastically reduced, by chains retailing stationery and novelties in equal measure to the limited range of popular titles stocked. Several of these chains have now passed into overseas ownership.

While the production of some classes of specialist publications may have attenuated, sports writing has continued to find a ready market. Notwithstanding the sustained, probably increasing, interest in the arts and other matters cultural, there is still a very long way to go before this matches New Zealanders' devotion to sport in all its forms. While little so far has been written on the sociology of sport in New Zealand, although Lloyd Jones' *Into the field of play* is suggestive, there can be little doubt of sport's hold on the public psyche. Sport has played a critical part in shaping New Zealand's national image, the country's sportsmen and women being held up as archetypal battlers succeeding against the odds. A win by, or defeat of, the All Blacks, the national rugby team, still has the power to lift national spirits or to plunge them into depression. Warwick Roger's *Old heroes* probes why historically rugby has had this hold, while in *The game of our lives* Finlay MacDonald surveys how rugby and New Zealand have shaped each other. The implications, however, have not always been socially healthy. In 1981, for example, New Zealand was a country divided, the Springbok tour of that year, enmeshed in conflicts over South Africa's apartheid policies, being played out behind barbed wire barricades, with police battling with protesters in the streets. But public adulation of sports heroes extends far beyond rugby, even minority sports, when successful, mesmerizing the populace. The national soccer team's unexpected 1982 progression to the finals of the World Cup in Spain (see John Adshead and Kevin Fallon's *New Zealand's world cup*) occasioned widespread work absences, large numbers who had never kicked a soccer ball being glued to television screens. In the 1960s and 1970s, as books by Peter Heidenstrom and Joseph Romanos show, middle-distance athletes were on a pedestal. So were motor racers. More recently squash players and golfers have enjoyed similar status. Americas Cup yachtsmen, participants in perhaps the ultimate in rich men's sports, received ticker tape welcomes when bringing their trophy home in 1995. Yet, despite media attention being focused primarily on high performance areas, New Zealanders like to think of themselves more as a nation of doers than watchers, a philosophy actively encouraged by government agencies. Currently the New Zealand Assembly for Sport, which represents over 50 national sporting organizations, claims a membership of over 1.5 million. However, there are signs that mass participation may be slipping, and that watchers may soon greatly outnumber doers. It is likely that this trend is linked to the increasing professionalization, and consequent commercialization, of sport in the 1990s, especially at the elite level. Sport has become big business, show business. Its administration, at the top, has embraced corporate trappings and, largely on the basis of television fees, augmented by corporate sponsorship, players are being paid unprecedented fees. The concentration is on saleable product. The concomitant is that at lower levels sport is under stress, in some instances withering, voluntary support dropping away. The full ramifications of the transition have yet to be determined, but an indication of the possible future is a planned new stadium for the nation's capital. Though there is generous provision for corporate facilities, the seating available for traditional supporters will be appreciably less than at existing venues. To cover costs, admission prices must rise steeply. Hence, while the elite will continue to watch contests live, the masses may be relegated to television coverage, often delayed telecasts. That indigenous sport could become just one electronic offering among many, and not necessarily the most popular, is suggested by New Zealand youngsters' growing enthusiasm for Chicago Bulls regalia and their identification with overseas superstars.

It is possible, too, that other forms of outdoor recreation may in future be enjoyed by fewer New Zealanders. There have been serious suggestions that use of the country's national parks and wilderness areas, even some beaches, should be regarded as saleable rights and be put up to tender. To do so would reverse longstanding traditions. Recent surveys indicate that over half the population participates in at least one outdoor activity monthly, more than a third more frequently. Easy access to mountains and coast, to a range of wilderness areas, the diversity of climates, above all the low density of population, have all encouraged a multitude of outdoor activities. Those most written about have been hunting and fishing. While hunting was important as a supplementary source of food in colonial days, the continuing enthusiastic pursuit of game – birds, pigs, deer – may be symbolic of the desire of many New Zealanders to project a rugged, individualistic image. This is suggested by the enduring popularity of the writings of the late Barry Crump, who devoted a lifetime to purveying yarns about 'the good keen man', alone against the elements save for his dogs and a gun. Writers such as Philip Holden and Rex Forrester have figured prominently in general publishers' lists, while such books are the staple of at least one boutique publishing house. Generally, there has been a more genteel air to books on fishing, whether fly-fishing for trout and salmon or big-game fishing in the seas off the northern North Island. Yet, while blood sports have the higher profile, walking and tramping are enjoyed by far greater numbers. Since 1976 designated walking tracks have been established in rural and urban areas throughout the country. The 'walkways system' offers walking opportunities over private land and is a complementary network to the back-country tramping tracks overseen by the Department of Conservation. These latter are primarily for the physically fit, and a selection are described in Colin Moore's *New Zealand wilderness walks*. Since the early 1980s mountain-biking has also become popular on these back-country tracks, although tensions between trampers and bikers have arisen. At higher altitudes, the mountains also exert other recreational pulls. Both rock and ice climbing have had adherents from the early years of colonization, and the exploits of Sir Edmund Hillary, conqueror of Everest, and more recent New Zealand international climbers, have ensured a steady stream of new recruits. Hugh Logan's *Great peaks of New Zealand* explores the features of sixteen major mountains. In the post-Second World War years, and particularly in recent decades, skiing has attained a new importance, the season extending from June to October in both the North and South Islands. New Zealand has twelve commercial ski fields and a similar number of fields are operated by clubs. The habitual summer playgrounds of New Zealanders, however, are the country's beaches, whether for swimming, surfing, boating, or simply lazing in the sun. Stephen Barnett and Richard Wolfe evoke vividly 'the beach' as the place where people mix, whatever their status in life, the place where cares are cast aside. An icon of the beach lifestyle has been *The bach*, humble, often ramshackle, beachside accommodation in which holiday makers roughed it and convinced themselves they were enjoying the privations. The bach, however, is now becoming a thing of the past, being replaced by the substantial holiday homes of the wealthy and regulated camping grounds or cabin accommodation for others.

Prior to the 1980s, domestic lifestyles in New Zealand were relatively simple, at least for most. Those with more opulent tastes tended to hide, rather than flaunt, them. As late as the early 1980s, then Prime Minister Muldoon's preference for vacations at a simple bach owned for decades, to devote his few leisure hours to the cultivation of lilies, mirrored the aspirations of the preponderance of his constituents. The myth of egalitarianism was thus perpetuated. As disparities visibly grew, however, as the gap between ordinary New Zealanders and the small emergent commercialist elite effectively exercising power widened, it was the latter that imposed its stamp on social customs and mores. Conspicuous, often extravagant, consumption became not only acceptable but something to be envied and aspired to, even if full emulation was beyond the means of most. For those who could afford it, the traditional house in the suburbs was traded in for the semi-rural, ten-acre lifestyle block, or more recently the expensive inner-city apartment, sometimes both. Where retained, the suburban house was remodelled, sometimes rebuilt, to mansion proportions, in a number of cases adjacent properties being acquired to provide additional gardens or tennis courts. In imitation, home improvement became a national preoccupation of the masses. And there were other indicators. Consumption of beer, the national beverage, while still substantial by world standards, fell away, and there was a taste switch from local draught to canned and bottled, often imported, beers. Even where loyalty to local product remained, beers from boutique breweries were in greater demand. Conversely, wine drinking increased, and to accommodate more sophisticated palates the range, and price, of local wines increased remarkably. A recent guide lists more then 1,200 New Zealand wines. Significantly, however, bottle stores in affluent areas are well stocked with imported vintages. Under a variety of pressures, New Zealand cuisine also changed. The standard home fare became more innovative, employing new cooking methods and a new range of raw foodstuffs. In many households the traditional 'meat, spud and two veg' yielded way to what were conceived as more healthy dishes, even if these often came pre-packaged from supermarkets. Dining out, reserved for most in earlier decades for the celebration of special occasions, became commonplace for younger New Zealanders. Silver-service establishments for the few were matched by a mushrooming of more modest bistros, brasseries and café bars. At the humblest level, the local fish and chip shop, the takeaway mainstay for generations, encountered new opposition from Chinese takeaways, Kentucky Fried Chicken, Pizza Hut and the ubiquitous McDonalds. New preferences were also discernible in house interiors. While the truly affluent purchased handcrafted furniture and antiques, the less well off made do with cheap veneered imitations bought from large furnishing chains. While the kitchens of the affluent were stocked with an amazing variety of new appliances imported from Europe or the United States, mass-produced cut-price versions of Taiwanese or Korean origin were available for others from bargain warehouses. House exteriors were also refashioned. In imitation of the spacious grounds of the new mansions, gardening experienced a revival, exotic and native plants becoming available from competing chains of garden centres. Even personal attire was transformed. The elite insisted upon genuine Gucci or Pierre Cardin, but others eagerly purchased ersatz designer labels sourced from Indonesia, the Philippines and Brazil. It was symptomatic that even the traditional New Zealand holiday should lose its appeal. While those of means opted for a fortnight in London or Provence, augmented by occasional shopping weekends in Sydney, there was also widespread marketing of budget tour packages to Norfolk Island or Fiji.

New Zealand's somewhat stolid traditional image was rooted in its history. From the beginnings of European settlement its citizens were more concerned with making livings than international waves. Yet, as a country dependent on overseas markets, the task was not always straightforward. Mindful of the potentially adverse impacts of international economic fluctuations, from the late 1930s New Zealand governments actively pursued policies of insulationism. The result was 'Fortress New Zealand' (or 'Godzone'), the state, through trade barriers and progressive social policies seeking to guarantee New Zealanders' lifelong security. In the early post-Second World War decades sheltering behind the fortress walls was comforting, but by the 1980s, with many born after 1945 succeeding to positions of authority, the afforded protection also came to be regarded as stultifying. In consequence, the fortress was systematically demolished, the insulating packing being discarded and the outer ramparts removed stone by stone. Effectively, since the mid-1980s New Zealand has been globalized. It has been fully exposed to overseas economic and cultural forces. Its political leaders have been prepared to cede a remarkable degree of their authority to the marketplace. The population, or so it has been claimed, has been dragged into the late 20th century and, theoretically, has been more appropriately positioned for life in the 21st century. The full impact of the changes has yet to be determined.

What is clearly apparent is that, despite widespread interest in 'the New Zealand experiment', few other countries have been prepared to so uncritically adopt textbook solutions, to push structural reforms so far and so fast. For many New Zealanders, the reforms have been, and remain, an uncomfortable venture into the unknown. New choices are being constantly presented, and new ways of doing things demanded, for new reasons, but new constraints are also becoming obvious. The question is whether, as a result of the upheaval, New Zealand in the late 1990s is a better place to live, work, and bring up families. Any answer to this depends on the respondent's perspective, largely shaped by personal circumstances and income. For a relatively small number – the winners and the elite – New Zealand has been transformed into an exciting land of opportunity. For many, perhaps a majority, the changes have almost certainly brought some tangible material benefits, but these have been offset by deep-seated uncertainties; about increasingly frenetic lives, about the threat of unemployment, and about their future prospects in ill health and old age. For those at the bottom of the social pile – the clear losers, the unemployed and displaced, and beneficiaries – contemporary New Zealand is beginning to bear an uncomfortable resemblance to the countries many of their 19th-century European forbears forsook in search of better lives.

Brad Patterson

Acknowledgements

Thanks must be expressed to all those who offered suggestions, shared their specialist knowledge in particular subject areas, or who provided constructive comment on the introductory essay in draft. In particular, the compilers wish to indicate their gratitude to Brian Easton, Ray Grover, Bill Renwick, Adrienne Simpson, and Ian Wards. No less acknowledgement is due to Anna Fabrizio, ABC-CLIO Ltd., who as volume editor has been a model of patience, courtesy and helpfulness.

---

[1] Since the Introduction was written, Brian Easton's *In Stormy seas: the post-war New Zealand economy* has subsequently been published (Dunedin: University of Otago Press, 1997. 343p.).

The Country and Its People

1 **The commercialisation of New Zealand.**
Brian Easton.   Auckland: Auckland University Press, 1997. 288p.
bibliog.
Based on a course in public policy for second-year undergraduate political studies
students, this work is a critique of the application of business (or commercial) principles to the public sector, and to New Zealand generally, over the last decade.
Commencing with an examination of the economic policies of the 1970s and early
1980s, many of which created the problems which led to the 'crisis' of 1984, the
resulting opportunity to introduce commercialization is then explored under three
sections: the ideas, the politics and case-studies. The author, a well-known economist
and commentator, brings valuable, informed and sometimes controversial insights to
an examination of the 'more-market' policies prevalent in New Zealand from the
mid-1980s.

2 **Cul de sac: the question of New Zealand's future.**
Harvey Franklin.   Wellington: Unwin Paperbacks/Port Nicholson Press,
1985. 184p.
The author offers 'unorthodox' suggestions as to how New Zealand could emerge
from an 'endless circle of high borrowing and growing inefficiency'. He challenges
the accepted tenet that New Zealand has an egalitarian society and suggests that those
who have power will dictate the direction the country will move in. This study builds
on some of the arguments advanced in Franklin's earlier analysis of New Zealand in
the mid-1970s, *Trade, growth and anxiety: New Zealand beyond the welfare state*
(Wellington: Methuen, 1978. 402p.).

3 **New territory: the transformation of New Zealand, 1984-92.**
Colin James.   Wellington: Bridget William Books, 1992. 367p.
This sequel to the author's *The quiet revolution: turbulence and transition in contemporary New Zealand* (Wellington: Allen & Unwin/Port Nicholson Press, 1986. 212p.)
examines the influences on New Zealand politics in the 1980s and 1990s, a period of

'booms and busts and sharp, disruptive changes in every field of government policy' (cover). Not just an examination of the changes internally, James examines the international scene and sets the New Zealand experiences into the global setting. This is the new territory shaped by the uncertainties and insecurities of the depression of the 1930s (which reappeared in the 1980s) and a desire to shake off the restraints of the comfort of the years 1940 to 1980. The last chapter considers whether it is possible for New Zealanders to set up home in this new territory and make it theirs.

4 The New Zealand experiment: a world model for structural adjustment?

Jane Kelsey. Auckland: Auckland University Press/Bridget Williams Books, 1997. 2nd ed. 433p. bibliog.

The author, an associate professor of law at the University of Auckland, critically examines the impact of the brand of economic fundamentalism practised in New Zealand since 1984, questioning whether this approach should be accepted as the 'success story' disciples claim it to be. The work raises questions about the effects of the new regime on the lives of New Zealanders, on their communities, the government and the country. It considers 'how and why economic fundamentalism took hold in New Zealand after 1984, . . . examines what was done, and the attempts to embed the neo-liberal regime against change . . . [and] describes the economic, social, democratic and cultural deficits that were left in its wake' (Preface). Concluding chapters consider possible alternatives. The Epilogue to the second edition is written in a more optimistic vein.

5 The big con: the death of the Kiwi dream.

Gordon McLauchlan. Wellington: GP Publications, 1992. 222p.

A hard-hitting examination of the period since 1984 written in a lively style by a popular columnist and social critic. No aspect of society is immune to his acerbic pen and he challenges the reader to re-examine his or her understanding of this period. His previous title, *The passionless people* (Auckland: Cassell New Zealand, 1976. 216p.), performed a similar analysis on the 1970s.

6 The cross-leased chardonnay cellphone paradise.

John Ruck. Auckland: Harper Collins, 1996. 154p.

Purporting to be a successor to Austin Mitchell's *The half-gallon, quarter-acre, pavlova paradise* (Christchurch: Whitcombe & Tombs, 1972. 184p.) – Mitchell provides a Preface – this book whimsically seeks to assess the impact of the 'New Zealand recovery' on the country, its life and people. The author, absent from New Zealand for thirty years, travelled extensively in both main islands. He concludes that, while the dreary country depicted by Mitchell has become more vibrant, the downside of the reforms is clearly obvious. If paradise status is to be attained, there is much further to go.

7 Revolution: New Zealand from fortress to free market.

Marcia Russell. Auckland: Images Ink/Hodder Moa Beckett/TVNZ, 1996. 255p.

Memories and anecdotes put a rarely seen human face on the 'New Zealand experiment', the transformation from welfare state to post-welfare state between 1984 and 1993.

Journalistic in style (the author admits that she found it difficult because of her training to express any personal assessment of the 'revolution'), and relatively uncritical, the book makes no claim to provide academic analysis. Neither does it include interviews with leaders of current political parties which might have been expected given its derivation from a television series.

8 A vision betrayed: the decline of democracy in New Zealand.

Tony Simpson. Auckland: Hodder & Stoughton, 1984. 304p.

'From the commencement of self-government ours has been a society ruled by an elite which has perceived access to power as an opportunity for enrichment and financial advancement' (Introduction). The author looks at the exercise of power by the elite in government, the public service, business, farming and the professions and assesses the effect it has had on the character of the society within which it is located. He examines the belief that New Zealand has an egalitarian society and concludes that this is a myth. The work is prescient as it was published before the changes that occurred in New Zealand, but the author makes predictions, which subsequent events have upheld, about the existence of a power elite.

General Descriptions and Travel Guides

Promotional literature

9 **Werner Forman's New Zealand.**
Werner Forman, introduction by C. K. Stead.   London: Harvill, 1994.
223p. map.

In 1968, Werner Forman, while working on a book on Cook's voyages of coastal explo-ration, became entranced by New Zealand and undertook a journey from the north to the south which he recorded with his camera. 'His journey amounts to a magnificent portrait of a country, its people, architecture, historic sites, antiquities, landscapes and sky-scapes' (cover). The introduction by C. K. Stead provides biographical information on the photographer as well as a brief history of New Zealand related in a poetic style. The photographs emphasize the unique Maori dimension to New Zealand.

10 **Readers Digest guide to New Zealand.**
Maurice Shadbolt, photographs by Brian Brake.   Sydney: Readers
Digest, 1993. rev. ed. 352p. maps.

The country is divided into twenty regions which are identifiably different, and practi-cal information for the tourist is provided on each, including useful addresses, opening hours and details of scenic drives and walks, historic sites, viewpoints and picnic spots. Unusual and revealing photographs open up the regions explored. An introduc-tory essay covers the early geological history of New Zealand, general information on the country, the people, flora and fauna, and arts of the Maori, all very much in overview.

11 **Timeless land.**
Grahame Sydney, Brian Turner, Owen Marshall.   Dunedin: Longacre
Press, 1995. 160p.

Introduced by actor Sam Neill, this is a unique collaboration, with painter Grahame Sydney, poet Brian Turner and writer Owen Marshall depicting New Zealand through fifty paintings, poetry and prose. Each contributor complements the others, and the result is a memorable pastiche.

12   New Zealand Geographic.

Kennedy Warne.   Auckland: New Zealand Geographic, [1996?]. 192p.

A selection of the 'finest' images and articles drawn from the magazine *New Zealand Geographic*. The result is a more diverse work than the usual promotional literature, and contains sections on the land, the people, the wildlife and 'Beyond these shores', which includes the Pacific. The essays are interesting and packed with information while the photographs make the ordinary seem extraordinary.

Guides

13   Tramping in New Zealand: a Lonely Planet walking guide.

Jim Dufresne, J. Williams.   Hawthorn, Victoria: Lonely Planet, 1995. 3rd ed. 314p. maps.

Provides facts about the country as well as details on possible walks that might be undertaken. Each is rated to suggest the level and experience necessary for tackling it.

14   AA explorer New Zealand.

Nick Hanna.   Auckland: Hodder Moa Beckett, 1997. 288p. maps.

Divided into five sections – 'New Zealand is' (life and living today), 'New Zealand was' (historical information), A to Z sections (places to visit), travel facts and hotels and restaurants – this is an attractively presented racy introduction to the country for the overseas visitor. Attractions are rated using stars. The book is a most useful compendium of information for the traveller.

15   New Zealand wilderness walks.

Colin Moore.   Auckland: Hodder Moa Beckett, 1996. 141p.

Beautifully illustrated with colour photographs, this work shows the prospective walker what is likely to be encountered on eight 'wilderness walks' in New Zealand. The book is intended 'to inspire people to make one, or all, of these Great Walks; to see and touch the pyramids and cathedrals of New Zealand; to feel the great forces of nature at work' (Introduction). With this intention, it does not include details of the walks, the deficiency being met by the hut-to-hut descriptions provided by Pearl Hewson's *New Zealand's great walks* (Auckland: Hodder Moa Beckett, 1996. 112p.) which also contains detailed maps.

16   Mobil New Zealand travel guide.

Diana Pope, Jeremy Pope.   Auckland: Reed, 1998. 768p.

Covering the North Island in one volume and the South Island in a second, these are information-packed guides to New Zealand travel which are regularly updated. Freely admitting that their choices are subjective, the authors grade with stars the attractions described. Accommodation information is not provided and can be obtained from works such as *The New Zealand bed and breakfast book, 1997: homestays, farmstays, bed and breakfast inns,* compiled by J. & J. Thomas (Mahina Bay, Eastbourne, New Zealand: Moonshine Press, 1997) or *Friars guide to New Zealand accommodation for the discerning traveller: city homes, country estates, farms, lodges, inns, hotels, cottages, bed and breakfast* (Auckland: Hodder Moa Beckett, 1997. 224p.).

17   New Zealand by bike: 14 tours geared for discovery.
Bruce Ringer.   Auckland: Reed, 1994. 315p. maps.

Commencing with good basic information on New Zealand – covering the climate, the currency, what is needed for touring by bike and the kind of accommodation that is available – this guide then describes eight North Island, and six South Island, tours. Plenty of detail is provided for each tour, including the number of days to allow, possible side trips that might be included and alternative routes.

Geography

General

18 **Changing places in New Zealand: a geography of restructuring.**
Edited by Steve Britton, Richard Le Heron, Eric Pawson.
Christchurch: New Zealand Geographical Society, 1992. 328p. maps.

This work seeks to redress the fact that commentary on the changes in New Zealand over the last decade has tended to be from economists. 'There has been no comprehensive assessment of the context and results of restructuring for companies and workers, nor its impact upon people and places, the environment and regions' (Preface). Fifty geographers, working from both within and beyond the universities, contribute their views in a work that is extensively referenced. Their conclusions are supported by case-studies. Chapter headings include 'Internationalisation of the economy', 'The companies', 'The workers', 'Manufacturing, services and tourism' and 'Local government reform'.

19 **The invasion of New Zealand by people, plants and animals: the South Island.**
Andrew Hill Clark.   Westport, Connecticut: Greenwood Press, 1970.
Reprint of 1949 ed. 465p. maps. bibliog.

'This book is a report on a revolutionary change in the character of a region, which occurred in a period of less than two centuries. One of the most important factors in the change was the invasion of the area by armies of plants and animals, which with help of man, mingled with or displaced native flora and fauna' (Preface). The work is divided into four sections: the land; the people; the invading animals; and the invading plants. The author concluded that the South Island was facing serious land management issues which could not be answered by looking back to Britain but required new initiatives to be developed both from within the country and from other similar 'new raw lands'. Now clearly historical in nature, the work remains surprisingly relevant and readable.

7

20 **Landmarks.**
Kenneth B. Cumberland.   Surry Hills, New South Wales: Readers
Digest, 1981. 304p. maps.

A lavishly illustrated production, written by an academic with experience as a soil
conservator and in pastoral agriculture as well as time served on town planning committees. Through all these opportunities the author has been able to study the
landscape from a number of different viewpoints. He has brought these to this work.
Based on a television series, he presents 'the history of the evolution of the landscape
[and] of the men who left their mark on it' (p. 7). He also looks forward to the future
and believes that the landscape will undergo further modifications as social and economic changes inevitably occur. An attractive work to simply browse, this is also
highly instructive through its informed text.

21 **New Zealand: a geography.**
Peter Dent, Fiona McEwan.   Auckland: Heinemann, 1986. 208p. maps.

An example of a textbook used almost exclusively by college students, but with interest also as an introduction to New Zealand's geography. It is clearly divided into
sections on natural hazards, the natural environment, farming and forestry, population
and settlement, and renewable and non-renewable resources. Short illustrative case-
studies are a valuable feature.

22 **Aotearoa and New Zealand: a historical geography.**
Alan H. Grey.   Christchurch: Canterbury University Press, 1994. 476p.
bibliog.

Focusing on the transformation of the landscape from uninhabited wilderness to a
mosaic of grasslands and moderate-sized towns, this book attempts to place the New
Zealand colonization experience in the wider context of 19th-century European overseas expansion. The author, an expatriate, detects two continuous negative trends: the
well-intentioned despoiling of unique natural environments by both Polynesians and
Europeans; and the less well-intentioned displacing of the Maori people by the
Europeans.

23 **Southern approaches: geography in New Zealand.**
Edited by P. G. Holland, W. B. Johnston.   Christchurch: New Zealand
Geographical Society, 1987. 361p. maps.

'This work commemorates 50 years of geography as a separate university discipline.
Seventeen original scholarly essays review past achievements, identify, challenge and
evaluate ways ahead for the subject. The essays report on the state of geography in
relation to debates on environment and society in New Zealand, and suggest how traditional concepts and new ways of thinking may be applied to the formulation of
public policy' (abstract). The contributors are all well known in their field. 'Each
author was asked to look back over 50 years of academic writing and research, to
assess what geographers working in New Zealand have done and are doing, to identify
research and professional challenges, and to evaluate possible new ways forward'
(Introduction). The result is a wide-ranging presentation which looks at geography in
New Zealand from numerous viewpoints.

24   **Changing places: New Zealand in the nineties.**
Richard Le Heron, Eric Pawson.   Auckland: Longman Paul, 1996.
447p. maps.

A successor to *Changing places in New Zealand: a geography of restructuring* (q.v.), this work uses the same model and 'concentrates around 90s issues, globalisation, corporate strategies, labour flexibility, social policy, sustainability, urban and regional futures, patterns of consumption, and how all these are affecting people's sense of place' (cover). Case-studies are once again an important basic component and findings are compared with the earlier work. Although not easy reading, this collates much useful information.

Maps, atlases and gazetteers

25   **Atlas of New Zealand boundaries.**
Jan Kelly, Brian Marshall.   Auckland: Auckland University Press, 1996. 325p. maps.

The way the country is divided for administrative purposes differs from body to body depending on their particular needs. This atlas explores these different divisions – thematic, territorial, environment, land, employer/employee organizations, judicial, welfare and services, to list a few. 'As a reference and information guide it will be a vital resource to government departments, government corporations and local bodies; to private institutions; and to consultants and contractors in engineering and planning' (cover).

26   **Heinemann New Zealand atlas.**
Edited by D. W. McKenzie.   Auckland: Heinemann/Department of Survey and Land Information, 1987. 118 maps.

'An essential home reference book', this atlas, using cartography from the Department of Survey and Land Information, presents a series of topographical maps (scale 1:250,000) covering New Zealand and its outlying islands. Additional information is supplied through the introduction and the extensive gazetteer.

27   **New Zealand historical atlas: Ko papatuanuku e takoto nei.**
Edited by Malcolm McKinnon, with Barry Bradley, Russell Kirkpatrick.
Auckland: David Bateman/Historical Branch, Department of Internal Affairs, 1997. [300]p.

This atlas, the first of its kind to be published in New Zealand and the fruit of a 7-year project, consists of 100 double-page spreads containing 228 full-colour plates; maps are the predominant feature on each plate but text and a range of other graphics are also included. Each plate deals with a discrete topic; ten of the plates consist of dramatic three-dimensional maps which present Maori oral tradition in relationship to the land. Plate 1 looks at New Zealand's position at the juncture of two tectonic plates and plate 100 examines the country's external relations over the last thirty to forty years. In between, the topics cover the whole range of New Zealand history from geological time through Maori settlement, contact with Europeans, colonization and the 20th century. This was an ambitious project, which has been beautifully realized.

28 New Zealand electoral atlas.
Alan McRobie. Wellington: Government Print Books, 1989. 154p. maps.

The changing mosaic of the country's electoral districts is traced in maps from 1853 to 1987. An introductory essay outlines the basis upon which boundaries were initially determined, and explains the creation of a politically independent Representation Commission in 1887. Each map is accompanied by information upon which the Commission's subsequent decisions were based.

29 AA atlas and touring guide of New Zealand.
New Zealand Automobile Association. Auckland: Lansdowne Press, 1985. 196p. maps.

More than just a collection of road maps to guide the visitor around New Zealand, this volume provides a textual snapshot of each area written by an authority on that particular region. Extensively illustrated with photographs, it thus presents a view of the country that surpasses a collection of road maps, or photographs and commentary on their own.

30 AA New Zealand illustrated atlas.
New Zealand Automobile Association. Auckland: Hodder Moa Beckett, 1995. 112p.

'Fifteen double-page spreads feature maps focusing on the major highways and tourist routes with additional information on walkways, golf courses, ski fields, thermal areas, motor camps and national parks' (cover). Additional information is provided on more than twenty cities, towns and districts, together with illustrations to assist in identifying flora and fauna. The book also includes sections on parks, walking tracks, horticulture, agriculture and history. As a publication of the Automobile Association, information to assist the motorist – road rules, accident and emergency first aid and breakdown advice – is also provided.

31 Place names of New Zealand.
A. W. Reed. Wellington: Reed, 1975. 510p. bibliog.

With the *Supplement* (Wellington: Reed Trust, 1979. 177p.), which contains additions and corrections, these two volumes provide explanation of the origins of most New Zealand place-names which people are likely to enquire into. 'In the case of Maori names, incidents important, epoch-making, or trivial are often enshrined. . . . In such cases legend and history come to life, in others speculation is inevitable . . . with European names which come from a variety of sources, the origin is either known or unknown. . . . There is often more than one possible explanation' (Introduction).

32 New Zealand atlas.
Edited by Ian Wards. Wellington: Government Printer, 1976. 292p. maps.

Although originally intended as a revision of *A descriptive atlas of New Zealand* (Wellington: Government Printer, 1959. 109p.) this became an entirely new work. 'It aims to explain New Zealand, its history, its shape and substance, its people and its economy in a series of articles, maps and photographs' (Foreword). Containing many photographs of landscapes and nature history, and also including a lengthy text about many aspects of New Zealand in the 1970s, this book is as much a descriptive account of New Zealand as it is strictly an atlas. The photographs, whether black-and-white or colour, are some of the finest published of New Zealand – '. . . the goal has been clarity and a high regard to the unifying and enhancing quality of a discriminating use of colour' (Introduction). Of particular interest is the binding technique used to ensure information on maps covering two pages is not lost in the 'gutter' of the book.

New Zealand Geographer.
See item no. 892.

New Zealand Geographic.
See item no. 893.

Landforms, Geology and Climate

General

33 **Stars of the southern skies: an observer's guide for New Zealand.**
Patrick Moore. Auckland: David Bateman, 1994. 190p. maps.

The world-famous astronomer has produced a practical, illustrated guide to the skies above New Zealand, Australia, southern Africa and South America, both for the curious and for dedicated astronomers. Information and advice sit side by side with an explanation of the stars visible in the southern skies. This is an introductory work that could easily inspire the reader to delve more deeply.

34 **Lands in collision: discovering New Zealand's past geography.**
G. R. Stevens. Wellington: Scientific Information Publishing
Centre/DSIR, 1985. 128p. maps.

Written especially for the general reader, this comprehensive 'atlas' illustrates in text, maps and drawings, New Zealand's development through geological time. 'Paleogeographic maps depict the evolution of New Zealand's flora and fauna, its climate and geography, and its position in relation to the continents of the Southern Hemisphere through the ages' (cover). Of particular interest are artists' reconstructions of how ancient environments and life forms may have looked.

35 **New Zealand adrift: the theory of continental drift in a New Zealand setting.**
G. R. Stevens. Wellington: Reed, 1980. 442p. maps.

The theory that New Zealand was once part of a vast super-continent, Gondwanaland, is here explored through text and illustrations by an authority in the field. Of interest to teachers, students, and lapidaries, this theory is so fascinating that anyone with an interest in the formation of New Zealand will find much to intrigue them. The use of Landsat photographs assists in explaining the rock formations of different parts of the country.

36   **Prehistoric New Zealand.**
G. R. Stevens, M. McGlone, B. McCulloch.   Auckland: Heinemann
Reed, 1995. rev. ed. 128p. maps.

A most appealingly presented introduction to prehistoric New Zealand, in which man
is seen as having been a force for destruction. Some of the contributions may be controversial but the whole is stimulating in its approach.

Landforms

37   **The mountain lands of New Zealand.**
J. T. Holloway.   Christchurch: Lincoln College, Tussock Grasslands
and Mountain Lands Institute, 1982. 105p. maps.

A slim, but attractive, and informed, survey of the characteristics of New Zealand's
mountain lands. The intent is to provide 'an introduction to the subject, lending perspective to more learned contributions' (p. 2). There are short chapters on geology,
geomorphology, climate, soils, mountain forests, high-altitude shrublands and tussock
grasslands. Up to a third of the North Island, and between half and two-thirds of the
South Island, may be classified as mountain lands.

38   **Waters of New Zealand.**
Edited by M. Paul Mosley.   Wellington: New Zealand Hydrological
Society, 1992. 431p. maps.

Written by a group of New Zealand's leading hydrologists, this work 'provides a
wide-ranging coverage of the freshwaters of New Zealand, from precipitations as rain
or snow through to groundwater and geothermal waters' (Introduction). The book is
intended to be used as an essential reference text for professionals working in the
environmental and engineering fields, and as a text for students of geography, natural
resources and civil engineering, environmental studies and related subjects.
References throughout the text aid further study. Although technical in nature, an
effort has been made to present the information in simple terms.

39   **A field guide to New Zealand's lakes and rivers.**
Brian Parkinson, Geoffrey Cox.   Auckland: Random Century, 1990.
176p.

A beautifully presented aid to the identification of a variety of different freshwater
habitats and their inhabitants. Covering both the North, and the South, Island, the
authors also consider the effects of pollution on these bodies of water and explain how
the flora and fauna have adapted to handle these new conditions. The illustrations by
Geoffrey Cox are a particular feature of this book, which is designed to accompany
the reader as he/she explores the countryside.

40 **Landforms of New Zealand.**
Edited by J. M. Soons, M. J. Selby. Auckland: Longman Paul, 1992. 2nd ed. 531p. maps.

Although essentially a geomorphological textbook, even the casual reader will find much of interest in this comprehensive and authoritative examination of the physical geography of New Zealand. The early chapters take a thematic approach, looking at broad subjects such as the age and development of the New Zealand landscape, the stability of hillslopes and the effects of erosion. Later chapters provide regional perspectives which contrast such landforms as the Volcanic Plateau with the strongly glaciated landscape of Fiordland. Bearing the potential wider readership in mind, the authors have kept technical language to a minimum, and the provision of an extensive glossary assists where this cannot be avoided. The second edition takes into account the studies of the intervening ten years that have provided further understanding of the earth sciences.

41 **Wetlands: discovering New Zealand's shy places.**
Gordon Stephenson. Wellington: Government Printing Office, 1986. 117p.

Bogs, swamps, estuaries, and other wet places, are the subject of this slim book. Taking the reader to areas not normally thought of as attractive and interesting, the author opens up a fascinating hidden life. These are 'the shy places, where secrets are not easily yielded'. In selecting which wetlands to include, the major criteria were ease of access and covering a wide range. The author readily acknowledges that there are many areas he has not been able to cover. An enthusiastic text is supported by colour plates and line-drawings.

Geology and soils

42 **The great New Zealand fossil book: pictures of ancient life in an evolving land.**
Ron Brazier, Ian Keyes, Graeme Stevens. Lower Hutt, New Zealand: DSIR, 1990. 112p. maps.

Although there are more colourful 'fossil books', the pen-and-wash drawings included in this volume are outstanding. 'The fossils featured in the illustrations are considered to be as anatomically accurate as it is possible to make in any life-like reconstructions, and in the majority of cases represent the first ever attempts to reconstruct some of New Zealand's own prehistoric animals and plants from their fossil remains' (p. 5). The accompanying text is also authoritative. For an account of one woman's search to prove dinosaurs once lived in the hills of Hawke's Bay through examination of fossils, see Joan Wiffen's *Valley of the dragons: the story of New Zealand's dinosaur woman* (Auckland: Random Century, 1991. 128p.).

43 New Zealand soils: an introduction.

H. S. Gibbs. Wellington: Oxford University Press, 1980. 115p. maps.

This text 'describes types of soils and their suitability for use in such economic activities as farming and forestry, and discusses different methods of soil management and their effect on environmental conditions' (Introduction). Professor Gibbs, a soil chemist, has written a work aimed at students of physical geography, but which nevertheless contains much of general interest.

44 Soils in the New Zealand landscape: the living mantle.

Les Molloy. Wellington: Mallinson Rendel/New Zealand Society of Soil Science, 1988. 239p. maps.

Attractively illustrated in colour, this authoritative book explores the soils which cover the remarkable diversity of landscapes that make up New Zealand. 'This book is about the soils of New Zealand – what they are like, why there are so many different sorts of soils, how they fit into our landscapes, and how we use them' (Foreword). Commissioned by the New Zealand Society of Soil Science, the work traverses twelve soil landscape regions, from the volcanic soils in the centre of the North Island to the peaty soils of Stewart Island, and including loamlands, clay hills, shattered hills, mountain terrains and plains. An introductory chapter explains how soils are formed and the final chapters look to the future and consider 'soils and land use' and 'soil and society'.

45 The geology of New Zealand.

Edited by R. P. Suggate, G. R. Stevens, M. T. Te Punga. Wellington: Government Printer, 1978. 2 vols. maps.

Developed over some fourteen years as a co-operative effort by Geological Survey staff, this remains the definitive, and most authoritative, work on the geology of New Zealand. It describes the stratigraphy of the country but also deals with the geological events that the stratigraphy records and the results of those events as they may be observed today. 'The attempt has been made to bring together in two volumes concise summaries of the stratigraphy, paleontology, petrology, and structure of New Zealand' (Foreword). References are provided throughout the work to allow further study in particular areas. While much of the same ground is covered in Maxwell Gage's *Legends in the rocks: an outline of New Zealand geology* (Christchurch: Whitcoulls, 1980. 426p.) this work is much less detailed and has been written with the layman in mind. An additional feature of this work, however, is the chapter entitled 'Geology serves New Zealand: the economic incentive' which examines the role of geology in the economic life and development of the country.

46 The field guide to New Zealand geology: an introduction to rocks, minerals and fossils.

Jocelyn Thornton. Auckland: Reed, 1995. Reprint of 1985 ed. 226p. maps.

The geological history of New Zealand is covered 'from its beginnings on the sea floor some 600 million years ago to its present patchwork landscape of volcano, range and plain'. This book attempts to answer questions about geology using simple terms and illustrations of New Zealand's more common rocks, minerals and fossils. The specimens illustrated are particularly clear in their depiction and very wide in their coverage. Sufficient information is provided to encourage interested readers to explore for themselves.

Climate

47 **The New Zealand weather book: a guide to the forces that shape our climate.**
David Beatson. Christchurch: Whitcoulls, 1985. rev. ed. 87p. maps.

Explains in clear language where New Zealand's weather comes from as well as how to read a weather map and set up a weather station. Additionally, this guide shows why it is not easy to predict New Zealand's weather and thus why it is important to be prepared for all types of conditions, particularly if boating or out walking. This is a particularly useful work for those who enjoy the outdoors.

48 **Greenhouse New Zealand: our climate: past, present and future.**
Jim Salinger. Dunedin: Square One Press, 1991. 104p. maps.

The 'greenhouse effect' is almost a household discussion point in New Zealand. The author explains the way the climate works, outlining past climates, describing possible future climate scenarios, given enhanced greenhouse warming, and exploring potential impacts for New Zealand. Clear prose and plenty of diagrams and illustrations assist the reader to understand the phenomenon and its possible effects on not only weather patterns but also plants, crops, animals and the natural environment. The author's enthusiasm for his subject is apparent.

49 **The weather and climate of Australia and New Zealand.**
A. P. Sturman, N. J. Tapper. Melbourne: Oxford University Press, 1996. 476p. maps.

Written for both meteorology students and professionals from other disciplines with an interest in atmospheric processes, this book treats Australasia as a climatic region. After sections on climatic systematics, the book focuses on 'selected aspects of the mesoscale, regional and local weather systems, and on climate patterns commonly observed across urban and rural areas of Australia and New Zealand' (cover). Past climate change, contemporary variability and future scenarios are examined, and possible links between human activity and climate variability are outlined.

Special features

50 **Earthquakes.**
G. A. Eiby. Auckland: Heinemann Reed, 1989. rev. ed. 166p. maps.

A New Zealand authority (now deceased) writes about earthquakes in general. However, New Zealand examples are cited throughout the book and an appendix lists major New Zealand, as well as world, earthquakes. Many of the illustrations show the effects of earthquakes in New Zealand.

51   **Antarctica: the Ross Sea region.**
Edited by Trevor Hatherton.   Wellington: DSIR, 1990. 287p. maps.
With the contributions written by experts in their fields, this superbly produced book describes the early exploration of the Ross Sea region, then details current scientific knowledge of this part of Antarctica. Considerable attention is devoted to the landforms underlying the ice sheet, the climate, ice forms and the adaptations by animals and lower plants to the harsh physical environment. The book also examines the need to protect the environment from inappropriate human intrusion.

52   **Tarawera: the volcanic eruption of 10 June 1886.**
R. F. Keam.   Auckland: The author, 1988. 472p. maps.
A superbly presented and exhaustively researched volume on an eruption in the centre of the North Island which has been a lifetime's study for the author, a University of Auckland physicist. Probably best known for the fact that the catastrophe caused the destruction of the world-famous 'pink and white terraces' (a fan-like staircase in delicate shades of pink and white on the shores of Lake Rotomahana – it was formed over thousands of years by a geyser, which had played over the mountain slope leaving deposits of silica), the effects of the eruption were much more widespread. The eruption fundamentally transformed the local landscape, covering it with ash and splitting the mountain in two. This work provides a scholarly, yet readable, 'analytical and comprehensive historical account' of the event, and of the physical and human impacts.

53   **Volcanoes of the south wind: a field guide to the volcanoes and landscape of Tongariro National Park.**
Karen Williams.   Wellington: Tongariro Natural History Society, 1989. 132p. maps.
Acknowledging their power, mystery and fascination, the author provides a basic explanation of the processes behind the formation and activity of volcanoes, using the central North Island cones as case-studies. Beautifully illustrated with colour photographs, many explanatory drawings also support the text.

54   **Yesterday's new earth: New Zealand's geothermal landscape.**
Peter Wood, photographs by Craig Potton.   Nelson, New Zealand: Craig Potton Publishing, 1990. 138p.
A geologist and a photographer combine expertise to present the Taupo volcanic zone in words and images. Their exploration ranges from the volcanic cones in Tongariro National Park to White Island in the Bay of Plenty, with hot springs and mud pools along the way. The fact that these sometimes haunting, sometimes fear-engendering, landscapes are at risk is stressed.

Island volcano: White Island, or Whakaari, New Zealand.
See item no. 189.

Fauna and Flora

General

55   The concise natural history of New Zealand.

Harriet Fleet.   Auckland: Heinemann, 1986. 275p. bibliog.

An enthusiastic preface by R. M. Lockley, well-known naturalist, introduces this attractively presented introduction to the natural history of New Zealand. A comprehensive coverage is arranged by main habitat areas, beginning in the alpine regions and progressing down to the sea, with additional chapters on the offshore islands.

56   New Zealand's nature heritage.

Edited by Ray Knox.   Hong Kong: Paul Hamlyn, 1974-76. 105 nos. in 7 vols. maps. bibliog.

For the interested layman, this remains a comprehensive, well-illustrated work in its field. The whole ambit of New Zealand's natural history is covered, from its geology to the impact of Maori and Pakeha on the habitat, including landforms, soils, natural and introduced flora and fauna, and inland and sea-water forms and life. The articles have been written by authorities in the various fields.

57   Biogeography and ecology in New Zealand.

Edited by G. Küschel.   The Hague: Dr. W. Junk, 1975. 689p. bibliog. maps. (Monographiae Biologicae, vol. 27).

'The volume contains seventeen chapters, the first three dealing with the geological history, climate and soils . . . the following ones . . . are devoted to the plants, the vertebrates, the surrounding seas, the lakes and ponds, the terrestrial and freshwater invertebrates and some aspects on the Maoris and man's influence on nature . . . Two . . . chapters are dedicated specifically to . . . the kiwi (*Apteryx*) and the tuatara (*Sphenodon*)' (Introduction). All the authors are recognized authorities in their scientific fields.

58 **The natural history of New Zealand: an ecological survey.**
Edited by Gordon R. Williams.   Wellington: Reed, 1973. 434p. maps.
The first *general* natural history of this country, 'the aim of the book has been to produce a text informative to the expert, helpful to the student, and informative, helpful and interesting to the layman' (Preface). Each chapter has been written by an expert in the field and is supported by diagrams, where appropriate, and a list of references. Very few aspects of natural history in New Zealand appear to have been neglected (although the editor admits that it is impossible to be entirely comprehensive) and the work remains a very useful reference source.

Fauna

59 **The southern ark: zoological discovery in New Zealand, 1769-1900.**
J. R. H. Andrews.   Auckland: Century Hutchinson, 1986. 237p. maps.
Not only does this work survey 130 years of discovery, description and illustration of New Zealand's unique fauna, beginning with Captain Cook and concluding at the end of the Victorian era, but it also describes the science scene in the country in the 1850s. Writings from famous naturalists of the time – Sir Joseph Banks, Sir Richard Owen, the Reverend Richard Taylor – are matched with illustrations from such noted artists as Sydney Parkinson, Edward Lear, George Forster, and John Gould. Substantial footnotes accompany the text of this unusual and inviting work.

60 **Collins guide to birds of New Zealand and outlying islands.**
R. A. Falla, R. B. Sibson, E. G. Turbott.   Auckland: Harper Collins, 1993. 247p. maps.
The continuing revisions and reprintings of this work testify to its popularity and usefulness. Each of the noted authors covers certain families or natural groups, providing information including a description of the bird, its voice, the habitat and range it can be found within and breeding information.

61 **New Zealand spiders: an introduction.**
R. R. Forster, L. M. Forster.   Auckland: Collins, 1973. 254p. bibliog.
Written for the enquiring layperson, this volume offers a general description of the structure and behaviour of New Zealand spiders and their life, then deals with various groups found in the country. The feeding, mating and breeding of spiders is covered, and accompanied by well-presented diagrams and illustrations in black-and-white and colour. The work will not only assist the reader in gaining an understanding of these often maligned creatures but will also aid in the identification of specimens.

62 **New Zealand butterflies: identification and natural history.**
George W. Gibbs.   Auckland: Collins, 1980. 207p. maps.
Written by the grandson of one of New Zealand's foremost naturalists, George Hudson Gibbs, this book seeks to remedy the lack of readily available information on the butterflies of New Zealand. Systematically laid out according to the various

families represented, the work presents the life history of the butterflies, illustrated with 197 colour plates. Distribution maps accompany the information on each species.

63 **New Zealand amphibians and reptiles in colour.**
Joan Robb. Auckland: Collins, 1986. 128p. maps.

An enchanting and informed account of the amphibians and reptiles of New Zealand, both native and introduced. There are detailed descriptions of all New Zealand frogs and lizards, while a particular feature to note is the section on the country's most ancient creature, the tuatara. The text is accompanied by 145 colour photographs, diagrams, a glossary, notes on scientific names and useful distribution maps.

64 **New Zealand insects and their story.**
Richard Sharell. Auckland: Collins, 1982. rev. ed. 268p.

This book is principally concerned with 'live insects, their biology and their relationship to each other, to their environment and to man' (p. 18). Written for the interested layperson, the work nevertheless incorporates a catalogue of New Zealand insects and a glossary. It also includes notes on the life of George Hudson Gibbs (1867-1946), pioneer New Zealand entomologist. There are 200 colour photographs.

Flora

65 **Flora of New Zealand.**
Edited by H. H. Allan (vol. I); L. B. Moore, E. Edgar (vol. II);
A. J. Healy, E. Edgar (vol. III). Wellington: Government Printer, 1961-80. 3 vols. maps.

Volume I of this three-volume work 'deals with all the indigenous vascular plants except the monocotyledons; volume II includes all the monocotyledon families except Gramineae; and volume III describes the introduced wild plants belonging to the rush, sedge, lily, iris, arum and related families. The volumes are identification manuals intended for agriculturalists and botanists; scientific descriptions are provided in careful detail. 'Special attention has been paid to keys to families, genera and species and line drawings . . . should assist identification in some difficult groups' (cover, volume I). This is an authoritative, comprehensive, descriptive account of the plants native to this country.

66 **The mosses of New Zealand.**
Jessica Beever, K. W. Allison, Jean Child. Dunedin: University of Otago Press, 1992. 214p.

Photographs and line-drawings assist in the identification and description of 75 of the commonest species. Distinguishing characteristics are given for a further 380. 'All the genera and all the common species known to occur on the New Zealand mainland, or its close offshore islands are included' (Preface). This is an appealing volume which is interesting to browse.

67   **New Zealand ferns and allied plants.**
     Patrick J. Brownsey, John C. Smith-Dodsworth.   Auckland: David
     Bateman, 1989. 168p. bibliog.
'Covers all the ferns and allied plants, both native and introduced, which can be found
in New Zealand, a country particularly renowned throughout the world for the abun-
dance and variety of its ferns' (cover). Providing information to the botanist as well as
the interested layperson, colour and black-and-white photographs, line-drawings and
silhouettes ensure ease of identification. A more technical presentation can be found in
H. B. Dobbie's *New Zealand ferns* (Auckland: Southern Reprints, 1987. 3rd ed.
489p.), the work of a lifelong enthusiast and authority on ferns.

68   **Native New Zealand flowering plants.**
     J. T. Salmon.   Auckland: Reed, 1991. 254p. maps.
A comprehensive guide to over 600 species of native flowering plants, grouped
according to their habitat, lavishly illustrated with colour photographs.

69   **The native trees of New Zealand.**
     J. T. Salmon.   Auckland: Reed, 1996. rev. ed. 384p. maps.
'There are more than 220 species of indigenous New Zealand tree, and they are all
covered in this book: its scope is complete' (cover). A number of introductory chapters consider the role of the tree in the ecosystem, look at the structure of trees, and
how they grow and reproduce, discuss the role of forests and the threats facing them,
and examine the particular character and types of New Zealand forests. The species
are then described and illustrated in detail from the juvenile to the mature appearance.
The superb colour photographs, the result of many years of dedicated effort by the
author, make this a fascinating work to browse as well as providing information for
those wishing to identify a particular tree.

70   **Early New Zealand botanical art.**
     F. Bruce Sampson.   Auckland: Reed Methuen, 1985. 142p.
The journals and diaries of explorers, botanists and early settlers, as well as publications of the time, have been researched to provide this collection of paintings and
drawings from 1769 to 1914. Botanists and artists represented include Johann and
George Forster, Sir William and Sir Joseph Hooker, Thomas Kirk and Thomas
Cheeseman, and the author has also covered some lesser-known illustrators. The volume is of interest for the light it sheds on the illustrators noted as well as for the
botanical detail of their drawings.

71   **New Zealand fungi: an illustrated guide.**
     Greta Stevenson.   Christchurch: University of Canterbury, 1994. 122p.
     bibliog.
Lists more than 300 species of common fungi with line-drawings and photographs to
aid identification. The book also provides general chapters to guide the novice on what
fungi are and what they do, and how to collect, preserve and identify them, together
with a useful bibliography.

72 **Vegetation of New Zealand.**
Peter Wardle. Cambridge, England: Cambridge University Press, 1991. 672p. maps.

A compendious and profusely illustrated account of the present-day vegetation of New Zealand in terms of the environmental factors and historical events that have shaped it. Chapters 1-4 describe the New Zealand environment, fauna and flora, and discuss the origins, relationships, life forms and reproductive aspects of the indigenous vegetation. Chapter 5 is a synopsis of vegetation types, habitat classes and environmental processes, while chapter 6 is an outline of the country's geographic divisions. Chapters 7-13 contain expanded descriptions of plant communities. Chapters 14-16 discuss ecological functions and processes.

Marine life

73 **Seaweeds of New Zealand: an illustrated guide.**
Nancy Adams. Christchurch: Canterbury University Press, 1994. 360p.

This is the first comprehensive guide to New Zealand seaweeds, over 600 species being concisely, yet precisely, described. Of these, 441 are illustrated with the author's vivid water-colour paintings, while pencil sketches provide further anatomical detail. Introductory sections describe the distribution, ecology, collection and study of seaweeds, there being also an extensive glossary. The book is the result of a lifetime's study and research.

74 **Collins guide to the sea fishes of New Zealand.**
Tony Ayling. Auckland: Collins, 1987. rev. ed. 343p. maps. bibliog.

Colour plates supported by almost 500 line-drawings by the author provide a useful identification guide to the sea fishes of New Zealand. Accompanying information includes a guide to using the book to identify fish and an essay on the distribution of fishes.

75 **New Zealand freshwater fishes: a natural history and guide.**
R. M. McDowall. Auckland: Heinemann Reed; Wellington: MAF Publishing Group, 1990. rev. ed. 553p. maps.

This revised edition greatly expands the natural history content of the original text while still maintaining the goal of assisting readers to identify fish. The author consciously seeks to satisfy the needs of both the specialist and the non-specialist, and in so doing may provide more information than the interested lay reader wants. Nevertheless, the work offers a fascinating range of detail, with black-and-white and colour photographs and line-drawings helping to elucidate the text.

6 **The New Zealand sea shore.**
John Morton, Michael Miller.   London; Auckland: Collins, 1973. 2nd
ed. 653p. maps. bibliog.

comprehensive and fully illustrated guide to New Zealand marine life by leading
authorities on the subject. 'We have tried to present the story of living communities
and the species that compose them, not from a structural or taxonomic viewpoint, but
to show how they adapted to live where they do, in harmony and in contest with each
other' (Preface). Some 200 plants and animals have been painted specifically for the
book by Michael Miller and photographs and drawings also supplement the text. 'The
treatment is habitat-by-habitat, so that the reader may know *what* plants and animals
to expect in any one type of locality, *where* to look for them, and *how* and *why* they
are there' (cover).

New Zealand forest parks.
See item no. 644.

Wild Fiordland: discovering the natural history of a world heritage area.
See item no. 645.

Heritage: the parks of the people.
See item no. 646.

Botanic gardens and parks in New Zealand: an illustrated record.
See item no. 647.

The black robin: saving the world's most endangered bird.
See item no. 652.

Little Barrier Island: New Zealand's foremost wildlife sanctuary.
See item no. 653.

Threatened plants of New Zealand.
See item no. 655.

To save a forest: Whirinaki.
See item no. 657.

New Zealand and the Pacific

77 Pacific neighbours: New Zealand's relations with other Pacific Islands.

Ron Crocombe. Christchurch: Centre for Pacific Studies, Canterbury University; Suva, Fiji: Institute for Pacific Studies, University of the South Pacific, 1992. 290p. maps.

An overview of the post-colonial ties linking New Zealand with the Pacific Islands. The author distinguishes the movements of people in both directions, resource flows and the transfer of ideas through education and media penetration, as well as more formal and diplomatic linkages. A concluding section ponders the possible nature of future relationships. 'New Zealand and its neighbour states will continue to interact because they have little choice but to do so' (p. 235).

78 Samoa mo Samoa: the emergence of the independent state of Western Samoa.

J. W. Davidson. Melbourne: Oxford University Press, 1967. 467p. maps.

Explores the political evolution of Western Samoa, from early contact with missionaries and traders, through colonial rule, to recognition of its sovereignty. The work is a classic in its field, describing this evolution from the point of view of the islanders themselves, not from that of those who came to conquer. The author has drawn on documentary sources but has also brought his long association with Samoan affairs to bear on his analysis. 'His sympathy with Samoan aspirations, and his deep affection for the country and its people, are apparent throughout the book' (cover).

79 Mau: Samoa's struggle for freedom.

Michael J. Field. Auckland: Polynesian Press, 1991. rev. ed. 263p. maps. bibliog.

The story of New Zealand's acquisition of German Samoa following the First World War, the setting up of New Zealand rule on the island, the clashes between ruler and

24

ruled and the eventual securing of independence, is here related by a white New Zealander married to a Samoan. As he states, 'I am faced with the reality that I can tell the story only from a New Zealand point of view' (Introduction), but accepting this caveat, this is a moving and at times impassioned account of an episode that has received little attention from New Zealand historians.

80 The Cook Islands, 1820-1950.

Richard Gilson, edited by Ron Crocombe. Wellington: Victoria University Press; Suva, Fiji: Institute of Pacific Studies of the University of the South Pacific, 1980. 242p. maps. bibliog.

The editor completed this work after the author died. He comments in the Preface, 'It is a great pity that Gilson did not live to undertake the further research he intended, particularly to give greater attention to questions of local government, social organisation and culture change in the smaller islands'. Accepting these limitations, this is a most useful commentary on the history of the Cook Islands, from early times, through the mission period and New Zealand annexation, to independence in 1965. For an alternative, much more critical view see D. Scott's *Years of the Pooh-Bah* (Auckland: Hodder & Stoughton, 1991. 320p.).

81 Tokelau: a historical ethnography.

Judith Huntsman, Anthony Hooper. Auckland: Auckland University Press, with assistance from Creative New Zealand, 1996. 355p. maps. bibliog.

The outcome of more than two decades of research, this is the most comprehensive account of three atolls entrusted to New Zealand care in 1925, and included within the nation's territorial boundaries in 1948. It is 'both a comparative ethnographic study of the islands and a narrative record of their past' (Introduction). Not only was much of the research conducted on the islands themselves but documents housed in the Pacific, United States and New Zealand were intensively examined. The resulting, attractively presented work will be the authority in this area for many years to come.

82 New Zealand's record in the Pacific Islands in the twentieth century.

Edited by Angus Ross. Auckland: Longman Paul, for the New Zealand Institute of International Affairs; London: Hurst; New York: Humanities Press, 1969. 362p. maps. bibliog.

Deals mainly with New Zealand's relations with its former Pacific territories: the Cook Islands, Western Samoa, Niue, and the Tokelaus. The authors concentrate on New Zealand's administrative record, generally from a point of view sympathetic to New Zealand. More space might have been given to social and economic changes and New Zealand's role in them. For an understanding of the relationships in the 19th century, Angus Ross's *New Zealand aspirations in the Pacific in the nineteenth century* (Oxford: Clarendon Press, 1964. 332p.) 'seeks to fill a gap which has existed for too long in New Zealand's history' (Preface).

83 **Would a good man die? Niue Island, New Zealand and the late Mr Larsen.**
Dick Scott.   Auckland: Hodder & Stoughton/Southern Cross Books, 1993. 176p. map.

Built around an account of the assassination of the Resident Commissioner in 1953, this book is a scathing indictment of New Zealand's 20th-century administration of Niue Island. While the New Zealand Government mourned the death of 'an outstanding officer', the author sets out to present a different view. In a book based on archival research and interviews in three countries, he tells how three young Niueans believed they were ridding the island of a tyrant. Saved from the gallows on three occasions, they were to serve unusually long prison sentences. In typical Scott style, this relates another previously untold episode in New Zealand's history.

84 **The phosphateers: a history of the British Phosphate Commissioners and the Christmas Island Phosphate Commission.**
Maslyn Williams, Barrie Macdonald.   Melbourne: Melbourne University Press, 1985. 586p. plates. bibliog.

A comprehensive examination of the role of the British Phosphate Commissioners and the Christmas Island Commission written from the authors' advantageous position of having access to the records of both. Not simply a history of these bodies, however, the authors have woven their activities into an assessment of the happenings in the local and world environment. The product was an extremely valuable component in agricultural development in New Zealand. This is an important work in view of the subsequent legal actions initiated by the islands involved in phosphate production.

The challenge of change: Pacific Island communities in New Zealand, 1986-1993.
See item no. 277.

Pacific migrant labour, class and racism in New Zealand: fresh off the boat.
See item no. 278.

Prehistory and Archaeology

85 **Prodigious birds: moas and moa-hunting in prehistoric New Zealand.**
   Atholl Anderson.   Cambridge, England: Cambridge University Press, 1989. 238p. maps.

One hundred and fifty years of research into the moa, and the Maori who hunted it, are summarized in this book. Evidence from palaeontology, biology, archaeology and ethnography is reviewed. Part one discusses moa systematics. Part two describes the field evidence of moa hunting in detail. The book is an indispensable guide to moa historiography, the formative debates and methods of analysis used in earlier studies being detailed.

86 **The tattooed land: the southern frontiers of the pa Maori.**
   Barry Brailsford.   Wellington: Reed, 1981. 262p. maps. bibliog.

Concentrating on the South Island Maori, the author links oral tradition with archaeological discoveries to present a picture of the life of this group of people before Europeans arrived in New Zealand. The origins of the people studied are examined and then, moving from north to south, specific areas are examined in some detail. Measured site plans are provided, together with drawings of artefacts unearthed. The quotations from Europeans arriving in this land provide a different dimension and illuminate the archaeological evidence.

87 **The prehistory of New Zealand.**
   Janet Davidson.   Auckland: Longman Paul, 1987. new ed. 270p. maps. bibliog.

An authoritative review of what is known about life in New Zealand before the coming of the European, this book brings together in an easily accessible form information previously only available in specialist publications. There are sections on the origins of the Maori, the natural and modified environments, economic and settlement patterns and the rise of warfare. An extensive bibliography is provided, together with a list of scientific names of plants and animals and of sites and places of archaeological interest mentioned in the text. The work is the best short introduction to the subject. However, a more general, popular survey can be found in *Digging up the past: New Zealand's archaeological history,* edited by Michael Trotter and Beverley McCulloch (Auckland: Penguin, 1997. rev. ed. 128p.) which provides a well-illustrated and pithy introduction to recent investigations in New Zealand archaeology.

88 The prehistoric exploration and colonisation of the Pacific.
Geoffrey Irwin. Cambridge, England: Cambridge University Press, 1992. 240p. maps. bibliog.

Described variously as 'one of the most innovative and interesting works on Polynesian prehistory', 'an important and influential contribution to Pacific prehistory' and 'an excellent reference work', this book draws on the author's sailing experiences to set out a new model which shows the purposeful nature of Polynesian exploration. Two distinct periods of voyaging and colonization, the Pleistocene period and the period of systematic exploration of the remote Pacific, are examined. Although a somewhat specialized work, this book nevertheless has a fascination, as the author shares his theory of the nature of the exploration by these island people. It is a natural successor to C. A. Sharp's *Ancient voyagers in Polynesia* (Hamilton, New Zealand: Pauls Book Arcade; Sydney: Angus & Robertson; Berkeley, California: University of California Press, 1963-64. 159p.).

89 Nga tohuwhenua mai te rangi: a New Zealand archaeology in aerial photographs.
Kevin L. Jones. Wellington: Victoria University Press, 1994. 294p. maps.

The author employs aerial photographs from official collections to delineate important archaeological sites on the land surface. Recorded Maori historical and archaeological features from every region in New Zealand are included, as well as a selection of 19th-century post-European settlement sites. The aerial photographs are augmented by photographs taken on the ground, by line-drawings which explain key points, and by an informed text.

90 The first thousand years: regional perspectives in New Zealand archaeology.
Edited by Nigel Prickett. Palmerston North, New Zealand: Dunmore Press, 1982. 204p. maps.

Published to commemorate the twenty-fifth anniversary of the New Zealand Archaeological Association, the eight contributors to the volume emphasize the recent professionalization of the discipline, the new questions being formulated, and the new methodologies embraced. The ten discrete regional studies focus on the nature and variety of Maori adaptations to the New Zealand environment, both the continuities and the differences between regions being distinguished. The book, presented in easily absorbed format, is intended to help bridge the gap between practising archaeologists and the interested public.

91   The great New Zealand myth: a study of the discovery and origin
     traditions of the Maori.
     D. R. Simmons.   Wellington: Reed, 1976. 504p. bibliog.
Controversial when published, this work is a re-evaluation which casts serious doubt on
the generally accepted versions of Maori migration myths. 'This doubt is the outcome,
not of any appeal to extra-traditional evidence such as that provided by archaeology,
but simply of re-examination of the traditional material itself' (Introduction). In his
search for authentic, traditional myths, Simmons subjects surviving sources and contemporary informants and recorders to rigorous examination.

92   The origins of the first New Zealanders.
     Edited by Douglas G. Sutton.   Auckland: Auckland University Press,
     1994. 269p. maps.
This multi-disciplinary volume presents fresh views of New Zealand's prehistory.
Contributors re-examine the orthodox scenario of Polynesian colonization, and, by
studying Eastern Polynesian, Maori and Moriori languages, the climate, archaeologi-
cal evidence, geomorphology – even by building a canoe and 'rediscovering' New
Zealand – create new challenging models for the date, type and source of New
Zealand colonization. The papers were originally presented to a symposium at
Auckland University in 1988.

Prehistoric New Zealand.
See item no. 36.

Two worlds: first meetings between Maori and Europeans, 1642-1772.
See item no. 109.

Moriori: a people rediscovered.
See item no. 187.

**Traditional lifeways of the southern Maori: the Otago Museum
Ethnological Project, 1920.**
See item no. 195.

**The pa Maori: an account of the fortified villages of the Maori in pre-
European and modern times: illustrating methods of defence by means
of ramparts, fosses, scarps and stockades.**
See item no. 196.

The coming of the Maori.
See item no. 198.

Economics of the New Zealand Maori.
See item no. 199.

Prehistoric rock art of New Zealand.
See item no. 772.

Journal of the Polynesian Society.
See item no. 882.

New Zealand Journal of Archaeology.
See item no. 897.

European Discovery and Exploration

93   The discovery of New Zealand.
J. C. Beaglehole.   London, Wellington: Oxford University Press, 1961.
rev. ed. 102p. maps.

This work first appeared in 1939 as one of a series entitled 'New Zealand Centennial Surveys'. Though dated, it remains the best concise account of both the Polynesian and European discovery of New Zealand.

94   The journals of Captain James Cook on his voyages of discovery.
Edited by J. C. Beaglehole.   Cambridge, England: Hakluyt Society,
1955-74. 4 vols. in 5. maps. bibliog. (Hakluyt Society. Extra Series
nos. 34-37).

Edited by one of New Zealand's most renowned scholars, these journals contain the earliest detailed descriptions of New Zealand and the people who lived there. Cook's observations are clear and painstakingly made. Few other discoverers matched his ability to observe and record.

95   The farthest corner: New Zealand – a twice discovered land.
Harry Morton, Carol Morton Johnston.   Auckland: Century
Hutchinson, 1988. 315p. maps. bibliog.

Acknowledging New Zealand's isolation, even in the Pacific world, the authors contrast the experiences of the Polynesian and later European explorers, first in discovering the islands, then in assessing their potential. The text is supported by a series of 'features' highlighting the practical details of survival in an alien land, and the demands placed on human endurance and ingenuity.

96   Explorers and travellers: early expeditions in New Zealand.
John Pascoe.   Wellington: Reed, 1983. rev. ed. 158p. maps.

The author, a distinguished mountaineer, drawing from written accounts by European adventurers and from his own experiences in travelling the routes described, presents a vivid picture of the excitement and privations of the life of the early explorers portrayed in this book. Illustrated with photographs from the Alexander Turnbull Library (part of the National Library, Wellington) and other collections, this provides interesting insights into the determination of these men.

Settlement History of New Zealand

General

97 **Making peoples: a history of the New Zealanders: from Polynesian settlement to the end of the nineteenth century.**
James Belich.   London: Allen Lane; Auckland: Penguin Press, 1996. 497p.

The first of a projected two-volume revisionist history of New Zealand, this book covers the period from Polynesian settlement to the end of the 19th century. It examines Maori origins and pre-contact history in unusual detail for a general study, as well as interracial relations up to 1900, and the myths and realities of European colonization. The dominant theme is the making of two peoples, Maori and Pakeha, their changing economic and social structures, and their relationships with each other. While the book is immensely readable, a number of the author's sometimes provocative theories have yet to be tested.

98 **The future and the past: themes in New Zealand history.**
Edited by Colin Davis, Peter Lineham.   Palmerston North, New Zealand: Department of History, Massey University, 1991. 141p.

In the wake of the 1990 sesquicentenary celebrations, six younger historians review the state of New Zealand historiography. Recognizing that a shift in academic interest to the country's past has been relatively recent, they pose several critical questions. What so far has been achieved? What gaps remain? What are the future challenges for those interested in the subject? The essays address six broad themes: religion; Maori history; rural life; women's history; society and social welfare; and war. An extensive bibliography is attached to each.

99 **The making of New Zealand: an economic history.**
G. R. Hawke.   Cambridge, England: Cambridge University Press,
1985. 362p. map.

A survey of New Zealand's economic history by the country's leading cliometrician. Prepared as a text, the book endeavours to place the New Zealand experience within the context of international development. Particular emphasis is placed on the development and performance of different sectors of the economy, and on the role of government. Coverage is uneven, nearly two-thirds of the book being devoted to trends in the second half of the 20th century, and the sometimes awkward prose does not make for easy reading.

100 **Historical dictionary of New Zealand.**
Keith Jackson, Alan McRobie.   Auckland: Longman, 1996. 313p.
maps. bibliog.

Produced as part of an international series, this dictionary places primary emphasis on entries related to history and politics, with recent events and individuals being accorded greater prominence than those from the more remote past. There is a useful introductory essay and an extended bibliography.

101 **New Zealand's heritage: the making of a nation.**
Edited by Ray Knox.   Auckland: Paul Hamlyn, 1971-73. Reprinted
with minor amendments, 1977-79. 2,940p. maps.

First published in the 1970s in 105 weekly parts, this remains the most accessible general history of New Zealand. Inevitably, with around 180 contributors, the quality of the articles varies. Some are by acknowledged authorities in their fields; others are rewrites of material readily available elsewhere. But on the whole the information is reliable. Many illustrations enhance the text. Topics covered include: natural history, Maori and European settlement, exploration, famous people, sport, science, wars, economics, the arts and culture, and social and political history.

102 **The Oxford history of New Zealand.**
Edited by Geoffrey W. Rice.   Auckland: Oxford University Press,
1992. 2nd ed. 755p. maps. bibliog.

Acclaimed as a standard scholarly reference work when first published in 1981, this edition has been updated to encompass the turbulent 1980s and more recent research. Six new chapters have been added, and others have been enlarged or revised. As before, the book draws upon the work of archaeologists, social scientists, economists, historians and critics, to provide a comprehensive account of New Zealand's past from the first Polynesian settlement to the present day. Valuable appendices include summarizing tables, graphs and maps, while there are exhaustive bibliographies for each chapter.

103 **A history of New Zealand.**
Keith Sinclair.   Auckland: Penguin, 1991. 4th rev. ed. 364p. maps.

Revised and reprinted many times since it was first published in 1959, and initially written for an international audience, this book is already the classic short history of New Zealand. Though criticized by some as exhibiting a North Island bias, it views New Zealand as distinctively a Pacific country. As the narrative moves through different stages of the nation's development, the centre of interest shifts according to whether race relations, economic changes, political ideas or politics seem to the author to have been most significant. 'He sees the appearance of an indigenous literature and the growth of national consciousness as being as noteworthy as the price of butterfat' (cover).

104 The Oxford illustrated history of New Zealand.
Edited by Keith Sinclair. Auckland: Oxford University Press, 1996.
2nd ed. 408p. maps.

This book has been written for the general reader seeking a greater understanding of New Zealand's past. Each chapter has been written by a specialist in his or her field, drawing on the most recent research. Considerable attention has been paid to the history of the Maori, with chapters on the Polynesian settlers, the Maori in colonial times, Maori prophet leaders, and the Maori in the 20th century. There are also chapters on New Zealand as a Pacific nation and New Zealand in the world. The well-chosen illustrations, all in black-and-white, complement the text.

105 The quest for security in New Zealand 1840 to 1966.
W. B. Sutch. Wellington; London: Oxford University Press, 1966.
512p. bibliog.

'This is the story of the struggle of the people of New Zealand for personal, social and economic security. It tells of the forces developing poverty, unemployment, insecurity and depression . . . (and) . . . describes the measures taken to protect the country against these hazards' (Preface). A social and economic history by a left-wing economic nationalist, who was himself involved in many of the events described from the mid-1930s, it has become a period-piece in the light of more recent history. Unorthodox in interpretation, sometimes careless in detail, it is nevertheless history with passion.

Early contact (-1853)

106 Fatal success: a history of the New Zealand Company.
Patricia Burns, edited by Henry Richardson. Auckland: Heinemann Reed, 1989. 327p. maps.

Directly involved in the foundation of four New Zealand settlements in the 1840s, and associated with the establishment of two others, the New Zealand Company was an enigma. Though launched with high-sounding rhetoric in Britain, its colonial preoccupations were more venal. Its business was the transportation of migrants to the colony to take up lands purchased from the Maori, the principal objective being to make profits for shareholders. The conduct of the business is examined, as well as the effects on relations between Maori and Pakeha. The book is a useful synthesis of knowledge about the Company and the man with which it is almost synonymous, Edward Gibbon Wakefield.

107 **Early Victorian New Zealand: a study of racial tension and social attitudes 1839-1852.**
John Miller.   Wellington; London: Oxford University Press, 1974. Reprint of 1958 ed. 217p. maps. bibliog.

Racily written, this book provides a portrait of the New Zealand Company settlements at Wellington, Nelson, Wanganui and New Plymouth in their founding decade. The author has a keen eye for the eccentric, the bizarre and the grotesque. One of the first books to debunk myths surrounding the New Zealand Company, it also deals with race relations, changes to Maori life, the emergence of pastoralism as an economic base for the settlements, colonial society, and the fostering of political feeling. There are serious messages beneath the froth.

108 **The whale's wake.**
Harry Morton.   Dunedin: McIndoe for University of Otago Press, 1982. 396p. maps.

A lively account of whaling in New Zealand waters, discussing the whales, whalers and whaling techniques, ships, the market for whale products, and whaling from shore stations. The author places the industry in its social context, showing the role that whaling played in early 19th-century New Zealand development. With the decline of the industry in the 1840s, many of those involved sought new lives ashore. Authoritative, the book was exhaustively researched in New Zealand and on three continents.

109 **Two worlds: first meetings between Maori and Europeans, 1642-1772.**
Anne Salmond.   Auckland: Viking, 1991. 477p. maps.

This book is a provocative synthesis of two previously separate views of the first meetings of Maori and Europeans in New Zealand. Until the present, European perspectives, those of the voyagers of discovery, have taken precedence. Drawing from local tribal knowledge, the author sets out to redress the balance. She finds that 'both Maori and European protagonists were active . . . following their own practical, political and mythological agendas' (cover). Many popular misconceptions and bigotries relating to traditional Maori society are revealed. This is a large, attractive and well-illustrated book.

110 **The shadow of the land: a study of British policy and racial conflict in New Zealand 1832-1852.**
Ian Wards.   Wellington: Historical Publications Branch, 1968. 422p. maps. bibliog.

A most detailed examination of the British occupation of New Zealand, based on research in the official archives. Commencing with a discussion of the circumstances in which the Treaty of Waitangi was signed, the book moves on to consider the establishment of British rule and the role of the military, particularly the pacification campaigns in the Bay of Islands and the southern North Island in the mid- and late 1840s. Though controversial when first published, its importance is now widely recognized.

111 **From Hongi Hika to Hone Heke: a quarter century of upheaval.**
Ormond Wilson. Dunedin: McIndoe, 1985. 330p.
This book casts fresh light on Maori attitudes at the time of the 1840 Treaty of
Waitangi, both of those who endorsed and those who opposed it. Based on an intensive study of contemporary sources, it compares the relative impacts of the two classes
of Europeans who had already settled in New Zealand: on the one hand the missionaries, on the other runaway seamen and convicts escaped from New South Wales,
Australia. It contrasts the reactions to these new influences on three Maori leaders who
reacted in very different ways: Hongi Hika, Te Rauparaha and Hone Heke.

Colonial period (1853-1914)

112 **New Zealand's burning: the settlers' world in the mid 1880s.**
Rollo Arnold. Wellington: Victoria University Press, 1994. 319p.
maps. bibliog.
'I believe that we need, but do not yet have, a comprehensive overview of what it was
that emerged from the founding years. This book aims to provide such a comprehensive overview; a summing up of the nature and quality of what had been achieved'
(Preface). Taking the fires that flared in the North Island bush districts in the summer
of 1885-86 as a peg, the author, through settler responses to the emergencies, analyses
how life worked, the forces shaping settler minds, the institutions being crafted, and
the new rural and urban landscapes. This work is a masterly study of late-19th-century
New Zealand, based on painstaking research.

113 **The New Zealand wars and the Victorian interpretation of racial
conflict.**
James Belich. Auckland: Penguin, 1988. 396p. maps.
A very different picture of the Anglo-Maori wars from that propounded in earlier
works is presented in this book. According to Belich, honours were at least even in
early conflicts, the true turning-point in race relations being the Waikato War of 1863-
64, when the British finally triumphed through superior numbers and fire power. Apart
from demonstrating the strength of Maori resistance, the book also seeks to explain
previous interpretations, concluding that Victorian perceptions laid down what should
happen in war between Europeans and other races.

114 **Lands for the people?: the highland clearances and the
colonisation of New Zealand: a biography of John McKenzie.**
Tom Brooking. Dunedin: University of Otago Press, 1996. 363p.
maps. bibliog.
Not simply a superior political biography, this book is also a unique summary of current knowledge about the intense 19th-century debate as to how land should be
apportioned, to whom, and on what terms. With the career of land reformer John
McKenzie providing the linkages, the author examines the extent of land monopoly
and the state's role in making land more widely available. He also addresses the questions

of how far land hunger was assuaged by the subdivision of existing estates, and how far by the sequestering of Maori land.

115 A southern gentry: New Zealanders who inherited the earth.
Stevan Eldred-Grigg. Wellington: Reed, 1980. 192p.

The emergence of a colonial elite – the 'wool kings' of the South Island – is related in this book. The author reconstructs how the elite lived: how they garnered their wealth, the exclusive social circles, the town houses and rural mansions, the hierarchical arrangements on properties and how wealth translated into power. The opulence of their lifestyles is contrasted with that of contemporary ordinary New Zealanders; often uncertain, sometimes wretched. Written from a committed left-wing viewpoint, and dismissed by some critics on this account, the story is both colourful and challenging.

116 The ideal society and its enemies: the foundations of modern New Zealand society, 1850-1900.
Miles Fairburn. Auckland: Auckland University Press, 1989. 316p.

What were the characteristics of 19th-century New Zealand? Did that society differ markedly from other frontier societies? In this original and innovative study the author, utilizing techniques of the 'new social history', seeks to answer these questions. Rejecting the views of other social historians, he advances his theory that in these years New Zealand was an atomized society, i.e., rapid frontier expansion scattered the settlers as transient strangers. The results, despite comparatively high material living standards, were weak interpersonal relationships and high degrees of loneliness and individual licence. This work was warmly reviewed by some critics, roundly criticized by others.

117 The New Zealand Liberals: the years of power, 1891-1912.
D. A. Hamer. Auckland: Auckland University Press, 1988. 418p.

The twenty-one years of Liberal rule (1891-1912) has been regarded as a watershed in New Zealand's development. The provision of land for modest settlers and the credit to keep them on it, compulsory arbitration and other new labour laws, old age pensions, all helped to establish a conviction that the state should solve economic and social problems. Taken with reforms such as women's suffrage, the measures helped to give the country a reputation as a 'social laboratory'. 'My purpose has been . . . to write a history of Liberal politics and of the political origins, implications and consequences of Liberal policy and governmental activity' (Introduction).

118 The history of policing in New Zealand.
Richard S. Hill. Vol. 1, Wellington: Government Printer, 1986. 1,141p. Vol. 2, Wellington: Historical Branch, Department of Internal Affairs/GP Books, 1989. 386p. Vol. 3, Palmerston North, New Zealand: Dunmore Press/New Zealand Police, with the assistance of the Historical Branch, Department of Internal Affairs, 1995. 532p.

Packaged as a three-volume history of policing in New Zealand (to 1917), this work is far more. It is no less than an alternative view of 19th-century social history, particularly the seamy side. Interwoven with the organizing themes of social and racial control, and enormous detail on the mechanics of policing, are tales of battles and murders, strikes and scandals, riots and tragedies. Volume 1, *Policing the colonial frontier*, covers the period up to the late 1860s. Volume 2, *The colonial frontier tamed*, covers the ensuing two decades. The third volume, *The iron hand in the velvet glove*, carries the story up to the First World War.

119   Frontier New Zealand: the search for Eldorado, 1800-1920.

Duncan Mackay.   Auckland: Harper Collins Publishers NZ, 1992. 159p.

This book is an attempt to develop an integrated history of 19th-century New Zealand as an extractive frontier. The various phases – sealing and whaling, mining, and logging – are reconstructed, and the long-term influences of these phases on the subsequent development of the country are assessed. Significantly, the agricultural frontier, in many respects also extractive by nature, is excluded from consideration. The many photographs indicate the rawness of the towns and communities formed.

120   The forgotten worker: the rural wage earner in nineteenth century New Zealand.

John E. Martin.   Wellington: Allen & Unwin/Trade Union History Project, 1990. 228p.

Little has previously been written about the rural workers – shearers, labourers, musterers – who formed a critical part of the 19th-century New Zealand labour force. In this study their daily work rounds are described, as are their relations with employers, their living conditions, and their expectations. A central theme of the book is the growth of unionism as the large estates declined and family farms emerged.

121   Colonial sweat and tears: the working class in nineteenth century New Zealand.

Julia Millen.   Wellington: Reed, 1984. 160p.

Surprisingly little is known of the lives of New Zealand's colonial working class. Yet from 1840 until the end of the century the colony was hailed as 'a glorious country for the working man', one where manual labourers could work free from oppression, and domestic servants enjoy comforts and prospects previously reserved for the wealthy. The author demonstrates that reality was a little different; that, for many, freedom and fortune were illusions. Special attention is paid to the lot of single women, servants and children.

122   The immigrants: the great migration from Britain to New Zealand, 1830-1890.

Tony Simpson.   Auckland: Godwit, 1997. 240p. map.

In this general history of 19th-century British immigration to New Zealand, the author considers the reasons people left their home country and why they chose New Zealand. Against the economic, social and political backgrounds in both countries, he discusses the schemes devised and the incentives offered. The harrowing journeys undertaken and the difficulties of adjustment figure prominently. In a concluding section the part immigration has played in the development of New Zealand's political culture and social agendas is analysed. Related, but more specialized, studies include Rollo Arnold's *The farthest promised land* (Wellington: Victoria University Press/Price Milburn, 1981. 408p.), which probes the immigration boom of the 1870s, and Charlotte Macdonald's *A woman of good character* (Wellington: Allen &

Unwin/Historical Branch, Department of Internal Affairs, 1990. 283p.), which focuses on single women as assisted immigrants in the 19th century.

123 **Makers of fortune: a colonial business community and its fall.**
Russell C. J. Stone. Auckland: Auckland University Press; London: Oxford University Press, 1978. 240p. maps. bibliog.

Focusing on urban dynamics, and the interrelations between town and country, this history of Auckland's 19th-century business community provides a counterpoint to the dominant theme of rural development in New Zealand colonial history. After sketching the rise of the community in the first four settlement decades, the author analyses its virtual collapse in the 1880s, the result of depression conditions and banking crises. His recounting of the fates of individuals, firms and industries, drawn largely from legal and business records, illuminates much about colonial business. After two decades, this is still a unique work.

20th century

124 **The new dominion: a social and political history of New Zealand 1918-39.**
R. M. Burdon. Wellington: A. H. & A. W. Reed, London: George Allen & Unwin, 1965. 382p.

Often overlooked, this survey of New Zealand's development between the two world wars remains a useful assemblage of information not otherwise readily available. Though the presentation is a little disjointed, few topics of significance in the two decades are not at least touched upon. As a contemporary observer, the author is particularly strong on political and economic changes, but he is also enlightening on matters as divergent as the 1918 influenza epidemic, the rise of the motor car, and penal reform.

125 **New Zealand working people, 1890-1990.**
Stevan Eldred-Grigg. Palmerston North, New Zealand: Dunmore Press/Trade Union History Project, 1990. 251p.

A study in words and photographs of the lives, interests and preoccupations of New Zealand's working families over the past century. Part one, dealing with the period up to 1935, examines lifestyles both in rural districts and the growing towns. The limited impact of the Liberal labour reforms of the 1890s is suggested. Part two emphasizes the changes arising from the reforms of the first Labour Government (1935-49), what the author terms 'the revolution of oil and electricity', and the accelerated urbanization of the working population. That further disappointments were in store is made clear.

126 **The rake's progress?: the New Zealand economy since 1945.**
J. D. Gould. Auckland: Hodder & Stoughton, 1982. 247p.

New Zealand's senior economic historian reviews the country's post-Second World War history. 'The time seemed ripe to put on record some of the developments in the

New Zealand economy, its successes and failures' (Preface). A short general survey is followed by chapters dealing with the period in five-year segments. Later chapters examine New Zealand's growth record, the role of government in the economy and the experience of racial minorities. While acknowledging that New Zealand staggered from crisis to crisis, only coming up with temporary solutions to long-term problems, the author's outlook is guardedly optimistic.

127   After the war: New Zealand since 1945.

Michael King.   Auckland: Hodder & Stoughton/Wilson & Horton, 1988. 208p.

Presents a collage of incidents and pictures chosen to indicate the changing preoccupations of New Zealanders after 1945, the transformations in their way of life, and even the differences in appearances. The sections are by decades, each opening with a short introductory essay. The photographs, the core of the book, are copiously annotated.

128   Gallipoli: the New Zealand story.

Christopher Pugsley.   Auckland: Spectre, 1990. 2nd ed. 412p. maps.

Anzac Day, the day each year when New Zealanders remember their war dead, commemorates the participation of New Zealand troops in 1915 landings at Gallipoli, in the Dardanelles. The actions have been portrayed as the crucible from which a sense of nationhood first emerged and, in the author's view, have become 'perhaps our most enduring national myth'. Through documentary research and interviews with survivors he evaluates the impact upon those who fought and upon the country which sent them. The object is to strip aside the myth and reveal reality.

129   The slump: the thirties depression: its origins and aftermath.

Tony Simpson.   Auckland: Penguin, 1990. 181p.

'In conversations the subject of the Depression of the thirties comes up again and again as a central and significant life event' (Preface). The author, previously the compiler of a much republished oral history of New Zealand in the 1930s, *The sugarbag years* (Auckland: Godwit, 1997. rev. ed. 205p.), sets out to establish what the experience meant for New Zealanders. The early chapters probe the origins of the crisis, laying stress on the volatile international economy. The greater part of the book, however, is devoted to New Zealand responses, in particular the responses of governments. Also considered are the longer-term outcomes: political, economic and cultural. A conviction that history may be repeating itself is expressed.

130   The New Zealand people at war: the Home Front.

Nancy M. Taylor.   Wellington: Historical Branch, Department of Internal Affairs/Government Printer, 1986. 2 vols.

The final title in the 'Official History of New Zealand in the Second World War' series, this book provides a comprehensive account of the experiences, attitudes and concerns of ordinary New Zealanders between 1939 and 1945. There are detailed descriptions of the many war-imposed tasks and restrictions – shortages, rationing, direction of labour and censorship. The experience of various groups whose role or attitudes were influenced by the war, such as women, churches, trade unions and educational authorities, is clearly outlined. Attention is also paid to those who opposed the conflict, whether from conscientious or political motives. Complementary volumes are J. V. T. Baker's *War economy* (Wellington: War History Branch, Department of

Internal Affairs, 1965. 660p.) and F. L. W. Wood's *Political and external affairs* (Wellington: War History Branch, Department of Internal Affairs, 1958. 395p.).

131 **Her work and his: family, kin and community in New Zealand, 1900-1930.**
     Claire Toynbee.   Wellington: Victoria University Press, 1995. 260p.
Based on interviews with New Zealand men and women whose childhood spanned the early decades of the 20th century, this book focuses on the work done by women, men and children as members of families and communities in those years. Bringing together new information, it looks at tasks done individually or together, for pay or for free. 'The main aim is to fill in some gaps in our knowledge about Pakeha family and kinship relationships in New Zealand' (Introduction). The book concludes with comment on more recent developments in family life in New Zealand.

Aotearoa and New Zealand: a historical geography.
See item no. 22.

Coates of Kaipara.
See item no. 223.

Sir Joseph Ward: a political biography.
See item no. 224.

Edward Stafford: New Zealand's first statesman.
See item no. 225.

Julius Vogel: business politician.
See item no. 229.

From the cradle to the grave: a biography of Michael Joseph Savage.
See item no. 237.

Walter Nash.
See item no. 257.

The rich: a New Zealand history.
See item no. 312.

New Zealand: a handbook of historical statistics.
See item no. 632.

The unauthorized version: a cartoon history of New Zealand.
See item no. 722.

New Zealand Journal of History.
See item no. 900.

Studying New Zealand history.
See item no. 972.

Regional History

North Island

Northland

132 **'I have named it the Bay of Islands . . .'.**
Jack Lee. Auckland: Reed, 1996. 2nd ed. 329p. maps.
The early European history of New Zealand is the history of the Bay of Islands. It was there that the first tentative contact between Maori and European took place, the first missions were established, and the first European settlements sprang up. Significantly, it was also at the Bay of Islands that the Treaty of Waitangi was signed in 1840 – and armed conflict first broke out. This carefully researched study seeks to correct the imbalance of earlier books, which stressed missionary influence to the virtual exclusion of the settlements' commercial ascendancy. Similarly, it places the role of Maori in these events in a new light. A companion volume, also by Jack Lee, entitled *Hokianga* (Auckland: Reed, 1996. 319p.) examines parallel developments at the primary harbour on the western coast.

133 **The story of Northland.**
A. H. Reed. Wellington: Reed, 1975. Reprint of 1956 ed. 395p. maps. bibliog.
Essentially a popular history, with minimal documentation, this volume nevertheless remains the only overview of the 19th-century development of New Zealand's northern peninsula. Much of the book deals with the missionary and early colonization periods, ground traversed elsewhere, but there are valuable summaries of attempts by the Auckland Provincial Government to open up the districts, including the planting of Nova Scotians at Waipu, the Bohemians of Puhoi, and the Albertlanders. Thematic chapters cover other aspects of 19th-century life. Florence Keene's *Between two mountains: a history of Whangarei* (Auckland: Whitcombe & Tombs, 1966. 319p.) is a standard history of the region's main city.

Auckland

134 **Decently and in order: the government of the City of Auckland 1840-1971: the centennial history of the Auckland City Council.**
G. W. A. Bush. Auckland; London: Collins, for the Auckland City Council, 1971. 637p.

Written as the history of a local authority, this book tells much about the developing hub of New Zealand's largest city. The author shows convincingly that throughout its life the Auckland City Council has been concerned with morals, aesthetics, and better lives for its citizens, as well as with roads, water supply and sewerage. The account is set out in four chronological sections – pre-1871, 1871-1918, 1919-45 and 1945-71 – while a fifth section surveys the changing machinery of local government. Relentlessly scholarly, the book is exhaustively documented. A sequel by the same author, *Advance in order; the Auckland City Council from Centenary to reorganisation* (Auckland: Auckland City Council, 1991. 304p.) updates the story.

135 **The heart of colonial Auckland, 1865-1910.**
Terence Hodgson. Auckland: Random Century, 1992. 127p. map.

'I have attempted a lively look at aspects of what is now central Auckland but which for many years *was* Auckland . . . I have not tried to be exhaustive but with the assistance of contemporary photographs and press reporting have sought to capture some of its fabric and flavour for delectation some hundred or so years on' (Introduction). The main source for the information has been the *New Zealand Herald.* A thematic approach is adopted in this attractive overview, with separate sections considering commerce, banking and insurance, warehousing and manufacturing, the poor, and the rich.

136 **The lively capital: Auckland, 1840-1865.**
Una Platts. Christchurch: Avon Fine Prints, 1971. 271p. maps.

An attractive illustrated account of Auckland in the twenty-five years it was the capital of the colony. Originally conceived as a collection of paintings and drawings, the author located many complementary letters and journals, and resolved to let the settlers speak for themselves. 'They tell of their day-to-day doings, they gossip, they report social gaieties, or speak their minds seriously on the worrying affairs of the time' (Preface). Two major themes are emphasized: the youth of the settler population, and the relative closeness of Maori and European in those years.

Waikato, Thames, Coromandel

137 **The view from Pirongia: the history of Waipa county.**
L. H. Barber. Auckland: Richards Publishing/Waipa County Council, Te Awamutu, 1978. 195p. map.

Focusing on the heart of the Waikato's 'cow country', this short social history recounts the settlement of the district by Maori, then the subsequent losing battle with Europeans for possession of the land. The greater part of the book is concerned with the way bog and scrub was converted into pasture, laying the foundation for a thriving dairying industry. How changes in that industry later dictated further changes in the landscape and social structure is briefly surveyed.

138 **No easy riches: a history of Ohinemuri County, Paeroa and Waihi: 1885-1985.**
Laurie Barber.   Auckland: Ray Richards Publisher/Ohinemuri County Council, 1985. 216p. map.

The Ohinemuri, part of the Thames district, has been built on gold and grass. The initial stimulus, in the 1870s, was quartz mining, and for more than forty years ore was hammered from the hills. From the early 20th century, with a decline in the price of gold and other problems, grasslands farming attained greater importance. But the author shows that the farmers also encountered problems. Ordinary folk have had to work hard for their rewards. The mining industry, recently resuscitated, is more comprehensively covered in J. B. McAra's *Gold mining at Waihi* (Waihi, New Zealand: Martha Press, 1988. rev. ed. 352p.).

139 **Astride the river: a history of Hamilton.**
P. J. Gibbons.   Christchurch: Whitcoulls, for Hamilton City Council, 1977. 381p. maps.

A soundly researched history of the major city of the region. 'It began as a small imperial outpost in conquered territory during 1864 . . . The text has been divided into three parts . . . Hamilton as a village . . . as a growing town, and as an embryo city . . . In most chapters I discuss four themes . . . the dimensions of growth . . . the changes in leadership . . . the refashioning of physical environment . . . and the initiation and development of cultural institutions' (Preface).

Bay of Plenty

140 **Tauranga 1882-1982.**
Edited by A. C. Bellamy.   Tauranga, New Zealand: Tauranga City Council, 1982. 296p. maps.

A miscellany of short contributions compiled to celebrate the 100th anniversary of the incorporation of the coastal borough, now city, of Tauranga. 'There has been insufficient time to compile a definitive history. An attempt has been made to cover a wide range of topics although it is realised that some matters that should have been covered have been omitted' (Introduction). The work is intended to complement W. H. Gifford and H. B. Williams's *A centennial history of Tauranga* (Christchurch: Capper Press, reprinted 1976. 351p.).

141 **The founding years in Rotorua: a history of events to 1900.**
Don Stafford.   Auckland: Ray Richards/Rotorua District Council, 1986. 448p. maps.

Located at the centre of the North Island's thermal region, and with a substantial Maori population, from the 1880s Rotorua drew an increasing stream of tourists. In less than twenty years a steaming, scrub-covered wilderness was transformed into a bustling little township, which soon also became a hub for the timber industry and farming. This book, by a respected local historian, reliably records the development of town and district up to 1900. Rotorua's later years are covered in a sequel by the same author and publisher, *The new century in Rotorua* (1988. 428p.).

142 **A history of Tauranga County.**
Evelyn Stokes. Palmerston North, New Zealand: Dunmore Press,
1980. 489p. maps.

The settlement and development of the western Bay of Plenty coastal lands as viewed
by an historical geographer. 'In the process of colonisation, three distinct phases can
usually be identified: 1. Exploration and infiltration; 2. Invasion and dispossession; 3.
Consolidation of immigrant settlement' (Introduction). The author effectively applies
this model to Tauranga County, studying both Maori and European colonization
waves. Of particular interest are the sections on the confiscation of Maori lands in the
1860s, and subsequent special settlement schemes, including the Ulster plantation at
Katikati. Throughout the author exhibits sensitivity to the inevitable clash of cultures.

King Country

143 **King Country: New Zealand's last frontier.**
Dick Craig. Mount Maunganui, New Zealand: R. S. Craig, 1990.
219p. map.

A history of the King Country, 'the territory extending south from the Punui River
near Te Awamutu to encompass the Taupo and Waimarino regions' (Foreword). A
standard account which covers the era from prehistoric times through the missionary
period to the Maori Wars (1860s), this '. . . tells how the tribes of the King Country
were [subsequently] . . . left unmolested for nearly two decades, and how eventually
the territory was opened to the Pakeha' (Introduction). This work is slight, and lacks
footnoting and a bibliography, but there are few other works on this area.

144 **The after-breakfast cigar.**
Spencer Westmacott, edited by H. F. Westmacott. Palmerston North,
New Zealand: Dunmore Press, 1983. 167p. map.

Westmacott was an early European settler in the King Country, taking up land there in
1910. These edited memoirs are an accurate record of his first four years. They
describe the leasing of the land and its survey; then the hard jobs of cutting and burning off the bush and of establishing sheep. The trials of body and spirit are evident.
There are also glimpses of life in the nearest township, Te Kuiti. The memoirs also
suggest that, once the barriers had been broken, surprisingly close relations developed
between the European newcomers and local Maori.

Taranaki

145 An illustrated history of Taranaki.
Gail Lambert, Ron Lambert. Palmerston North, New Zealand: Dunmore Press, 1983. 167p. maps.

'This history of the province of Taranaki has been compiled in response to a long-felt need . . . for a general work that interrelates developments and events' (Introduction). While a detailed scholarly study has yet to be written, this work provides a useful interim overview. Taranaki today is a peaceful dairying province. with an expanding industrial base, and with oilfields and gasfields assuring its immediate future. It was not always so. For much of the first three decades of settlement the province was beset by tensions and occasional outbursts of interracial warfare. The authors chart the transformation in words and photographs.

146 Days of darkness: Taranaki, 1878-1884.
Hazel Riseborough. Wellington: Allen & Unwin/Historical Branch, Department of Internal Affairs, 1989. 267p. maps.

Faced with the reality of land confiscation following the wars of the 1860s and early 1870s, the Taranaki tribes offered passive resistance – most notably at Parihaka, under the leadership of prophet Te Whiti. The settler government chose to interpret the Maori protest as a further challenge to European supremacy, dealing with it severely. The author reconstructs the circumstances, also describing how the government sought to obviate further resistance through the settlement of a close European population in the disaffected areas. 'Present day Maori claims to land are based on real and lasting grievances' (Preface).

147 The industrious heart: a history of New Plymouth.
J. S. Tullett. New Plymouth, New Zealand: New Plymouth City Council, 1981. 350p. maps.

Not merely a chronological listing of events and roll of dignitaries – here relegated to appendices – this account of the development of New Plymouth, Taranaki's sole city, presents the standard fare of local history in much more readable form. The author adopts a thematic approach, chapters on town planning, the growth of business, the implications of rural change, and the oil industry, being juxtaposed with others on education, religious persuasions and cultural life. He seeks at all times to relate his narrative to the lives of New Plymouth citizens, offering occasional pen-portraits.

East Coast, Poverty Bay

148 Challenge and response.
W. H. Oliver, Jane M. Thomson. Gisborne, New Zealand: East Coast Development Research Association, 1971. 251p.

A synoptic view of the development of the East Coast districts, with a well-known academic historian as senior author. Unusually, the authors endeavour to relate the experience of one of New Zealand's later frontiers to contemporary events elsewhere in the country. The book is in three parts. The first, 'Maori and Pakeha', extends roughly to the end of the wars of the 1860s, the foci being European incursions and early race relations. In part two, 'An outlying district', attention turns to the European occupation of rural land, to around 1900. The emphasis is on sheepfarming. Part three, 'The nationalisation of regional life', tenders a brief survey of 20th-century trends.

Hawke's Bay

149 City of the plains: a history of Hastings.

M. B. Boyd. Wellington: Victoria University Press, for Hastings City Council, 1984. 464p. maps.

Laid out on the fertile Heretaunga Plains in 1873, the subsequent history of Hawke's Bay's inland city has been largely shaped by changing land use in its hinterland. In the beginning it serviced pastoralists producing wool for export. With refrigeration, meat- and butter-packing plants appeared. In the 20th century new technologies turned the district into 'the vegetable basket and fruit bowl of New Zealand'. In this well-researched, well-illustrated and engagingly written study, the author details these changes in Hastings's economic base, discussing the implications for urban form and the social structure which developed.

150 Story of Napier, 1874-1974: footprints along the shore.

Michael Campbell. Napier, New Zealand: Napier City Council, 1975. 252p.

A more narrowly conceived account of Hawke's Bay's port city, established in the 1850s. While broader regional trends are not overlooked, emphasis is placed on local government and the provision of public amenities within the boundaries. There is useful discussion of the longstanding rivalry with the adjacent city of Hastings, while several chapters are devoted to the disastrous earthquake of February 1931, and the reconstruction which followed. The post-Second World War expansion of the city is well covered.

151 Hawke's Bay: the history of a province.

Mathew Wright. Palmerston North, New Zealand: Dunmore Press, 1994. 215p. maps.

A fresh approach to the history of one of New Zealand's most affluent regions by a younger historian. Arguing that Hawke's Bay's middle-class elite of the 19th century – runholders and businessmen – shared much with their peers of Canterbury or Otago, and that the elite's influence was pivotal to the way Hawke's Bay developed, Wright also traces the fortunes of the privileged in the 20th century. For a more conventional view, see *History of Hawkes Bay* (Christchurch: Capper Press, 1976. Reprint of 1939 ed. 468p.) by J. G. Wilson, W. J. Prentice and others. The rise of the pastoral industry is elaborated in Miriam Macgregor's *Early stations of Hawkes Bay* (Wellington: Reed, 1970. 312p.).

Wairarapa

152 Wairarapa: an historical excursion.

A. G. Bagnall.   Masterton, New Zealand: Hedley's Bookshop, for the Masterton Trust Lands Trust, 1976. 607p. 10 maps. bibliog.

Monumental in scope and execution, and written by a doyen of New Zealand local historians (also a distinguished librarian and bibliographer), this book provides the only comprehensive account of the North Island's southeastern districts. Themes such as Maori occupation and sale of land to the Pakeha, the taking up of the country's first pastoral runs, and the extension of settlement into bushlands to the north, are lovingly covered in exhaustive detail. Particularly impressive are the reconstructions of land-ownership patterns from previously unconsulted manuscript records. This is a reference work as much as it is a history.

Wanganui, Rangitikei

153 The Wanganui story.

Maxwell J. G. Smart, Arthur P. Bates.   Wanganui, New Zealand: Wanganui Newspapers, 1972. 320p. maps.

The authors, local enthusiasts and residents, have assembled a workmanlike account of 'the river city' in the 19th and early 20th centuries. As late as 1900, Wanganui ranked seventh amongst New Zealand's urban centres, but in subsequent decades it slipped back. The coverage is broad, if a little idiosyncratic, encompassing Maori history, missionaries, the foundation of the settlement, wars, fires and floods, commercial development, early industries and transport. While documentation is scanty, this book may be accepted as a generally reliable history of the city and its immediate environs.

154 From sand to papa: a history of Wanganui County.

Rex H. Voelkerling, Kevin L. Stewart.   Wanganui, New Zealand: Wanganui City Council, 1986. 296p.

Nicely allusive, the title of this book refers to the spread of European settlement in the Wanganui country districts from coastal flatlands to the rugged back-country hills. Despite a wide-ranging brief, largely accommodated, the authors maintain their developmental focus, both through general survey chapters and the judicious use of case-studies. The experiences of individual settlers and families are drawn upon to illustrate trends. In contrast to earlier studies of the district, discussion moves well beyond the pioneering days, extending to the late 20th century.

155 **Early Rangitikei: a few notes, collected from various sources of the settlement on the Rangitikei river of a number of Maoris of different tribes: a short history of the purchase and colonization of the land between the Turakina and Oroua rivers and an account of the various pioneers.**

James G. Wilson. Christchurch: Capper Press, 1976.

Reprint of 1914 ed. 270p. 2 maps.

Although dubious on some points of detail, this discursive work nevertheless provides human insights into the settlement of the Rangitikei not available elsewhere. A resident from the 1870s, the author reports both what he personally witnessed and what he heard from older identities. Maori tradition is summarized, but the emphasis is on settler families. Most valuable are the sections on the accelerated European influx in the 1870s. A complementary work, which is more prosaic, if more reliable on later events, is S. G. Laurenson's *Rangitikei: the day of striding out* (Palmerston North, New Zealand: Dunmore Press, 1979. 225p.). It surveys the history of Rangitikei County up to the late 1970s.

Manawatu, Horowhenua

156 **Horowhenua County and its people: a centennial history.**

A. J. Dreaver. Palmerston North, New Zealand: Dunmore Press, on behalf of Horowhenua County Council, 1984. 316p. maps.

One hundred and fifty years ago the Horowhenua, the tapering wedge of coastal plain immediately to the northwest of Wellington, was largely covered by dense bush. That bush held back European settlement, thus protecting the Maori inhabitants, for several decades. This elegantly written and attractively presented book is about Maori leaders, bushmen and sawmillers, flaxcutters, the early settlers on their small bush-clad holdings, railwaymen and roadbuilders, and, given its sponsorship, the local government which presided. The 20th century, when the bush had long disappeared, is also well covered.

157 **The line of the road: a history of Manawatu County 1876-1976.**

M. H. Holcroft. Dunedin: John McIndoe, for the Manawatu County Council, 1977. 216p. map.

After a short chapter setting the scene, this work focuses on the opening-up of the Manawatu lowlands after 1876. It is a tale of land division and subdivision, of bush-felling and swamp drainage, and of the roads and bridges built as farming developed. Early families are introduced, and their working lives sketched. There is an intriguing account of the construction and operation of the Sanson Tramway, an enterprise unique in the history of New Zealand local government. 'The flavour is recovered of village life in an earlier time, and the book gains the momentum of a wider history as Manawatu shares the rigours of war and depression' (cover). The style is that of the literary craftsman, rather than the historian.

158   **Palmerston North: a centennial history.**
G. C. Petersen.   Wellington: Reed, 1973. 254p. maps.

Palmerston North is known to New Zealanders today as the urban centre of the prosperous Manawatu lowlands, and as a growing university city. The author traces the development of the city from its 1871 origins in a natural forest clearing. Looking back as well as forwards, he also examines earlier European settlement of the Manawatu. The greater part of the book, however, is concerned with the transition from mill town to rural servicing centre, then to wider urban functions. Although the organization of material might have been tighter, most aspects of the city's growth are canvassed. There is some comment on the fortunes of nearby townships and villages.

Wellington

159   **Petone: a history.**
Susan Butterworth.   Petone, Hutt City, New Zealand: Petone Borough Council/Ray Richards Publisher, 1988. 270p. maps.

The small borough of Petone (now absorbed into Hutt City) has a colourful history. The site of the New Zealand Company's first town-building attempt, it was soon abandoned, lying dormant until the 1870s. In the late decades of the 19th century it was transformed into an industrial town by the coming of the railway, a woollen mill and a major meat-packing plant. The establishment of motor assembly plants and other industries between the two world wars made it one of the most densely industrialized areas in New Zealand. The author describes Petone's evolution, at the same time probing the relationship with the greater Hutt Valley and the Wellington Region.

160   **The making of Wellington, 1800-1914.**
Edited by David Hamer, Roberta Nicholls.   Wellington: Victoria University Press, 1990. 319p. map.

Published to mark the 150th anniversary of the founding of Wellington, this collection of 11 original essays seeks to isolate the forces which moulded the city in its early decades. The topics are eclectic, ranging from specific historical sites to wider issues of social organization, political intrigue and the problematical idea of settlement itself. The editors acknowledge that there is not as yet a fully researched history of Wellington City. 'What this book offers is a sampling of current research into Wellington's history, a snapshot of some of the issues that are currently engaging the attention of its historians' (Introduction).

161   **Colonial capital: Wellington, 1865-1910.**
Terence Hodgson.   Auckland: Random Century, 1990. 182p. map.

Transfer of the seat of government from Auckland to Wellington in 1865 boosted a previously sluggish town. Shops, offices, factories and warehouses multiplied, augmenting the Parliament Buildings, Government House and many new administrative buildings. Mansion-like houses and imposing business premises – visible manifestations of the wealth and power of the elite – contrasted starkly, however, with the squalid living conditions of the poor. The new libraries, parks and pleasure gardens for the well-to-do were matched by prisons, asylums and charitable institutions for the less privileged. In a brisk text, the author draws attention to the disparities, illustrating his findings with more than 130 contemporary photographs.

South Island

Nelson, Golden Bay

162 **Nelson: a history of early settlement.**
Ruth M. Allan. Wellington: Reed, for Nelson City Council, 1965.
458p. maps.

Already a classic of New Zealand historiography, the manuscript of this book was left incomplete at the author's death. Hence discussion is confined to the founding 1840s. Uncompromisingly scholarly, but vigorously written, after due obeisance to Maori Nelson and the early navigators, the text traverses the Wakefield system of colonization, the emigrant voyages, urban and rural development, the life and struggles of the colonists, and the leading personalities involved. The book contains a judicious account of the 'Wairau Massacre' of 17 June 1854, when the settlement's leadership was wiped out by Maori, also a chapter on German settlers who came to the province. Two additional chapters are provided by colleagues of the author.

163 **Nelson: a regional history.**
Jim McAloon. Whatamango Bay, New Zealand: Cape Catley/Nelson City Council, 1997. 261p. maps.

A lively account of the history of Nelson, town and province, from the beginnings of European settlement. The author declares his bias early on: 'If there is a heavy emphasis on economics in this book, that is because economic problems – in the basic sense of getting a living – have dominated Nelson's history' (p. 1). At a rollicking pace, he takes the reader through the early attempts to set up an agricultural base, the diversion of gold in the provincial years, and the consolidation of the rural economy in the later 19th century. Atypically, he devotes as much space to the 20th century, to specialist crops (hops and tobacco), to forestry and to tourism. Coverage of other aspects of Nelson's development is moulded around these imperatives. McAloon succeeds in making the book both a good read and a signpost for further enquiry.

164 **Collingwood. A history of the area from earliest days to 1912.**
J. N. W. Newport. Christchurch: Caxton Press, 1971. 294p.

Gold brought Golden Bay to transient prominence in 1857, Collingwood becoming the port for the workings. While the initial rush was soon over, quartz mining, timber and flax milling, coal mining, and later farming, ensured the continued existence of the township. All of these activities are surveyed in this book. While in the 20th century the district descended to sleepy hollow status, more recently it has become a seasonal tourist centre, Collingwood being the gateway to both the celebrated Heaphy Track (a walking route across the top of the South Island) and Farewell Spit (a long extension of sand at the top of the South Island).

Marlborough

165   Gold in a tin dish.
M. R. (Mike) Johnston.   Nelson, New Zealand: Nikau Press, 1992-93.
2 vols. maps.

Historian by inclination and geologist by training, the author meticulously reconstructs the province's goldmining history, successfully marrying examination of the technological aspects of gold extraction with an assessment of social impacts. Volume one highlights the Wakamarina Field, located about midway between Nelson and Blenheim, where the 1864 rush was shortlived, independent alluvial miners soon being replaced by mining companies. Few fortunes were made. The Eastern Marlborough Goldfields are the focus of volume two – from the alluvial reef mining of the 1860s, to dredging around 1900, and the Depression diggings of the 1930s. The second volume concludes with a history of other mining ventures, in particular antimony and coal.

166   Marlborough: a provincial history.
Edited by A. D. McIntosh.   Christchurch: Capper Press, 1977.
Reprint of 1940 ed. 431p. maps.

Originally compiled as an official history for the 1940 Centennial, this book retains its value as a source of information on the 19th-century European settlement of Marlborough. There is also a short section on Maori history. Much space is devoted to the taking up of runs in the district from the late 1840s, it being an adjunct of the Nelson settlement. The establishment of the rival townships of Blenheim (originally called Beaver) and Picton is likewise considered. The ultimately successful struggle of the Marlborough settlers for separation from Nelson, and the creation of a new province in 1860, occupy several chapters. The later decades of the century are dealt with in three chapters.

167   Kaikoura: a history of the district.
J. M. Sherrard.   Christchurch: Capper Press, 1980. Reprint of 1966 ed.
373p. maps.

Comparatively isolated until the mid-20th century, the rugged Kaikoura district was, nevertheless, attractive to Maori, offering a haven for fugitive tribes driven from the north. After the advent of the European, however, while the coast became the preserve of shore whalers, and sheep spread onto the steep hills and the bare rock and shingle ridges of the mountains behind, the district was apportioned among a handful of large runholders. It took the introduction of refrigeration and wholesale Crown subdivision of land to bring greater diversity to the farming landscape, increase the population, and spur communications development. In the author's view, Kaikoura's past is 'a microcosmic history of New Zealand'. The biannual J. M. Sherrard Award in Regional History recognizes the author's contribution to the genre.

West Coast

168 **The golden reefs: an account of the great days of quartz-mining at Reefton, Waiuta and the Lyell.**
Darrell Latham.   Nelson, New Zealand: Nikau Press, 1992. 2nd ed.
461p. maps.

After the madcap years of the alluvial gold rushes of the 1860s, reef mining in the Buller district followed almost as a footnote. Nevertheless, mining companies invested heavily, hauling imported crusher batteries across rough country, building water races (artificial channels to carry water to a mine or claim), and honeycombing the hills with shafts and drives. The author's objective is to distinguish legend from reality: 'The Coast has suffered enough already from romantic distortions of its history' (p. 14). He seeks to establish the successes, which were few, and the disappointments, which were many. The focus is on the Reefton-Inangahua area up to 1880, but later developments are noted in outline.

169 **The West Coast gold rushes.**
Philip Ross May.   Christchurch: Pegasus, 1967. 2nd ed. 560p. maps.

One of the landmark works of New Zealand regional history. Gold changed the West Coast from a no-man's-land to a settled district in just three years. Before 1865 the region was almost uninhabited. By 1867 it was dotted with townships, criss-crossed with tracks and tramways, its population numbered 30,000, and its chief port was the busiest in the colony. This is the story of those three years, magisterially detailed. No other part of New Zealand has been subjected to such intense scrutiny over so short a period. *Miners and militants: politics in Westland* (Christchurch: Whitcoulls, for the University of Canterbury, 1975. 174p.), edited by the same author, picks up later themes in the history of the West Coast up to 1918. Among the topics covered are local politics, railway construction and the place of coal mining.

170 **Jackson's Bay: a centennial history.**
Irvine Roxburgh.   Wellington: Reed, 1976. 198p. maps.

Gold played little part in the history of lonely south Westland, the site of Jackson's Bay Special Settlement, established with enthusiasm in 1874. From the beginning the enterprise was ill-fated, and within ten years most of the introduced settlers had drifted away. Thereafter, until the 1960s, the district was largely abandoned to a few struggling farmers, occasional prospectors, timber millers, trappers and fishermen. The opening of the Haast highway, linking the district to Otago, provided new opportunities, particularly in tourism. This is a competently written and documented study.

Canterbury

171 The early Canterbury runs.
L. G. D. Acland, revised by W. H. Scotter, with annotations by G. R. Macdonald. Christchurch: Whitcoulls, 1975. 4th ed. 417p. maps. bibliog. Originally published, Christchurch: Whitcombe & Tombs, 1951. 427p.

A standard work on pioneer station life and sheepfarming in Canterbury. This edition has been thoroughly revised and, in some instances, the material has been reassembled. The book contains short histories of over 150 early properties, also details of the individuals who took them up. Designed for reference rather than general reading, the book is well indexed. More detailed coverage of the South Canterbury runs is provided by Robert Pinney's *Early South Canterbury runs* (Wellington: Reed, 1971. 330p.).

172 A new history of Canterbury.
Stevan Eldred-Grigg. Dunedin: McIndoe, 1982. 252p.

The author addresses 'the idea of Canterbury', noting the strong parochial attachment of the province's sons and daughters. In contrast to most such regional histories, this work concentrates on ordinary people: '. . . their experience of migration, childbirth, marriage, sickness and death, the houses they lived in, their work and workplaces, and the changing and often hostile social classes into which they were grouped'. Employing many of the modern social historian's techniques, the book is as much concerned with town as country, thus helping offset the absence of a modern history of Christchurch.

173 The Amuri: a county history.
W. J. Gardner. Culverden, New Zealand: Amuri County Council, 1983. 2nd ed. 492p. maps.

Presents the Canterbury pastoral experience in microcosm. Taking a North Canterbury county as his study area, the author retraces how, in the 19th century, it was occupied by a dozen great sheep runs, the realms of 'the Amuri wool kings'. The depiction of the industry, compiled from run records, is vivid. Around the turn of the century, run began to give way to farm as state settlement and private subdivision produced a pattern of smaller properties on plain and hills. New sections added to this revised edition carry the story up to the 1980s. The same author's *A pastoral kingdom divided* (Wellington: Bridget Williams Books, 1992. 247p.) examines this sequence with reference to one property. Both books are models of their type.

174 A history of Canterbury.
Edited by James Hight, C. R. Straubel, W. J. Gardner, W. H. Scotter. Christchurch: Whitcombe & Tombs, for Canterbury Centennial Historical and Literary Committee, 1957-72. 3 vols.

The most ambitious, and probably the most successful, of the mid-20th-century provincial histories, this monumental work was over thirty years in the making. It remains a first port of call for enquirers into Canterbury's past. Volume one covers early penetration and the establishment of a settlement by the Canterbury Association. Volume two is a general history of the years of provincial government (1854-76), with wider chapters on the cultural life of Canterbury appended. Volume three surveys the history of the province from 1876 to the centennial of settlement in 1950.

175 **French Akaroa: an attempt to colonise southern New Zealand.**
Peter Tremewan.   Christchurch: University of Canterbury Press, 1990.
383p. maps.

This book provides a variant on the standard themes of Canterbury history. While the British were concluding the Treaty of Waitangi in the North Island in early 1840, the French were sending an expedition to the South Island. The author examines the elaborate, government-backed French plans to settle 'Southern New Zealand', and the reactions of the settlers once they discovered they were under a foreign flag. Their lives in the remote settlement of Akaroa, and the accommodations they had to make, are central to the study. Extensive use is made of French sources.

Otago

176 **Aspiring settlers: European settlement in the Hawea and Wanaka region to 1914.**
John H. Angus.   Dunedin: John McIndoe, 1981. 93p. bibliog.

Distinctive physical features, dominated by alternate ranges and enclosed basins, some with lakes, together with a varied cultural pattern, make Central Otago unique in New Zealand. The area's tussock grasslands naturally proved attractive for grazing, but the discovery of gold, and the realization that parts of the district were suited to intensive agriculture, ensured long-running conflicts over the use of resources. This small, but professionally written, book surveys the conflicts in the Upper Clutha basin to 1914. The beginnings of a tourism industry are also noted. Similar themes are analysed in respect of the better-known Queenstown district, but with greater emphasis on gold, in F. W. G. Miller's *Golden days of Lake County* (Christchurch: Whitcombe & Tombs, 1973. 299p.).

177 **White stone country.**
K. C. McDonald.   Christchurch: Capper, 1977. 304p.

Cut off from the rest of its parent province by a mountain wall, North Otago has also fostered its own distinctive identity. Inland lie a chain of upland basins. Having been used as sheep pasture for most of the district's European history, more recently these basins have been the site of hydroelectric power developments. Nearer the coast are more densely settled rolling downs, which are given over to mixed farming. This volume provides a routine account of the settlement process. Farming in the district receives closer attention in W. H. Scotter's *Run, estate and farm* (Christchurch: Capper Press, 1978. reprint ed. 142p.).

178 **The history of Otago: the origins and growth of a Wakefield class settlement.**
A. H. McLintock.   Christchurch: Capper, 1975. Reprint of 1949 ed.
829p. maps.

Widely considered the most readable of the mid-20th-century provincial histories, this substantial book is primarily concerned with the 19th-century development of the settlement established under the aegis of the Free Church of Scotland in 1848. Beset by problems, the settlement's early progress was slow, but it was transformed by the discovery of gold in the interior in 1861. Almost overnight, the main town, Dunedin, became the colony's foremost commercial and industrial centre, while rural expansion was stimulated. Though the settlement became more cosmopolitan, and was later overtaken by more northerly settlements, the dour Presbyterian influence was never completely lost. Written by a former parliamentary historian, the work is immaculately documented.

179   **A history of Otago.**
   Erik Olssen.   Dunedin: McIndoe, 1984. 270p. maps.

This lively, modern, synoptic history takes as its organizing theme 'the complex issue of provincial identity'. The author seeks to show what is distinctive about Otago and its people through exploration of the province's past. All the common ingredients are produced: the Maori, whalers and sealers, the Scots settlers with their dreams of a godly community, and the profitably disrupting effects of sheep and gold. But the author also explains more recent trends of stagnation and decline, and is at pains to be inclusive in his treatment. 'Each generation writes its own history and I start from where . . . [A. H. McLintock] . . . ended'. The volume is well illustrated with photographs and colour reproductions.

180   **Building the New World: work, politics and society in Caversham, 1880s-1920s.**
   Erik Olssen.   Auckland: Auckland University Press, 1995. 297p.
   maps.

A ground-breaking study of Dunedin's industrial-residential suburb of Caversham around the turn of the century, bringing together the perspectives of historical sociology and the new cultural history. After sketching the origins of the suburb, the author analyses the labour process in various skilled trades, the gendering of skill and work, and the forces moulding the evolution of a socialist political movement. The findings are extrapolated from a mass database assembled by scholars at the University of Otago. Caversham is placed in its wider urban setting in K. C. McDonald's *City of Dunedin: a century of civic enterprise* (Dunedin: Dunedin City Corporation, 1965. 434p.).

Southland

181   **Port Preservation.**
   A. C. Begg, N. C. Begg.   Christchurch: Whitcombe & Tombs, 1973.
   398p. maps.

At the southwestern tip of New Zealand, in Fiordland, Preservation Inlet was the scene of sporadic extractive activity – sealing, whaling, timber and flax cutting – prior to the permanent European settlement of the southern districts. With the exception of subsequent attempts to wrest mineral wealth, particularly gold, from the environs, the inlet was largely ignored in later years. Bush now clothes the scars. The authors have compiled a well-illustrated geographical and historical account, based on personal observation and investigation of (mainly published) historical sources.

182 **The south explored: an illustrated history of New Zealand's deep south.**
John Hall-Jones.   Wellington: Reed, 1979. 165p. maps.
The wild, often inhospitable, lands of 'the far South' were among the first to be probed by Europeans. 'This is the story of the discovery of Foveaux Strait; of Bluff, the oldest town in New Zealand; the early whaling stations of the south . . . It is also the story of the first Europeans to penetrate to the great lakes of the interior' (Prologue). The author draws extensively from the accounts of contemporary travellers and the volume is profusely illustrated with paintings, maps and photographs. An earlier work, *Fiordland explored: an illustrated history* (Wellington: Reed, 1976. rev. ed. 148p.) examines the western coast.

183 **Old Invercargill.**
M. H. Holcroft.   Dunedin: John McIndoe, 1976. 128p. map.
A largely impressionistic survey of the growth of New Zealand's southernmost city up to 1914. Surveyed in 1857, Invercargill was the capital of the short-lived province of Southland. It later became the servicing and processing centre for an extensive hinterland. The author argues that the rigorous environment has fostered a sturdy spirit of independence. The progress of the immediately adjacent rural lands and townships is sketched in F. W. G. Miller's *King of counties* (Invercargill, New Zealand: Southland County Council, 1977. 187p.).

184 **Catlins pioneering.**
A. R. Tyrrell.   Dunedin: Otago Heritage Books, 1989. 164p. maps.
Known today as an isolated rural district of scenic beauty, Catlins, situated on the far southeastern coast of the South Island, was a busy place in the late 19th century. Its lands and forests drew settlers who were excluded from elsewhere and, against the odds, small villages sprang up, each with its mill, dairy factory, school and post office. Despite the fact that improved communications have caused many of the villages to shrivel, the district continues to contribute significantly to the regional economy. The text, compiled by a local enthusiast, is uneven, but the illustrations are fresh.

Offshore islands

185 **Beyond the roaring forties: New Zealand's subantarctic islands.**
Conon Fraser.   Wellington: Government Printing Office Publishing, 1986. 213p. maps.
Mere dots in the Southern Ocean, New Zealand's subantarctic islands – the Antipodes, Bounty, Snares, Campbell and Auckland Islands – are among the remotest and wildest on earth. Despite their isolation, however, they have been plundered since their discovery. The author recounts the depredations of the whaling and sealing days, also noting several ill-fated attempts to plant permanent settlements on the islands. Today all five island groups are managed as nature reserves, and are acknowledged as being of worldwide ecological importance. Readable and superbly illustrated, this is the first

book to encompass all the subantarctic islands. A more detailed study is Ian S. Kerr's *Campbell Island: a history* (Wellington: Reed, 1976. 182p.).

186   **Rakiura: a history of Stewart Island, New Zealand.**
      Basil Howard.   Dunedin; Wellington: Reed, 1974. Reprint of 1940 ed.
      415p. maps.

Based on manuscript and published sources, this remains the authoritative history of Stewart Island. It covers events from European discovery until the 1930s. 'The story of the Island must be regarded not as local history, but as a . . . narrative of a territory which was not admitted to political equality with its neighbours . . . The economic development was likewise characteristically different from that of the remainder of New Zealand' (Preface). The story is amplified by photographs and sketches in John Hall-Jones's *Stewart Island explored* (Invercargill, New Zealand: Craigs, 1994. 216p.). Subjects include early settlements, sheep stations and sawmills, while there are previously unpublished pictures of New Zealand's only tin mine and Norwegian whaling stations.

187   **Moriori: a people rediscovered.**
      Michael King.   Auckland: Viking, 1989. 226p. maps.

Long regarded as one of the mystery peoples of the Pacific, and depicted as primitive forerunners of the Maori, the Moriori of the Chatham Islands were considered extinct. In this book, the author strips aside the myths, rehabilitates the Moriori, and reveals that descendants are very much alive. An impressive exercise in historical, archaeological and literary detective work, it presents the history of the Chathams from the viewpoint of the pre-European inhabitants. A European perspective is provided by Sheila Natusch's *Hell and high water: a German occupation of the Chatham Islands, 1843-1910* (Christchurch: Pegasus, 1977. 173p.).

188   **Waiheke Island: a history.**
      Paul Monin.   Palmerston North, New Zealand: Dunmore Press, 1992.
      229p. maps.

Just twenty kilometres from Auckland, Waiheke is the only substantially populated island close to a New Zealand metropolitan centre. Numerous ancient Maori sites confirm that it was attractive to Maori also. The author, a resident, engagingly sketches the island's history, paying particular attention to the impact of the European settlement on the indigenous inhabitants and the natural environment. He suggests parallels between the removal of land from Maori ownership and the damage inflicted by miners and timber fellers.

189   **Island volcano: White Island, or Whakaari, New Zealand.**
      W. T. Parham.   Auckland; London: Collins, 1973. 211p. maps.

Off the Bay of Plenty coast, White Island, New Zealand's only live marine volcano, is both unpredictable and fascinating. Fishermen, mutton-bird hunters, sulphur miners, scientists and conservationists have all been drawn to the sometimes hostile environment – but few have stayed long. The author, as well as outlining the island's volatile history, also considers its geological formation and its fauna and flora. Some of the illustrations are striking.

Antarctica

190 **Scott Base, Antarctica: a history of New Zealand's southern-most station, 1957-1997.**
David L. Harrowfield. Christchurch: New Zealand Antarctic Society, 1997. 48p.
Written to commemorate the fortieth anniversary of Scott Base, New Zealand's permanent station in Antarctica, this short work conjures up the atmosphere, difficulties and rewards of working in such a remote area. The author succinctly describes why the base was established, lists the achievements over the years, examines the reasons for changes in the programmes over time and discusses developments that are likely to occur in the future. The volume is well illustrated with black-and-white photographs.

191 **New Zealand and the Antarctic.**
L. B. Quartermain. Wellington: Government Printer, 1971. 269p. maps. bibliog.
'The sole aim of this book is to provide the general reader with a balanced and accurate . . . account of the part played by New Zealand in the discovery of Antarctica and the unveiling of its secrets' (Preface). Already a standard reference work, this volume deals briefly with the early expeditions which made a New Zealand harbour a last port of call, but the emphasis is on direct New Zealand involvement in the 1950s and 1960s. There is extensive discussion of the establishment of Scott Base, the Trans-Antarctic Expedition of 1956-57, and subsequent scientific programmes.

Antarctica: the Ross Sea region.
See item no. 51.

Tarawera: the volcanic eruption of 10 June 1886.
See item no. 52.

In crude state, a history of the Moturoa oilfield, New Plymouth.
See item no. 589.

Wellington Harbour.
See item no. 601.

Maori History

General

192 Maori: a photographic and social history.
Michael King.   Auckland: Heinemann, 1997. rev. ed. 287p.

Newly revised, this book combines the findings of the most recent scholarship with a range of images illustrating every aspect of Maori life since the advent of photography. The photographs, employed as evidence, not decoration, clearly indicate the changes that have occurred in Maori life in response to the European presence.

193 Te haurapa: an introduction to researching tribal histories and traditions.
Te Ahukaramu Charles Royal.   Wellington: Bridget Williams
Books/Historical Branch, Department of Internal Affairs, 1992. 111p.
bibliog.

'There is no such thing as Maori history, only tribal history' (p. 9). Having defined his terms, Royal sets out a practical guide for researchers. He outlines techniques for recovering oral history and tradition, for the consultation of relevant documentary records and for the appropriate presentation of results.

194 Struggles without end = Ka whawhai tonu matou.
R. J. Walker.   Auckland: Penguin, 1990. 334p. maps.

A new history of Aotearoa (the Maori name for New Zealand meaning 'Land of the long white cloud'), from the origins of human settlement to the present day, recounted from a Maori perspective. For the author, a Maori academic who has won distinction as a teacher and writer in both his own and the European worlds, the past 150 years have witnessed a continuing struggle by Maori for social justice, equality and self-determination. The second half of the book, surveying the mid- and late-20th-century Maori revival, provides useful keys to an understanding of current Maori preoccupations and aspirations.

Traditional life

195 **Traditional lifeways of the southern Maori: the Otago Museum Ethnological Project, 1920.**
James Herries Beattie, edited by Atholl Anderson.   Dunedin: University of Otago Press/Otago Museum, 1994. 636p. maps.
Comprises the collected research papers of an amateur ethnologist who in the 1920s travelled extensively in the South Island collecting information about traditional customs, material culture and settlement patterns. The book is divided into two parts, Murihiku (Otago-Southland) and Canterbury, with shorter sections on Nelson and Westland. A current tribal leader notes in his Foreword: '. . . this volume is full of fascinating details, many of which will challenge, in some respect, what are now received truths' (p. 7).

196 **The pa Maori: an account of the fortified villages of the Maori in pre-European and modern times: illustrating methods of defence by means of ramparts, fosses, scarps and stockades.**
Elsdon Best.   Wellington: GP Books, 1996. Reprint of 1927 ed. 459p. bibliog. (Dominion Museum Bulletin no. 6).
An account of traditional Maori fortifications based on first-hand observation, the knowledge of informants, and wide reading, by perhaps New Zealand's foremost recorder of Maori ways. While subsequent archaeological work has modified many of Best's findings, his bulletins contain a wealth of information not readily available elsewhere. Other reprinted titles (all from GP Books, Wellington) of continuing importance include: *Maori agriculture* (first edition, 1925. 315p.); *Forest lore of the Maori* (first edition, 1942. 421p.); *Fishing methods and devices of the Maori* (first edition, 1929. 264p.); and *The Maori canoe* (first edition, 1925. 452p.).

197 **Maori marriage: an essay in reconstruction.**
Bruce Biggs.   Wellington: Reed, for the Polynesian Society, 1970. Reprint of 1960 ed. 108p. bibliog. (Polynesian Society Maori Monographs, no. 1).
An exercise in cultural reconstruction using traditional sources, '. . . the aim of the study is to present a coherent, systematic account of marriage in indigenous Maori culture. For the most part the text will be confined to the results of the research, that is, to decisions finally reached after weighing the evidence' (p. 10). Topics raised include the personal and social factors determining marriage, types of marriage, the social and economic aspects of marriage, and Maori attitudes to sex.

198 **The coming of the Maori.**
Peter Buck (Te Rangi Hiroa).   Wellington: Maori Purposes Fund Board/Whitcombe & Tombs, 1974. Reprint of 2nd ed., 1950. bibliog.
Buck was the leading Maori and Polynesian ethnologist of his age, and in this book, which was originally published in 1949, he seeks to present an overview of pre-European Maori people. The topics covered include origins, language, material culture, social organization and religion. He combines his own extensive research

results with the findings of others. Although some of the information has been aug-mented, in some instances modified, the book has worn well. It remains a standard reference work.

199   **Economics of the New Zealand Maori.**
       Raymond Firth.   Wellington: Government Printer, 1972. Reprint of
       2nd ed., 1959. 519p. map. bibliog. Originally published as *Primitive
       economics of the New Zealand Maori*, London: Routledge, 1929. 505p.
Although first published seventy years ago, Firth's story is unrivalled as an exposition of pre-European Maori economic organization. While the accumulation and disposal of wealth is considered, greater attention is given to the means by which '. . . food, cloth-ing, shelter, tools, and objects of wealth . . . are secured to the service of man' (p. 16). In this revised edition there is an examination of the changes resulting from the contact of Maori with Europeans.

200   **Maori women.**
       Berys Heuer.   Wellington: Reed, for the Polynesian Society, 1972.
       66p. bibliog. (Polynesian Society Maori Monographs no. 3).
Collating references to Maori women from English and Maori texts, the author seeks to define their role in traditional family and tribal life. Discussion covers such aspects as cultural attitudes towards women, marriage contracts and the division of labour, women's role in procreation and socialization, property rights, the special roles and duties of women, and ritual functions.

201   **The natural world of the Maori.**
       Margaret Orbell.   Auckland: David Bateman, 1996. rev. ed. 128p.
       maps.
Drawing upon the work of archaeologists and historians, quoting extensively from the myths and songs recorded by Maori, an anthropologist seeks to recreate the pre-European landscape and to evoke the Maori experience of Aotearoa (New Zealand). 'Their closeness to nature and the immediacy of their dependence upon it, their inti-mate and profound knowledge of plants, animals and landscape, led to a view of the world which recognised . . . the sacredness of other life forms and the landscape itself' (p. 216).

202   **Maori warfare.**
       A. P. Vayda.   Wellington: Reed, for the Polynesian Society, 1970.
       Reprint of 1960 ed. 141p. maps. bibliog. (Polynesian Society Maori
       Monographs, no. 2).
A clear and carefully documented attempt '. . . to organise the data on Maori warfare and to see them in relation to the New Zealand environment in which the Maori peo-ple worked and fought' (p. 1). The author, an American anthropologist, also discusses related matters: cannibalism, slavery, the exploitation of conquered land, and, not least, peace-making.

Tribal histories

203 Horowhenua, its Maori placenames and their topographic and historical background.
G. L. Adkin.   Christchurch: Capper, 1986. facsimile ed. 446p. maps.

Presented as an area study, there is much information in this work on the Muaupoko, Ngati Raukawa and Ngati Toa tribes. An introductory sketch of the general history of the district precedes a detailed discussion and explanation of Maori place-names. The book is based on many years of archaeological work by the author, the testimony of local informants and study of Maori Land Court Minute Books.

204 Tuhoe, the children of the mist: a sketch of the origin, history, myths and beliefs of the Tuhoe tribe of New Zealand: with some account of other early tribes of the Bay of Plenty district.
Elsdon Best.   Auckland: Reed, 1996. 4th ed. 2 vols. Originally published, Wellington: Board of Ethnological Research, for the author, 1925. 2 vols.

Probably the most comprehensive study of the traditional history of a tribe to date, the book is the result of many years residence in the Urewera by the author. Isolated from the remainder of New Zealand, the people still retained a large number of their indigenous customs. Volume one (1,211p.) deals with Tuhoe history myths and religion. Volume two (94p.) contains maps and genealogical tables. While recent research suggests that Best's interpretations were flawed by the framework he adopted, the information he collected remains valuable.

205 The Kapiti Coast: Maori history and its place names.
W. Carkeek.   Christchurch: Capper Press, 1978. Reprint of 1966 ed. 187p. maps. bibliog.

Unusually, this book focuses on the post-1819 arrival of the Ngati Toa, Ati Awa and Ngati Raukawa tribes on the Kapiti Coast and their subjugation of the tribes then in possession of the area. Equally unusually, there are chapters on early European contact and the pressures resulting from European colonization. Notes on the place-names of the district are usefully appended.

206 Tuwharetoa: the history of the Maori people of the Taupo district.
John Te H. Grace.   Wellington: Reed, 1992. facsimile of 1959 ed. 567p. map. bibliog.

This book, written by a tribal leader, is in three parts: the first recounts the early traditional history to the end of the 17th century; the second runs to the mid-19th century; and the third carries the story to the present day. While parts one and two are fashioned from verbal accounts and Maori Land court documents, part three is supplemented from documents in the possession of the author's family. He concedes that 'there may be versions of sub-tribal history recorded here that differ from those possessed by some families' (p. 17).

207 **Nga iwi o Tainui: the traditional history of the Tainui people: nga koorero tuku iho a nga tuupuna.**
Compiled by Pei Te Hurinui Jones, edited and annotated by Bruce Biggs. Auckland: Auckland University Press, 1995. 402p. maps.

A collection of the histories, genealogies, songs and chants of the Tainui people, who arrived at and settled the area around Kawhia Harbour about 1300 AD. The original text, embodying the researches of Dr Jones over many years, was written in Maori. A parallel text in English was prepared by Professor Biggs, who brought the book to publication. The two texts are presented on facing pages.

208 **Whakatohea of Opotiki.**
A. C. Lyall. Wellington: Reed, 1979. 220p. map. bibliog.

Written by a European with tribal connections, this is a brief history of the tribe and its residence in the eastern Bay of Plenty. 'There is much of Whakatohea history to be added to that which follows here. Further research will disclose it, elaborate on some chapters here written and improve the accuracy of others' (p. xii).

209 **Rangitane: a tribal history.**
J. M. McEwen. Auckland: Heinemann Reed, 1990. 292p.

Drawing on all available written and oral sources, this work traces the history and traditions of the Rangitane tribe, now based in the Manawatu but with links extending through central New Zealand. Of particular interest is the tribe's interaction over the centuries with its neighbours, the author demonstrating the fluctuating fortunes of tribal groupings who, only by absorption, invasion, conquest or alliance, have established the identities they bear today. Having been in preparation for half a century, the book is a labour of love.

210 **Takitimu.**
Tiaki Hikawera Mitira, also named J. H. Mitchell. Gisborne, New Zealand: Te Rau Press; Papakura, New Zealand: Southern Reprints, 1990. Reprint of 1944 ed. 271p.

A history of the Kahungunu people of the North Island's east coast districts from the migration period to the 20th century. The book is in four main parts: the discovery of the land by the Maori, with record of landfalls; the settlement of the districts by Kahungunu; the history of certain leaders of the Wairoa people in more recent times (James Carroll, Tamihana Huata); and appendices relating to important charms, proverbial sayings and signs in common use by the people.

211 **The puriri trees are laughing: a political history of the Nga Puhi in the inland Bay of Islands.**
Jeffrey Sissons, Wiremu Wi Hongi, Pat Hohepa. Auckland: Polynesian Society, 1987. 165p. maps.

A political history of two Nga Puhi descent groups attempting '. . . to bring together traditional history and early European accounts in a way that respects the integrity of Nga Puhi traditions while opening up possibilities for these and the European accounts to inform each other' (p. 5). Part one draws largely upon European accounts relating to the period 1815-19, providing a platform for the reader to view the deeds of the ancestors, related in parts two and three. Traditional narratives in Maori are accompanied by translations in English.

212   **Te Arawa: a history of the Arawa people.**
Don Stafford.   Auckland: Reed, 1991. 2nd ed. 573p. maps.

The result of more than twenty years of intensive study, this history of the tribes who today occupy the Rotorua lakes district and part of the central Bay of Plenty coastline combines traditional evidence and that from post-settlement records. While the traditions are sympathetically ordered and presented, the greater part of the book focuses on the 19th century. The inter-tribal wars of the early decades are considered, and the first incursions reconstructed. The conflicts of the 1860s are then discussed at length. Some later developments are briefly dealt with in appendices.

Post-European

213   **Nga morehu = The survivors.**
Judith Binney, Gillian Chaplin.   Auckland: Auckland University Press/Bridget Williams Books, 1996. 2nd ed. 218p.

A very moving collection of the life histories of eight Maori women, all of whom have been associated with the Ringatu faith, led by Te Kooti Arikirangi Te Turuki, all of whom are from the eastern part of the North Island of New Zealand. The introduction sets the scene for the background that produced these women; the subsequent chapters present the women themselves, the forces that made them 'survive', the experiences they have weathered, their expectations and the changes they have endured in their personal worlds and in the world around them. This is a refreshing and humbling work.

214   **Redemption songs: a life of Te Kooti Arikirangi Te Turuki.**
Judith Binney.   Auckland: Auckland University Press/Bridget Williams Books, 1995. 666p. maps. bibliog.

Though couched as a biography of Te Kooti Arikirangi Te Turuki, remembered principally as a guerilla fighter, but a leader in peace as well as war, and founder of the Ringatu church, this book provides fresh perspectives on many aspects of 19th-century Maori history. The causes of Te Kooti's struggles are analysed against the backdrop of land confiscations and illegal land purchases, while his role in renewing Maori pride after the wars of the 1860s is assessed. Produced with the blessing of Ringatu elders, this big book draws on many sources previously unavailable to researchers.

215 **'Hauhau': the Pai Marire search for Maori identity.**
Paul Clark. Auckland: Auckland University Press; London,
Wellington: Oxford University Press, 1975. 186p. map. bibliog.

A detailed study of the origins and theology of the 'Hauhau' movement of the 1860s,
based on contemporary documentation, including Maori records. While the movement
has been depicted previously as a bloodthirsty and fanatical cult, this book is an
attempt to interpret it in a more positive light. The author presents it as a search for
ways of coming to terms with European settlement and domination, and of using
European skills and literacy, without compromising Maori identity.

216 **Te mamae me te aroha = The pain and the love: a history of the
Kai Tahu Whanui in Otago, 1844-1994.**
Bill Dacker. Dunedin: University of Otago Press/Dunedin City
Council, 1994. 154p.

This book tells the story of Kai Tahu Whanui in Otago since the commencement of
European settlement in 1844. While it is an account of dispossession and marginaliza-
tion, it also demonstrates '. . . the faith and determination that countered disease and
despair, and indicates what might have been if the people had retained sufficient land
for an economic resource in the new world' (p. 1). In the light of changing official
attitudes, the author perceives new windows of opportunity for Kai Tahu Whanui.

217 **Te wai pounamu, the greenstone island: a history of the southern
Maori during the European colonisation of New Zealand.**
Harry C. Evison. Christchurch: Aoraki Press/Ngai Tahu Trust Board,
1993. 582p. maps.

Arising from the author's lifetime of research on behalf of Ngai Tahu Treaty
claimants, this large book tells the story of the 19th-century penetration, annexation
and colonization of southern New Zealand by Europeans, and the implications for the
local Maori inhabitants. Evison also attempts to place his story in the broader contexts
of New Zealand history and imperial politics. An epilogue traces the history of Ngai
Tahu claims for reparation to the present day. While the contents might have been
more tightly organized, the narrative is disturbing.

218 **A new Maori migration: rural and urban relations in northern
New Zealand.**
Joan Metge. London: University of London, The Athlone Press;
Melbourne: Melbourne University Press, 1964. 300p. maps.

Until 1939 the Maori remained almost wholly based in rural communities, but during
and after the Second World War increasing numbers migrated to the towns and cities
in search of work. Distinctively urban Maori groups developed. This migration
significantly affected relationships, both between Maori and Europeans, and within the
Maori people as a whole. In this pioneering study, the author, an anthropologist, presents comparisons of two Maori communities, one in a traditional rural area and the
other in Auckland, New Zealand's largest industrial centre.

219 **Kinds of peace: Maori people after the wars, 1870-85.**
Keith Sinclair. Auckland: Auckland University Press, 1991. 161p.
maps.

Having earlier studied the origins of the Anglo-Maori Wars of the 1860s, the author, probably the best-known writer on New Zealand history, devotes his last major work to the aftermath of those wars for the Maori people. He uncovers the political and cultural reactions of Maori to the impact of European settlement and armed conflict: religion and prophecy; the King movement (Maori resistance movement to create a counterpart sovereign); Maori entry into the parliamentary system; Maori communities; and the Hawke's Bay Repudiation movement (Maori resistance movement to stop the sale of land). Often, in the process, little-known personalities are highlighted. Sinclair presents a vivid picture of a dramatic and painful period of Maori history.

220 **A show of justice: racial 'amalgamation' in nineteenth century New Zealand.**
Alan Ward. Auckland: Auckland University Press, 1995. updated ed.
382p. maps.

The author sets out 'to examine the nineteenth century antecedents of Maori-Pakeha relations, both in their ideology and with regard to the practical, legal and administrative provisions relating to the Maori' (Preface). He shows how, in practice, the settlers both refused to recognize Maori political and judicial institutions and, lest it enabled them to keep their lands closed to settlement, limited their participation in the new state. He also demonstrates how, under settler pressure, the special machinery set up to involve Maori was hastily dismantled. Considered an angry book when first published (1973), this work established a benchmark for later studies.

221 **Politics of the New Zealand Maori: protest and co-operation, 1891-1909.**
John A. Williams. Auckland: Auckland University Press; London, Wellington: Oxford University Press, 1977. Reprint of 1969 ed. 204p.

By 1890 Maori had accepted the permanence of military defeat, and thereafter they became more articulate, united and effective in their use of acquired political techniques. Disadvantaged by their small representation in the national parliament, they formed their own, which, although without legal power, was able to exert moral and political pressure. The author shows how a conquered people acquired a voice in determining the disposition of their land, and in deciding how, and to what extent, they would be assimilated into the society which enveloped them.

Prodigious birds: moas and moa-hunting in prehistoric New Zealand.
See item no. 85.

The tattooed land: the southern frontiers of the pa Maori.
See item no. 86.

The great New Zealand myth: a study of the discovery and origin traditions of the Maori.
See item no. 91.

Days of darkness: Taranaki, 1878-1884.
See item no. 146.

Te Rangi Hiroa: the life of Sir Peter Buck.
See item no. 227.

Te Puea: a biography.
See item no. 244.

Whina: a biography of Whina Cooper.
See item no. 245.

Eruera: the teachings of a Maori elder.
See item no. 258.

Te iwi Maori: a New Zealand population, past, present and projected.
See item no. 267.

Ratana: the man, the church, the political movement.
See item no. 402.

Rua and the Maori millennium.
See item no. 403.

Journal of the Polynesian Society.
See item no. 882.

He pukaki Maori – Te Wharė Tohu Tuhituhinga o Aotearoa: a guide to Maori sources at National Archives.
See item no. 960.

A bibliography of publications on the New Zealand Maori and the Moriori of the Chatham Islands.
See item no. 967.

Biographies, Autobiographies and Memoirs

222 The life of Katherine Mansfield.

Antony Alpers. Oxford: Oxford University Press, 1982. 467p. bibliog.

The standard biography of New Zealand's pre-eminent international literary icon. In a short, but productive, life – she died from tuberculosis in 1923, aged thirty-four – Mansfield revolutionized the English short story. Combining material from previously closed manuscript collections with personal information from friends and contemporaries, the author has grafted perceptive character analysis onto impeccable literary scholarship. See also *The collected letters of Katherine Mansfield*, edited by Vincent O'Sullivan and Margaret Scott (Oxford: Clarendon Press, 1984-96. 4 vols.).

223 Coates of Kaipara.

Michael Bassett. Auckland: Auckland University Press, 1995. 325p. map. bibliog.

A timely reassessment of the career of one of New Zealand's more enigmatic 20th-century politicians, who was publicly idolized in the 1920s, but reviled in the 1930s. An appealing war hero, Coates was a successful Reform minister in the early 1920s, becoming Prime Minister in 1925. As Finance Minister in the Coalition Ministry of the 1930s, while making decisions of critical future importance, he was a lightning rod for the unpopularity of the administration. He died in 1943, alienated from his party, but a valued member of the War Cabinet. The author seeks to explain some of the conundrums of Coates's career, and to explore the private man.

224 Sir Joseph Ward: a political biography.

Michael Bassett. Auckland: Auckland University Press, 1993. 330p. bibliog.

Ward was a leading figure in New Zealand's Liberal Party. His career in public life lasted more than half a century, he was New Zealand's longest-serving Cabinet minister (over twenty-three years), and he was the only prime minister since 1900 to win office on two separate occasions. He was still a minister at his death in 1930. His long political career was not, however, without its controversies – he survived both an early bankruptcy and the loss of his seat through sectarian prejudice (he was of Irish Catholic descent) in 1919. While Ward probably stayed in politics too long, he contributed substantively to 20th-century development.

225 Edward Stafford: New Zealand's first statesman.

Edmund Bohan. Christchurch: Hazard Press, 1994. 432p. bibliog.

The author argues that New Zealand's youngest-ever Prime Minister, who led the colony for ten of the first twenty years of responsible government (1856-61, 1865-69 and 1872), brought to the chaotic and factional world of colonial politics a 'vision of an independent democratic and racially tolerant nation'. His joustings with less liberal contemporaries are reconstructed against a backdrop of racial wars and bitter interprovincial rivalries.

226 Gadfly: the life and times of James Shelley.

Ian Carter. Auckland: Auckland University Press/Broadcasting History Trust, 1993. 339p. bibliog.

Shelley, an Englishman, took up appointment as Professor of Education at Canterbury University College in 1920. For more than a decade he was an ebullient and sometimes controversial Christchurch personality, sponsoring innovative adult education schemes and generally promoting the arts. In 1936, he became Director of Broadcasting under the first Labour Government, endeavouring to force public broadcasting into the BBC mould. A major legacy was the creation of the New Zealand Symphony Orchestra. In addition, by the time he retired in 1949, the broadcasting service had become the country's largest arts patron. The book offers insights into New Zealand's cultural life between the wars, including comment on other influential personalities.

227 Te Rangi Hiroa: the life of Sir Peter Buck.

J. B. Condliffe. Christchurch: Whitcombe & Tombs, 1971. 314p. bibliog. maps.

'This book attempts to tell the story of an Irish Maori. Born in a small village in a troubled area of New Zealand soon after the Maori wars, he became Director of the Bishop Museum at Honolulu and Professor of Anthropology at Yale University' (p. 19). Buck's overseas academic distinction, however, came after an already distinguished New Zealand career. An early Maori medical graduate, briefly a parliamentarian (and more briefly a minister), with Sir Apirana Ngata he helped to stimulate the post-1900 Maori revival. Further light on the man is shed in *Na to hoa aroha = From your dear friend: the correspondence between Sir Apirana Ngata and Sir Peter Buck, 1925-50*, edited by M. P. K. Sorrenson (Auckland: Auckland University Press/Alexander Turnbull Endowment Trust and the Maori Purposes Fund Board, 1986-88. 3 vols.).

228 The life and times of a good keen man.

Barry Crump. Auckland: Hodder Moa Beckett, 1996. 191p.

By far New Zealand's best-selling male author, for more than thirty years Crump combined the spinning of episodic outdoors 'yarns' with the cultivation of an image as the archetypal, larger than life, 'Kiwi bloke'. Variously a deer culler, possum trapper, bushman, crocodile hunter, gold miner, television presenter and actor, as well as writer, Crump recounts his adventures and characters along the way.

229 **Julius Vogel: business politician.**
Raewyn Dalziel.   Auckland: Auckland University Press/Oxford
University Press, 1986. 386p. bibliog.

Although he spent only eighteen years in New Zealand, during his ten years as
Colonial Treasurer (and three years also as Premier) Vogel initiated the 1870s' programme of extensive public works and settlement that set the colony on the path
towards national unity and economic growth. From 1876 to 1880 he was Agent-
General representing New Zealand in London. This meticulously researched
biography also unveils the private Vogel – his Jewish background, his career as a journalist, and his entrepreneurial adventures in Australia and New Zealand.

230 **Bread and roses: her story/ Sonja Davies.**
Sonja Davies.   Auckland: David Bateman, 1993. 2nd ed. 309p.

The frank autobiography of a battler who, despite illness and personal disasters,
achieved impressively in several fields. As a housewife, she was prominent in local
politics. She founded the New Zealand Association of Child Care Centres. She was
the first woman to be elected to the Executive of the Federation of Labour and, in
1983, the first woman to become FOL vice-president. She later served two terms as an
MP. A champion of women's rights, she mixed with leading feminists and political
figures, both in New Zealand and overseas.

231 **Kate Sheppard: a biography: the fight for women's votes in New
Zealand.**
Judith Devaliant.   Auckland: Penguin, 1992. 242p. bibliog.

At the heart of this book lies the dramatic seven-year battle for the vote for women in
New Zealand, which was ultimately successful in 1893. Sheppard, a founder of the
New Zealand Women's Christian Temperance Union, led the campaign, later also
helping to establish the National Council of Women. She was also influential, through
her writings and as a touring speaker, in promoting women's rights overseas. In later
life she promoted a broad programme of humanitarian and social reforms. The author
seeks to determine the formative influences which shaped the career of this remarkable woman.

232 **An eye for country: the life and work of Leslie Adkin.**
Anthony Dreaver.   Wellington: Victoria University Press, 1997. 312p.
bibliog.

Adkin was one of those extraordinary New Zealanders who, self-taught and operating
outside professional and academic structures, made significant contributions in several
areas of scholarship. As a geologist, anthropologist and historian, his sometimes controversial views continue to challenge; as a keen tramper, he mapped large areas of
mountain country; and he was also a photographer of the first rank. Utilizing the
extensive research materials left by his subject, the author draws the threads of
Adkin's life together.

233 Salmond: southern jurist.

Alex Frame. Wellington: Victoria University Press, 1995. 294p. bibliog.

Salmond was one of New Zealand's most acute legal minds, his texts on Torts and Jurisprudence being well known throughout the English-speaking law world. The book, utilizing previously untapped legal files, including those of the Solicitor-General, traces the development of his ideas on the law and their application to the social and political problems of the country in the first quarter of the 20th century. Of particular interest is his approach to Maori claims arising out of the Treaty of Waitangi.

234 Autobiography.

Janet Frame. Auckland: Century Hutchinson, 1989. 437p.

Brings together into one volume the three parts of novelist and poet Janet Frame's autobiography, *To the is-land*, *An angel at my table* and *The envoy from mirror city*. These volumes detail the life of one of New Zealand's best-known modern authors – from her childhood in a poor but intellectually intense railway family, to her time as a student and a long period in mental hospitals, and finally the fulfilment she found through writing. This work allows a glimpse of her traumas, tribulations and achievements in a very readable and involving way.

235 Walter Buller: the reluctant conservationist.

R. A. Galbreath. Wellington: GP Books, 1989. 336p. maps. bibliog.

Buller is best known for his *History of the birds of New Zealand* (London: John Van Voorst, 1873. 384p.). The son of a missionary, he made his career in the Native Department and later also practised as a barrister. As an ornithologist, he won international recognition. Yet as the author, himself a zoologist, points out, Buller's contribution was riddled with contradictions. While his publications captured for posterity New Zealand's disappearing birds, his involvement in the trading of specimens helped drive some to extinction. While he advocated the establishment of sanctuaries, he believed native flora and fauna must inevitably be displaced by European introductions.

236 The seven lives of Lady Barker: author of Station Life in New Zealand.

Betty Gilderdale. Auckland: David Bateman, 1996. 312p. bibliog.

The life of a much travelled Victorian woman, best remembered in New Zealand for her account of mid-19th-century life on a Canterbury sheeprun. Born in the West Indies, prior to arriving in New Zealand she had accompanied her first husband to India. In later life she and her second husband, Sir Frederick Broome, served in other parts of the Empire, the culmination being the latter's appointment as Governor of Western Australia. Others of her eighteen books achieved similar legendary status in the countries in which she had been resident.

237 From the cradle to the grave: a biography of Michael Joseph Savage.

Barry Gustafson. Auckland: Penguin, 1988. 369p. bibliog.

Arguably New Zealand's most loved Prime Minister, Savage became the personification of the social security system created by the first Labour Government to raise the living standards of all citizens and provide security and dignity 'from the cradle to the grave'. While this image has been questioned subsequently, the author investigates the intellectual, political, economic and social influences that shaped Savage's personal philosophy and political direction. He also analyses the internal party clashes immediately preceding his subject's death in 1940. 'The intention is to record, explain and evaluate Savage's life, not to honour it' (p. 2).

238 **Diary of the Kirk years.**
     Margaret Hayward.   Wellington: Reed; Queen Charlotte Sound, New
     Zealand: Cape Catley, 1981. 322p.

A personal record, prepared by his private secretary, of the last thirty-four months in the life of the Rt. Hon. Norman Kirk, Prime Minister of New Zealand, 1972-74. Distilled from millions of words jotted down virtually daily, it seeks to contribute to an understanding of how he thought, how he worked, how he coped in his personal and political life, and his vision of a more just society. Although abridged for legal reasons, when it came out the book was considered 'the most detailed and accurate of its kind ever published in New Zealand' (publisher's note).

239 **Richard Henry of Resolution Island.**
     Susanne Hill, John Hill.   Dunedin: McIndoe/New Zealand Wildlife
     Service, 1987. 364p. bibliog.

A reclusive bushman and casual labourer who spent nearly twenty-five years in remote Fiordland, Richard Henry (1845-1929), through his keen intelligence and acute powers of observation, turned himself into one of New Zealand's foremost field naturalists. Concerned at the plight of the country's flightless birds, he was instrumental in having Resolution Island proclaimed a national sanctuary in 1891. In 1894, he was appointed curator and caretaker. While the practical results were mixed, he published many research notes and articles. This elegantly written book is the result of more than eight years of research.

240 **Nothing venture, nothing win.**
     Edmund Hillary.   Auckland: Coronet Books/Hodder & Stoughton,
     1988. rev. ed. 396p.

The revised and updated life story of one of the greatest adventurers of the 20th century – conqueror of Everest, Antarctic explorer, friend of the Sherpas and a tireless traveller. Hillary reveals himself as a man of outstanding bravery and skill, yet one also characterized by his modesty. In a new Epilogue, he reviews the years after 1975, the culmination of which was his appointment as New Zealand's High Commissioner to India. Written in clear, straightforward prose, the book reflects the man.

241 **Sylvia!: the biography of Sylvia Ashton-Warner.**
     Lynley Hood.   Auckland: Penguin, 1990. 264p. maps. bibliog.

The very personal biography of a troubled and contradictory woman who, while believing herself rejected in New Zealand, nevertheless achieved international acclaim. A major educational innovator, her 'key vocabulary' literacy technique having been developed in remote rural schools, in later life she taught in North American universities. Also a novelist of standing, she typically published all her major works overseas. The book reads 'like a novel' as the author intended.

242 Memories of Muldoon.
Bob Jones.   Christchurch: Canterbury University Press, 1997. 224p.

Not a biography, rather a lively account of the author's often turbulent relationship with a Prime Minister who stamped his mark on New Zealand in the 1970s and early 1980s as no other 20th-century politician, before or since. Jones threw his efforts behind Muldoon in his bid for office, then a decade later, through his leadership of the short-lived New Zealand Party, played a major part in the Prime Minister's 1984 downfall. He assesses Muldoon's record and concludes that the man has been unfairly demonized. This is a sometimes quirky view of a politician who was both idolized and loathed, but who could never be ignored. The book complements the several volumes of Muldoon autobiography, commencing with *The rise and fall of a young Turk* (Wellington: Reed, 1974. 203p.). A scholarly biography is in preparation.

243 Frank Sargeson: a life.
Michael King.   Auckland: Viking, 1995. 478p. bibliog.

Sargeson was the first major author to remain in New Zealand, and from the 1930s he steered New Zealand writing in new directions. For fifty years, from a primitive cottage on Auckland's North Shore, he turned out short stories, which earned him a worldwide reputation for their compression and power, as well as plays and novels. As the author skilfully teases out, Sargeson was a man of contradictions. While rejecting his puritan upbringing, he was puritan in his total commitment to his calling. At times quarrelsome, even malicious, he could also be a generous mentor to younger writers. King provides a superior literary biography.

244 Te Puea: a biography.
Michael King.   Auckland; London: Hodder & Stoughton, 1977. 331p. 2 maps. bibliog.

The most formidable female Maori leader of the first half of the 20th century, Te Puea Herangi secured the survival of the Maori King Movement and fought to improve the condition of her Waikato people, winning recognition from successive governments. More than any contemporary, she succeeded in strengthening Maori values and institutions by the controlled accommodation of European influences. The book, which draws heavily upon oral sources, documents events unfamiliar to most non-Maori. While the author is European, he exhibits great sensitivity to matters Maori.

245 Whina: a biography of Whina Cooper.
Michael King.   Auckland: Penguin, 1991. 2nd ed. 285p. maps. bibliog.

Referred to at her death as 'the mother of New Zealand', Whina Cooper became the most visible Maori woman of the later 20th century. Though raised in a traditional rural environment, she came to epitomize a new urban leadership. Foundation President of the Maori Women's Welfare League, she was a sometimes controversial activist, leading the 1975 Maori Land March in her eightieth year. As the author notes: 'once made leader, she led – in a manner to which she was incurably accustomed' (p. 9).

246 Student at the gates.
Elsie Locke.   Christchurch: Whitcoulls, 1981. 180p.

Describes the early life of a noted leftwing activist, whose choices were influenced by the Depression, and who went on to become a writer of popular history and children's literature. The turbulent days of Auckland in the 1930s are recalled, and interwoven through this important social history is the author's own story, which in itself has the fascination of a survival narrative. Many of the author's acquaintances became well-known literary names, but the limited opportunities for women become glaringly obvious.

247 The life of James K. Baxter.
Frank McKay.   Auckland: Oxford University Press, 1992. 320p. maps. bibliog.

New Zealand's most widely read poet, also a penetrating literary critic, Baxter was a wanderer for most of his life. By turns student, labourer, teacher and editor, by inclination for many years a roisterer, he drew greatest public notice in late life as the ascetic founder of a community for the casualties of society at a remote settlement called Jerusalem. 'His long hair and beard, his bare feet and general messianic appearance could not fail to attract attention' (p. vii). This is a literary biography in the best tradition of the genre.

248 McMeekan: a biography.
Gordon McLauchlan.   Auckland: Hodder & Stoughton, 1982. 242p. bibliog.

One of the most brilliant scientists New Zealand has produced, Campbell McMeekan was prominent in the development of truly scientific agricultural research. While he taught at both Massey and Lincoln Colleges, and published prolifically, his zenith was as head of the Ruakura Agricultural Research Station, which he made the most efficient livestock research centre in the Commonwealth. His career, however, was tempestuous, and when he failed to be appointed Director-General of Agriculture he left New Zealand in 1962 for employment with the World Bank.

249 Our lesser stars: twelve New Zealand family biographies.
Edited by Colleen Main.   Auckland: New Zealand Society of Genealogists, 1990. 328p.

Comprised of twelve short-listed essays from the New Zealand Society of Genealogists' sesquicentennial family biography competition, this book provides insights into the lives of ordinary New Zealanders in the 19th and early 20th centuries. While the essays vary in quality, and the coverage is less than national, collectively the vignettes help offset professional biographers' natural preoccupation with the famous and infamous.

250 Memoirs.
John Marshall.   Auckland: Collins, 1983-89. 2 vols.

Elected to Parliament in 1946, Marshall was to be a member continuously for three decades. Early marked for high office, he held senior portfolios for more than twenty years, being also Deputy Prime Minister for eleven of those years. His tenure of the Prime Ministership, however, was short, less than ten months, the National Party losing office in 1972. Known to friends and foes alike as 'Gentleman Jack', elegant and invariably courteous, Marshall was, nevertheless, an enigma. While widely regarded as a liberal, many of his views were rigidly conservative.

251 Accidental life.
Phoebe Meikle.   Auckland: Auckland University Press, 1994. 311p.

The autobiography of a woman who, despite adversities, became a respected educationalist, then carved a career in publishing, both at times when it was unusual for women to reach the top in these professions. Meikle also became a public figure, lecturing in New Zealand and overseas on feminist and pacifist issues. Frank and often moving, this book addresses ideas and emotions, as well as happenings.

252 The story of Suzanne Aubert.
Jessie Munro.   Auckland: Auckland University Press/Bridget Williams Books, 1996. 464p. bibliog.

A sympathetic and beautifully written portrait of a small French nun who arrived in New Zealand as a missionary in 1860. Her calling was to span six decades. There was scarcely one of those decades, first in Hawke's Bay, then up the remote Whanganui River, later in the capital, in which she did not make a distinctive contribution. Striding the roads and streets on behalf of the poor and neglected, she won popular support, respect and affection. Her lasting legacy was the order she founded, the Sisters of Compassion.

253 The riddle of Richard Pearse.
Gordon Ogilvie.   Wellington: Reed, 1973. 251p. maps. bibliog.

There is evidence to suggest that Pearse, a South Island farmer, made himself airborne in a powered machine in March 1903, nine months prior to the Wright brothers' flight. Though he received little recognition during his lifetime, Pearse continued to experiment for a further fifty years. This is a competent biography of a talented, but lonely and frustrated, inventor.

254 A fighting withdrawal: the life of Dan Davin, writer, soldier, publisher.
Keith Ovenden.   Oxford: Oxford University Press, 1996. 469p. bibliog.

A well-documented, well-written biography of a writer who, while he may not have reached quite the status of Baxter or Sargeson, is nevertheless one of New Zealand's significant literary figures. Additionally, that his life was more than this has assured an interesting biography. Through access to the papers of Davin and his wife, the author is able to present a very full picture of his university life, his war years, his years with Cambridge University Press, and his later period of decline following retirement.

255 Born to New Zealand: a biography of Jane Maria Atkinson.
Frances Porter.   Wellington: Bridget Williams Books, 1995. Reprint of 1989 ed. 416p. bibliog.

A woman's informed view of important events in 19th-century New Zealand. A member of the Richmond-Atkinson clan, influential in Taranaki politics and nationally, the sister-in-law of sometime Premier Henry Atkinson, the subject was on intimate terms with both those who made policy and those who executed it. Insights were conveyed in letters to friends and relatives, along with observations on her domestic situation. Nothing that touched her life escaped her vigorous commentary.

256   Halfway round the harbour: an autobiography.
Keith Sinclair. Auckland: Penguin, 1993. 228p.

Prolific, penetrating, often controversial, Sinclair is generally regarded as New Zealand's most influential historian. Generations of students have been reared on his *History of New Zealand* (Auckland: Penguin, 1991. 320p.), originally published in 1959, while he also enjoyed high standing as a poet and social commentator. In this candid autobiography, published shortly before his death, the strongest sections recount his interwar childhood, war service and development of the study of New Zealand history as more than a subplot of British imperial history. There are also observations on contemporary literary figures.

257   Walter Nash.
Keith Sinclair. Auckland: Auckland University Press; Wellington, London: Oxford University Press, 1976. 439p. bibliog.

A biography based on the most extensive collection of papers yet left by any politician in New Zealand. Nash was a Member of Parliament for almost forty years, Minister of Finance for fourteen years, and Prime Minister for three (1957-60). He was among the most influential of the group who from 1935 created the New Zealand welfare state. The book is also informative on the origins and history of the New Zealand Labour Party and its influence on the development of modern New Zealand.

258   Eruera: the teachings of a Maori elder.
Eruera Stirling, as told to Anne Salmond. Auckland: Oxford University Press, 1990. Reprint of 1985 ed. 288p.

Combining ancestral knowledge entrusted in childhood and personal reminiscences spanning eighty years, this book is a unique recording of the influences shaping one respected elder's life. It is in three parts. Concerned that younger generations be aware of the ancestral ways, he first sets down traditions of his Whanau-a-Apanui tribe. He then goes on to give a vivid description of the Bay of Plenty in the era of whaling, maize cropping and kumara growing, during which Stirling worked with Sir Apirana Ngata. The third section covers his later years in Auckland, touching upon the revival of Maori activism. For a complementary view, see his wife's story, also as told to Anne Salmond, *Amiria* (Auckland: Reed, 1995. 184p.).

259   The father and his gift: John Logan Campbell's later years.
R. C. J. Stone. Auckland: Auckland University Press, 1987. 309p. bibliog.

This book and its predecessor, *Young Logan Campbell* (Auckland: Auckland University Press; Oxford University Press, 1982. 287p.), present a portrait of a New Zealand-domiciled Victorian businessman which is unparalleled in scope and depth. Known as 'the Father of Auckland', for seventy years Campbell's name was almost synonymous with the city, the various firms of which he was a principal contributing to its growth. Despite business vicissitudes, Campbell was also a generous benefactor. The work is an outgrowth of Professor Stone's earlier studies of the Auckland business community.

260 **Ettie: a life of Ettie Rout.**
Jane Tolerton. Auckland: Penguin, 1992. 283p. bibliog.

A biography of a woman variously described as 'the guardian angel of the ANZACs' and 'the wickedest woman in Britain', one whose First World War efforts centred on actively protecting soldiers from venereal disease. As the author reveals, however, there were other important dimensions to her life. A feminist and a committed socialist, she was instrumental in the 1910 founding of a leftwing newspaper, the *Maoriland Worker* (Wellington: New Zealand Federation of Labour, 1910-23. weekly). Later she promoted birth control and dabbled in ethnography.

261 **Fairburn.**
Denys Trussell. Auckland: Auckland University Press, 1984. 320p. bibliog.

A carefully documented life of a poet, satirist and critic whose varied career (insurance clerk, freelance journalist, Farmers' Union secretary, radio scriptwriter, craftsman, English tutor and art lecturer) only hints at the range of his interests. The account is woven into a narrative of New Zealand's development in his lifetime, Fairburn being involved in many public issues. Far from hagiographic, the book explores the dilemmas of a man of sensibility in a raw, young culture.

262 **Turnovsky: fifty years in New Zealand.**
Fred Turnovsky. Wellington: Allen & Unwin, 1990. 256p.

An immigrant from Czechoslovakia, Fred Turnovsky built up a life for himself in his adopted country, particularly in the manufacturing industry, coming to prominence as President of the New Zealand Manufacturers' Federation. His contribution to the performing arts through his role on the Queen Elizabeth II Arts Council is legendary. This is a 'rags to riches' story that is modestly told and incorporates many insights into the country and the society he adopted.

Lands for the people?: the highland clearances and the colonisation of New Zealand: a biography of John McKenzie.
See item no. 114.

Redemption songs: a life of Te Kooti Arikirangi Te Turuki.
See item no. 214.

The book of New Zealand women: ko kui ma ta kaupapa.
See item no. 287.

A stand for decency: Patricia Bartlett and the Society for the Promotion of Community Standards, 1970-1995.
See item no. 357.

Ratana: the man, the church, the political movement.
See item no. 402.

Rua and the Maori millennium.
See item no. 403.

Made in New Zealand: the story of Jim Fletcher.
See item no. 537.

Brierley: the man behind the corporate legend.
See item no. 539.

The biography of an idea: Beeby on education.
See item no. 661.

Ngaio Marsh: the woman and her work.
See item no. 705.

Colin McCahon, artist.
See item no. 726.

Southern voices: international opera singers of New Zealand.
See item no. 752.

Biographical dictionary of New Zealand composers.
See item no. 753.

Belliss on bowls.
See item no. 814.

Sandra Edge: full circle: an autobiography.
See item no. 817.

Rhythm and swing: an autobiography.
See item no. 819.

Arthur's boys: the golden era of New Zealand athletics.
See item no. 828.

Who's who in New Zealand.
See item no. 934.

Dictionary of New Zealand biography.
See item no. 942.

A dictionary of New Zealand biography.
See item no. 944.

New Zealand who's who in Aotearoa.
See item no. 947.

Population

263 **Without issue: New Zealanders who choose not to have children.**
Jan Cameron. Christchurch: Canterbury University Press, 1997.
240p.

In New Zealand during the 1980s one woman in nine was childless; that figure is likely to double by the end of the century. This book explores some of the myths surrounding the decision not to have children. The information has been compiled through interviews and case-studies of women and men. The author concludes there is no one reason for this approach – a whole raft of reasons came to light, including image and social preferences. This work complements her earlier investigation: *Why have children? A New Zealand case study* (Christchurch: University of Canterbury Press/New Zealand Demographic Society, 1990. 142p.).

264 **Trans-Tasman migration: trends, causes and consequences.**
Edited by Gordon A. Carmichael. Canberra: Australian Government Printing Service, 1993. 435p. maps. bibliog.

The two-way flow between Australia and New Zealand is by far the most significant factor in determining New Zealand's annual net migration gain. Nine contributors – demographers, economists and geographers – examine the development of policy, the pattern of flows between the two countries and associated economic factors, and the characteristics of New Zealanders in Australia and Australians in New Zealand. An agenda for further research is suggested.

265 **Fertility and family formation in the 'second demographic transition': New Zealand patterns and trends.**
Natalie Jackson, Ian Pool. Christchurch: New Zealand Institute for Social Research and Development, 1994. 192p. bibliog. (Family and Societal Change: Research Report no. 2).

'This study looks at the current demographic dynamics and structures of New Zealand families and reviews the recent changes' (Introduction). Supported by the New

80

Zealand Foundation for Research Science and Technology and initially prepared under a contract for the New Zealand Institute for Social Research and Development, this is an academic examination of the issues but the presentation makes the information accessible to a wider audience. Both Pakeha and Maori studies are included.

266 The population of New Zealand: interdisciplinary perspectives.
R. J. Warwick Neville, C. James O'Neill.   Auckland: Longman Paul, 1979. 339p. maps. bibliog.

Covers a wide range of issues relating to population: international migration, internal migration, mortality, marriages and families, fertility, sex and age distribution, race and ethnicity, population and the economy, social policy and the environment. All of the topics are dealt with by authorities in the particular field. Although the data is now dated, it provides a picture of the New Zealand population in the 1970s, and historically.

267 Te iwi Maori: a New Zealand population, past, present and projected.
Ian Pool.   Auckland: Auckland University Press, 1991. 271p. maps. bibliog.

Intended initially as an update of the author's earlier work, *The Maori population of New Zealand, 1769-1971* (Auckland: Auckland University Press; Wellington, London: Oxford University Press, 1977. 266p.), this is instead a completely new evaluation of the subject. He found that there was now a larger body of research to draw on, Maori fertility had declined markedly in the 1970s, a different range of demographic tools was now available and that, also, through wider experience, his own perspectives had changed. The result is a valuable analysis of the Maori as a component of the New Zealand population.

268 International migration and the New Zealand economy: a long-run perspective.
Jacques Poot, Ganesh Nana, Bryan Philpott.   Wellington: Victoria University Press for Institute of Policy Studies, 1988. 217p. bibliog.

The authors, all based at the time of this study at Victoria University in Wellington, have pooled their research on international migration to produce a thoughtful examination of the consequences of emigration and immigration on the 'long-run path of the economy'. The *Joanna* model of the New Zealand economy (which estimates the effects of changes in net migration on prices, quantities and macroeconomic aggregates after markets have had time to adjust), is described. Its application is considered in terms of a range of scenarios. There are also comparisons with an Australian model.

269 New Zealand and international migration: a digest and bibliography, number 2.
Edited by Andrew D. Trlin, Paul Spoonley.   Palmerston North, New Zealand: Department of Sociology, Massey University, 1992. 162p. bibliog.

The first volume explored the 'growing awareness over the last two or three decades that international migration is an important factor influencing almost all aspects of social life' (Preface). The second volume considers how policy has evolved, examines the effect of immigration on the domestic economy and outlines the changed nature of immigration. A thoughtful and thought-provoking work, it details the strengths and inadequacies of the new policies, questions whether there are people being disadvantaged and suggests what the gains to New Zealand, economically and socially, might be. The chapters fall into two categories: those dealing with the nature of immigration policy and its relationship to economic concerns, and those examining the issues surrounding Pacific Island migrants and their descendants in New Zealand. The extensive bibliography is a feature of both volumes.

270 Population of New Zealand.
United Nations. New York: United Nations, 1985. 2 vols. (ESCAP Country Monograph Series no. 12).

'The purpose is to provide . . . an understanding of existing population problems as well as a scientific basis for decision making, policy formulation and determination of development goals and targets. An immediate objective . . . is to encourage the analysis and maximum utilization in planning of the data collected through censuses, vital registration systems and sample surveys' (Preface). Prepared essentially for overseas consumption, this is nevertheless an extremely useful compendium covering a wide range of population issues: migration, population redistribution, urbanization, fertility regulation, mortality trends, ethnicity, population projections, the law and population. It provides a sound basis for any further general work or for more in-depth analysis of the topics covered.

Immigration and national identity in New Zealand: one people, two peoples, many peoples?
See item no. 275.

New Zealand's ageing society: the implications.
See item no. 379.

New Zealand Population Review.
See item no. 908.

Minorities

271 **Half the world away from home: perspectives on the Irish in New Zealand, 1860-1950.**
Donald H. Akenson.   Wellington: Victoria University Press, 1990. 250p.

The author considers first in general terms the flow of migrants from the British Isles, more particularly Ireland. He then examines the impact of immigration through case-studies in the form of a person (an Irish Catholic writer), Dan Davin, a settlement, Katikati, and a closer look at education. While acknowledging the importance of the discussions about the relationships between Maori and Pakeha, Akenson considers it is time the Pakeha group be examined more closely as to its makeup and that the different components are worthy of study in their own right.

272 **Far from the promised land?: being Jewish in New Zealand.**
Ann Beaglehole, Hal Levine.   Wellington: Pacific Press, 1995. 146p.

Based on tape-recorded interviews with people of widely varying background. Those interviewed include: religious and secular Jews; men and women who identify strongly as Jews and others whose Jewish identity is weak, sometimes nonexistent. The authors conclude that while New Zealand has generally welcomed Jews, it has been a hard country in which to remain Jewish. Assimilation and out-migration have been central to the New Zealand Jewish experience.

273 **Danish emigration to New Zealand.**
Edited by Henning Bender, Birgit Larsen.   Aalberg, Denmark: Danes Worldwide Archives, 1990. 132p. map. bibliog.

A random collection of essays, principally by Danes and drawn from Danish sources, prepared to commemorate New Zealand's sesquicentenary in 1990. While a number of the themes are familiar, of particular interest are essays on the Danish contribution to New Zealand dairy technology, and the pre-First World War Danish view of New Zealand as a 'workers' paradise'.

274 **Alla fine del mondo = To the ends of the earth: a history of Italian migration to the Wellington region.**
Paul Elenio. Petone, New Zealand: Petone Settlers' Museum and the Club Garibaldi, 1995. 85p. map.

Although the history of one particular group of immigrants to one particular area, much of what is recorded in this slim volume is likely to be true of other Italian communities in New Zealand. Written for the descendants of the first settlers and for the people of New Zealand generally, the work aims to show the reasons for migration, the aspirations of the migrants, and their determination to succeed in the new land. The volume is illustrated with many historical black-and-white photographs.

275 **Immigration and national identity in New Zealand: one people, two peoples, many peoples?**
Edited by Stuart William Greif. Palmerston North, New Zealand: Dunmore Press, 1995. 343p. bibliog.

Arguments over immigration are as old as New Zealand itself. This book seeks to fill in the background to the current debate, both through overview chapters and case-studies of specific migrant groups. Particular attention is paid to the current wave of immigration from Asia, the thorny question of whether New Zealand should be a monocultural, bicultural or multicultural society being also raised. Maori objections to present immigration policy are canvassed. 'No government policy should be too far ahead of public opinion or out of step with a substantial majority' (p. 20).

276 **Dragons on the long white cloud: the making of Chinese New Zealanders.**
Manying Ip. North Shore City, New Zealand: Tandem Press, 1996. 168p.

'This book is a study of the ethnic Chinese community in New Zealand based on the oral-history accounts of local-born Chinese New Zealanders' (Preface). The largely self-contained nature of Chinese communities has meant that many of those interviewed have had to negotiate their way between two worlds. In this work they describe how they have managed the resulting tensions. Other works on Chinese immigration to New Zealand are this author's *Chinese New Zealanders: from market garden to boardrooms* (Auckland: Tandem Press, 1996. 276p.) and James Ng's multi-volumed *Windows on a Chinese past* (Dunedin: Otago Heritage Books, 1993- . 4 vols.).

277 **The challenge of change: Pacific Island communities in New Zealand, 1986-1993.**
Vasantha Krishnan, Penelope Schoeffel, Julie Warren. Wellington: New Zealand Institute for Social Research and Development, 1994. 100p.

Intended as the first of a series of studies of Pacific Island communities in New Zealand, this slim volume provides detailed analysis of a range of factors which contribute to the group's ability to manage the transition from migrant communities to New Zealand-born communities. Age and gender analysis, educational qualifications, self-employment statistics, unemployment rates, income analysis; all contribute to the picture of the 'changing structure of Pacific Island people's lives' (Preface).

278 **Pacific migrant labour, class and racism in New Zealand: fresh off the boat.**
Terrence Loomis. Aldershot, England: Avebury, 1990. 235p. map. bibliog. (Research in Ethnic Relations Series).
Acknowledging the role that Pacific Island migrant labour has played in the development of the New Zealand economy, the author seeks to explain why this group's economic and political position has remained relatively constantly disadvantaged over time. Concentrating particularly, but not exclusively, on Cook Islanders, work and class relations, housing, and the social forces surrounding the group are examined.

279 **Immigrants and citizens: New Zealanders and Asian immigration in historical context.**
Malcolm McKinnon. Wellington: IPS/Victoria University of Wellington, 1996. 86p.
'This book provides a valuable contribution to the current debate about Asian immigration by discussing it in the context not of Asian actions but of long standing New Zealand attitudes and policies' (Introduction). Using the concept of 'kin-migration' – that is, immigration primarily from the original source, in New Zealand's case, Great Britain – this work discusses how Asian immigrants are being accepted and what changes New Zealanders have to make to feel more comfortable with this change in immigration patterns. A companion work is Raj Vasil and Hong-Key Yoon's *New Zealanders of Asian origin* (Wellington: IPS/Victoria University Press, 1996. 60p.).

280 **Tasman's legacy: the New Zealand-Dutch connection.**
Hank Schouten. Wellington: New Zealand-Netherlands Foundation, 1992. 264p. maps.
Photographs of people bring a very human aspect to this collection of stories about the Dutch who emigrated to New Zealand. Covering the early contacts such as Abel Tasman (1642), Joel Samuel Polack (1831), Petrus van der Velden (1890), but concentrating on the more recent migrations after the Second World War, the work provides a picture of the contribution of the Dutch to New Zealand, through interviews, writings and photographs. In 1945 there were only 128 Dutch-born residents in New Zealand. Two decades later the Dutch had become by far the largest single group of residents of non-British origin.

281 **Indians in New Zealand: studies of a sub-culture.**
Edited by Kapil N. Tiwari. Wellington: Price Milburn, for the New Zealand Indian Central Association Inc., 1980. 244p.
Nine essays by a range of mainly New Zealand-based authors consider not only the different Indian communities in New Zealand but also set these communities in the context of Indian philosophy, religion and culture. At the time of writing, Indians constituted New Zealand's third minority group. The collection 'reflects the relatively new awareness among scholars of various disciplines of the wealth of original historical and cultural materials concerning ethnic groups' (Introduction). A more detailed study of one community is W. H. McLeod's *Punjab to Aotearoa: migration and settlement of Punjabis in New Zealand, 1890-1990* (Taumaranui, New Zealand: New Zealand Indian Association, Country Section, 1992. 60p.).

282 **Now respected, once despised: Yugoslavs in New Zealand.**
Andrew Trlin. Palmerston North, New Zealand: Dunmore Press, 1979. 255p. bibliog.

Although the presentation of this information shows its age, the book is nevertheless a well-researched study of Yugoslavs in New Zealand, examining their origins, the areas of industry which became uniquely theirs (digging for the fossilized gum from kauri trees, wine making), the attitudes displayed towards them when war broke out in 1914, and the assimilation process. Throughout, notes and references guide the reader to further sources of information. The research is given a human face by case histories of a number of families.

Ethnic groups in New Zealand: a bibliography. An annotated bibliography of New Zealand material of particular interest to the Ethnic Sector.
See item no. 968.

Women

General

283 Women in history: essays on European women in New Zealand.
Edited by Barbara Brookes, Charlotte MacDonald, Margaret Tennant.
Wellington: Allen & Unwin/Port Nicholson Press, 1986. 202p. bibliog.

Ten essays look at aspects of the life of women in New Zealand between 1860 and 1930. The editors acknowledge that much of importance in the history of women in this country is not yet covered; nevertheless, this work provides interesting glimpses of a life that modern-day women would find extraordinary. A follow-up work, *Women in history no. 2* (Wellington: Bridget Williams Books, 1992. 321p.) draws on studies being undertaken in a variety of fields and suggests that since 1986 books about women have been a feature of the lists of New Zealand publishers.

284 Standing in the sunshine: a history of New Zealand women since they won the vote.
Sandra Coney, et al.   Auckland: Viking, 1993. 332p. bibliog.

Published to mark the centenary of women's suffrage in New Zealand, this book provides resource material for those studying women's history. Arranged thematically, but by no means claiming to be comprehensive, the work ranges through women's contributions to suffrage, politics, health, education, sport, family life, arts and crafts, the land, war and the home. Acknowledgements are made to the many people who assisted in the accumulation of the material. The short essays are supported by appropriate illustrations.

285 Public and private worlds: women in contemporary New Zealand.
Edited by Shelagh Cox.   Wellington: Allen & Unwin/Port Nicholson Press, 1987. 235p.

'We all inhabit two realms, the public and the private, and they shape our lives' (Introduction). This thesis is the basis for the essays in this book. The private and public worlds inhabited by a range of 20th-century women are explored and contrasted. Significantly, Rose Pere, a contributor from a Maori background, presents a world that is not so divided, one in which women are of 'paramount importance'.

286   **Women in the economy: a research report on the economic position of women in New Zealand.**
Anne Horsfield.   Wellington: Ministry of Women's Affairs, 1988. 434p.

New Zealand women have always played a major part in the economy, but in recent years their role has been changing as more women enter the paid workforce. At the same time they are affirming the importance of family life through continued work in the home, and are active in promoting the services they need (childcare, healthcare, education). This study was commissioned by the Ministry of Women's Affairs to provide a clear picture of the economic position of women in New Zealand today. Comprehensively surveying existing research, the author suggests areas for future enquiry. There is a companion volume, *Maori women in the economy: a preliminary review of the economic position of Maori women in New Zealand* (q.v.).

287   **The book of New Zealand women: ko kui ma te kaupapa.**
Edited by Charlotte Macdonald, Merimeri Penfold, Bridget Williams.
Wellington: Bridget Williams Books, 1991. 772p.

A wide-ranging collection of short portraits, arranged alphabetically, of over 300 women who have contributed to the history of New Zealand. The time span covered is very wide, from the 12th century through to the 1980s. The work does not claim to be comprehensive, and does not deal with any living women, but it must surely rank as the most complete grouping of women to have made an impact within New Zealand.

288   **'My hand will write what my heart dictates': the unsettled lives of women in nineteenth century New Zealand, as revealed to sisters, family and friends.**
Edited by Frances Porter, Charlotte Macdonald, with Tui Macdonald.
Auckland: Auckland University Press/Bridget Williams Books, 1996. 518p.

Short excerpts with introductory commentary, presented thematically and drawn mainly from collections at the Alexander Turnbull Library, Wellington, collectively present a powerful portrait of the life of women in 19th-century New Zealand. Most of the writers represented are Pakeha, but some Maori writing is included, both in Maori and translation.

Suffrage

289 Women's suffrage in New Zealand.
Patricia Grimshaw. Auckland: Auckland University Press/Oxford
University Press, 1987. new ed. 156p. bibliog.

In 1893, New Zealand was the first national state to allow women the vote. This many times reprinted work seeks to show that the concession was not an isolated event, but rather one which was contemporaneous with other parallel changes in the position of women in New Zealand. The volume also sets out to demonstrate that the issue itself was forced into prominence by an organization, the Women's Christian Temperance Union, whose motives in campaigning for the vote were basically feminist. There is a thoughtful 'Afterword' to this revised edition.

290 The woman question: writings by the women who won the vote.
Margaret Lovell-Smith. Auckland: New Women's Press, 1992. 256p.
bibliog.

Some eighty articles from sixteen women writing in the period 1869-1910, covering issues ranging from winning the vote through the economic independence of women and equal rights to training and prison reform, are conveniently gathered in this volume. Predominantly sourced from *The Prohibitionist* (1890-1907), and *The White Ribbon* (1895-1934), this work provides insights from the pens of the women of the day. It is not as broad in its coverage as *The vote, the pill and the demon drink: a history of feminist writing in New Zealand, 1869-1993* (q.v.).

291 Women in the House: Members of Parliament in New Zealand.
Janet McCallum. Picton, New Zealand: Cape Catley, 1993. 284p.
bibliog.

Published to mark the centenary of female suffrage in New Zealand, also the sixtieth anniversary of the election of the country's first woman Member of Parliament, this book brings together short biographies of all thirty-six women taking seats in the House of Representatives to 1993. While the individual essays are a useful reference source, collectively they highlight common patterns, as well as striking differences. They provide insights into female attitudes towards politics.

292 The vote, the pill and the demon drink: a history of feminist writing in New Zealand, 1869-1993.
Edited by Charlotte Macdonald. Wellington: Bridget Williams
Books, 1993. 260p.

The history of women's rights in New Zealand is explored through the writings of groups and individuals. The 'collection has been put together to provide a broader base for reflection on New Zealand's feminist history, and to provide an historical account of the development of feminism both as a set of ideas and as a political movement' (Introduction). Each section commences with an essay to set the scene and concludes with a list of references for further reading. Covering a longer period and a wider range of sources, it supplements *The woman question: writings by the women who won the vote* (q.v.).

Feminism

293 **Changing our lives: women working in the women's liberation movement, 1970-1990.**
Edited by Maud Cahill, Christine Dann. Wellington: Bridget Williams Books, 1991. 186p.

'Twenty-one women speak . . . about the way in which the women's movement has affected their lives' (Introduction). This is a candid, moving, sometimes disturbing account.

294 **Up from under: women and liberation in New Zealand, 1970-1985.**
Christine Dann. Wellington: Allen & Unwin/Port Nicholson Press, 1985. 152p.

The author, one of the committed leaders of the women's movement, considers the differences between the women's liberation movement, the women's movement and feminism in New Zealand between 1970 and 1985. Thematic perspectives are presented: historical, political, health, work, education and so on. For the enquirer interested in the development of these movements in New Zealand, the work provides an introduction with a strong sense of authenticity.

295 **Feminist voices: women's studies texts for Aotearoa/New Zealand.**
Edited by Rosemary Du Plessis, with Phillida Bunkle, Kathie Irwin, A. Laine, Sue Middleton. Auckland: Oxford University Press, 1992. 358p.

Two dozen contributors – Maori and Pakeha, lesbian and heterosexual, older and younger – present their feminist analyses of Aotearoa/New Zealand. 'It is a pot-pourri of texts, written by women whose ordinary lives have shaped what they have to say and the voices they bring to the telling' (cover). The book is organized in five sections: women's studies, politics of culture, the politics of work, women and the state, and feminist politics.

296 **Women and economics: a New Zealand feminist perspective.**
Prue Hyman. Wellington: Bridget Williams Books, 1994. 256p.

Challenging orthodox economic analysis and theory, this book explores the impact of economic policy on New Zealand women since 1984. There is a detailed study of pay equity in the contemporary environment of the Employment Contracts Act, individual contracts, and reduced levels of collective bargaining. The role of the state in relation to economic independence and income maintenance is discussed, with particular reference to women's experience within and outside the paid workforce. Special consideration is given to two areas of particular concern to women – the position of older women and housing policy.

297 **Heading nowhere in a navy blue suit: and other tales from the feminist revolution.**
Sue Kedgley, Mary Varnham. Wellington: Daphne Brasell Associates Press, 1993. 206p.

'Has feminism done what it set out to do? Had it improved the lives of all women or just a few? Had men got the message? Had women? Would the world be different for our daughters and granddaughters? These questions led to this book' (Introduction). Women involved in the feminist movement in the 1970s and 1980s look back reflectively and consider the positive and negative outcomes, what has been achieved and what still remains to be done.

298 **Three masquerades: essays on equality, work and hu(man) rights.**
Marilyn Waring. Auckland: Auckland University Press/Bridget Williams Books, 1996. 205p.

Following her earlier works on the worth of women – *Counting for nothing: what men value and what women are worth* (Wellington: Allen & Unwin/Port Nicholson Press, 1988. 290p.) and *If women counted: a new feminist economics* (London: Macmillan, 1989. 386p.) – this sometime politician turned university lecturer considers the masquerades that abound in discussions of equality, work and human rights. In each of the three essays, the author draws on her experiences as a politician and activist and adds to these her knowledge of economics, development studies and law to discuss whether the theory of equality provided by domestic and international law measures up against the reality of day-to-day life. The first essay looks at the issue of parliamentary representation as well as representation generally for women at the domestic and international level; the second considers the invisibility of women's work and raises questions about what would happen if the economic value of this work was recognized; and the third further develops the themes of representation and equality.

Women's organizations

299 **Women together: a history of women's organizations in New Zealand: Nga ropu wahine o te motu.**
Edited by Anne Else. Wellington: Historical Branch, Dept. of Internal Affairs/Daphne Brasell Associates Press, 1993. 610p. bibliog.

One hundred and thirty-two short histories of women's organizations are described under thirteen headings in this compendious volume. The organizations range from the Onehunga Ladies' Benevolent Society to unions, health councils and religious groups. The well-researched essays are supported by thorough indexing and a chronological list of the groups identified.

300 **The National Council of Women: a centennial history.**
Dorothy Page. Auckland: Auckland University Press/Bridget
Williams Books/National Council of Women, 1996. 240p. bibliog.

Emerging from the successful campaign for women's suffrage, the National Council
of Women has been consistently involved in causes relating to women over the subsequent 100 years. This is a history not only of the organization but also of the women
who as part of the organization gave so much to women's issues. The work is sourced
from primary and secondary material.

Maori women

301 **Maori women in the economy: a preliminary review of the
economic position of Maori women in New Zealand.**
Anne Horsfield, Miriana Evans. Wellington: Ministry of Women's
Affairs, 1988. 123p.

The companion volume to *Women in the economy: a research report on the economic
position of women in New Zealand* (q.v.), which 'was developed from a project to can-
vass data and literature on New Zealand women to identify gaps in our knowledge
about their economic position'. The particular information relating to Maori women is
extrapolated and here presented under the headings, 'The Treaty of Waitangi', 'Paid
work', 'Unwaged work', 'Unemployment', 'Incomes and wealth', and 'Education services'. Although the information is now becoming dated, it does provide a base from
which a picture can be formed and upon which further information can be established.

302 **Toi wahine: the worlds of Maori women.**
Edited by Kathie Irwin, Irihapeti Ramsden. Auckland: Penguin,
1995. 143p.

A collection of writings by Maori women which 'explores the dreams, lives, thoughts,
experiences and reflections of Maori women as well as the concerns and issues facing
[them]' (Introduction). It includes fiction and non-fiction, autobiography, analysis,
poems and speeches. Particularly apposite illustrations are provided by Robyn
Kahukiwa.

303 **Mana wahine Maori: selected writings on Maori women's art,
culture and politics.**
Ngahuia Te Awekotuku. Auckland: New Women's Press, 1991.
174p.

Brings together a number of essays written over some twenty years, some previously
published, which look at the emergence of Maori women, and their movement into
areas previously the domain of men, from a variety of viewpoints. A reinforcement
for Maori women of the direction they are taking, this is also a point of reference for
New Zealanders generally.

304 **Mana wahine: women who show the way.**
Edited by Amy Wood. Auckland: Reed, 1994. 208p.
Presents profiles of twenty-four Maori women who are considered to have contributed
to changing New Zealand. Often moving and very sincere, this is a celebration of
women, many of whom would not have pushed themselves forward for recognition
but whose contribution should not go unrecorded.

Nga morehu = The survivors.
See item no. 213.

Bread and roses: her story/Sonja Davies.
See item no. 230.

Kate Sheppard: a biography: the fight for womens' votes in New Zealand.
See item no. 231.

The seven lives of Lady Barker: author of Station Life in New Zealand.
See item no. 236.

Te Puea: a biography.
See item no. 244.

Whina: a biography of Whina Cooper.
See item no. 245.

Student at the gates.
See item no. 246.

Accidental life.
See item no. 251.

The story of Suzanne Aubert.
See item no. 252.

Born to New Zealand: a biography of Jane Maria Atkinson.
See item no. 255.

Ettie: a life of Ettie Rout.
See item no. 260.

Women and politics in New Zealand.
See item no. 422.

Women and education in Aotearoa 2.
See item no. 664.

Women's Studies Journal.
See item no. 918.

**Directory of women's organizations and groups = Te rereangi ingoa o
nga ropu wahine kei Aotearoa nei.**
See item no. 932.

**Victoria's furthest daughters: a bibliography of published sources for
the study of women in New Zealand, 1830-1914.**
See item no. 966.

Society and Social Structure

General

305 Social process in New Zealand: readings in sociology.
Edited by John Forster.   Auckland: Longman Paul, 1969. 307p. maps.
bibliog.

Those interested in an historical analysis of the social arrangements of New Zealand society will find information in part two of this publication of value. Under the broad heading, 'Community', three essays ('The village and the bush', 'The nature of community', and 'Social ecology of New Zealand cities') all provide historical and sociological background to the evolution of New Zealand society and national character. The importance of these essays is that they contain well-documented material largely unpublished elsewhere. The other sections of the book – on demography, differentiation, and attitudes towards research – are now dated.

306 New Zealand society: a sociological introduction.
Edited by P. Spoonley, D. Pearson, I. Shirley.   Palmerston North, New Zealand: Dunmore Press, 1994. 381p.

Twenty-three contributors provide brief but useful introductions to selected aspects of contemporary New Zealand society. The initial chapters focus on key institutions, the family and community, both urban and rural. These are followed by chapters dealing with the structural inequalities arising from class, racism and ethnicity, and gender. The book then turns to the state, and to matters of social policy and service delivery. The last section includes chapters which focus on ideology and its reproduction in forums as various as the arts and religion.

Social strata

307 Respectable lives: social standing in rural New Zealand.
Elvin Hatch.   Berkeley, California: University of California Press, 1992. 214p.

An ethnography by an American social anthropologist of a small South Island sheep-farming community. The central argument is that 'the local system of social standing and conceptions of self are grounded in historically variable, cultural systems of meaning' (Introduction). These systems are explored through analyses of the occupational structure and patterns of landholding. Fieldwork for the study was undertaken in 1981.

308 Models of society: class, stratification and gender in Australia and New Zealand.
F. L. Jones, Peter Davis.   Sydney: Croom Helm, 1986. 174p.

The book functions on two levels. On one, it presents the results of research into the features and patterns of class mobility and class structure in Australia and New Zealand. A status attainment model shows how jobs and earnings depend on school origins and early socialization, and compares the process for women and men. On the other level, it is a demonstration of analytical and modelling methods utilizing primary data drawn from national surveys. Although the tables presented are useful, the text is dense for the non-specialist reader.

309 Eclipse of equality: social stratification in New Zealand.
David G. Pearson, David C. Thorns.   Sydney: George Allen & Unwin, 1983. 287p. (Studies in Society).

Although aimed primarily at university students, this work is nevertheless deserving of a wider audience. 'Inequality, the level of poverty and extent of social differentiation are increasingly debated topics in contemporary New Zealand faced with inflation, unemployment and signs of increasing social stress' (Introduction). The range of opinions as to what causes differences between individuals, ranging from inherent ability, through to the division of labour within society, social class and economic and political systems, are explored. The authors consider the differences to fall more within the class perspective and analyse this approach in detail.

310 Social class in New Zealand.
Edited by David Pitt.   Auckland: Longman Paul, 1977. 139p. bibliog. (Studies of Small Societies).

This collection of essays sets out to explore 'the official and intellectual ideology that New Zealand is, was, and should be, an egalitarian society, and certainly that there is little poverty' (Introduction). The contributors, all academics, conclude, however, that this prevailing ideology is largely a myth, and that social differentiation does exist in New Zealand. They present evidence suggesting an increasing polarization of classes, this being linked closely to the socio-economic structure.

Occupations and income distribution

311 Income distribution in New Zealand.
Brian Easton. Wellington: New Zealand Institute for Economic Research, 1983. 281p.

Utilizing all statistical information available to 1980, the author seeks to determine broad trends in New Zealand personal income distribution for the post-Second World War decades. His unexpected finding, with caveats, is that inequalities were, in fact, lessening. Subsequent work by the same author clearly demonstrates that the trend has now been reversed. See the chapter by B. Easton in B. Silverstone, A. Bollard and R. Lattimore's *A study of economic reform: the case of New Zealand* (q.v.).

312 The rich: a New Zealand history.
Stevan Eldred-Grigg. Auckland: Penguin, 1996. 266p.

Using examples from the wool barons of the 19th century through to the finance capitalists of the late 1980s, the author explores the development of a wealthy elite in New Zealand society. No bibliography is provided but the wide range of sources used (from scholarly works to material from the gossip writer Felicity Ferret) is indicated in the acknowledgements. The lively writing style makes this a work to enjoy as much as to learn from. With such a broad coverage, the work inevitably lacks depth, and displays both insights and prejudices.

313 Who gets what?: the distribution of income and wealth in New Zealand.
Income Distribution Group, New Zealand Planning Council.
Wellington: New Zealand Planning Council, 1990. 158p.

A snapshot of the distribution of wealth and income in New Zealand for the year ended March 1988; by gender, race, age and family type. The report's conclusion is that income became less equally distributed among New Zealand households during the late 1980s, and that this was directly linked to a reduction in paid employment opportunities. The report also found that a larger proportion of Maori households than of all households was in the lower income bracket, and that a gap between male and female incomes persisted. 'Whether income is considered to be distributed fairly, or unfairly, is a matter for community judgement' (p. 128).

314 Work in New Zealand: a portrait in the '80s.
Roy McLennan, David Gilbertson. Wellington: Reed, 1984. 303p.

The compilers perceived 'a need to understand what the work and days of contemporary New Zealanders are like' (p. 1). Over 130 interviews were conducted over several years with citizens from all walks of life. Fifty are presented in this book. Selection was on the basis of the kind of work people do, where they do it, their sex and ethnicity, and the particular story each has to tell. While the 'microbiographies' are of varying interest, it is unfortunate that no generalizations are attempted.

Families

315 **A question of adoption: closed stranger adoption, 1944-1974.**
Anne Else. Wellington: Bridget Williams Books, 1991. 241p.
bibliog.

Commencing with a brief historical background, the author examines the decades in New Zealand history in which closed adoption (where neither party has knowledge of, or contact with, the other) was most widespread. Drawing on contemporary material but also influential international books and articles, and through interviewing Child Welfare officers for unwritten practices, the author examines sympathetically the issues surrounding this type of adoption.

316 **Common purse.**
Robin Fleming, in association with Julia Taiapa, Anna Pasikale, Susan Kell Easting. Wellington: Bridget Williams Books, 1997. 160p.

An exploration of the allocation of money within family households in New Zealand, focusing on ethnic and gender differences in the access of individual family members to family money. The book discusses issues such as different banking arrangements, control of the family budget, access to money for personal spending, the costs of participating in *whanau* or Pacific Island communities and the way major spending decisions are made. The work opens up the debate about some fast-changing social structures and makes a particular contribution to cross-cultural research in New Zealand.

317 **Mum's the word: the untold story of motherhood in New Zealand.**
Sue Kedgley. Auckland: Random House, 1996. 359p.

'A popular history which outlines the changes that have taken place in the ideology and practice of motherhood over the past century, and the theories of motherhood that have gone in and out of fashion, as a background to better understanding motherhood today' (Introduction). This is a lively and compelling account of motherhood in New Zealand from 1880 to 1996. A wide range of sources has been consulted and the result is a very readable compendium on a subject that has not hitherto received a great deal of attention. It considers traditions, influences and changes in areas relating to motherhood for Pakeha women. The author expresses her regret that she was unable to find a Maori writer to work on the research that had been undertaken on Maori women.

318 **Families in New Zealand society.**
Edited by Peggy G. Koopman-Boyden. Wellington: Methuen, 1978.
184p.

This remains an important collection of essays on the family in New Zealand. A number of the essays are intentionally historical, and others that were not originally intended to be, have become so with the passage of time. In many respects the book has become a reference point for other studies. Chapters on Maori and Samoan families ensure that multiple dimensions of New Zealand society are recognized. References to aid further exploration of the issues are appended to each chapter.

319 **Divorce in New Zealand: a social history.**
Roderick Phillips. Auckland: Oxford University Press, 1981. 154p. bibliog.

'It is the aim of this book to provide a broad historical overview of divorce in New Zealand, partly because such a survey is of considerable social and historical interest in its own right, partly to facilitate a more comprehensive appreciation of divorce in modern New Zealand' (Introduction). The author argues that, while divorce rates continue to rise, and while legal frameworks for the dissolution of marriage have become less judgemental, attitudes towards divorce remain rooted in historical experience.

320 **The next generation: child rearing in New Zealand.**
Jane Ritchie, James Ritchie. Auckland: Penguin, 1997. 248p.

The authors' earlier study, *Growing up in New Zealand* (Sydney: Allen & Unwin, 1978. 212p.) has become a classic in its field. This work builds on the research begun some forty years ago and looks at similarities and changes in patterns of child rearing over the intervening years. Sometimes controversial in their approach, the authors are particularly critical that physical punishment is still commonplace. Their work is extended in a companion volume, *The dangerous age: surviving adolescence in New Zealand* (Sydney; Wellington: Allen & Unwin/Port Nicholson Press, 1984. 157p.).

321 **A history of children's play: New Zealand 1840-1950.**
Brian Sutton-Smith. Wellington: New Zealand Council for Educational Research, 1982. 331p. maps.

Based on a thesis presented in 1950, this book comprehensively surveys the nature of children's play, organized and spontaneous, at home and at school, from the beginnings of European settlement. The author suggests that the advent of state schooling in the 1870s brought increasing formalization and control, and that there has been even greater organization in the 20th century. In an epilogue, bringing the coverage up to the 1980s, he expands his argument that children's play and games may help illustrate important lines in contemporary history.

322 **The best years of your life: a history of New Zealand childhood.**
Mary Trewby. Auckland: Viking, 1995. 176p.

More an album with accompanying text than a social history, this book records many memories, some affectionate, others less so. The progression from babyhood to adolescence is captured in over 250 photographs, most of 20th-century origin. Play at home and school, domestic chores, holidays, food, clothes – all have their place.

Communities

323 Tokoroa: creating a community.
D. L. Chapple.   Auckland: Longman Paul, 1976. 160p. maps. bibliog. (Studies of Small Societies).

Tokoroa represents a particular kind of New Zealand community, a company town created to serve the needs of industry, in this instance forestry. It is synthetic and isolated from traditional urban New Zealand. Chapple looks at problems the new residents face – housing, welfare, community services and cultural differences – and outlines those features which make Tokoroa a unique community, as well as those which make it similar to other new towns faced with rapid change and industrialization.

324 Community formation and change: a study of rural and urban localities in New Zealand.
Bob Hall.   Christchurch: Department of Sociology, University of Canterbury, 1983. 216p. maps.

A comparative study of the development of rural and urban communities based on fieldwork in widely varying localities. In each instance the fieldwork has been preceded by extensive documentary research and particular emphasis has been placed on land ownership issues. 'Our aim is to understand the historical pattern of community in a number of different localities in New Zealand' (Introduction). Overtly academic, the emphasis on the historical has produced some interesting vignettes.

325 Johnsonville: continuity and change in a New Zealand township.
David G. Pearson.   Sydney: Allen & Unwin, 1980. 204p. maps. bibliog.

'This book is based on a local study of a contemporary New Zealand suburb, Johnsonville, which has emerged from a small-town history which extends back to the earliest days of European settlement' (Introduction). The objective is to show the social evolution which inevitably occurs when a community is subject to rapid and ongoing changes, and from this to develop a model. The approach is thematic – 'Bush clearing to suburbia', 'The contemporary scene', 'Property and inequality', 'Local politics and participation', 'Class, community and change' – and, where appropriate, historical data is juxtaposed with the present reality.

326 Littledene: patterns of change.
H. C. D. Somerset.   Wellington: New Zealand Council for Educational Research, 1974. enlarged ed. of 1938 ed. 224p. bibliog. (NZCER Research Series, no. 51).

The original *Littledene* was published in 1938 (Wellington: New Zealand Council for Educational Research); combining imagination with research, it has become a New Zealand sociological classic. This edition includes 'Littledene revisited', a work written twenty years after the first. The combined work presents an unrivalled study of a rural New Zealand community, its composition and nature, and its relationship with the rest of society. Included in the volume are charming and apposite illustrations.

A vision betrayed: the decline of democracy in new Zealand.
See item no. 8.

A southern gentry: New Zealanders who inherited the earth.
See item no. 115.

The forgotten worker: the rural wage earner in nineteenth century New Zealand.
See item no. 120.

Colonial sweat and tears: the working class in nineteenth century New Zealand.
See item no. 121.

New Zealand working people, 1890-1990.
See item no. 125.

Building the New World: work, politics and society in Caversham, 1880s-1920s.
See item no. 180.

New growth from old: the whanau in the modern world.
See item no. 334.

The family and government policy in New Zealand.
See item no. 378.

Incomes policy in New Zealand.
See item no. 609.

False economy: New Zealanders face the conflict between paid and unpaid work.
See item no. 616.

New Zealand Sociology.
See item no. 910.

Contemporary Maori Society

327 Tikanga whakaaro: key concepts in Maori culture.
Cleve Barlow. Auckland: Oxford University Press, 1991. 187p.
Words like *aroha* (love), *mana* (prestige) and *tapu* (sacred, forbidden, taboo) are familiar to most New Zealanders, but what do they really mean? This book provides explanations in English and Maori of seventy terms which are important in Maori culture. Each term is clearly defined, and its significance explained with reference to tradition, custom, myth and ritual, as well as present-day understanding. 'I have selected concepts that I feel are important for understanding Maori culture as it is practised today, and concepts which are likely to be relevant in the future' (Preface). The author, an anthropologist of Nga Puhi descent, has published papers in linguistics and cognitive psychology.

328 Kotahitanga: the search for Maori political unity.
Lindsay Cox. Auckland: Oxford University Press, 1993. 238p. maps.
Since the onset of European colonization there has been a continuing search by Maori for unity, manifested in a series of religious, political and social movements. By examining these movements, seeking common threads and differences, the author provides background to the developing notion of collective Maori sovereignty. There is extended discussion of the origins, structure and goals of the most recent movement, the National Maori Congress, founded in 1990.

329 Maori: the crisis and the challenge.
Alan Duff. Auckland: Harper Collins Publishers NZ, 1993. 122p.
A forthright author, noted for his powerful novels, looks at the issues facing Maori. He concentrates particularly on the tensions between a crisis of under-performance and the challenge to overcome this. Duff analyses the problems, as he sees them, which face his people and lead them to crime; at the same time he questions why Maori do not take advantage of educational opportunities. The work was regarded as controversial by both Maori and Pakeha.

330 **Maori land tenure: studies of a changing institution.**
I. H. Kawharu. Oxford: Clarendon Press, 1991. 363p. maps. bibliog.
From the first settlement of New Zealand, land has been a source of identity and purpose for Maori. The author, both a distinguished scholar and a tribal leader, first discusses the traditional tenure system, then traces how the system has been eroded in the past 150 years, with consequent major land losses. The greater part of the book, however, is devoted to the administration of Maori land in the 20th century. 'So long as the Maori retains an interest in the residue of his patrimony so long will that be a determinant of some part of his social life' (Preface). A short supplementary survey is George Asher and David Naulls's *Maori land* (Wellington: New Zealand Planning Council, 1987. 96p. Planning Paper no. 29).

331 **Te ao hurihuri: aspects of Maoritanga.**
Edited by Michael King. Auckland: Reed, 1992. rev. ed. 191p.
The original edition (1975) was conceived to 'convey information and feeling about the way in which Maori . . . relate to one another and to the places in which they live and meet'. Apart from the editor, all contributors were Maori. The present volume contains the principal essays, plus those from a sequel *Tihe mauri ora: aspects of Maoritanga* (Wellington: Methuen New Zealand, 1978. 111p.). Topics covered include: the language and protocol of the *marae* (formal meeting place); Maori views of land; death; Maori religious movements; *kingitanga* (kingship); and the relevance of Maori myth and religion. The essays, as proven, are of enduring value.

332 **Landmarks, bridges and visions: aspects of Maori culture: essays.**
Sydney Moko Mead. Wellington: Victoria University Press, 1997. 266p. maps.
A collection of essays, articles and speeches written over the last thirty years, a time of tumultuous change for Maori and the New Zealand nation as a whole. While the topics are wide-ranging, the central concern is always the importance of Maori language and education in fostering a living tradition and promoting social and political change. The author, foundation Professor of Maori Studies at Victoria University, Wellington, asks some hard questions: whether Maori have been too willing to go along with whatever paid officials advise; whether Maori are so colonized in their thinking that they can no longer think for themselves; or whether they are now awakening from a long sleep on a soft assimilated bed.

333 **Maori sovereignty: the Maori perspective.**
Edited by Hineani Melbourne. Auckland: Hodder Moa Beckett, 1995. 187p.
While Maori sovereignty is a confusing, and often disturbing, concept for many New Zealanders, there is growing consensus amongst Maori that they should control their own affairs and resources. In this book, seventeen Maori from diverse backgrounds and differing political persuasions share their views of Maori aspirations in the mid-1990s. There are indications that some of these aspirations are being realized, and that the changes may benefit not only Maori communities but also the wider population of New Zealand. Pakeha (European) views, by no means all sympathetic, are set out in a companion volume, Carol Archie's *Maori sovereignty: the Pakeha perspective* (Wellington: Hodder Moa Beckett, 1995. 189p.).

334 New growth from old: the whanau in the modern world.

Joan Metge. Wellington: Victoria University Press, 1995. 342p. bibliog.

For most of the past 150 years policies and laws relating to the family and the care and protection of children were based on European practice, Maori forms and practices being either attacked or ignored. Since the late 1970s, however, there have been significant changes, the existence of *whanau* (or extended families) being officially recognized. 'There is an urgent need for a knowledge base about Maori family forms that is broader, better grounded and more accessible' (Preface). The author also intends the book as a contribution to the debate about the causes of current problems affecting Maori families, and she suggests strategies for handling such problems more effectively.

335 Hui: a study of Maori ceremonial gatherings.

Anne Salmond. Auckland: Reed Methuen, 1987. rev. ed. 226p. maps.

A *hui* is a ceremonial gathering on the *marae* (formal meeting place) and 'it is in this context that *Maoritanga* (Maori culture) is most deeply expressed . . . The aim of this study is to give a full portrait of the *hui*; not only its rituals, but its background, setting and staging as well' (Introduction). Throughout the *hui* Maori is the ceremonial language, Maori people dominate, Maori food is eaten, and Maori rituals are practised. Occasions include birthdays, weddings, funerals, unveilings of tombstones, tribal gatherings and meetings of Maori organizations. The work is based on two years field-work on North Island *marae*.

336 Te marae: a guide to customs and protocol.

Hiwi Tauroa, Pat Tauroa. Auckland: Reed, 1993. 2nd ed. 168p.

'This is the *marae*. It is not just a place where people meet. It is the family home of generations that have gone before' (p. 19). But how many New Zealanders know what they should or should not do when invited to a *marae*? 'In order to prevent personal embarrassment and to avoid insulting one's host by saying or doing the wrong thing, it is necessary that a visitor know something of the basic ritual and procedures of a *marae*' (Introduction). This is a straightforward introduction to Maori protocol for Pakehas.

337 Nga pepa a Ranginui = The Walker papers.

Ranginui Walker. Auckland: Penguin, 1996. 215p.

A collection of media columns and lectures by one of the most prolific Maori writers on issues affecting Maori and Pakeha today. All drawn from his work over the past decade, the pieces retain their topicality. Most of the issues canvassed – Maori inter-generational tensions, Treaty of Waitangi settlements, education and power, intellectual property and 'cultural safety' – remain close to the headlines. An earlier collection is *Nga tau tohetohe = Years of anger* (Wellington: Penguin, 1987. 239p.).

Whaiora: Maori health development.

See item no. 388.

Maori political perspectives: he whakaaro Maori mo nga to kanga kawanatanga.

See item no. 426.

Maori, Pakeha and democracy.
See item no. 441.

Justice, ethics and New Zealand society.
See item no. 442.

Justice and identity: antipodean practices.
See item no. 444.

Return to sender: what really happened at the fiscal envelope hui.
See item no. 460.

Justice and the Maori: Maori claims in New Zealand political argument in the 1980s.
See item no. 468.

Te hurihanga o te ao Maori: te ahua o te iwi Maori kua whakatatautia. A statistical profile of change in Maori society since the 1950s.
See item no. 633.

He paepae korero: research perspectives in Maori education.
See item no. 669.

He Pukenga Korero: A Journal of Maori Studies.
See item no. 879.

Takoa 1996: te aka kumara o Aotearoa = Directory of Maori organisations & resource people.
See item no. 946.

Social Issues

General

338 **The decent society? Essays in response to National's economic and social policies.**
Edited by Jonathan Boston, Paul Dalziel.   Auckland: Oxford University Press, 1992. 226p.

The title borrows from the National Party's 1990 election campaign slogan, 'Creating a decent society', and the essays are built around the perception that 'the economic and social policies pursued by National during its first year in office seem inconsistent with what most people regard as a "decent", "good" or "fair" society' (Introduction). The various contributors, all academic, outline the policy changes and critically assess their strengths and weaknesses.

339 **Studies in New Zealand social problems.**
Edited by Paul F. Green.   Palmerston North, New Zealand: Dunmore Press, 1994. 2nd ed. 366p.

A collection of short studies focusing on problems such as inequality, sexism, racism, violence, deviance and substance abuse. The problems discussed include not only those issues or current controversies that negatively affect most members of society, but also issues where future problems may be anticipated. 'Each study considers the interaction of economic structures, power relations, and the role of ideology in defining, analysing and remedying persistent social problems' (cover). The tone is academic.

340 **New Zealand in crisis: a debate about today's critical issues.**
Edited by David Novitz, Bill Willmott.   Wellington: GP Publications, 1992. 254p.

An innovative attempt to inform on major issues facing New Zealand. In each case two essays conveying different viewpoints are presented, followed by commentary intended to point up gaps in the arguments. Topics covered include sovereignty, nationhood, peace and war, government, the workforce, race, education, justice and the family. 'The aim in the end, is to increase rational public debate, not diminish it' (Introduction). The book suffers from the fact that some of the proposed chapters were not written, thus reducing the coverage and leaving some noticeable gaps, for instance, on the subjects of the role of the state and of gender.

341　**The tragedy of the market: a social experiment in New Zealand.**
　　　Mike O'Brien, Chris Wilkes.　Palmerston North, New Zealand:
　　　Dunmore Press, 1993. 201p.

'The purpose of this book is to make an assessment of the fourth Labour Government and the social experiment in monetary economics which it introduced between 1984 and 1990 . . . by drawing on the imagery of a famous debate in sociology concerning radical changes in the economics of advanced societies, the movement from Fordism [mass production, full employment, high growth, equity-directed society] to post Fordism [niche production, high unemployment, low growth, hierarchical society]' (p. 9). The authors see the focus on 'the market' as a vehicle for delivering economic and social objectives as a tragedy.

Unemployment and poverty

342　**Wages and the poor.**
　　　Brian Easton.　Wellington: Unwin Publications/Port Nicholson Press,
　　　1986. 100p.

Advancing the proposition that the poor of New Zealand can be found amongst wage earners, the author first seeks to define poverty as it can be understood in New Zealand. From this base, he then considers the issue from several perspectives, utilizing survey material. 'The final chapter outlines a taxation benefit and social service reform to modify wages [which would allow] the highest level of employment, [and] ensure incomes that are adequate for today's poor' (Introduction). This is an important work in that it highlights a problem that is often hidden.

343　**Unemployment in New Zealand.**
　　　Ian Shirley, Brian Easton et al.　Palmerston North, New Zealand:
　　　Dunmore Press, 1990. 191p.

Prepared by a research team based in the Social Policy Research Centre, Massey University, Palmerston North, this report examines the New Zealand employment experience since the Second World War, the underlying causes of present-day unemployment, the nature and extent of unemployment, and unemployment's economic and social implications. Official explanations of the problem are exposed to critical scrutiny. 'Although there is no easy way out of the current unemployment crisis, the predicament . . . can be attributed . . . to the absence of an employment policy, and the fact that full employment is no longer the major objective of social and economic policy' (p. 169).

344   **Poor New Zealand: an open letter on poverty.**
Charles Waldegrave, Rosalynn Coventry.   Wellington: Platform
Publishing, 1987. 158p.

At the time this polemic was published it attracted considerable professional and media attention both in praise of the authors' attempt to bring out into the open an aspect of society that was considered by many to be hidden, and in condemnation of the approach taken by the work. Nevertheless, the work fulfilled a purpose in encouraging and inspiring debate. It is illustrated by the well-known cartoonist, Tom Scott.

Gender relations

345   **Growing up gay: New Zealand men tell their stories.**
Edited by James Allan.   Auckland: Godwit, 1996. 192p.

Twelve gay men talk to the author about their lives, the problems they have encountered and how they have solved them. The voices of the men interviewed come through clearly, although the introduction makes it clear that careful editing has been required to bring these stories to the public. The story behind the book, as presented in the Preface, is also of interest.

346   **Out front: lesbian political activity in Aotearoa, 1962 to 1985.**
Julie Glamuzina, edited and designed by Jenny Rankine.   Hamilton,
New Zealand: Lesbian Press, 1993. 76p.

The author states, 'I decided to put this booklet together because I wanted to start recording some of the political activities of lesbians in Aotearoa since the 1960s'. This short work is based on written documentation and the information is presented chronologically as summaries of the activity that occurred year by year through to 1985.

347   **Gender, culture and power: challenging New Zealand's gendered culture.**
Bev James, Kay Saville-Smith.   Auckland: Oxford University Press,
1994. 120p. (Critical Issues in New Zealand Society).

The authors 'explore the notion that New Zealand is a "gendered culture", a culture in which the structures of masculinity and femininity are central to the formation of society as a whole' (Introduction). In taking this view they state that they are not regarding sex inequalities as paramount but that 'the gendered culture should be challenged because it enables hierarchies of sex, race, and class to be maintained' (Introduction). Issues explored include: 'Race, class and sex: land and the struggle for power'; 'Creating a gendered culture'; 'The contemporary practice of masculinity and femininity'; 'The costs of a gendered culture'; 'Vested interests in a gendered culture'; and 'Contesting a gendered culture'.

348　The sexual wilderness: men and women in New Zealand.
Sue Kedgley.　Auckland: Reed Methuen, 1985. 122p.

Twelve men and twelve women are interviewed in an attempt to explore the changes
that occurred in male/female relationships over the fifteen years between 1970 and
1985. Although further changes have undoubtedly occurred since the book was written, it nevertheless provides a snapshot in time. Not all the women interviewed are
feminists.

349　One of the boys?: changing views of masculinity in New Zealand.
Edited by Michael King.　Auckland: Heinemann, 1988. 255p.

The editor writes, 'I have not been concerned solely with aspects of masculinity that
lead to "problems" . . . I am interested equally in what makes people good, responsible, integrated human beings and in the processes of change which some men have
instituted in their lives to bring about such a result'. A selection of well-known New
Zealand men write about what being male means for them, and about the influences on
their development. The book provides an interesting counterpart to the works on
women and is notable in that all of the writers are identifiable. An historical overview
of similar issues is Jock Phillips's *A man's country?: the image of the pakeha male, a
history* (Auckland: Penguin, 1996. rev. ed. 321p.).

350　Minding children, managing men: conflict and compromise in the
lives of postwar Pakeha women.
Helen May.　Wellington: Bridget Williams Books, 1992. 371p.

In this study of two generations of Pakeha (European) women, those born at the end of
the First World War and those at the end of the Second World War, the author examines the ways in which sample groups ordered their lives and relationships as mothers,
as workers and with men. Drawing on interviews and contemporary media commentary, she considers the expectations and experiences that have defined women's views
on motherhood, child rearing and sexual equality.

Race relations

351　Proud to be white?: a survey of Pakeha prejudice in New Zealand.
Angela Ballara.　Auckland: Heinemann, 1986. 205p.

The book examines the nature and development of ethnocentric prejudice as displayed
by European New Zealanders, especially towards Maori. It traces its presence through
colonial history to the 1980s, principally through quotations from publications.
Provocative, often strident, the work provides a sobering counterbalance to the notion
that New Zealand has enjoyed model race relations.

352 **Talking past each other: problems of cross-cultural communication.**
Joan Metge, Patricia Kinloch. Wellington: Victoria University Press/Price Milburn, 1978. 56p. bibliog.

A paper presented to the New Zealand OECD (Organization for Economic Co-operation and Development) conference on Early Childhood Care and Education, February 1978. 'We hope that increased awareness of the possibility of cultural differences will, first, help improve communication between Pakehas, Maoris and Samoans involved in formal and informal encounters and co-operation, and secondly enable them to act to reduce the conflict between the communication codes presented to children, at home and outside institutions' (p. 41).

353 **A dream deferred: the origins of ethnic conflict in New Zealand.**
D. G. Pearson. Wellington: Allen & Unwin/Port Nicholson Press, 1990. 301p. bibliog.

After establishing a theoretical framework, the author, a sociologist, sets out to explain the historical foundations of relations between the major ethnic groups in New Zealand: Maori and European, Pacific Islanders and those of Asiatic ancestry. Two themes are the ways in which dominant groups have maintained their advantage, and the strategies adopted by ethnic minorities to redress the balance. The new wave of Maori assertiveness since the 1960s, and the responses of Europeans and other ethnic groups, are also examined.

354 **Nga Patai: racism and ethnic relations in New Zealand.**
Edited by Paul Spoonley, David Pearson, Cluny MacPherson. Palmerston North, New Zealand: Dunmore Press, 1996. 300p.

The third in a series which began in 1984, the two predecessors being *Tauiwi: racism and ethnicity in New Zealand* (Palmerston North, New Zealand: Dunmore Press, 1984. 250p.) and *Nga Take: ethnic relations and racism in Aotearoa/New Zealand* (Palmerston North, New Zealand: Dunmore Press, 1991. 218p.). This volume examines social issues (migration, the new assertiveness of Maori, sovereignty questions, and the ownership of New Zealand resources) in the 1990s and links these to racism and ethnic relations. The essays are clustered around three general headings: 'Migration, political economy and racialisation'; 'The politics of difference'; and 'Institutional policies and options'. The three volumes open up these issues for debate.

355 **The politics of nostalgia: racism and the extreme right in New Zealand.**
Paul Spoonley. Palmerston North, New Zealand: Dunmore Press, 1987. 318p.

Academic in approach, this work arises out of research undertaken by the author for his doctoral thesis. The book records the growth of groups that offer racist arguments in the public arena, 'the forms they have taken and their different belief systems, and has attempted to explain why this growth has taken place' (Introduction). The study provides a different perspective on the land of milk and honey, and includes comparisons between the experiences of New Zealand, Australia, the United Kingdom and Canada.

Moral concerns

356 **Working girls: women in the New Zealand sex industry talk to Jan Jordan.**
Jan Jordan. Auckland: Penguin, 1991. 275p.

A Wellington criminologist talks to seventeen workers in the New Zealand sex industry. The informants describe how they entered the industry, how they cope with the pressures, their dealings with police, perceived health dangers and their personal relationships. The accounts challenge many popular stereotypes about women who enter the industry.

357 **A stand for decency: Patricia Bartlett and the Society for the Promotion of Community Standards, 1970-1995.**
Carolyn Moynihan. Wellington: The Society, 1995. 216p.

An overtly sympathetic account of New Zealand's most visible late 20th-century morals campaigner, and of the organization she fronted for more than two decades. Their collective targets were many: pornography, abortion, the dissemination of contraception information to the young, and homosexual law reform. Admired by her supporters, loathed by others, Bartlett secured the grudging respect of many for the tenacity with which she advanced her views, if not for the views themselves.

358 **The right to live: the abortion battle of New Zealand.**
Marilyn Pryor. Auckland: Harlen Books, 1986. 303p.

Appointed National Executive Officer of the Society for the Protection of the Unborn Child (SPUC) in 1975, the author worked full-time for the Society in various capacities, including as President, until 1982. Here she sets out her views on abortion and details the Society's implacable opposition to abortion law reform. For an alternative view see Erich Geiringer's *Spuc 'em all* (Waiura, New Zealand: A. Taylor, 1978. 109p.).

359 **The great brain robbery.**
Tom Scott, Trevor Grice. Wellington: The Public Trust, 1996. 112p.

Scott, well-known satirical cartoonist, combines efforts with the national director of the Life Education Trust to produce a straightforward, clearly presented, and hard-hitting description of the effect of drugs on the human brain. Although aimed at teenagers, this is, equally, a good general introduction to the subject for adults. A number of moving personal stories lend impact.

360 **New Zealand green: the story of marijuana in New Zealand.**
Redmer Yska. Auckland: David Bateman, 1990. 184p. bibliog.

'This book tells of a century of marijuana use and abuse in New Zealand; how it continues to unite users and divide society' (cover). Sources included Police, Customs and Health Department records, newspaper files and published works. Yska offers a serious consideration of the subject which shows that marijuana has been part of the New Zealand way of life since at least 1880 when it was routinely used as a medicine.

Crime and violence

361   Straight to the point: angles on giving up crime.
Julie Liebrich.   Dunedin: University of Otago Press/Department of
Justice, 1993. 310p.

The author regards desistance from crime as a neglected area of research. To remedy
this situation she interviewed forty-eight randomly selected former offenders who had
not reoffended over the preceding three years. The work presents them as ordinary
men and women. 'Above all the decision to go straight is a personal one. It cannot be
imposed' (Preface). The Epilogue sums up the difficulties of this type of research: 'the
study, by its very design, is open to many interpretations' (p. 240).

362   Crime and deviance.
Greg Newbold.   Auckland: Oxford University Press, 1992. 158p.

According to the author, social, economic and political changes over the last thirty
years must provide a context for the major changes not only in crime, but in patterns
of behaviour, such as homosexuality and gang membership. He considers the issues
under a number of headings: Property crime, Women and deviance, Sexual deviance,
Violence, Drugs, Crime, Control and Inequality. This work contributes to the available
information in the area by bringing together facts and statistics from a variety of scattered sources.

363   Punishment and politics: the maximum security prison in New
Zealand.
Greg Newbold.   Auckland: Oxford University Press, 1989. 310p.
bibliog.

From his first-hand knowledge of the prison system, the author, now a lecturer in sociology, studies the history of prison security in New Zealand. He writes with three
objectives in mind: firstly, to set out the historical context, with particular emphasis on
the events of the past forty years; secondly, to set these events into a social context;
and thirdly, to comment on international similarities and disparities. Often blunt in his
assessments, the author presents a prison system in crisis. While suggesting remedies
for the future, he acknowledges that this is a difficult area in which to predict changes
with any degree of accuracy.

364   Staunch: inside New Zealand's gangs.
Bill Payne.   Auckland: Reed, 1997. new ed. 156p.

What is the significance of the gang to its members? The author attempts to answer
this question through his association with a number of gangs throughout New Zealand,
providing a rounded picture of gang life. The image he presents is more perceptive
than the usual fearsome image held by most New Zealanders. The volume is well supported by oral interviews and photographs.

365 **Violence in New Zealand.**
Jane Ritchie, James Ritchie. Wellington: Huia Publishers/Dorothy
Brasell Associates Press, 1993. 2nd ed. 189p.

Examines violence from the viewpoint that it is a part of the cultural conditioning that surrounds each individual. This is a disturbing and somewhat pessimistic work, which nevertheless takes a frank look at a difficult subject. The authors argue that social mores must change before violence can be dealt with adequately.

Her work and his: family, kin and community in New Zealand, 1900-1930.
See item no. 131.

A new Maori migration: rural and urban relations in northern New Zealand.
See item no. 218.

A show of justice: racial 'amalgamation' in nineteenth century New Zealand.
See item no. 220.

Social Services, Health and Welfare

General

366 **Social policy in Aotearoa/New Zealand: a critical introduction.**
Christine Cheyne, Mike O'Brien, Michael Belgrave. Auckland:
Auckland University Press, 1997. 282p.

From the mid-1980s there has been a rapid and radical redesign of social policy in New Zealand, this having major impacts on the community. 'A key feature of this book is an emphasis on bringing together theoretical and conceptual frameworks for understanding social policy . . . and linking these with the activity of policy analysis' (Preface). The book also identifies the values and perspectives that continue to influence policy proposals and how they are implemented. Illustrative examples include the recognition of indigenous entitlements, the shift from social security to income support, social services for children and families, and health policy reform.

367 **Social work in action.**
Edited by Robyn Munford, Mary Nash. Palmerston North, New
Zealand: Dunmore Press, 1994. 446p.

Social work in New Zealand is in a state of flux, statutory social service agencies being restructured and the tasks and goals of social services being redefined. After providing background on the development of social work as a profession, the book seeks to illustrate the diverse range of contemporary social work practice through case-studies. There are chapters on social work practice with families, women, the disabled and the elderly, as well as survivors of violence and abuse.

368 **In the public interest: health, work and housing in New Zealand society.**
Edited by Chris Wilkes, Ian Shirley. Auckland: Benton Ross, 1984. 307p.

Published just prior to the onset of New Zealand's radical reform programme, this book highlights three social policy areas already of concern. 'State action in the public interest . . . implies a form of intervention taken on behalf of the whole community whereas action on behalf of a private interest implies that certain sections of society will benefit, but that equally other groups will suffer as a consequence' (Introduction). The conflict between private and public interests in health, work and housing is examined, while there are chapters on the history of policy developments and the effect of state activity (or lack of it) on the consumer.

Welfare state

369 **The working class and welfare: reflections on the development of the welfare state in Australia and New Zealand, 1890-1980.**
Francis G. Castles. Wellington: Allen & Unwin/Port Nicholson Press, 1985. 128p.

This study explores the political development of social policy in both Australia and New Zealand in the period 1880-1980. 'Today, in both Australia and New Zealand, there is much discussion of welfare issues – of the desirability and costs of superannuation, of the equity of a system still heavily imbued with the ethos of selectivity and of the continuing problem of poverty in the midst of plenty' (p. xii). The author argues that such issues can only be comprehended fully against the background of the historical development of social policy practice in these countries.

370 **Social policy and the welfare state.**
Brian Easton. Auckland: Allen & Unwin, 1980. 182p.

By the early 1980s the welfare state in New Zealand was under strain. The author attempts to explain 'the idea of the welfare state', the reasons for its existence and its mode of functioning. He remains strongly supportive. 'The welfare state has been a community response to historical change. To go against this historical thrust would be to abandon New Zealand as a community' (p. 177).

371 **From welfare state to civil society: towards welfare that works in New Zealand.**
David G. Green. Wellington: New Zealand Business Roundtable, 1996. 228p.

More a polemic than a researched and reasoned discussion, this book sets out a New Right agenda for reform of New Zealand's benefit system, health care and education. Responsibility for most of the country's social ills is attributed to the welfare state. 'The principle underlying the proposals advocated . . . is that individuals should accept responsibility for their own upkeep, wherever possible' (p. 199).

372 Social policy.
Pat Shannon. Auckland: Oxford University Press, 1991. 117p.
(Critical Issues in New Zealand Society).

An analysis of recent developments in social policy in New Zealand, this book takes a hard look at the welfare state, using the criterion of 'social well-being' developed by the 1988 Royal Commission on Social Policy, both from the point of view of the kinds of help provided, and its effects on those who receive it. The author concludes that all policy development is part of a continuing struggle over the distribution of resources, and that only when the consumers of policy – ordinary people – can control its development and implementation will the goal of social well-being be achieved.

373 Selfish generations?: the ageing of New Zealand's welfare state.
David Thomson. Wellington: Bridget Williams Books, 1991. 233p.

This book examines the theory that the welfare state no longer benefits the young but is directed towards the old. The author contends that the 'selfish generation' has taken for itself and left little for today's children. At times controversial, the question that remains is 'Does such a welfare state have a future?'.

374 Social welfare and New Zealand society.
Edited by A. D. Trlin. Wellington: Methuen New Zealand, 1977. 235p. bibliog.

Rather than a definitive text, this work is a series of original essays on social welfare ideals, provisions and policies, implementation within the welfare state, and the effect on social organization in New Zealand. The contributors, many of whom are New Zealand academics of repute, examine the origin and development of welfare policies from the late 19th century to 1975. Particular emphasis is given to full employment, state housing and race relations. The essays vary in style and approach. W. H. Oliver's article, for example, 'The origins and growth of the welfare state', is not merely descriptive, but is evaluative. It would serve well those seeking a concise account of the welfare system in New Zealand before the Second World War.

Social services

375 Disability, family, whanau and society.
Keith Ballard. Palmerston North, New Zealand: Dunmore Press, 1994. 346p.

Maori and Pakeha parents, care-givers and researchers describe their experiences of disability, in particular intellectual disability, in present-day New Zealand. Around 12,000 people are reputed to be so disabled. Individuals who have an intellectual disability present their accounts of issues that impact on their lives. 'As the writers reflect on their lives and on their interactions with education, health and welfare agencies, two particular themes stand out: the oppressive effects of segregation and the liberating experience of integration and inclusion' (p. 12).

376 **Compensation for personal injury in New Zealand: its rise and fall.**
Ian B. Campbell. Auckland: Auckland University Press, 1996. 286p.
'The book looks at the three issues of compensation, prevention and rehabilitation and how the government's failure to address these issues has led to many of today's problems' (Introduction). A well-researched evaluation of the issues relating to accident compensation in New Zealand, this provides an historical background as well as critical commentary on the more recent developments in the field. The developments that have taken place in New Zealand since the original workers' compensation legislation of 1900 are documented and those that led to the Woodhouse Royal Commission of Inquiry 1967 and the subsequent accident compensation legislation are reviewed. The future of the New Zealand Accident Compensation Commission is now in question, its conversion to a contestable insurance scheme having been proposed.

377 **Building the New Zealand dream.**
Gael Ferguson. Palmerston North, New Zealand: Dunmore Press, 1994. 344p. bibliog.
Since the late 19th century, when New Zealand governments first provided cheap and easily accessible loan finance for the purchase of houses, state support for housing has been an intrinsic part of New Zealand life. Government promotion of the suburban family home reached its greatest heights in the early 1960s, when the state financed more than half of the houses being built annually. Since that time, however, support has been steadily withdrawn, with the idea of state involvement in the housing market being all but abandoned. The book provides a chronological history of housing policies in New Zealand and examines the effect these policies had on people and the environment.

378 **The family and government policy in New Zealand.**
P. G. Koopman-Boyden, C. D. Scott. Sydney: Allen & Unwin, 1984. 234p.
'Caring for the day-to-day physical and emotional needs of children including their education and socialisation is the shared responsibility of family, community and state.' The authors explore the issues arising out of this belief and conclude with some personal views on how to resolve the problems.

379 **New Zealand's ageing society: the implications.**
Edited by Peggy Koopman-Boyden. Wellington: Daphne Brasell Associates Press, 1993. 257p.
Contributions by ten experts in the field combine to provide a number of perspectives on the issues surrounding the welfare of the elderly in New Zealand. These include family, community support and superannuation, and address particular concerns for Maori and women. Extensive references are provided with each chapter. At a time when the elderly population of New Zealand is increasing the book is a timely assessment of the problems of dealing with an ageing population.

380 **Private pensions in New Zealand: can they avert the 'crisis'?**
Susan St John, Toni Ashton. Wellington: Institute of Policy Studies, 1993. 224p.

As the New Zealand population ages, the sustainability of state-funded superannuation has been questioned. The authors briefly review the historical background to 1987, then examine more recent policy changes. Possible future options are considered. 'An integrated mix of policies for private and public provision is desirable so that the elderly can be supported next century in a cost-effective way, consistent with economic conditions and fair shares for all citizens' (p. 6).

381 **Childcare in New Zealand: people, programmes, politics.**
Anne B. Smith, David A. Swain. Wellington: Allen & Unwin/Port Nicholson Press, 1988. 218p.

A developmental psychologist and a family sociologist combine expertise to look at the issues surrounding childcare in New Zealand. The book covers the need for childcare arrangements, the effect of childcare on children, administrative and policy background, family daycare and *nga kohanga reo* (Maori language nest), the role of the childcare worker, international comparisons and the future. The information provided remains as relevant in the 1990s as it was when the book was written.

Health

382 **New Zealand health policy: a comparative study.**
Robert H. Blank. Auckland: Oxford University Press, 1994. 166p.

This book attempts to put New Zealand's health policy in an international context, comparing New Zealand developments with those taking place in other countries, especially the United States. It discusses such trends as ageing populations and the diffusion of expensive medical technologies, together with such intractable issues as the problems of cost containment and difficult resource allocation and rationing policies. 'New Zealand policy makers . . . must be aware of the potential dangers as well as the presumed benefits of current changes' (p. ix). For another perspective on the role of the state in the practice of medicine and the market's association with medicine, see *The caring community: the provision of health care in New Zealand* by I. M. Hay (Auckland: Oxford University Press, 1989. 207p.) in which the author seeks to explain the changing relationships between providers and recipients.

383 **A healthy country: essays on the social history of medicine in New Zealand.**
Linda Bryder. Wellington: Bridget Williams Books, 1991. 252p.

This collection of essays examines the history of medicine and health care in New Zealand from the early days of settlement to the present day. 'It is not intended as a comprehensive study, but as an introduction to various aspects of that history.' The work centres on four particular areas: the medical and ancillary professions, hospitals, public health policies and women's health. Pointers to further information in each area are provided by the extensive references for each chapter.

384 **Second opinion: the politics of women's health in New Zealand.**
Phillida Bunkle. Auckland: Oxford University Press, 1988. 194p.

A collection of essays ranging from the polemical to the personal, touching on many women's health issues. Topics covered include the abortion debate, birth technologies, contraception and health, and cervical cancer. 'Together these essays form a kind of history of the women's health movement in New Zealand in recent years' (cover). The author, long a women's health activist, now an MP, is the New Zealand Alliance's spokesperson on health.

385 **For health or profit?: medicine, the pharmaceutical industry and the state in New Zealand.**
Edited by Peter Davis. Auckland: Oxford University Press, 1992. 298p.

A number of specialists in their field examine the role of the pharmaceutical industry in New Zealand, assessing whether the driving force for the industry is health or profit. As might be anticipated, the industry is found not to be a disinterested partner for the clinician. The conclusion is that the conventional medical model is deficient. Within the chapters of the book a number of institutional changes are canvassed.

386 **Intimate details and vital statistics: AIDS, sexuality and the social order in New Zealand.**
Edited by Peter Davis. Auckland: Auckland University Press, 1996. 234p.

This book offers a history of AIDS in New Zealand and sets out important research into the disease and into areas of social life that have previously been obscured by myth, taboo and legal prohibition. Contributors discuss the epidemic from the perspectives of the groups involved, and outline the responses of the New Zealand government and public. These have generally been panic-free, and characterized by the early mobilization of a preventative approach, together with substantial involvement of the gay community.

387 **Safeguarding the public health: a history of the New Zealand Department of Health.**
Derek A. Dow. Wellington: Victoria University Press/Ministry of Health/Historical Branch, Department of Internal Affairs, 1995. 302p. bibliog.

An authoritative overview of the evolution of New Zealand's public health system since 1840, focusing particularly on the work of the New Zealand Department of Public Health, which was established in 1900, and its successors, the Department of Health (1920) and the Ministry of Health (1993). While these institutions provide the organizational framework for the work, the author seeks to ensure a well-rounded picture is presented by including the contributions of individuals and other agencies. Well researched and written, the book contains many illustrations, including cartoons, to enliven the text.

388   **Whaiora: Maori health development.**
      Mason Durie.   Auckland: Oxford University Press, 1994. 238p.

This book is about Maori health (*whaiora*) development over the past 100 years, but
with particular emphasis on the decade 1984-94. 'My task has been to bring together
many strands and weave them into a *whariki,* a fabric, upon which rests the results of
all those early labours, the lost and recovered opportunities, and the tasks which
remain to be completed if future generations are to be strong and confident' (p. vii).
The author links changes in Maori leadership, political power and government health
policy. Using the twin standards of the Treaty of Waitangi and biculturalism he examines past policies, the recent health reforms, Maori health leadership, and the major
health problems currently facing Maori.

389   **Social dimensions of health and disease: New Zealand perspectives.**
      John Spicer, Andrew Trlin, JoAnn Walton.   Palmerston North, New
      Zealand: Dunmore Press, 1994. 368p.

Researchers, principally from the social sciences, show how social factors – cultural,
psychological, demographic, political – help define and explain health and disease.
'Theories and findings inform . . . such diverse aspects as: the determinants of ill
health; the processes by which health care is sought, provided and received; the paths
to recovery and rehabilitation; even the very nature of health itself' (p. 7).

New Zealand Medical Journal.
See item no. 906.

**Annotated bibliography for the history of medicine and health in New
Zealand.**
See item no. 953.

Religion

General

390 **Voices for justice: church law and state in New Zealand.**
Edited by Jonathan Boston, Alan Cameron. Palmerston North, New Zealand: Dunmore Press, 1994. 188p.

A collection of essays from a one-day symposium held at Victoria University of Wellington in 1993. 'The purpose of the symposium was to provide an opportunity for considered responses to the church leaders' *Social justice statement* issued in July of that year' (Preface). Academics, policy makers and those who were involved in drafting the statement were invited to the symposium. Five papers were presented with each having a respondent.

391 **Religion in New Zealand society.**
Brian Colless, Peter Donovan. Palmerston North, New Zealand: Dunmore Press, 1985. 2nd ed. 260p. bibliog.

A series of twelve essays by leading authorities studies the many influences that have had a bearing on the overall development of religious belief and practice as they now exist in New Zealand society. The collection deals with historical aspects, the contributions from Maori, Catholics, Protestants, the charismatic movement, sectarians, Jews, Indians, the Islamic community, the pluralist tendency and academics. It is 'a unique conflux of distilled waters of knowledge' (Introduction).

392 **Religions of New Zealanders.**
Edited by Peter Donovan. Palmerston North, New Zealand: Dunmore Press, 1996. 2nd ed. 277p.

The majority of the contributors to this work are academics connected with university departments of religious studies, but this is more than a purely academic exercise. A range of religions practised in New Zealand are studied. The chapter on the future, entitled 'Zeal and apathy', is a plea for tolerance. Well presented and arranged, the book can be dipped into or carefully read.

393 Bible and society: a sesquicentennial history of the Bible Society in New Zealand.
Peter J. Lineham.   Wellington: The Society/Daphne Brasell Associates Press, 1996. 320p.

A history published to mark the 150th anniversary of the Auckland Auxiliary of the British and Foreign Bible Society, established in Auckland in 1846. Other branches were later established in different parts of the country. As much a celebration of people as of the Society itself, this attractively produced and illustrated book also includes comment on wider social and religious issues. These range from 19th-century theological controversies over the authority of the Bible to reflections on its place in the 20th century.

394 Religion in New Zealand.
Edited by Christopher Nichol, James Veitch.   Wellington: Religious Studies Department/Victoria University of Wellington, 1983. 2nd ed. 313p.

Comprises essays prepared as a study resource for courses in religious studies, but which are of much wider interest. Despite the title, the focus is on Christianity. 'For many of us Christianity in New Zealand is so much a matter of fact, and for others so much a matter of history, that we are genuinely blind to its existence distinct and apart from ourselves . . . This series of essays may well help some to find out a little more about the club of which they are members, or as it may be, the club they have quit!' (Introduction). Part one, containing four essays, explores some of the strands which have been influential in moulding the particular direction New Zealand's religious history has taken. Part two contains other perspectives on Christianity as it was practised, or ignored, in New Zealand in the 1980s.

395 Faith in an age of turmoil: essays in honour of Lloyd Geering.
Edited by James Veitch.   London: Oriental University Press, 1990. 247p.

'Lloyd Geering has played a key role in trying to create a New Zealand response to the radical changes taking place in the Western world. The crisis of theology which culminated in the famous "trial" [of Lloyd Geering] . . . in 1967, saw the awakening of a New Zealand theological consciousness, even though it was stirred by some acrimony and fierce debate' (Foreword). This set of essays has been published to honour the man and the tremendous influence he has had on the religious development of New Zealand.

Denominations

396 Fight the good fight: the story of the Salvation Army in New Zealand, 1883-1983.

Cyril R. Bradwell. Wellington: Reed, 1982. 216p.

Widely respected by many New Zealanders for its social work, the Salvation Army was reviled in its early years in New Zealand. This is a well-researched history of the growth of the Army in New Zealand, and sets that development in its worldwide context.

397 The way ahead: Anglican change and prospect in New Zealand.

Brian Davis. Christchurch: Caxton Press, 1995. 235p.

The primate of the Anglican Church in Aotearoa/New Zealand and Polynesia discusses the wide-ranging changes that have occurred in the church and society since the 1960s. His views and opinions about the church and its role in secular societies like New Zealand, and his comments on areas in which New Zealand has been world leading (the ordination of women, the admission of children to communion at an early age, liturgical renewal, bicultural partnership and multicultural expression), are thoughtfully presented. Davis also examines the work of contemporary theologians, including Lloyd Geering. For an official history of the Anglican Church in New Zealand see *The Anglican Church in New Zealand: a history* (Dunedin: McIndoe, for the Anglican Church of the Province of New Zealand, 1973. 277p.) by W. P. Morrell, a distinguished academic historian.

398 'Be ye separate': fundamentalism and the New Zealand experience.

Edited by Bryan Gilling. Hamilton, New Zealand: University of Waikato/Colcom Press, 1992. 162p. (Waikato Studies in Education vol. 3).

This work 'illuminates some key periods, events and issues within the development of Christian Fundamentalism in New Zealand. At the same time it also promotes insights into both the broader contexts with which the phenomenon has been associated – and from which it has been, at least in part, derived – and how Christian Fundamentalists have been influenced by, and themselves tried to influence, New Zealand society around them' (Introduction). The authors are New Zealand scholars and the work presents some of the academic reflection and discussion which is taking place but which might not otherwise be available to a wider audience.

399 God's farthest outpost: a history of Catholics in New Zealand.

Michael King. Auckland: Penguin, 1997. 208p. bibliog.

An overview rather than a detailed analysis, this work is still a highly competent, fact-filled account which covers first Catholic contacts, the influence of the French and the impact of the Irish, as well as a number of controversies. These last include the 1922 trial and acquittal of Bishop James Liston for supporting the Dublin uprising of 1916, and the issue of state support for Catholic parochial schools. Well-chosen and presented illustrations add immeasurably to the text.

400 **Presbyterians in Aotearoa, 1840-1990.**
Edited by D. McEldowney. Wellington: Presbyterian Church of New
Zealand, 1990. 203p.

The work of five authors, co-ordinated by an editor, which looks at the Presbyterian
Church, warts and all. The authors look back to the historical links with Scotland and
forward to the growing involvement with Maori and Pacific Islanders and the church's
commitment to women. The book is attractively presented with many black-and-white
photographs.

Maori religious movements

401 **Mana from heaven: a century of Maori prophets in New Zealand.**
Bronwyn Elsmore. Tauranga, New Zealand: Moana Press, 1989.
398p. maps. bibliog.

'Attempts to increase understanding of the Maori religious response of the past and
present . . . by giving an account of the large numbers of religious movements which
arose . . . [and by showing] . . . how the beliefs of particular movements were affected
by the notions presented in the scriptures available at the time of their formation'
(Introduction). The book is divided into eras: before 1830, 1830-50, 1850s, 1860-
1900, 1900-20 and after 1920. Movements both well known and little known are
examined.

402 **Ratana: the man, the church, the political movement.**
J. McLeod Henderson. Wellington: Reed/Polynesian Society, 1972.
2nd ed. 128p. map. bibliog. (Polynesian Society Memoir no. 36).

An historical account of a most influential 20th-century Maori leader and the church
and religion he founded in the 1920s. Explanations of Ratana's religious principles
could be more detailed and greater research into written Maori sources might have
resulted in more information.

403 **Rua and the Maori millennium.**
Peter Webster. Wellington: Price Milburn, for Victoria University
Press, 1979. 328p. maps. bibliog.

A study by an anthropologist of the Ringatu religious movement of Rua Kenana, the
Maori prophet in the early years of the century. 'This book is an account of Rua as a
messiah, and the emergence and development of his cult, set in the context of the
times . . . I have concentrated upon a detailed explanation of the reasons for, and the
background relevant to, his emergence as a messianic leader and have tried to interpret
and understand his millennial dream in some depth' (Introduction).

Redemption songs: a life of Te Kooti Arikirangi Te Turuki.
See item no. 214.

'Hauhau': the Pai Marire search for Maori identity.
See item no. 215.

The story of Suzanne Aubert.
See item no. 252.

Far from the promised land?: being Jewish in New Zealand.
See item no. 272.

Religious history of New Zealand: a bibliography.
See item no. 958.

Maori Language

General

404 He whiriwhiringa: selected readings in Maori.
Edited by Bruce Biggs.   Auckland: Auckland University Press, 1997.
263p. maps.
Maori texts from a variety of sources, some not previously published, are presented in
Maori and English on facing pages, with numbered paragraphs to link one to the other.
The work, enabling easy comparison of the texts, is designed for those learning the
language.

405 The Reed pocket Maori proverbs.
A. E. Brougham, A. W. Reed, revised by Timoti Karetu.   Auckland:
Reed Consumer Books, 1996. rev. ed. 175p.
Lists Maori proverbs or *whakatauki* by subject, in both Maori and English, together
with an explanation of their derivation. The work 'provides both a useful reference
and an insight into Maori humour and values' (cover).

406 Te Matatiki: contemporary Maori words.
Maori Language Commission.   Auckland: Oxford University Press,
1996. 289p.
This regularly updated listing has been produced to help promote Maori as a living
language. In this edition over 2,000 previously unpublished terms have been added.
Each entry is provided with its Maori derivation. While the Commission has an objective of extending 'the linguistic range of Maori by weaving together into new
combinations current speech, and words and phrases which have fallen out of everyday use' (Preface), it acknowledges other bodies which are also producing new terms,
particularly in specialist areas, for instance, mathematics.

Dictionaries

407 English-Maori dictionary.
H. M. Ngata. Wellington: Learning Media, 1993. 559p.

The author identified the need for a dictionary which illustrated the usage of Maori, rather than simply supplying definitions or equivalents in English and Maori. Material was selected from a wide range of sources including Acts of Parliament, deeds from the Maori Land Court, translated records of Maori school files, the Maori Bible, and utterances from Maori orators, as well as everyday usage.

408 The Reed dictionary of modern Maori.
P. M. Ryan. Auckland: Reed/Television New Zealand, 1995. 648p.

A useful reference volume, containing 40,000 entries arranged in two sections, Maori-English and English-Maori. Words for new inventions are included, together with metric terms, modern concepts and some scientific, technological and legal terms. Separate lists for proverbs, Christian names, months, days of the week, points of the compass, parts of the body, colours, countries and continents are also provided.

409 A dictionary of the Maori language . . . seventh edition revised and augmented by the Advisory Committee on the teaching of the Maori language, Department of Education.
Herbert W. Williams. Wellington: GP Publications, 1992.
Reprint of 7th ed. 499p. bibliog.

The standard dictionary of the Maori language, scholarly and authoritative. Included is an eleven-page list of words corrected from earlier editions, an appendix containing 'Some of the more important words adopted from non-Polynesian sources', a brief introduction to the language, and the prefaces to the fifth and sixth editions.

Grammars

410 The Reed reference grammar of Maori.
Winifred Bauer, with William Parker, Te Kareongawai Evans, Te Aroha Noti Keepa. Auckland: Reed, 1997. 703p.

The first comprehensive grammar of Maori, this work is divided into five parts: preliminaries, particle grammar, syntactic structures, complex sentence structure and discourse functions. It is intended for teachers and adult and advanced students of Maori. The work adds to the author's previous extensive descriptive grammar, *Maori* (London: Routledge, 1993. 608p.).

411 **Teach yourself Maori.**
K. T. Harawira, revised by Timoti Karetu.   Auckland: Reed Books, 1994. 3rd ed. 142p. (Teach Yourself Books).

The usual basic introduction typical of this series. It assumes no prior knowledge of the language and provides lessons, exercises, pronunciation, advice and a vocabulary list.

412 **Maori language: understanding the grammar. A guide to the differences between English and Maori.**
David Karena-Holmes.   Dunedin: The author, 1995. 168p.

'This book aims to provide clear explanation of the differences between English and Maori in the ways words are used and phrases and sentences are constructed' (Introduction). Clearly set out, this is an aid for English-speaking students of Maori but does not profess to be a course in learning the language.

413 **Te reo rangitira: a course in Maori for sixth and seventh forms.**
T. S. Karetu.   Wellington: Government Printer/Department of Education, 1974. 196p.

This volume is designed to be used by those who have mastered both volumes of *Te rangatahi* (q.v.).

414 **Te rangatahi, tuatahi 1: a Maori language course for adult students. 'Ka hao te rangatahi', 'The new net goes fishing'.**
Hoani R. Waititi.   Wellington: GP Publishing, 1992. A reprint of 1974 ed.

One of the standard books for learning the Maori language. A more advanced stage of learning Maori is found in the second volume, *Te rangatahi, tuatahi 2: a Maori language course*, edited by Beth Ranapia (Wellington: Government Printer/Department of Education, 1972. rev. ed. 170p. First published, 1964).

New Zealand English

General

415 New Zealand ways of speaking English.
Edited by Alan Bell, Janet Holmes. Wellington: Victoria University Press, 1990. 305p.

A scholarly and well-referenced examination of the way New Zealanders speak and why they speak that way. The author admits that sociolinguistic research is still in its infancy in New Zealand. The work is divided into three sections: 'Attitudes to NZE [New Zealand English]', 'Variation and change in NZE', and 'Pragmatic analysis of New Zealand discourse'.

416 New Zealand English: an introduction to New Zealand speech and usage.
Elizabeth Gordon, Tony Deverson. Auckland: Heinemann, 1985. 88p. maps.

In this short, but lively and thoughtful, text, the authors provide an account of the distinctive accent and vocabulary of New Zealand English. In addition, they examine such topics as the origins of the New Zealand accent and vocabulary, influences from Australia and America, the pronunciation of Maori names, social and regional variation within New Zealand English, and changing attitudes towards New Zealand speech. A variety of media is employed to demonstrate many points. Although designed for instructional purposes, the book is of much wider interest.

417 Threads in the New Zealand tapestry of language.
Edited by Janet Holmes, Ray Harlow. Auckland: Linguistic Society of New Zealand, 1991. 121p.

Intended to demonstrate the degree of linguistic diversity in New Zealand, the papers in this volume present the results of research on the languages used by three different

128

Wellington ethnic communities: the Cantonese Chinese, the Greek and the Tongan. Examining three sociological areas – language proficiency, domains of language use and language use – the studies assess the extent of language loss over three to four generations.

Dictionaries

418 The New Zealand dictionary: a dictionary of New Zealand words and phrases.
Edited by Elizabeth Orsman, Harry Orsman. Auckland: New House Publishers, 1995. 2nd ed. 321p.

According to its editors, '*The New Zealand dictionary* sets out to present for the first time a broad selection from all registers of a distinctive New Zealand English vocabulary'. Coverage is restricted to the language which is used 'distinctively, but not exclusively, by New Zealanders'. Derivations have been provided for each word and also the first-known usage where this has been able to be identified.

419 The dictionary of New Zealand English: a dictionary of New Zealandisms on historical principles.
Edited by H. W. Orsman. Auckland: Oxford University Press, 1997. 965p.

The product of a lifetime's lexicographical work, this is a giant of a book. It provides a unique historical record of New Zealand words and phrases from their earliest use to the present day. The dictionary's 6,000 main headword entries and 9,300 separate subentries provide insights into New Zealand's diverse linguistic heritage. The definitions are illustrated by 47,000 select quotations arranged in chronological order. Beyond its contribution to the study of the English language, this book is an invaluable resource for studies of New Zealand society, history and culture.

420 Heinemann New Zealand dictionary: the first dictionary of New Zealand English and New Zealand pronunciation.
H. W. Orsman. Auckland: Heinemann, 1989. 2nd ed. 1,412p.

A standard home and school dictionary. The second edition contains a much larger selection of Maori words now used by, or of use to, speakers of English in New Zealand.

421 Heinemann dictionary of New Zealand quotations.
Harry Orsman, Jan Moore. Auckland: Heinemann, 1988. 1,050p.

'Contains almost 3,000 fascinating, amusing, and often surprising, quotations by New Zealanders or about New Zealand' (Introduction). It includes oral as well as published material, although the authors admit it does not include a great deal of satire because of a belief that New Zealanders are able less and less to laugh at themselves! The one index covers keywords, ideas, themes and references.

Politics

General

422 Women and politics in New Zealand.

Helena Catt, Elizabeth McLeay. Wellington: Political Science/Victoria University Press, 1993. 151p.

'These essays illuminate women's involvement in political life and so reveal the diverse views, history and lifestyles of New Zealand's women' (Introduction). Topics include a variety of feminist views, consideration of the proportion of women MPs, the gender gap in delegations to party conferences, women's success as elected representatives to Hospital and Area Health Boards, the groups involved in the abortion debate during the fourth Labour Government, and the gender gap in voting behaviour.

423 New Zealand politics in perspective.

Edited by Hyam Gold. Auckland: Longman Paul, 1994. Reprint of 3rd ed. 532p.

Covers a range of issues: institutional fundamentals, dominant actors (including the Executive, Parliament, key parties of the time, groups, the judiciary and the state) and electoral choice. Each chapter is supported by references. The work provides a practical review of the political situation as at 1985, with earlier chapters providing background for the following chapters to build on.

424 The New Zealand politics source book.

Paul Harris, Stephen Levine. Palmerston North, New Zealand: Dunmore Press, 1994. 2nd ed. 496p.

Comprises selections from a number of basic documents which throw light on the evolution of New Zealand politics. The work begins with historical material such as the Magna Carta, the Bill of Rights and the Treaty of Waitangi, then moves to more recent material, including the Ombudsmen Act 1975, the Privacy Commissioner Act 1991 (the forerunner of the Privacy Act 1993) and material relating to elections, political parties, Parliament, cabinet, the state sector, local government and international relations. Although such a work can never be completely up to date, the bringing together of such a range of material provides a valuable first reference.

425 The fourth Labour Government: politics and policy in New Zealand.
Edited by Martin Holland, Jonathan Boston.   Auckland: Oxford University Press, 1990. 2nd ed. 296p.

'In this study [of the fourth Labour Government] twelve specialists in the fields of economics, political science, public administration, sociology and law examine and critically assess some of Labour's key policy initiatives' (cover). The areas discussed range from the Bill of Rights, to Parliamentary reform, the economic strategy, tax reform, ANZUS and the nuclear issue. In his Foreword, David Lange notes, 'the essays are more in the nature of political commentaries than "scientific" analysis'.

426 Maori political perspectives: he whakaaro Maori mo nga ti kanga kawanatanga.
Stephen Levine, Raj Vasil.   Auckland: Hutchinson, 1985. 206p.

With most political writing examining the aspirations of white New Zealand, it is refreshing to turn to this work based on interviews with a number of articulate Maori men and women about their views of Maori political and social problems and their assessment of possible solutions. The principle areas identified are identity, legitimacy, participation, penetration and distribution. More a raising of the issues than a presentation of solutions, there is much in the book, however, that is challenging and worth further examination.

427 New Zealand politics in transition.
Edited by Raymond Miller.   Auckland: Oxford University Press, 1997. 446p.

A timely re-assessment of New Zealand politics in the aftermath of the 1996 election, the first conducted under the MMP (Mixed Member Proportional Representation) system. The book explores the causes and consequences of political change in the 1990s, and presents the research and sometimes differing viewpoints of some forty writers, all with expertise in specific areas of New Zealand politics. As well as the evolving political system, contributors consider the implications for institutions and parties. Other topics canvassed include: elections and the media, theories of the state, public policy, Maori politics, and inequality and power.

428 Politics in New Zealand.
Richard Mulgan.   Auckland: Auckland University Press, 1997. 2nd ed. 344p. bibliog.

Designed as a tertiary student text, this work is a clear and concise introduction to the key concepts and academic controversies surrounding New Zealand politics. This edition includes the results of the first MMP (Mixed Member Proportional Representation) election in 1996. General theories of the state, including pluralism, public choice market liberalism and Marxism, are discussed. Lists of further readings with each chapter, and an extensive bibliography, lead the enquirer to sources of further information.

429 **New Zealand parliamentary record, 1840-1984.**
J. O. Wilson. Wellington: Government Printer, 1985. 4th ed. 337p.

A most useful reference work relating to the New Zealand Parliament. 'This edition lists all the information in the earlier editions with the exception of the records of Provincial Councils, and the lists of High Commissioners and Ambassadors . . . the lists of Governors-General, Ministers, Members of Parliament and the officials connected with Parliament have been brought up to date. A list of minor ministerial responsibilities, Ministers in charge, has been compiled and added' (Introduction). A more recent publication, *Ministers and members in the New Zealand Parliament*, edited by G. A. Wood (Dunedin: University of Otago Press, 1996. 2nd ed. 119p.) lists the ministries in chronological order since 1911 and the MPs alphabetically, and offers a number of appendices on a range of subjects from women MPs, to by-elections, third parties and party leaders.

Electoral behaviour

430 **New Zealand under MMP: a new politics?**
Jonathan Boston, Stephen Levine, Elizabeth McLeay, Nigel S. Roberts. Auckland: Auckland University Press/Bridget Williams Books, 1996. 206p.

Part of a three-year research project (begun in 1995), known as 'The New Zealand Political Change Project: the Impact of Electoral System Change in a Small Democracy', this work examines the effect of MMP (Mixed Member Proportional Representation) in its short history to date and assesses what the likely long-term impact on the electoral system might be. Chapters include 'New Zealand's changing political identity', 'The effects of MMP: the expectations of opinion leaders', 'Parliament: changing the rules of the game', 'The public service and the new environment' and 'The dynamics of policy making under MMP'. The work also considers whether MMP is likely to endure.

431 **Voter's choice: electoral change in New Zealand?**
Helena Catt, Paul Harris, Nigel S. Roberts. Palmerston North, New Zealand: Dunmore Press, 1992. 143p.

Produced prior to the referendum on the electoral system, three experts discuss the pros and cons of the Supplementary Member option, the Single Transferable Vote, Mixed Member Proportional Representation (MMP), and Preferential Voting. The work is useful for an understanding of the choices which confronted New Zealanders in 1992, and the background to the MMP system introduced in 1996. It also discusses whether New Zealand should have a senate, and whether referenda should be more extensively employed.

432 **Electoral behaviour in New Zealand.**
     Edited by Martin Holland.   Auckland: Oxford University Press, 1992.
     202p.

The first collective attempt to define the current status of voting analysis in New
Zealand. While studies of electoral behaviour have been a predominant concern of
New Zealand political scientists since the early 1960s, much of the early work was
descriptive rather than quantitative. The eleven contributors demonstrate new
approaches. As the chapters illustrate, while New Zealand may exhibit certain unique
characteristics, the similarities with other Western democratic regimes are striking.

433 **Towards consensus?: the 1993 general election in New Zealand and
     the transition to proportional representation.**
     Jack Vowles.   Auckland: Auckland University Press, 1995. 253p.

Seeks to explain the results of the 1993 election (which resulted in National losing
their large majority) and the referendum (which resulted in the selection of Mixed
Member Proportional Representation [MMP] as the preferred form of government)
and examines the implications of these two results for the future of New Zealand politics. The analysis is based on a survey of voters, political party activists and
parliamentary candidates.

434 **Voters' vengeance: the 1990 election in New Zealand and the fate
     of the fourth Labour Government.**
     Jack Vowles, Peter Aimer.   Auckland: Auckland University Press,
     1993. 264p.

An 'important and illuminating' examination of the 1990 election which resulted in a
landslide for National, from the perspective gained through survey of the voters themselves. The conclusion is that what occurred could be linked into an international
pattern.

Parties and credos

435 **The Labour Party after 75 years.**
     Edited by Margaret Clark.   Wellington: Department of Politics,
     Victoria University of Wellington, 1992. 129p.

1991 marked the seventy-fifth anniversary of the founding of the New Zealand Labour
Party. The party, New Zealand's oldest, was then in sombre rather than celebratory
mood, the fourth Labour Government having been heavily defeated in the 1990 general election. Contributors to a seminar held in that year, including party activists,
contemplated not only the Labour Party's past triumphs and disasters, but also its
future political and policy options. That the Labour Party would have to re-evaluate its
position and set about fashioning a new consensus with which to inspire voters was
acknowledged.

436 **Unfinished business.**
Roger Douglas, with Louise Callan. Auckland: Random House New Zealand, 1993. 305p.

A controversial figure during his four years as Minister of Finance in the fourth Labour Government, Roger Douglas looks forward in this book to 2020 and argues that the reforms he began (far-reaching structural reforms) would need to continue to achieve the positive results he anticipated for the country. This remains an important work in setting out the vision driving this influential politician. A description of the events that saw Douglas moving from the political wilderness to Minister of Finance can be found in *Towards prosperity: people and politics in the 1980s; a personal view*, by Roger Douglas and Louise Callan (Auckland: David Bateman, 1987. 256p.).

437 **The first 50 years: a history of the New Zealand National Party.**
Barry Gustafson. Auckland: Reed Methuen, 1986. 407p. maps. bibliog.

Written by a former Labour Party activist, one who has written three histories of the Labour Party, but who by this time had switched to National, this work describes in some detail the establishment, build-up and coming to power of the National Party. The author clearly states that it was his intention to provide an accurate and objective analysis, but that this approach has been tempered by concentration on the people involved with the National Party. Well researched and presented, the work offers insights both into the political and the social scene over the period 1936 to 1986.

438 **New Zealand the way I want it.**
Bob Jones. Christchurch: Whitcoulls, 1978. 278p.

Founder in 1983 of the short-lived New Zealand Party, Jones's discussion of political parties and personalities, the economy, unions, and business articulates the attitudes of many rightwing New Zealanders, even if it places greater emphasis on individualism than most might.

439 **I've been thinking.**
Richard Prebble. Auckland: Seaview Publishing, 1996. 113p.

The leader of ACT (Association of Consumers and Taxpayers), elected as part of the MMP (Mixed Member Proportional Representation) government in 1996, but a former Labour MP, presents his trenchant views on a range of subjects. He insists, 'I wrote the book not to get back into politics but as a guide to MMP. The reaction to the book persuaded me there is an appetite for a new style of politics: one based on values, not election promises' (Preface to fourth printing). ACT has been viewed as a vehicle for further dissemination of the views of Roger Douglas.

440 **Making a difference.**
Ruth Richardson. Christchurch: Shoal Bay Press, 1995. 248p.

'Politicians like me may be right or wrong, successful or unsuccessful, but we see ourselves as agents of change' (Introduction). With this philosophy, Ruth Richardson embarked on her career as a politician determined 'to make a difference'. In this work she details the highs and lows of her period as a politician. Critical, forthright, not afraid to face problems and present solutions, in some ways arrogant, the work presents the former National Finance Minister's perspective on politics in the 1980s and 1990s.

New territory: the transformation of New Zealand, 1984-92.
See item no. 3.

New Zealand electoral atlas.
See item no. 28.

Diary of the Kirk years.
See item no. 238.

Memories of Muldoon.
See item no. 242.

Memoirs.
See item no. 250.

Kotahitanga: the search for Maori political unity.
See item no. 328.

Political Science.
See item no. 914.

Constitution, Government and Legal System

General

441 Maori, Pakeha and democracy.
Richard Mulgan. Auckland: Oxford University Press, 1989. 159p.

Provides a useful background to many threateningly divisive issues relating to race relations in New Zealand. The author, a professor of political studies, sets out the issues for the ordinary New Zealander. His 'point of view is that of a Pakeha who accepts the need to protect Maori culture and identity, but who sees Pakeha people as having their roots firmly and legitimately planted in New Zealand as well' (Introduction). Chapters include 'Bicultural concepts', 'The legacy of colonial conquest', 'Democracy and the Maori', 'The role of the Treaty of Waitangi' and 'Biculturalism in action'.

442 Justice, ethics and New Zealand society.
Edited by Graham Oddie, Roy W. Perrett. Auckland: Oxford University Press, 1992. 233p.

Issues of sovereignty and whether it was ceded to the Crown by the Treaty of Waitangi, land confiscation, property rights, the value of an ecosytem, whether or not collectives, such as tribes, can bear moral responsibility, are debated in the New Zealand setting by a number of eminent philosophers, all of whom know and understand the New Zealand context. The result is very much a learned debate, but it is a valuable addition to discussion of such issues.

443 An introduction to New Zealand government: a guide to finding out about government in New Zealand, its institutions, structures and activities.
J. B. Ringer. Christchurch: Hazard Press, 1991. 335p.

A factual description of government in New Zealand which will be useful for anyone wishing to find out about 'what has been written about it, how to gain access to services, and the sweeping changes that have occurred in recent years' (Introduction). Described by reviewers as 'an invaluable bibliographical and reference tool', 'an indispensable first reference', and 'comprehensive in coverage and well-structured', it brings together information which might otherwise have to be sought from a number of sources.

444 **Justice and identity: antipodean practices.**
Edited by Margaret Wilson, Anna Yeatman. Wellington: Bridget Williams Books, 1995. 223p.

Traditional concepts of justice are challenged in this collection of essays arising from a seminar series sponsored by Waikato University's School of Law, in conjunction with the Department of Women's Studies. Questions of sovereignty, governance and democracy are debated, drawing on recent New Zealand and Australian experience. Obligations under the Treaty of Waitangi, the concept of partnership and the implications of officially sanctioned bicultural policies underlie the New Zealand contributions.

Parliamentary practice

445 **The dilemma of Parliament.**
Keith Jackson. Wellington: Allen & Unwin/Port Nicholson Press, 1987. 204p.

The author, a professor of political science, looks at the role of the New Zealand House of Representatives, the effects of a powerful caucus and party cohesion, the function of select committees and ministerial responsibility. The work provides a context of political life in the 1980s against which to set the rapid changes of the 1990s.

446 **Parliamentary practice in New Zealand.**
David McGee. Wellington: GP Publications, 1994. 2nd ed. 606p.

Answering some of the often-asked questions about the practices of New Zealand's Parliament, this book aims to improve public knowledge of a vital, but surprisingly poorly documented, institution. Compiled by the current Clerk of the House of Representatives, it traverses the structure and functions of the House, elections, members' responsibilities and conditions of service, the basis of parliamentary procedure, the conduct of business, and the form and classification of legislation. 'I have not consciously attempted to simplify parliamentary procedure for the reader although I have certainly not tried to expound every rule in its utmost complexity' (Preface).

447 **The Cabinet and political power in New Zealand.**
Elizabeth McLeay. Auckland: Auckland University Press, 1995. 256p. (Oxford Readings in New Zealand Politics: no. 5).

Based on original research undertaken over two decades, this book considers the nature of cabinet power in the light of New Zealand's constitutional arrangements, the party system, the post-1984 restructuring of the state sector, economic change, relationships between groups and ministers, and the changes to be expected with the introduction of proportional representation. The author concludes that, while the doctrines of collective and ministerial responsibility have been breached, cabinet itself is still identifiably the same sort of institution it has always been: the most important committee of the elected leadership.

Constitution

448 Essays on the constitution.
Edited by Philip A. Joseph. Wellington: Brooker's, 1995. 411p.

'These essays are a reflection of our national culture . . . a unique record of our constitutional and political life' (Introduction). Couched in legal language, and very much a legal view of our culture, this volume canvasses issues such as Maori sovereignty claims, proportional representation, republicanism and the future of the Privy Council appeal system. It provides a reference for constitutional meaning and debate in these areas.

449 Bridled power: New Zealand government under MMP.
Geoffrey Palmer, Mathew Palmer. Auckland: Oxford University Press, 1997. 340p. bibliog.

A revised edition of *Unbridled power* (Auckland: Oxford University Press, 1987. 2nd ed. 322p.), written by father and son, the former a professor of law and an ex-Prime Minister, the latter a senior bureaucrat. It remains a very useful guide to the way Government and Parliament work, with this time the addition of a description of the ways MMP (Mixed Member Proportional Representation) may change those processes. The new title relates to the fact that the authors consider MMP will place constraints on the powers of governments. They warn that the greater consultation they believe must occur on legislation and lawmaking will slow down the process and may result in political compromises. The work, ironically, also looks more closely at ministerial responsibility than did the earlier editions.

450 New Zealand's constitution in crisis: reforming our political system.
Geoffrey Palmer. Dunedin: McIndoe, 1992. 231p.

Believing that New Zealand's system of government is in urgent need of reform, the author sets out his views on the reform of Parliament, rights, freedoms and the Bill of Rights, Maori issues, the media, the electoral system and public law. Each chapter presents the current situation and analyses how issues could be better handled and what reforms may be needed. Not necessarily an easy read, the work does challenge accepted views.

451 **Referendums: constitutional and political perspectives.**
Edited by Alan C. Simpson. Wellington: Department of Politics, Victoria University of Wellington, 1993. 182p.

The contributors, from a variety of backgrounds, write about the constitutional and democratic issues relating to referenda, both from the New Zealand viewpoint and from comparative perspectives. While perhaps a specialized topic, the discussion is reasonably wide-ranging.

452 **Republicanism in New Zealand.**
Edited by Luke Trainor. Palmerston North, New Zealand: Dunmore Press, 1996. 190p.

Presents six viewpoints on a subject which, while not yet a matter of heated debate, does concern a growing number of New Zealanders. The arguments are presented for and against change, Maori attitudes are considered, and the symbolism involved is reflected upon. This is an interesting and challenging group of essays.

Constitutional safeguards

453 **Freedom of information in New Zealand.**
Ian Eagles, Michael Taggart, Grant Liddell. Auckland: Oxford University Press, 1992. 661p.

'*Freedom of information in New Zealand* analyses the growing New Zealand freedom of information jurisprudence, setting it against relevant international developments, and provides a comprehensive examination of this constitutionally significant legislation' (cover). The legislation is assessed from a wide range of perspectives including its relationship to the national economy to privacy, and to commercial and allied interests. The role of the ombudsman and the courts is also investigated. The scope and application of the legislation and issues raised by the legislation are covered in some depth, with theoretical and practical issues being examined. This is an authoritative work.

454 **The model ombudsman: institutionalizing New Zealand's democratic experiment.**
Lawy B. Hill. Princeton, New Jersey: Princeton University Press, 1976. 411p. bibliog.

In 1962 New Zealand decided to create a 'grievance man' modelled on the Scandinavian ombudsman. The New Zealand ombudsman, like his Scandinavian counterpart, was to ensure democracy in a bureaucratic society. Hill investigates, analyses and evaluates the first twelve and a half years of the ombudsman's existence in New Zealand. While now dated, this scholarly work nevertheless remains useful for the background it presents to the development of the ombudsman's office.

455 **Rights and freedoms: the New Zealand Bill of Rights Act 1990 and the Human Rights Act 1993.**
Edited by Grant Huscroft, Paul Rishworth. Wellington: Brooker's, 1995. 546p.

The New Zealand Bill of Rights Act 1990 and the Human Rights Act 1993 have already had a significant effect on criminal law, and changes to the general law are already occurring. Legislators and judges are increasingly required to take rights into account as they conduct the business of the nation. The essays in this book deal with current issues in race relations, police powers, defamation, health care, equality rights, privacy and religion. New Zealand's international law obligations are also discussed, along with the question of remedies for breaches of the Bill of Rights. The approach taken is comparative, with reference made to the law of North American and European jurisdictions.

456 **The Privacy Act: a guide.**
Elizabeth Longworth, Tim McBride. Wellington: GP Publications, 1994. 315p.

The Privacy Act is intended to protect an individual's privacy, and to provide legal protection in respect of personal information. It places legal limitations on the collection, storage, disclosure, and use of such information by public and private sector agencies. This comprehensive guide is a practical resource for those needing to know their responsibilities under the Act, and for individuals wanting to know their rights. The origins of the Act are explored, as well as its scope and applications. Case-studies are employed to demonstrate just what the Act means.

Law

457 **The New Zealand legal system: structures, processes and legal theory.**
Morag McDowell, Duncan Webb. Wellington: Butterworths, 1995. 404p.

The writers offer a thorough grounding in all aspects of the historical development, institutions, and working of the law in New Zealand. There are also useful sections on studying the law and on the rudiments of the legal method. The volume is particularly valuable in its treatment of the developing law on New Zealand's constitution, the status of the Treaty of Waitangi and the impact of the New Zealand Bill of Rights Act 1990. Another comprehensive introductory work in this area, a standard text for students, is *Introduction to the New Zealand legal system*, by R. D. Mulholland (Wellington: Butterworths, 1995. 8th ed. 422p.).

458 **New Zealand: the development of its laws and constitution.**
Edited by J. L. Robson.   London: Stevens & Sons, 1967. 2nd ed.
532p. bibliog. (The British Commonwealth; The Development of its
Laws and Constitutions, vol. 4).

'The aim of this book is to discuss how the law has responded to . . . [political, social
and material] changes and an endeavour has been made to relate legal development to
the social forces behind it' (Preface to first edition). In the second edition, several of
the chapters have been rewritten and major developments to the beginning of 1966 are
covered. A classic, the work presents a succinct account of the legal and constitutional
structure of New Zealand up to the date of publication.

459 **A New Zealand legal history.**
Peter Spiller, Jeremy Finn, Richard Boast.   Wellington: Brooker's,
1995. 308p. maps.

Conceived as 'a contribution to the store of historical jurisprudence in New Zealand',
this book does not purport to be a comprehensive account of all aspects of New
Zealand legal history. Rather it reflects the particular interests of the three authors, all
academic lawyers. It also deliberately places emphasis on the historical background to
legal issues and concerns of current importance. There are four main themes: the role
of New Zealand's distinctively English legal heritage; the development of New
Zealand law; the unique place of Maori values, as embodied in the Treaty of Waitangi;
and the part played by New Zealand judges and lawyers in the refinement of legal
institutions.

Salmond: southern jurist.
See item no. 233.

Women in the House: Members of Parliament in New Zealand.
See item no. 291.

Maori sovereignty: the Maori perspective.
See item no. 333.

The Maori Magna Carta: New Zealand law and the Treaty of Waitangi.
See item no. 463.

New Zealand Law Journal.
See item no. 902.

**Directory of official information = Te rangi whakaatu whakaere
kawanatanga 1995-97.**
See item no. 930.

New Zealand government directory.
See item no. 939.

**Bennett's government publications: a tool to help you identify the source
of government and related reports, publications and discussion
documents.**
See item no. 950.

Treaty of Waitangi

460 Return to sender: what really happened at the fiscal envelope hui.
Wira Gardiner. Auckland: Reed, 1996. 232p.

In early 1995 the New Zealand Government sought to limit Maori claims for compensation under the Treaty of Waitangi Act by imposing what it termed 'a fiscal envelope' (a sum of NZ$1 billion). The author, then a senior official, attended meetings and protests throughout the country. He identifies many of the deep-seated concerns of Maori lying behind their rejection of the Crown's proposals, and describes a growing power struggle in Maori society, young leaders challenging the authority of elders. 'In this book it is my intention to capture the mood of the times' (p. 11).

461 Waitangi: Maori and Pakeha perspectives of the Treaty of Waitangi.
Edited by I. H. Kawharu. Auckland: Oxford University Press, 1989. 329p. maps.

Attitudes to the Treaty of Waitangi have recently changed markedly, what was previously judicially dismissed as 'a simple nullity' being now recognized as 'a still valid compact of mutual obligation'. The essays in this volume seek to establish what the Treaty actually says, the nature of guarantees therein, and the extent to which such guarantees have been honoured by the Crown. Those in part one discuss aspects of the legal and historical significance of the document. Those in part two are studies of Maori reaction to the Crown guarantees, especially in the context of current claims for redress.

462 A question of honour?: Labour and the Treaty, 1984-1989.
Jane Kelsey. Wellington: Allen & Unwin, 1990. 297p.

The author, an academic lawyer, exposes the inherent contradictions in the 1984-90 Labour Government's commitment to honouring the Treaty, while at the same time pushing on its programme of economic reform (including the privatization of state assets) at breakneck speed. She concludes that Maori expectations were first raised, then frustrated. Passionate, and unashamedly partisan, the book raises important questions.

463 **The Maori Magna Carta: New Zealand law and the Treaty of Waitangi.**
Paul McHugh. Auckland: Oxford University Press, 1991. 392p.
While a little dry, this book is the most comprehensive discussion of the law surrounding the Treaty. It not only considers the constitutional nature of the relationship between Maori and Parliament, but also describes the legislative activities of Parliament regarding Maori, the role of the Waitangi Tribunal, and the laws affecting Maori land tenure. 'Students of constitutional and public law, Maori studies, jurisprudence, legal history, and political studies will find it an invaluable guide' (cover).

464 **Claims to the Waitangi Tribunal.**
W. H. Oliver. Wellington: Waitangi Tribunal Division, Department of Justice, 1991. 108p. maps.
An introduction to the work of the Waitangi Tribunal, set up in 1975, and a summary of the claims heard, and reported on, to 1991. The issues covered include land, water, fishing, cultural rights, access to the nation's resources and participation in decision making. Detailed individual claim reports, those summarized and others subsequent, are published independently by the Waitangi Tribunal. For a more extended study of the operations of the Tribunal see Paul Temm, QC, *The Waitangi Tribunal: the conscience of the nation* (Auckland: Random Century,1990. 129p.).

465 **The Treaty of Waitangi.**
Claudia Orange. Wellington: Allen & Unwin/Port Nicholson Press, 1987. 312p. maps.
The first comprehensive study of the making of the Treaty, and of its subsequent place in New Zealand history. 'The story covers the several Treaty signings and the substantial differences between Maori and English texts; the debate over interpretation of land rights and the actions of settler governments determined to circumvent Treaty guarantees; the wars of sovereignty in the 1860s and the longstanding Maori struggle to secure a degree of autonomy and control over resources' (cover).

466 **Sovereignty and indigenous rights: the Treaty of Waitangi in international contexts.**
Edited by William Renwick. Wellington: Victoria University Press, 1991. 248p. maps.
New Zealand and overseas contributors attempt to place the Treaty of Waitangi in an international context, asking whether it has a unique place in relationships between colonizing nations and indigenous peoples. 'Discussions about Maori rights under the Treaty of Waitangi are for the most part conducted as if the points at issue are somehow unique to New Zealand' (p. 7). Other perspectives are provided by comparative analyses of the relationships between English-speaking colonizers and indigenous peoples in North America and the Pacific.

467 **The travesty of Waitangi: towards anarchy.**
Stuart Scott. Christchurch: Campbell Press, 1995. 184p. bibliog.
'Examines the much cited Treaty in the context of its origin and the intentions and aspirations of its authors and asks whether the huge concessions and grants which the Maori people have received in its name are really justified in the light of natural justice

and common sense' (Preface). Highly controversial when published, this work, nevertheless, provides a viewpoint held by some New Zealanders. There is also a sequel, *Travesty after travesty* (Christchurch: Certes Press, 1996. 144p.), which examines 'the advances of Maori influence, property ownership and political and financial power since 1993' (Preface).

468 Justice and the Maori: Maori claims in New Zealand political argument in the 1980s.
Andrew Sharp. Auckland: Oxford University Press, 1990. 310p.

'This book is a history and analysis of recent demands for justice made against the Pakeha people and Government of New Zealand by and on behalf of the descendants of the country's aboriginal inhabitants, the Maori, it is also a history and analysis of responses to those demands' (p. 1). Should the Maori be compensated for past wrongs? Should special programmes be set up which treat Maori and Pakeha (Europeans) differently? Should there be one law, one justice, for all? The author, a political scientist, addresses these questions in a relentlessly scholarly fashion.

Kotahitanga: the search for Maori political unity.
See item no. 328.

Maori sovereignty: the Maori perspective.
See item no. 333.

Maori, Pakeha and democracy.
See item no. 441.

Justice, ethics and New Zealand society.
See item no. 442.

Justice and identity: antipodean practices.
See item no. 444.

Shaping the news: Waitangi Day on television.
See item no. 919.

Public Administration

469 Public management: the New Zealand model.
Jonathan Boston, John Martin, June Pallot, Pat Walsh.   Auckland:
Oxford University Press, 1996. 406p.

'This book . . . documents and analyses the sweeping public reforms introduced since
the mid 1980s' (Preface). Confining their attention to the core public sector at the
national level, the authors set out to define the features of the model embraced and 'to
identify the principles and administrative doctrines on which it is based and evaluate
its merits'. Topics covered include an overview of the revolution in public management, a description of the resulting structure, management at the centre and beyond
the centre, human resources and financial management and a consideration of what
constitutes responsible management. The work concludes with an optimistic assessment of 'the New Zealand model'.

470 The state under contract.
Edited by Jonathan Boston.   Wellington: Bridget Williams Books,
1995. 205p.

Since 1984 reform of the New Zealand state sector has been radical and far reaching,
and there has been an emphasis on contractualist modes of governance. The essays, all
by academic experts in the field, examine the benefits and pitfalls of this approach.
While most of the contributors concentrate on the New Zealand scene, comparisons
with state-sector reforms in Australia, Canada and the United States are offered. 'The
book concludes with an analysis of the philosophical foundations underpinning the
increasing reliance on market mechanisms and consumer preferences' (cover).

**471 The great experiment: Labour parties and public policy
transformation in Australia and New Zealand.**
Francis G. Castles, Rolf Gerritsen, Jack Vowles.   Auckland: Auckland
University Press, 1996. 262p.

With each chapter co-authored by an Australian and a New Zealander, the ways in
which public policies have been transformed in these two countries are compared and

contrasted. The work carefully considers the circumstances surrounding the election of Labour governments in Australia in 1983 and in New Zealand in 1984, and evaluates the extent of the resulting economic and social transformation programmes. The policy areas covered in the volume are economic, environmental, external and indigenous affairs, industrial relations, social policy and women's affairs.

472 Corporatization and privatization: lessons from New Zealand.
Ian Duncan, Alan Bollard.   Auckland: Oxford University Press, 1992. 194p.

Through a number of New Zealand case-studies (Coal Corporation, Electricity Corporation, N. Z. Post Ltd., State Insurance Ltd., Telecom Corporation), this book delves into the process of privatization via corporatization. The work considers what brought about the transformation of the Post Office and other state-owned organizations and what the objectives of public sector reform were. It also assesses whether these objectives have been achieved. For some, the verdict appears to be that it is too early to tell; for others a more positive result is recorded.

473 The making of Rogernomics.
Edited by Brian Easton.   Auckland: Auckland University Press, 1989. 212p.

A collection of essays solicited from 'young men and women whose work deserved wider notice' on aspects and arguments of economic policy during the term of the fourth Labour Government (1984-90). The antecedents of policies adopted by the Hon. Roger (Rogernomics) Douglas are examined critically, and the diffusion, under Treasury influence, of monetarized macroeconomics and commercialist microeconomics traced.

474 The quest for efficiency: the origins of the State Services Commission.
Alan Henderson.   Wellington: State Services Commission, 1990. 441p.

The Public Service Act 1912 transferred all responsibility for the staffing of the New Zealand public service from politicians to a Public Service Commissioner, who also assumed general responsibility for the efficiency and economy of the service's operations. This well-researched book outlines administrative practices under ministerial control prior to 1913, many of which were doubtful, and traces the origins of the Public Service Act. It then goes on to examine New Zealand's experience of apolitical public service personnel management and the pursuit of public service efficiency until the public administration 'reforms' of the 1980s, in particular, the State Sector Act 1988.

475 Rolling back the state: privatization of power in Aotearoa/New Zealand.
Jane Kelsey.   Wellington: Bridget Williams Books, 1993. 391p.

An examination and assessment of the change in the public sector since 1984, emphasis being placed on the relinquishment of power by the state and its transfer to private hands. The intention of the author is to initiate dialogue and promote debate on the issues and concerns arising from this approach. 'The plea . . . is that we debate these differences and provide contestable analysis and options to challenge the stranglehold that the liberal lobby has maintained over policy and politics in the past decade and that we do so soon' (Preface).

476 The spirit of reform.
Alan Schick. Wellington: State Services Commission, 1996. 87p.

An American professor of public policy, the author was commissioned by the State Services Commission and the Treasury 'to make an overall assessment of the extent to which public and political confidence in the current public administrative arrangements is justified, and to identify the key issues that should be given attention in the next few years' (Preface). The resulting report contains both plaudits and criticisms. Its objectivity makes it of particular interest to those examining state sector reforms in New Zealand since the late 1980s.

477 Leap into the dark: the changing role of the state in New Zealand since 1984.
Edited by Andrew Sharp. Auckland: Auckland University Press, 1994. 255p.

Based on the University of Auckland's 1992 Winter Lecture series, the essays in this volume focus on the changing role of the state in New Zealand. 'Maybe the reforming governments since 1984 believed they would take the electorate with them ... Or maybe the politicians and their advisers thought their simple and elegant market theories would produce the goods, and thus convince the people. If so, they were wrong ... things keep turning out contrary to their predictions' (Introduction). The changes are examined with sceptical eyes by experts in the various fields reformed. While the contributors do not always agree on the detail of their criticisms, all are united in the belief that the revolution has been characterized by clumsiness, ineptitude and lack of thought.

478 Reining in the dinosaur: the story behind the remarkable turnaround of N Z Post.
Vivienne Smith. Wellington: N Z Post, 1997. 232p. bibliog.

N Z Post, one of three businesses created by the corporatization of the New Zealand Post Office, commenced operation in 1987 in an atmosphere of expected failure. This work documents how the business was transformed to the point where it 'is considered a benchmark of excellence in the postal world for the management and measurement systems it has introduced to the mail business' (cover). Published by N Z Post, this is unsurprisingly a positive examination of the business. Nevertheless, it documents the growth of a business which corporatization forced into examining different approaches.

The commercialisation of New Zealand.
See item no. 1.

The New Zealand experiment: a world model for structural adjustment?
See item no. 4.

Changing places in New Zealand: a geography of restructuring.
See item no. 18.

Changing places: New Zealand in the nineties.
See item no. 24.

New Zealand health policy: a comparative study.
See item no. 382.

Out of the woods: the restructuring and sale of New Zealand's state forests.
See item no. 572.

A century of state-honed enterprise: 100 years of state plantation forestry in New Zealand.
See item no. 575.

The power to manage: restructuring the New Zealand Electricity Department as a state-owned enterprise.
See item no. 593.

Revisiting the 'reforms' in education.
See item no. 663.

A shakeup anyway: government and the universities in New Zealand in a decade of reform.
See item no. 678.

Public Sector.
See item no. 915.

Broadcasting in New Zealand: waves of change.
See item no. 926.

Local Government

479 **Local government & politics in New Zealand.**
Graham Bush.   Auckland: Auckland University Press, 1995. 2nd ed.
330p.

'The revolutionary restructuring of the [local government] system in 1989 and the
introduction of complementary managerial, operational and financial reforms have
invigorated local government as never before in New Zealand's history'
(Introduction). New Zealand's leading authority on local government has completely
rewritten his 1980 edition of this book to take into account the radical subsequent
changes. The intention is to impart a broad understanding of where local government
has come from, what it is now like and how it behaves, and the principles which will
probably guide it into the future.

480 **Reforming local government?: a critical analysis of the views of the
Business Roundtable on local government.**
Paul Harris.   Hamilton, New Zealand: Centre for Labour and Trade
Union Studies, 1996. 55p.

A response to the Business Roundtable document *Local government in New Zealand*
(Wellington: Business Roundtable, 1995. 86p.). 'We make no pretence that the report
is objective. It is a critical analysis of the Roundtable's position and is written on
behalf of those who are seeking other ways forward for our country than that of the
New Right' (Preface). The Centre for Labour and Trade Union Studies at Waikato
University was approached by the New Zealand Public Service Association to prepare
this critique. The information provided, however, is intended to contribute to the
wider debate on the future of local government and thus is directed both to the public
and to decision makers. The concluding chapter suggests alternative approaches that
might be considered.

481 **Governance and management in New Zealand local government.**
Robert Howell, Philip McDermott, Vicky Forgie. Palmerston North, New Zealand: Department of Management Studies, Business Studies Faculty, Massey University, 1995. 72p.

The Massey University programme relating to local government has been built around describing and interpreting the initiatives following the reform of local government from 1989, considering the underlying motivations and assessing the political and managerial issues that have arisen. This report examines a previously unresolved issue, governance, defined as the political structuring and strategic direction of organizations which determines their purpose and effectiveness. The paper concludes that its review of current practices in a number of councils provides insufficient evidence to justify proposals 'for enhancing the definition and practice of good governance in local government' (p. v).

482 **Local and regional government in New Zealand: function and finance.**
Claudia D. Scott. Sydney; Auckland; London; Boston, Massachusetts: Allen & Unwin, 1979. 154p. bibliog.

'This study . . . has come from the desire to provide a comprehensive framework within which to analyse alternative courses of action and developments. The articulation of important linkages between function, organization and finance of local authority sectors will be treated within a broader context which defines underlying philosophical and political principles concerning the roles of central and local government and intergovernment fiscal relations' (Introduction). Topics also discussed include rating, capital works, decentralization, and future developments. This is a useful study of New Zealand local government prior to the initiation of reform.

Decently and in order: the government of the City of Auckland 1840-1971: the centennial history of the Auckland City Council.
See item no. 134.

New Zealand Local Government.
See item no. 905.

Foreign Relations

483 In the field for peace: New Zealand's contribution to international peace-support operations, 1950-1995.
John Crawford. Wellington: New Zealand Defence Force, 1996. 84p. maps.

'Involvement in international peace-support operations was at first a peripheral activity for the New Zealand Armed Forces, but over recent years it has assumed an increasingly important place in the work of the New Zealand Defence Force' (Introduction). The role of the Force in twenty-one different peace-keeping situations is outlined. Photographs illustrate some of the difficulties and tensions under which the Force has had to work. Participation in these operations is seen as being within a range of activities which New Zealand undertakes as part of its efforts to be 'a good international citizen'.

484 On our own: New Zealand in the emerging tripolar world.
Bryce Harland. Wellington: Institute of Policy Studies, 1992. 112p.

'The aim is to assess the implications for New Zealand of recent changes in the world . . . taking economic as well as political factors into account, and trying to look ahead, past current crises and personalities, to see what sort of world New Zealanders will have to live in for the next decade or so' (Introduction). An extended essay, in which the author attempts to determine New Zealand's place in a world witnessing the realignment of allegiances and power in America, Asia and Europe. He looks at the dangers of both nationalism and dependency.

485 The New Zealand foreign affairs handbook.
Stephen J. Hoadley. Auckland: Oxford University Press/New Zealand Institute of International Affairs, 1992. 178p. maps.

Provides quick answers for those seeking information about New Zealand in world affairs. Maps, diagrams, documents and tables provide up-to-date information on diplomacy, aid, trade, capital flows, defence, immigration and cultural exchanges. In addition, the governmental and political institutions which make foreign policy are analysed, and the roles of parties, interest groups and public opinion are reviewed.

486 **The Trans-Tasman relationship.**

Frank Holmes. Wellington: Institute of Policy Studies, 1996. 58p.

An extended essay reviewing the current relationship between New Zealand and Australia, largely in response to the New Zealand Foreign Minister's suggestion that the two countries need to pause and consider what they want and expect from each other. Not just about the closer economic relationship (CER), though this is accorded due importance, the essay attempts to encompass all major facets of the wide-ranging set of relationships between the peoples of the two countries.

487 **Beyond New Zealand. II. Foreign policy into the 1990s.**

Edited by Richard Kennaway, John Henderson. Auckland: Longman Paul, 1991. 2nd ed. 250p.

There have been major changes in the world order since the first edition (1980) of this book: the end of the Cold War; the declining hegemony of the superpowers; and the new economic dynamism of the Asia-Pacific region. Partially reflecting these changes, recent years have witnessed the questioning of many long-held assumptions about New Zealand's security, manifested in the growth of the peace movement, promulgation of the non-nuclear policy, and the promotion of a wider network of contacts in trade and diplomatic representation. Contributors attempt to both trace the changing attitudes and assess the implications. The editors assume little prior knowledge of the issues on the part of readers.

488 **Rocking the boat: New Zealand, the United States and the nuclear-free zone controversy in the 1980s.**

Paul Landais-Sharp, Paul Rogers. Oxford: Berg Publishers, 1989. 185p.

The 1984 election of David Lange's Labour Government, and its subsequent stand on the issue of port visits by nuclear-armed vessels, led to a crisis in relations with the United States. Despite heavy pressure from its ANZUS allies, but with strong domestic support, the New Zealand government maintained its policy and went on to win a second election in 1987, the nuclear issue being a central part of the campaign. This volume examines the controversy and suggests some of the implications of New Zealand's stance. A collection of essays edited by Jacob Bercovitch, *ANZUS in crisis: alliance management in international affairs* (Christchurch: University of Canterbury Press/Macmillan, 1988. 267p.) offers Australian and American reactions to the crisis while Stuart Macmillan's *Neither confirm nor deny: the nuclear ships dispute between New Zealand and the United States* (Wellington: Allen & Unwin/Port Nicholson Press, 1987. 177p.) compares the New Zealand stance with that taken by its close neighbour, Australia.

489 **Nuclear free – the New Zealand way.**

David Lange. Auckland: Penguin, 1990. 212p.

A highly personal, partisan, eyewitness account by New Zealand's then Prime Minister of the events which led the government to ban visits by foreign nuclear warships, the consequence of which was the effective suspension of New Zealand from the ANZUS alliance. This is vintage Lange – lively, ironical, humorous – though the book has a serious justifying purpose.

490 **Peace people: a history of peace activities in New Zealand.**
Elsie Locke.   Christchurch; Melbourne: Hazard Press, 1992. 335p.
bibliog.

An extensively documented history of peace movements in New Zealand, stretching
back to the early days of colonial settlement but concentrating on the 20th century.
The book seeks to record the activities of many men and women now known to few.
'Heroes of war are celebrated in traditional societies, and their stories are told with
honour and respect. Heroes of peace are . . . quickly forgotten' (Introduction).
Roughly half of the work is devoted to discussion of building post-Second World War
opposition to nuclear weapons.

491 **New Zealand and the Korean War.**
Ian McGibbon.   Auckland: Oxford University Press/Historical
Branch, Department of Internal Affairs, 1992-96. 2 vols. bibliog.

An impressive account of New Zealand's involvement in the Korean War 1951-53.
Volume one covers the political, diplomatic and social aspects of the country's
involvement, and seeks to explain why it was considered necessary to contribute to the
United Nations' forces on the peninsula. A product of the situation was the ANZUS
Treaty of 1951, which was to have far-reaching implications for New Zealand's inter-
national relations in later decades. Volume two covers the military side of New
Zealand's involvement.

492 **Independence and foreign policy: New Zealand in the world since
1935.**
Malcolm McKinnon.   Auckland: Auckland University Press, 1993.
329p. maps.

The first interpretative study of New Zealand foreign policy for the period 1935-91.
Based on meticulous documentation, utilizing both public and private sources, this is an
original and thought-provoking work. The author looks critically at the idea of independence in New Zealand's foreign policy, exploring the way New Zealanders have thought
about independence, as well as the kinds of independence most commonly pursued and
their implications in practice. While the focus of the first part of the book is the Second
World War, later chapters provide insights into some recent issues in New Zealand foreign policy: the Vietnam War; relations with South Africa and the Pacific; and the
anti-nuclear debate. Economic as well as political international relations are analysed.

493 **The great debate: New Zealand, Britain and the EEC, the shaping
of attitudes.**
Robert McLuskie.   Wellington: Decision Research Centre, Victoria
University of Wellington/New Zealand Institute of International
Affairs, 1986. 175p.

In the Foreword to this book, Professor John Roberts describes Britain's decision to
join the Common Market 'and thrust a comfortable politico/economic associate into
the rough world of independence and competition for economic survival' as one of the
turning-points in New Zealand history. Although not an attractive presentation, this
study is a well-researched examination of the effects of that decision on New Zealand.
The author stresses his concern with the public debate, and with how the majority of
New Zealanders perceived the debate, not with official exchanges.

494 **Defending New Zealand: a study of structures, processes and relationships.**
James Rolfe. Wellington: Institute of Policy Studies, 1993. 186p. bibliog.

An analysis of the defence policy system which describes the organization of defence, the evolution of the policy-setting parts of the organization and the processes used to make policy decisions. The factors which are considered to be important to policy makers are also discussed. Examples are employed from a wide range of issues and events of the last twenty years. Alliance relationships and how they are managed, troop deployments and the background to equipment decisions inform the comments made. 'The study is explanatory rather than prescriptive . . . it does not set out to change policy or improve the policy-making process . . . rather it is an attempt to analyse the policy system as a means of achieving greater understanding of it' (Preface).

495 **New Zealand as an international citizen: fifty years of United Nations membership.**
Edited by Malcolm Templeton. Wellington: Ministry of Foreign Affairs and Trade, 1995. 176p.

A collection of essays, principally by former or present diplomats, assessing New Zealand's participation in the deliberations of the United Nations, in actions arising from those deliberations, and in the programmes of associated agencies. New Zealand's three terms on the Security Council are highlighted. While the summaries presented are useful, the views expressed are wholly orthodox.

496 **Fifty years of New Zealand foreign policy making.**
Edited by Anne Trotter. Dunedin: University of Otago, Foreign Policy School, 1993. 264p.

Marking the fiftieth anniversary of the establishment of New Zealand's Department of External Affairs, this book includes reflective contributions from politicians, officials and academics. Among the topics discussed are the country's relative isolation, its preoccupation with trade, the disparity in scale between its regional and global roles, the impact of public opinion on policy formation, and the new importance of Asia in New Zealand's world view. Four former departmental heads reminisce in an appendix.

497 **New Zealand and ASEAN: a critical overview of the relationship.**
Raj Vasil. Wellington: Institute of Policy Studies, 1995. 63p.

A slight work which critically explores New Zealand's relationships with the countries of the Association of Southeast Asian Nations (ASEAN). 'Raj Vasil recently visited ASEAN countries, talking with government leaders, officials and academics and this provides a unique perspective' (Foreword). The countries covered include Brunei Darussalam, Indonesia, Malaysia, the Philippines, Singapore and Thailand. The author concludes that, in spite of the distances, New Zealand's continued involvement in ASEAN can be beneficial to both sides.

Economy

498 The New Zealand economy: issues and policies.
Stuart Birks, Srikanta Chatterjee.   Palmerston North, New Zealand: Dunmore Press, 1997. 3rd ed. 356p.

Intended as an introductory outline of changes in the New Zealand economy after 1984 for the non-specialist. 'Our objectives are clear: to state, analyse and evaluate New Zealand's economic problems, policies and performance . . . We have tried, as much as possible, to avoid taking a party-political stance' (Preface). Overviews of the economy and economic growth are followed by chapters on the agricultural, manufacturing and services sectors, the labour market, finance and trade, the public sector, and welfare issues. Most of the contributors are from Massey University, Palmerston North.

499 Economic liberalisation in New Zealand.
Edited by Alan Bollard, Robert Buckle.   Wellington: Allen & Unwin/Port Nicholson Press, 1987. 364p.

A pioneering attempt to stimulate debate on the 'more market' reforms of the fourth Labour Government, this collection of essays is now primarily of historical interest, even if only as a progress report. The introduction seeks to put the first three reforming years in historical and economic context. The first half of the book focuses on microeconomic aspects of the reforms: industry deregulation, competition policy and regulatory change in individual industries. The second half directs attention to the macroeconomic aspects of liberalization. As the editors presciently noted: 'Economic liberalization is a continuing story' (Preface).

500 **The influence of United States economics on New Zealand: the Fullbright anniversary seminars.**
Edited by Alan Bollard. Wellington: New Zealand-United States Educational Federation/New Zealand Institute of Economic Research, 1989. 158p.

Many of New Zealand's radical structural economic changes have been attributed to United States economic thinking. How important have US-inspired policies been? How appropriate are they for New Zealand? Have they been satisfactorily filtered and adapted? What can be learnt from New Zealand experiences? The papers in this volume attempt to answer these questions. They systematically analyse the effects of US economic developments on New Zealand thinking and policy in the areas of competition and efficiency, regulation, monetary and financial policy, labour markets and social policy.

501 **Upgrading New Zealand's competitive advantage.**
Graham T. Crocombe, Michael J. Enright, Michael E. Porter.
Auckland: Oxford University Press/New Zealand Trade Development Board, 1991. 235p.

Part of an international study of the sources of national economic success overseen by Professor Michael Porter of the Harvard Business School, this work analyses the competitive position of New Zealand's top twenty export industries. It seeks to answer questions relating to the under-performance of New Zealand's economy over the preceding three decades and to establish a framework for remedying this situation.

502 **The New Zealand macroeconomy: a briefing on the reforms.**
Paul Dalziel, Ralph Lattimore. Auckland: Oxford University Press, 1996. 129p.

A concise, up-to-date record of New Zealand's economic performance during the twenty-five years leading up to 1984, of each of the major economic reforms that have been instituted since that date, and of the impact the reforms have had on more than forty-five key macroeconomic indicators. 'Writing the text has been an interesting experience . . . By reputation, one of us is a strong critic of aspects of the reforms, the other a strong advocate of the programme's basic principles . . . We agreed that we would not publish anything that we could not both support' (Preface). The text is amplified by graphs and diagrams.

503 **The Muldoon years: an essay on New Zealand's recent economic growth.**
J. D. Gould. Auckland: Hodder & Stoughton, 1985. 87p.

'Most (but not all) individual economists as well, apparently, as Treasury and the Reserve Bank, have espoused a "doom and gloom" view of New Zealand's recent economic history' (Introduction). In this extended essay the author, a distinguished economic historian, challenges the view and seeks to place New Zealand's economic performance in the 1970s and early 1980s in more realistic perspective. He considers a number of the criticisms of Sir Robert Muldoon's economic management to be exaggerated, sometimes unfair, and that insufficient credit is given for justifiable policies introduced. The essay is a thought-provoking counter to the 'there is no alternative' nostrums of the economic reformers.

504 **New Zealand: market liberalization in a developed economy.**
Patrick Massey. Basingstoke, England: Macmillan; New York:
St Martins Press, 1995. 245p. bibliog.

The author, a member since 1991 of Ireland's Competition Authority in Dublin,
worked in the New Zealand Treasury for almost two years (1989-91), drawn to the
country by the reports of radical economic reform. The purpose of the book is to
analyse the reform programme and its effects. 'It seeks to explain why a Labour government not only embarked upon the sort of reform programme normally considered
the preserve of right-wing administrations, but in fact surpassed them in the zeal with
which it embraced market-oriented policies' (Preface). He concludes that while there
are still some problem areas to be tackled, generally there are grounds for optimism
about the reforms. 'It appears that New Zealand is now a more internationally competitive and dynamic economy as a result of the reform programme' (p. 203).

505 **The New Zealand economy: a personal view.**
R. D. Muldoon. Auckland: Endeavour Press, 1985. 191p.

In the wake of the fourth Labour Government's first raft of structural reforms, the
author, recently ousted as Prime Minister, reiterated his personal manifesto:
'Economics, finally, is people, and economic management requires a knowledge and
understanding of the people who live inside the economy' (Preface). Arguing that any
country which allows its economy to run completely free would get the worst of all
worlds, and that there was little new in the panaceas being advanced, he reviews New
Zealand's economic performance in the preceding twenty-five years and the reasons
for decisions made. While, inevitably, the book is self-justifying, this is an enlightening insider account of the economic problems facing the country after Britain's entry
to the European Economic Community.

506 **State and economy in New Zealand.**
Edited by Brian Roper, Chris Rudd. Auckland: Oxford University
Press, 1993. 276p.

'Crisis, conflict, turmoil and transition have been characteristic features of New
Zealand's political economy from the late 1960s onwards. Major changes have taken
place in the underlying structure of New Zealand's economy and in the relationship of
this economy to the world economy' (Introduction). The contributors analyse these
changes, placing particular emphasis on the post-1984 paradigm shift from democratic
Keynesianism to New Right monetarism. Topics discussed include the development of
macroeconomic policy, the role of the Treasury and Reserve Bank, the extent of business influence in state policy formation, expert performance, industrial relations, and
the crisis of the Welfare State.

507 **New Zealand can be different and better: why deregulation does
not work.**
W. Rosenberg. Christchurch: New Zealand Monthly Review Society,
1993. 184p.

The author is well known for his alternative leftwing approach to politics in New
Zealand. In this work he 'demonstrates the falseness of the principles on which economic principles of liberalisation rest . . . that the application of so-called "Market"
principles . . . will destroy this country' (Introduction). He focuses on the vulnerability
of a small nation such as New Zealand and the costs, both social and economic, that

result from the abdication of financial power to offshore interests and the dismantling of all forms of protection for the domestic economy. The book is a sequel to *The magic square* (Christchurch: New Zealand Monthly Review Society, 1986. 128p.).

508　**A study of economic reform: the case of New Zealand.**
Edited by Brian Silverstone, Alan Bollard, Ralph Lattimore.
Amsterdam: Elsevier, 1996. 518p.

'During a decade of economic reform, beginning in 1984, New Zealand was transformed from one of the most interventionist OECD [Organization for Economic Co-operation and Development] economies to one of the most open, market-based . . . Probably no other OECD country has experienced so much concentrated change' (Preface). This book is probably the most comprehensive study of the reforms available. It covers areas ranging from growth, productivity, income distribution and unemployment, to labour and financial markets, fiscal and monetary policies, international trade, public and private industries, resource management and social services. A valuable introductory section places the contributions in context. All of the contributions are previously unpublished.

509　**Rogernomics: reshaping New Zealand's economy.**
Edited by Simon Walker.　Wellington: GP Books, 1989. 244p.

An examination of the impact of the economic reforms of the first four years of New Zealand's fourth Labour Government (1984-88). With the contributors largely enthusiastic about the reform programme, most being either committed advisers or participants, and with the volume being published by a right-leaning 'think tank', the laudatory tone is unsurprising. Several of the contributors make it clear that they consider further far-reaching changes, for instance labour market deregulation, to be required.

Cul de sac: the question of New Zealand's future.
See item no. 2.

Changing places in New Zealand: a geography of restructuring.
See item no. 18.

Changing places: New Zealand in the nineties.
See item no. 24.

The making of New Zealand: an economic history.
See item no. 99.

The rake's progress?: the New Zealand economy since 1945.
See item no. 126.

Women in the economy: a research report on the economic position of women in New Zealand.
See item no. 286.

Women and economics: a New Zealand feminist perspective.
See item no. 296.

Maori women in the economy: a preliminary review of the economic position of Maori women in New Zealand.
See item no. 301.

Making a difference.
See item no. 440.

The making of Rogernomics.
See item no. 473.

New Zealand Economic Papers.
See item no. 889.

Finance and Banking

510 **Kiwicap: an introduction to New Zealand capital markets.**
Roger J. Bowden.   Palmerston North, New Zealand: Dunmore Press,
1996. 186p.

A readable, and sometimes irreverent, account of the evolution of New Zealand's capital markets since financial deregulation. The book blends basic economic and
financial principles with a thorough understanding of the operations of the fixed interest, equity, derivatives and foreign exchange markets, as well as the mechanisms of
the New Zealand monetary system. Although primarily intended as an introductory
text in financial economics, the book is user-friendly for the general reader simply
wanting to know how the system operates.

511 **New Zealand's money revolution: a comprehensive, up-to-the-
minute guide to New Zealand's rapidly changing financial system.**
Edna Carew.   Wellington: Allen & Unwin/Port Nicholson Press,
1987. 188p.

The author's intention is to demystify the subject of financial deregulation, 'to explain
why the financial system has been reformed, so that everyone can understand the
changes and their implications and make the most of the benefits that the reform is
intended to bring' (Introduction). In clear language, with a minimum of jargon, chapters present information on the new role of government in the short-term money
market, the role of the Reserve Bank, banks generally, and non-bank financial institutions. The work looks at financial instruments such as commercial bills and promissory
notes, at the bond market and at futures trading and foreign exchange dealing.

512 **Tigers in New Zealand?: the role of Asian investment in the
economy.**
R. D. Cremer, B. Ramasamy.   Wellington: Institute of Policy
Studies/Asia 2000 Foundation, 1996. 115p.

Part of a series from the Institute of Policy Studies and the Asia 2000 Foundation on
New Zealand's linkages with the Asia-Pacific region. 'The book shows that Asian

160

investment is a necessary and positive part of the development and success of the New Zealand economy and a reflection of the leading role that Asia plays in the world economy' (cover). The work uses case-studies of Asian investment in New Zealand and then examines these and New Zealand in terms of the international economy. This is accessible information, attractively presented.

513 Bulls, bears and elephants: a history of the New Zealand stock exchange.
David Grant.   Wellington: Victoria University Press, 1997. 414p. map.

'Elephants, in times of excitement, charge in herds through the African bush, uprooting acacia trees as they go. New Zealanders, in times of fiscal excitement, charge in herds to their local stockbroker . . .' (Introduction). This book traces the development of the business of stockbroking in New Zealand and the growth of the Stock Exchange as an institution. It provides accounts of the stockbrokers' central roles in tumultuous episodes in the country's history, from the quartz-mining booms of the late 1860s to the boom and bust of the 1980s. The analysis included of the past two decades is particularly useful.

514 Between governments and banks: a history of the Reserve Bank of New Zealand.
G. R. Hawke.   Wellington: Government Printer, 1973. 244p. bibliog.

After an introduction describing the New Zealand banking system before the establishment of the Reserve Bank in 1934, the author describes the Bank's relations with the government, economic policy and exchange control, monetary policy, and relations with trading banks. The author has used the records of the Bank itself and, for the early years, Treasury records. He analyses and reviews the trials and tribulations of the early years of the Bank and looks at its adaptation and growth.

515 Competition and co-operation: the Insurance Council and the general insurance industry in New Zealand, 1895-1995.
Alan Henderson.   Wellington: Insurance Council of New Zealand/Historical Branch, Department of Internal Affairs, 1995. 80p.

A short history of the Insurance Council and the general insurance industry in New Zealand, 1895-1995, which explains the nature of insurance in clear terms. It is a well-illustrated work.

516 A new approach to central banking: the New Zealand experiment and comparisons with Australia.
Frank Holmes.   Wellington: Institute of Policy Studies/Victoria University of Wellington, 1993. 37p.

Discusses the differences between the New Zealand and Australian approaches to central banking, in easy-to-understand prose. With New Zealand's financial reforms attracting attention internationally, the report 'discusses the policy on prudential surveillance, but only as part of such wider issues as what the objectives of a central bank should be, how much independence it should be accorded in formulating and developing policy and how its relationships with government should be handled in a democratic system which in the past suffered from serious inflationary problems'

161

(Foreword). A more irreverent approach to the subject can be found in *Prosperity denied: how the Reserve Bank harms New Zealand*, by Bob Jones (Christchurch: Canterbury University Press, 1996. 100p.).

517 **Financial deregulation and disinflation in a small open economy: the New Zealand experience.**
Nicola Hunn, David Mayes, Neil Williams.   Wellington: New Zealand Institute for Economic Research, 1989. 221p.

Aimed at students of the subject, this is a textbook-like discussion of some of the implications of the key elements of the early financial policy moves of the 1984 Labour Government. The information is presented in two parts: the first introduces the macroeconomic effects of financial deregulation; the second some of the sectoral aspects of disinflation.

518 **An introduction to financial markets in New Zealand.**
Edited by Girol Karacaoglu.   Wellington: Victoria University Press, 1988. 142p.

Commencing with an overview of financial markets, each chapter looks at a different kind of market in more detail: the shares market, the money market, the futures market and the foreign exchange market. Arising out of a course for bank officers, this book provides good basic information at an easily assimilated level.

519 **New Zealand futures trading.**
Brent Layton.   Wellington: Allen & Unwin/Port Nicholson Press, 1987. 104p.

Futures trading is a recent development in New Zealand's financial market, a New Zealand Futures Exchange not being set up until early 1985. The author, a full-time futures trader, explains how futures trading works, and identifies a number of features unique to the New Zealand market. Written for both intending and practising traders, the text assumes a reasonable degree of technical knowledge.

520 **Financial policy reform.**
Reserve Bank of New Zealand.   Wellington: Reserve Bank of New Zealand, 1986. 220p. bibliog.

Thirteen articles 'explain the background to and the rationale for the changes in monetary policy and exchange rate policy that followed the change in Government in July 1984' (cover). The intention is that the information should be straightforward so as to appeal to a wide audience from students to the general public. Topics covered include financial sector policy reforms, monetary policy, the removal of the various controls on interest rates, the abolition of statutory ratios over financial institutions and the floating of the exchange rate.

521 **Monetary policy and the New Zealand financial system.**
Reserve Bank of New Zealand. Wellington: Reserve Bank/GP
Publications, 1992. 268p.

Since 1984 the New Zealand financial system and the framework for monetary policy
have changed almost beyond recognition. With the Reserve Bank being charged with
the formulation and implementation of monetary policy, this book may be regarded as
a statement of prevailing orthodoxies. The individual essays are collected in four
parts. Parts one and two set out how monetary policy is devised in New Zealand. Part
three analyses the structure of the New Zealand financial system, including the payments system; it also describes banking supervision policies and practices. Part four
provides a longer-term perspective of these issues, with an historical overview.

Trade

522 **Meeting the East Asia challenge: trends, prospects and policies.**
Alan Bollard. Wellington: Victoria University Press, for Institute of
Policy Studies, 1989. 186p. maps.

'This study acknowledges New Zealand's increasing dependence on [East Asia] and
the opportunities that arise from a region which is expected to experience strong
growth, higher incomes, greater mobility of its peoples and increasing demand within
those economies for a wide range of goods and services' (cover). The study is in two
parts. The first analyses trends and prospects in merchandise trade, services trade and
investment with the region; the second looks at pricing implications of these changes.
Though now becoming dated, the work sets the developing trade with this region in
context.

523 **Expanding our horizons: New Zealand in the global economy.**
Paul Callister. Wellington: New Zealand Planning Council, 1991.
52p.

A concise survey of the process of globalization and how it affects New Zealand. The
author examines the links between trade in goods, services and capital, as well as the
movement of people. He also raises some important issues. Is foreign investment
increasing and, if so, is this good for New Zealand? Is the concept of 'New Zealand-
made' valid any longer? Should barriers to the outside world be even further
reduced? 'New Zealand's future is certainly not guaranteed. In a global economy
companies and people will move towards the most profitable opportunities . . .'
(Conclusion, p. 48).

524 **Dismantling the barriers: tariff policy in New Zealand.**
Ian Duncan, Ralph Lattimore, Alan Bollard. Wellington: New
Zealand Institute of Economic Research, 1992. 94p. (Research
Monograph 57).

Theoretical in approach, this work provides historical perspectives on trade protection
through tariffs in New Zealand, considers the theory of tariff incidence, comments on

alternatives, assesses New Zealand's true rate of assistance and examines the pressures on industry in New Zealand to adjust to tariffs. The information is set in the light of the Government's decisions in the September quarter, 1991 on post-1992 tariffs. 'The main objective . . . is to examine the political economy of tariff policy, at least as it influenced the most recent set of decisions' (Introduction).

525 Fast forward: New Zealand business in world markets.
Peter Enderwick, Michele Akoorie.   Auckland: Longman Paul, 1996. 450p.

Acknowledging the need for management education in the field of international business in order to respond to the increased internationalization of the New Zealand economy, the authors have compiled a comprehensive set of original cases based on the experiences of New Zealand companies seeking to internationalize. Additional chapters provide comment and further information. The work is essentially designed as a senior level student resource. Topics include international marketing and management issues, how to assess and analyse case-studies and how to use case-studies to consider strategy formulation and implementation. The implications of internationalization of business are also considered.

526 New Zealand and Australia: negotiating closer economic relations.
J. Stephen Hoadley.   Wellington: New Zealand Institute of International Affairs, 1995. 134p.

An associate professor of political studies at the University of Auckland examines how closer economic relations (CER) were developed and fashioned through negotiations between New Zealand and Australia. The study considers how differences were resolved, bargains were made and what new arrangements were created to ensure mutual benefit. Experiences with NAFTA (New Zealand-Australia Free Trade Agreement) (1965-78) and ANZCERTA (Australia and New Zealand Closer Economic Relations Trade Agreement) (1978-83), in negotiating, are drawn on and lessons that may be learnt from the CER model are outlined. *CER and business competition: Australia and New Zealand in a global economy*, edited by Kerrin M. Vautier, James Farmer and Robert Baxt (Auckland: Commerce Clearing House New Zealand, 1990. 340p.), takes a more legalistic approach to the implications of CER. Chapter headings include 'Regulatory and judicial environment', 'Progress on current issues', 'Taxing issues' and 'The Pacific context'.

527 Meeting the European challenge: trends, prospects and policies.
Frank Holmes, Clive Pearson.   Wellington: Victoria University Press, for Institute of Policy Studies, with assistance from the Trade Development Board and Ministry of External Relations and Trade, 1991. 328p.

More detailed than *The great debate* by Robert McLuskie (q.v.), this work considers the implications of the European Community's developing associations with Eastern Europe and the USSR, and the implications for New Zealand of its growing influence in world trade and finance. The final chapter of the book 'explores what strategies need to be followed in both the public and private sectors to take advantage of the opportunities which will be available in the next decade'. The text is well supported with explanatory graphs, tables and diagrams.

Business and Business Conditions

General

528 Business and New Zealand society.
Edited by John Deeks, Peter Enderwick. Auckland: Longman Paul, 1994. 317p.

Looks at the concerns outlined in *Business in New Zealand society*, edited by George Hines (Wellington: Hicks Smiths & Sons, 1973. 307p.) and reassesses the debates in the contemporary context. 'The various chapters . . . touch upon a number of persistent themes . . . the inculcation of a market-based economic philosophy and its implications for efficiency versus equity, the concept of the firm responding to a range of stakeholder interests, the desire to see New Zealand maintain a pluralist democracy, the internationalisation of economic activity, the problems facing Maori enterprise and the need to hold managers accountable for their actions' (Introduction).

529 Controlling interests: business, the state and society in New Zealand.
Edited by John Deeks, Nick Perry. Auckland: Auckland University Press, 1992. 246p. maps.

A loosely connected collection of interdisciplinary case-studies on a diverse range of topics: the organization and reorganization of television; law firms; law enforcement and financial institutions; the Treaty of Waitangi and the fishing industry; the Employment Equity Act 1990; and the deregulation of the tobacco industry. A uniting thread is provided by changes introduced by the government in the period 1984 to 1990. References point to further reading on the various topics.

530 **The logic of New Zealand business: strategy, structure and performance.**
Robert T. Hamilton, Gurvinder Singh Shergill.   Auckland: Oxford University Press, 1993. 173p.

Builds up a picture of the reasons why some New Zealand companies have performed better than others, bringing together data on company strategies, structure, ownership and performance. There is an attempt to identify an underlying logic which has led to superior performance. Based on a PhD written by Shergill and supervised by Hamilton, this is a carefully considered academic study, not a book of handy tips.

531 **Behind the mirror glass: the growth of wealth and power in New Zealand in the eighties.**
Bruce Jesson.   Auckland: Penguin, 1987. 176p.

Hard-hitting and uncompromising in his approach, the author posits a shift in the 1980s in who holds wealth and power in New Zealand through both historical analysis and a careful examination of the contemporary scene. He believes that 'power has shifted, under the aegis of the fourth Labour Government, to a small group of hard-line right-wingers in Treasury, the Reserve Bank, business and some university departments' (Introduction). He then speculates on the probable effects of the shift and where it might take the country.

532 **The paradise conspiracy.**
Ian Wishart.   Auckland: Howling at the Moon Press, 1995. 363p.

What began as an investigation by two New Zealand business newspapers into claims of tax cheating quickly grew into a three-year investigation for a television documentary. The result was a Commission of Inquiry (the 'Winebox inquiry') into activities uncovered by the television team, and into 'whether some law enforcement agencies had acted lawfully or competently in their own probes into the alleged crimes' (Introduction). With the report of the Commission of Inquiry having now been presented, this is a racy account of what led to it being set up. *Lawyers, guns and money* (1997. 297p.), by the same author and publisher, examines some of the issues raised which were excluded from the enquiry.

Enterprises

533 **The Hawk: Allan Hawkins tells the Equiticorp story to Gordon McLauchlan.**
Allan Hawkins.   Auckland: Four Star, 1989. 183p.

The 1988 collapse of Equiticorp, one of New Zealand's fastest-growing businesses, became a *cause célèbre* because of the large number of investors who felt they had been misled and cheated. This is the story of the man behind Equiticorp, Allan Hawkins. Journalistic in approach, it provides insights into the business world of the 1980s and, specifically, the events leading up to the liquidation of the firm.

534   **Michael Fay: on a reach for the ultimate: the unauthorised biography.**
Iain Morrison, Grant Cubis, Frank Haden.   Wellington: Freelance Biographies, 1990. 285p.

Although disappointing as a biography, this book collates useful information on one of the leading contemporary figures in New Zealand merchant banking, also one of the principal private beneficiaries of deregulation and the sale of state assets post-1984. Considerable space is also devoted to Fay's repeated efforts to win the Americas Cup (yachting). The tone is excessively hagiographical.

535   **New Zealand's top 200 companies: rebuilding an economy, 1985-1995.**
Auckland: Profile Books, 1996. 325p. map.

The vital statistics of 200 top companies and 30 top financial institutions over the years 1985 to 1995 are detailed. At the same time the critical changes that have taken place in virtually every aspect of New Zealand's political, economic and social infra-structure are also recorded in an economic overview. The information is attractively presented with photographs enlivening the descriptions of the different areas reviewed. The whole provides a glowing picture of the changes that have occurred.

536   **Lost property: the crash of '87 – and the aftershock.**
Olly Newland.   Auckland: Harper Collins, 1994. 131p.

The stock-market crash of Black Monday, 19 October 1987, affected New Zealand as much as any other country. The author, 'wheeler and dealer supreme', gives an insider's view of what happened, conveniently laying the blame at the hands of the bankers and government of the day. For those who have wondered how it all hap-pened, this is a readable entree to the world of the stock and property markets.

537   **Made in New Zealand: the story of Jim Fletcher.**
Selwyn Parker.   Auckland: Hodder & Stoughton, 1994. 250p.

Fletcher Holdings is one of New Zealand's biggest and most well-known companies. Newsprint manufacturing, steel, timber processing, and manufacturing (from particle board to roofing) were all part of a kingdom which stretched beyond New Zealand's shores. Parker offers a sympathetic account of the man who developed this industrial empire. The picture painted is of a modest man, who through hard work rose from storekeeper to company director. Less sympathetic is Bruce Jesson's *The Fletcher challenge* (Pokeno, New Zealand: B. Jesson, 1980. 63p.).

538   **The Ariadne story: the rise and fall of a business empire.**
Bruce Ross.   Elwood, Victoria: Greenhouse Publications, 1988. 264p.

The stock-market crash of Black Monday (19 October 1987) signalled the overnight collapse of a NZ$2 billion conglomerate, Ariadne, the largest corporate loss in Australasian history. 'This book is about the arrogant treatment of shareholders by a management solely interested in its own personal gain and prepared to use any means to achieve it, and about those who should have protected the shareholders but did not' (Prologue). The author concludes that no part of the financial community was blame-less: regulatory bodies were lax and ineffectual; brokers preferred to bank their underwriting fees rather than question the merits of the investment; auditors meekly bowed to management pressure; and banks abandoned caution, lending against minimal collateral. The work is an indictment of the prevailing ethos, 'greed is good'.

539 Brierley: the man behind the corporate legend.
Yvonne van Dongen.   Auckland: Viking, 1990. 271p.

It is clear from the author's Preface that this is not an easy man about whom to write a biography. Essentially private, not willing to share much of himself, even with his closest friends, he was not even sure that he wanted a book written about his life. However, Sir Ron Brierley is something of a legend to most New Zealanders. From small beginnings he built Brierley Investment Limited (BIL) into a multi-million-dollar business through his skills as a 'corporate raider'.

Small businesses

540 Small businesses in New Zealand.
Alan Bollard.   Wellington: Allen & Unwin/Port Nicholson Press, 1988. 134p.

Not so much a 'how-to-do-it', as a history of the small business in New Zealand. The coverage extends from 'the early industry in New Zealand, through changes of the mid twentieth century to the factors influencing small business today' (cover). In describing the contribution small business makes to the New Zealand economy, a number of enterprises are profiled.

541   The New Zealand small business guide.
Richard Higham, Sara Williams.   Auckland: Penguin Books, 1994. rev. ed. 271p.

Described as practical, comprehensive and clearly presented, this guide is all of that. It offers good advice from buying a business through selling the product, financial preparation and control and tax issues. Another similarly useful volume is *The small business book: a New Zealand guide*, by Robert Hamilton and John English (Wellington: Bridget Williams Books, 1997. 3rd ed. 309p.).

Changing places in new Zealand: a geography of restructuring.
See item no. 18.

Changing places: New Zealand in the nineties.
See item no. 24.

Corporatization and privatization: lessons from New Zealand.
See item no. 472.

Fast forward: New Zealand business in world markets.
See item no. 525.

Turning it round: closure and revitalization in New Zealand.
See item no. 543.

Management.
See item no. 885.

A'Courts business handbook: products, brands, trades, companies.
See item no. 927.

The New Zealand business who's who.
See item no. 937.

New Zealand company register, 1996-97.
See item no. 938.

Newzindex: The Monthly Index of New Zealand Business and Commercial Publications.
See item no. 941.

A select bibliography of the business history of New Zealand.
See item no. 971.

Industry

General

542 **Manufacturing in the Wellington region, 1895-1995.**
Rex Monigatti. Wellington: Wellington Manufacturers Association, 1995. 62p.

A celebration of the work of the Wellington Provincial Industrial Association, established in 1895, and its successor, the Wellington Manufacturers Association. Well illustrated, the volume examines a number of the industries of the region, which includes within its ambit Taranaki, Wanganui, Manawatu, Gisborne, Hawkes Bay, Wairarapa, Nelson and Marlborough. This short introduction thus provides an overview of the development of manufacturing in the central portion of the country. Included is a final chapter which looks at key issues in 1995.

543 **Turning it round: closure and revitalization in New Zealand.**
Edited by John Savage, Alan Bollard. Auckland: Oxford University Press, 1990. 156p.

Economic deregulation has placed enormous pressure on New Zealand firms to rationalize their activities: by reorganizing, relocating, and in some instances by closing down completely. This book examines the responses to deregulation in five representative industries: meat processing, flour milling, carpet manufacturing, automobile assembly and petrol retailing. It analyses the factors, such as market and asset structure and firm ownership, which influence the rationalization strategies that firms employ, and also identifies the barriers they encounter.

544 **New Zealand manufacturing: a study of change.**
Richard Willis. Wellington: Department of Geography, Victoria University of Wellington, 1994. 23p. (Working Paper no. 23).

The author posits that over eighty per cent of the net increase in unemployment in the decade to 1994 may be explained by a severe shrinkage of manufacturing jobs, spread geographically and over all industry groups. 'It is fair to say that of all the sectors of the New Zealand economy, manufacturing has been most affected by the restructuring and deregulation politics of the last ten years' (Introduction). He reviews the background to the burgeoning pre-1984 development of New Zealand's industrial base, noting the protection afforded by isolation and tariff barriers. He also assesses the likely long-term impact of the recent changes.

545 **Well made New Zealand: a century of trade marks.**
Richard Wolfe. Auckland: Reed Methuen, 1987. 138p.
An informal history of trademarks in New Zealand, selecting from the enormous number registered over the past 100 years. While primarily of nostalgic appeal, the selection indicates the wide range of locally manufactured goods available from a comparatively early date. The author also shows how the symbolism employed in trademarks of different eras reflects New Zealand's developing sense of nationhood.

Case-studies

546 **Papermaking pioneers: a history of New Zealand Paper Mills Limited and its predecessors.**
John H. Angus. Mataura, New Zealand: New Zealand Paper Mills, 1976. 212p. bibliog.
'This is the story of paper making in the south of New Zealand where the industry in this country had its beginnings . . . the struggle against economic fluctuations; the problems of competition from imports . . . the role of manufacturing in New Zealand; the relationship between the industry and the government; and the interaction between NZPM and its competitors in New Zealand since the Second World War' (Preface).

547 **A century of achievement: a commemoration of the first 100 years of the New Zealand meat industry.**
Edited by R. A. Barton. Palmerston North, New Zealand: Dunmore Press, 1984. 205p. map.
Not a history in the usual sense, rather a gathering together of addresses by dignitaries and papers presented at four conferences. The result is a mix of scientific and general information, which nevertheless provides a picture of activities and achievements in the meat industry over the 100 years from 1882 to 1982 and also makes predictions of future developments. Given the fifteen years that have elapsed since the publication of this work, it is interesting to compare the predictions with the actuality.

548 **Watties: the first fifty years.**
Geoff Conly. Hastings, New Zealand: J. Wattie Canneries Ltd., 1984. 222p.
By the mid-1980s Wattie Industries Ltd. was a New Zealand industrial giant, dominating the country's processed fruit and vegetable industries and exporting worldwide.

This book is an informal account of the company's growth from its foundation as little more than a backyard enterprise in the 1930s, and a celebration of the family dynasty that steered it to success. Since the book was published the company was first merged into an Australasian conglomerate, then acquired as a subsidiary by the multinational Heinz Corporation.

549 A hundred million trees: the story of N. Z. Forest Products Ltd.

Brian Healy. Auckland: Hodder & Stoughton, 1982. 222p.

The development of New Zealand Forest Products Ltd., which in 1935 took over the trees planted by Perpetual Forests in the 1920s, is described in terms of the growth of the New Zealand economy and the people involved. Healy clearly shows the technology transfer based upon state experiment in the central North Island which underpinned the company's massive planting in the region. The result was the development of a company that became one of the biggest in New Zealand. Although the book has evidently been well researched, it unfortunately has neither an index nor a list of the sources consulted.

550 The people and the power: the history of the Tiwai Point aluminium smelter.

Clive Lind. Invercargill, New Zealand: N. Z. Aluminium Smelters Ltd., 1996. 252p.

'In words and pictures, this is the history of the Tiwai Point aluminium smelter. It tells the story of how one of New Zealand's largest industrial plants came to be, and its first twenty five years of operation. It is a story of potential, politics, power, potlines and, above all, people' (dedication). Attractively illustrated, well written, descriptive in nature, this is a positive presentation of Comalco Ltd. and its relationship with the New Zealand Government.

551 Super in the south: the early history of the Southland Co-operative Phosphate Co. Ltd.

Clive A. Lind. Invercargill, New Zealand: The Southland Co-operative Phosphate Co. Ltd., 1983. 194p. maps.

This history marks the first twenty-five years of production by the Southland Co-operative Phosphate Company Ltd., a company formed by a group of farmers in the late 1940s, who decided that instead of bringing in fertilizer from Dunedin some 100 miles away they would establish their own fertilizer industry in Southland. Unashamedly supportive of the company being written about, the author relates the battle to establish the business, relives the highs and lows experienced, discusses the new ventures considered, and looks at plans for the future.

552 Spinning yarns: a centennial history of Alliance Textiles Limited and its predecessors 1881-1981.

G. J. McLean. Dunedin: Alliance Textiles Ltd., 1981. 221p.

Covers not only the history of a particular company, but also explores the wider history of the woollen industry in New Zealand. 'The history is . . . the story of three separate mills and the company that was formed through their merger in the early 1960s' (Introduction). The work presents each of the three mills individually and then looks at the merged company, 'a very different venture, expansionary, capital-intensive and national in outlook . . . Yet . . . also a continuation of the earlier developments'. The author concludes that for the industry to survive it must develop international markets.

553 A command of co-operatives: the development of leadership, marketing and price control in the co-operative dairy industry of New Zealand.
Arthur H. Ward.   Wellington: New Zealand Dairy Board, 1975. 266p.

A history of the New Zealand Dairy Board written from official NZDB and dairy industry sources by a former General Manager who was associated with the Board for many years. The later chapters reflect, in an unbiased way, the author's personal involvement in the NZDB – perhaps the most successful producer board in New Zealand.

Agriculture

General

554 New Zealand agriculture: a story of the past 150 years.
Edited by Peter Cross.   Auckland: New Zealand Rural Press/Hodder
& Stoughton, 1990. 174p. maps.

Big and colourful, this book was published as a sesquicentenary celebration of the
New Zealand farming industry. It tells, often through the words of descendants of pioneering farming families, of the tribulations and triumphs. A regional approach is
adopted initially, then the plant and livestock industries, the marketing industries, the
servicing industries and the farming organizations are separately examined. In a concluding section eminent personalities associated with rural New Zealand look to the
prospects and challenges ahead. A book of similar type, if less lavish, is Gordon
McLauchlan's *The farming of New Zealand* (Auckland: Australia and New Zealand
Book Co., 1981. 256p.).

555 Agrarian restructuring in New Zealand.
John R. Fairweather.   Lincoln, New Zealand: Agribusiness and
Economics Research Unit, Lincoln University, 1992. 62p.

A brief review of structural changes in New Zealand agriculture between 1984 and
1990, by way of analysis of official statistics. Several major trends are discerned:
sheep numbers have decreased noticeably; dairy stock and deer numbers have
increased; farm incomes have fallen; the overall number of farms has declined, with a
'disappearing middle' most evident; and farm employment has stagnated, many being
compelled to take up supplementary off-farm work. Yet the author discerns no major
move to corporate farming: 'if anything, exposure to financial pressure has intensified
the family character of farming' (Conclusion, p. 57).

556 Practical small farming in New Zealand.

Trisha Fisk.   Auckland: Reed, 1996. rev. ed. 216p.

'This book is for realists – for those who want some space, to get away from the rat race, but who want to know how to do it right' (Introduction). Good, practical advice is provided for the prospective smallholder, in a well-presented work supported with illustrations. It covers land from buying to fencing, plants and their needs, including trees and weed management, and a variety of animals and their care.

557 White collars and gumboots.

Tony Nightingale.   Palmerston North, New Zealand: Dunmore Press, 1992. 277p. maps.

Concentrating on functions, this is a popular history of the Ministry of Agriculture and Fisheries. The author acknowledges that the focus is on 'the broader aims and policies of governments, scientists, and farm advisory officers rather than the development of the bureaucracy, its internal politics and personalities' (Preface). The text is supported by many interesting black-and-white and colour photographs.

558 Farming without subsidies: New Zealand's recent experiences.

Edited by Ron Sandrey, Russell Reynolds.   Wellington: Ministry of Agriculture and Fisheries/GP Books, 1990. 347p. (A MAF Policy Services Project).

'Investigates how New Zealand agriculture has been affected by the significant changes in government policies over the last five years' (cover). The book examines the situation under four headings: the setting, the reforms, the consequences and the future. It traces the origins, extent and effects of assistance to the agricultural sector, identifies who the real beneficiaries were, then describes the impact of removing this assistance. A disclaimer states that the views expressed are those of the authors and not necessarily those of the Ministry of Agriculture and Fisheries. Many of the same issues are covered in *Aspects of New Zealand's experience in agricultural reform since 1984* by Alan Walker and Brian Bell (Wellington: Ministry of Agriculture and Fisheries, 1994. 75p. MAF Policy Technical Paper 94/5), a popular summary of agricultural reform in New Zealand. As might be anticipated from a government paper, the tone is very positive.

Sheep and dairy farming

559 Sheep farming for profit.

Ralph Du Faur.   Wellington: Reed, 1966. 272p. map. bibliog.

Expertly trained and experienced in professional farm advisory work and practical sheep-farm management, the author covers every phase of sheep husbandry, including flock health, pasture management, soil fertility and fertilizers, farm layout and fencing. The work is now regarded as a classic.

560 The topdressers.

Janic Geelen.   Te Awamutu, New Zealand: New Zealand Aviation
Press, 1983. 367p. map.

A well-illustrated and researched history of the valuable role aerial topdressing has
played in New Zealand agriculture from the 1920s but particularly after the Second
World War. Significantly, aerial topdressing has declined in the past decade. A skilled
and often dangerous profession, this is the story of the aeroplanes and the men who
flew them, and the politics that lay behind this agricultural service industry. Many
illustrations, including cartoons, add to the general appeal of this book.

561 Milk production from pasture.

C. W. Holmes, G. F. Wilson.   Wellington: Butterworths Agricultural
Books, 1984. 319p.

'Intended for all those who are interested and involved in the principles and practices
of dairy farming on grazed pasture, including farmers, farm advisory officers, teachers, and students of agricultural and veterinary science' (cover). Up to date at the time
of publication, this book remains a useful overview of basic principles and practices.
It is divided into a section on practices and a further section on the principles which
lie behind the practices.

562 Pastures: their ecology and management.

Edited by R. H. M. Langer.   Auckland: Oxford University Press,
1990. 499p. maps.

As the basis of livestock production, pastures continue to be of vital importance to
New Zealand agriculture. This book covers all aspects of pastures, their ecology and
management. There are chapters on soil, climate, pasture plants, the establishment and
maintenance of pastures, livestock production, pests and diseases of plants and of animals at pasture, as well as the more specialized enterprises of seed production and hill
country pastures. Arising from Langer's earlier book, *Pastures and pasture plants*
(Wellington: Reed, 1973. 428p.), this volume takes account of subsequent scientific
advances, also some profound changes in approach.

563 The grasslands revolution in New Zealand.

P. W. Smallfield.   Auckland; London: Hodder & Stoughton/English
Universities Press, 1970. 151p. maps. bibliog.

An account of the developments in pasture improvement which greatly increased primary production in New Zealand in the years 1920 to 1970. The author was employed
by the New Zealand Department of Agriculture during that period, and was personally
associated with many of the developments. He is thus able to combine a survey of
general trends with his own experiences.

564 Top class wool cutters: the world of shearers and shearing.

Des Williams.   Hamilton, New Zealand: Shearing Heritage
Publications, 1996. 156p.

The major role of sheep farming in the economy of New Zealand has made the shearer
an individual whose skills are acknowledged and in demand. This collection of writing
seeks 'to open a little window on the world of shearers and shearing' (Introduction).
The author ranges widely in his coverage of the subject, from a historical glance at the

introduction of sheep to New Zealand, to the early writings about shearers and their craft and their equipment, to the hardships and rewards of shearing. He also covers shearing competitions in New Zealand and the records set.

565 **Empire of the dairy farmers.**
David Yerex. Petone, New Zealand: New Zealand Dairy Exporter Books/Ampersand Publishing Association, 1989. 200p. map.

A short personalized history of the New Zealand dairy industry, the early chapters based on a limited range of secondary sources. Around half the book is devoted to developments of the past three decades. Of particular interest are the accounts of the emergence of the Dairy Board as a multinational operation, the diversification of product, and economies of scale both on farms and in factories. The author forecasts further changes. An official history, *A history of the National Dairy Association of New Zealand, 1894-1984*, by G. F. Aldridge and C. W. Burnard (Masterton, New Zealand: Printcraft for The Association, 1985. 227p.), records the important part the National Dairy Association has played in dairying in New Zealand and the dedication of the people who have kept the Association going.

Other farming

566 **Profile of the New Zealand pork industry.**
David J. Dobson. Wellington: New Zealand Pork Industry Board, 1996. 73p.

Produced to answer the many requests for information for student projects, this slim volume sets out a general overview of the industry as at April 1996. Not only are the management and funding of the Pork Industry Board covered, but also the management, breeding, and housing of pigs, the economics of pig production, and how farmers are paid.

567 **Fruitful fields: the development of New Zealand's fruitgrowing industry, 1966 to 1991.**
Rex Monigatti. Wellington: New Zealand Fruitgrowers' Federation, distributed by GP Publications, 1991. 117p.

Celebrating the seventy-fifth anniversary of the New Zealand Fruitgrowers' Federation, this is a sequel to *Fruitful years* (Wellington: New Zealand Fruitgrowers' Federation, 1966. 115p.) published after fifty years. The intervening twenty-five years have witnessed tremendous growth and change in this industry, particular successes being the production and marketing of kiwifruit and pipfruit. The facilitating role of the Federation over these years is examined and the contributions of many people and organizations acknowledged.

568   **Te Mata: the first 100 years.**
   Keith Stewart.   Auckland: Godwit, 1997. 94p.

From the first plantings in 1892 to the award-winning wines of the 1990s, this is the history of a vineyard in Hawke's Bay in the foothills of Te Mata Peak. The vineyard produces wines that are well known nationally and internationally and this attractively presented and well-illustrated work details the highs and lows it has experienced. In many respects, this is a study of the New Zealand wine industry in microcosm.

569   **The farming of goats: fibre and meat production in New Zealand.**
   David Yerex.   Petone, New Zealand: Ampersand, 1986. 200p.

Drawing on the technical input of 'farmers, advisers, research scientists and people involved in the various processing and marketing sectors of this . . . industry', the author, an agricultural journalist, gives good practical advice on the farming of goats. The book covers breeds of goats, meat production, breeding, economics, marketing and many other useful topics – a chapter which looks forward to the year 2000 is included, incorporating a consultant's view of the outlook for goat farming in New Zealand.

570   **The kiwifruit story.**
   David Yerex, Westbrook Haines.   Masterton, New Zealand:
   Agricultural Publishing Associates, 1983. 96p.

A succinct description of the growth of the kiwifruit industry in New Zealand, 'from absolutely nothing, to international status' (Foreword). The authors place the explanation for the success 'on ordinary and determined people'. For the view of a leader in the industry see Roly Earp's *The kiwifruit adventure* (Palmerston North, New Zealand: Dunmore Press, 1988. 248p.).

571   **Modern deer farm management.**
   David Yerex, Ian Spiers.   Wellington: GP Books, 1990.
   rev. enlarged ed. 175p.

Building on previously published works, the authors resolved to bring into one volume all the then available information on new developments in deer farming and aspects of herd management. For those commencing this increasingly popular form of farming there is much here of practical use; for the general reader the work outlines the development of deer farming in New Zealand.

Straight Furrow.
See item no. 917.

Forestry, Fishing and Minerals Extraction

Forestry

572 Out of the woods: the restructuring and sale of New Zealand's state forests.
Reg J. Birchfield, I. F. Grant. Wellington: GP Publications, 1993. 250p.

Commissioned by the short-lived Board of the New Zealand Forestry Corp., this journalistic study outlines the corporatization of the Forest Service and the subsequent sale of the Crown forests. With the authors having access to all relevant governmental, Treasury and Corporation documents, and to the key players, this is an informed study of the privatization process. Regrettably, considering the sources used, there are no footnotes, nor a bibliography.

573 Pumice and pine: the story of Kaingaroa Forest.
Joan Boyd. Wellington: GP Publications Ltd., 1992. 198p. maps.

Planted in the friable, free-draining volcanic pumice of the Kaingaroa Plateau, the Kaingaroa Forest supplied the first New Zealand sawmill tailored to manmade forests. This is the story of the development of the forest and of the people who worked with it, from the first tentative plantings in the late 19th century. Particular attention is paid to the post-Second World War role of the forest in supplying both Kawerau's pulp and paper plant and the sawn timber trade. Numerous black-and-white photographs support the research presented.

574 New Zealand timbers: the complete guide to exotic and indigenous woods.
N. C. Clifton. Wellington: GP Publications, 1991. 171p.

A complete and well-illustrated guide to all millable timbers grown in New Zealand, indigenous as well as exotic. The author begins with a detailed examination of wood – the difference between softwood and hardwood, moisture content, wood density, shrinkage, growth stresses, decay, drying, preservative treatment and exterior finishes. He then covers each timber tree variety individually, explaining distribution, growth, characteristics and uses. 'In the interests of a wider audience . . . I have tried to keep scientific terms to a minimum' (Preface).

575 **A century of state-honed enterprise: 100 years of state plantation forestry in New Zealand.**
Andrew Kirkland, Peter Berg. Auckland: Profile Books, 1997. 176p. maps.

Both authors had long careers in the New Zealand Forest Service, and bring this experience to bear in their presentation and analysis of the history of plantation forestry in New Zealand. Commencing late in the 19th century, the massive programme of afforestation and reforestation by the Government finally ceased with the sale of the resource to the private sector 100 years later. This book presents an overview of that 100 years. While both pros and cons are distinguished in the divestment decision, state involvement in forestry is praised for the base it laid.

576 **History of forestry.**
M. M. Roche. Wellington: New Zealand Forestry Corporation/GP Books, 1990. 466p. maps. bibliog.

'This book provides an account of the origins and growth of the New Zealand timber industry, beginning with the spar trade of the 1790s to 1840s' (Introduction). Focusing first on the 19th-century regional timber industries, it records the milling of indigenous timbers until the natural forests began to disappear. The book also documents the revitalization of the industry through the planting of exotic forests from the late 19th century and the establishment of the New Zealand Forest Service. Developments of the 20th century are comprehensively discussed, including the foundations of post-Second World War industrial forestry. The book concludes with a perceptive survey of recent changes in New Zealand forestry. Exhaustively researched and well written, this will be the standard work on the topic for many years.

577 **Kauri to radiata: origin and expansion of the timber industry in New Zealand.**
Thomas E. Simpson. Auckland; London: Hodder & Stoughton, 1973. 442p. bibliog.

The author enlivens his text by drawing on his practical timber milling experience and the years he spent in both the governmental and private sectors of the industry. Archival and published sources have been researched for the work. 'This book makes no claim to being a complete history of the timber industry of New Zealand. It does, however, . . . trace from the earliest days and as nearly as possible in chronological order the expanding use of our timber trees to meet the needs of a growing population' (Preface).

Fishing

578 Market access issues for the New Zealand seafood trade.
Rory McLeod. Wellington: New Zealand Fishing Industry Board, 1996. 102p.

Looks at the New Zealand situation with regard to the fishing industry and compares it with the overall international situation and case-studies of North America, the European Union, Japan and Russia. The view is that 'the New Zealand fishing industry is in a quite different position to most of its overseas counterparts: it does not face the massive problems of overcapitalisation and lack of profitability that are evident in other countries; it is wholly unassisted; and it fishes from resources that are generally sustainably managed' (chapter 9, p. 83). The Quota Management system as applied to the industry is explained and the links between New Zealand's domestic fisheries management situation and the position New Zealand adopts on trade access issues are outlined.

579 Nets, lines and pots: a history of New Zealand fishing vessels.
Emmanuel Makarios. Wellington: IPL Books/Wellington Maritime Museum. Vol. 1, 1996. 112p. Vol. 2, 1997. 120p.

A quirky collection of well-written, very human articles on New Zealand fishing vessels and the people who pilot them. A regular contributor to *Seafood New Zealand: Incorporating New Zealand Professional Fisherman* (Wellington: New Zealand Seafood Industry Magazine Ltd., 1993- . 11 issues per year) and *New Zealand Marine News* (Wellington: D. F. Gardner, for New Zealand Ship and Marine Society, 1949-), the author has a deep interest in the sea and his enthusiasm is apparent.

580 The story of Sandford Limited: the first one hundred years.
Paul Titchener. Auckland: Sandford Ltd., 1981. 133p.

A history of the oldest and largest of New Zealand's fishing companies, now in its second century of operation. Albert Sandford, the founder of the company, jumped ship in Auckland in January 1864. The story of his, and his descendants', involvement in the fishing industry, at least in part, is also the story of the development of Auckland. Fishing boats and people are at the heart of the Sandford business and they are well represented in this work.

Mining

581 **The evolution of institutional arrangements for gold mining in New Zealand.**
Veronica Jacobsen. Hamilton, New Zealand: Department of Economics, University of Waikato, 1994. 41p. map. bibliog. (Working Papers in Economics no. 94/3).

'Models of the evolution of property rights have remained relatively underdeveloped since Demsetz' 1967 investigation . . . Legislative change in property rights in gold mining from 1847-1992 is seen to be influenced by the existing institutional structure, technological change, changes in the relative values of gold and the environment and political lobbying pressure' (abstract). The author seeks to explain the evolution of goldmining law on land in New Zealand which was largely unoccupied, but where the Crown's ownership of minerals was undisputed and where legislation was already in place. The conclusion reached is that 'a recent resurgence in mining has not resulted in pro-mining legislation largely because the mining industry is nationally insignificant and the environmental lobby is strong' (p. 38).

582 **Mineral deposits of New Zealand: a collection of papers summarising the results of mineral exploration in New Zealand 1974-87.**
Edited by David Kear. Parkville, Victoria: Australasian Institute of Mining and Metallurgy, 1989. 225p. maps. bibliog. (Monograph 13).

The geology of successful and unsuccessful exploration for minerals since 1974 is described in papers solicited from those most closely associated with the work. 'The collection deliberately excludes papers in the energy, construction materials and groundwater areas.' Technical in nature, the explorations detailed are presented regionally from Northland through to Otago and Southland and including offshore minerals. The first part of the work provides a general contextual overview.

583 **A history of goldmining in New Zealand.**
J. H. M. Salmon. Christchurch: Cadsonbury Publications, 1996. 315p. maps. bibliog.

A facsimile edition of a 1963 publication which has remained a classic study of the industry. The author provides a comprehensive and authoritative account of the rise and decline of goldmining in New Zealand from the first alluvial gold rushes, through quartz mining to the last days of the dredges. Particular mining sites are described, along with the technology relevant to those sites, often in the words of contemporary prospectors and miners. The romance of the boom days of the industry is evident, along with the privations and successes. The author also discusses in broad terms the impact of goldmining on New Zealand, economically, politically and socially.

584 **Mineral wealth of New Zealand.**
Bruce Thompson, Bob Braithwaite, Tony Christie.   Lower Hutt,
New Zealand: Institute of Geological and Nuclear Sciences, 1995.
170p. maps. (Institute of Geological and Nuclear Sciences Information
Series 33).

'Part one of this work describes the occurrence, exploration and mining of minerals in
New Zealand and the environmental impacts using the Golden Cross gold mines as a
case history. Part two details the location, geology, use and production of eighteen
metallic, twenty-two non-metallic and three energy mineral commodities important to
New Zealand' (cover). The last are coal, petroleum and gas, and geothermal energy.
This is an attractively presented 'mine of information'.

Gold in a tin dish.
See item no. 165.

**The golden reefs: an account of the great days of quartz-mining at
Reefton, Waiuta and the Lyell.**
See item no. 168.

The West Coast gold rushes.
See item no. 169.

**Steepland forests: a historical perspective of protection forestry in New
Zealand.**
See item no. 650.

New Zealand Forestry.
See item no. 890.

Energy

585   **Coal resources of New Zealand.**
J. M. Barry, S. W. Duff, D. A. B. MacFarlan.   Wellington: Energy
and Resources Division, Ministry of Commerce, 1993. 73p. maps.
Although providing technical information, this attractively presented report will
advise the reader more generally about coal resources, their location and why they
exist where they exist. Norman Crawshaw's *From clouds to sea: 100 years of coal
from Millerton and Stockton* (Westport, New Zealand: Coal NZ, 1996. 162p.) sets this
information into context by providing a case-study of the extraction of coal on the
Buller coalfields (West Coast, South Island).

586   **Geothermal resources of New Zealand.**
M. P. Cave, J. T. Lumb, L. Clelland.   Wellington: Energy and
Resources Division, Ministry of Commerce, 1993. 89p. maps.
A companion volume to Barry, Duff and MacFarlan's *Coal resources of New Zealand*
(q.v.), this volume is a well-presented introduction to geothermal resources in the
country. The information provided is technical but the illustrations and diagrams assist
in drawing the reader into a closer examination of the content.

587   **Power in New Zealand: a geography of energy resources.**
B. Farrell.   Wellington: Reed, 1962. 197p.
More useful for the historical information it now provides than as an analysis of present-day resources, this book reviews the history and development of coal,
hydroelectricity, geothermal steam, petroleum and natural gas in New Zealand. The
comments on the state of exploitation of these resources, and suggestions as to the
future place of each in the economy of New Zealand, are interesting to compare with
the actuality presented in more recent works.

588 **Coal in New Zealand: resources, mining, use infrastructure.**
Garth S. Harris. Auckland: New Zealand Energy Research and
Development Committee, 1985. 92p. maps.

Short, but information-packed, this research report provides quick answers to most
general questions about the New Zealand coal industry. The various sections deal with
coalfields, exploration, mining techniques, resources and reserves, transport, other
resources required by the industry, environmental questions, how coal is used, markets
and export. Passages relating to government policy have been rendered redundant by
the subsequent corporatization of State Coal Mines.

589 **In crude state: a history of the Moturoa oilfield, New Plymouth.**
Ron Lambert. New Plymouth, New Zealand: Methanex NZ/Taranaki
Museum, 1995. 67p. map. bibliog.

'A history of one of the oldest and certainly one of the smallest, commercially developed oilfields in the world' (Introduction). Commencing operations in a primitive
way, in 1865, the oilfield finally closed in July 1972. It was the forerunner of a thriving late 20th-century Taranaki oil and gas industry. Descriptive rather than analytical,
this is an appealingly presented work, well illustrated with black-and-white photographs.

590 **From threat to opportunity: moving to a sustainable energy
pathway.**
Ian McChesney. Lincoln, New Zealand: Centre for Resource
Management, Lincoln University, 1991. 72p.

This report develops a 'sustainable energy' pathway that takes into consideration the
Government's policy to reduce carbon dioxide emissions and the need to be able to
replace the energy currently tapped from the Maui gasfield when it is depleted. As
might be anticipated, the account is couched in technical language.

591 **People, politics and power stations: electric power generation in
New Zealand, 1880-1990.**
Edited by John E. Martin. Wellington: Bridget Williams
Books/ECNZ, 1991. 316p. maps.

Drawing on an unpublished work (by Peter O'Connor and Mary Ronnie) commissioned by the then Electricity Division of the Ministry of Energy in 1985, this book
looks at the planning for, and construction of, power stations by the state. It is set out
in three sections: the beginnings, roughly between 1880 and 1917 when electricity
generation was pioneered in New Zealand and government involvement first began;
the expansion period from 1918-45; and the period of consolidation through to 1990,
when power stations – hydro, thermal and geothermal – mushroomed throughout the
country. Copiously illustrated, this work can be seen as a companion volume to Neil
Rennie's *Power to the people* (Wellington: Electricity Supply Association of New
Zealand, 1989. 256p.) which documents the national reticulation of electric power.

592 **The point at issue: petroleum energy politics in New Zealand.**
Mike Paterson. Auckland: Collins, 1991. 243p.

Through eyewitness accounts, supplemented by the public record, this book examines
thirty-five years of debate, political dealing, shifting fortunes and conflict relating to

the New Zealand Refining Company's development of the Marsden Point (Whangarei) oil refinery. 'It offers insights and first-hand accounts of both the personalities and the behind-the-scenes action which helped to shape New Zealand's first controversial "Think Big" project' (cover). The study provides useful background to changing official energy policies.

593   **The power to manage: restructuring the New Zealand Electricity Department as a state-owned enterprise.**
    Barry Spicer.   Auckland: Oxford University Press, 1991. 181p.
Following the passing of the State-Owned Enterprises Act in 1986, managers of state trading organizations were given 'the power to manage'. This study documents the changes which transformed the New Zealand Electricity Division of the Ministry of Energy into the Electricity Corporation of New Zealand Ltd. The work looks at the reform process, what drove the competitive strategy, and the social and political pressures. It appraises the financial performance of Electricorp and reflects on the experience of restructuring. The authors conclude that Electricorp has been able to show a much improved performance, both in rates of return and levels of profitability.

Coal, class and community: the United Mineworkers of New Zealand, 1880-1960.
See item no. 628.

An abuse of power: the story of the Clyde Dam.
See item no. 659.

Transport

594 Coastal shipping policy in New Zealand.

R. Y. Cavana. Wellington: Graduate School of Business and Government Management, Victoria University of Wellington, 1993. 25p. (Working Paper Series no. 6/93 – July 1993).

'A brief review of the coastal shipping industry in New Zealand and an overview of international cabotage laws. An alternative open coast shipping policy proposed by the New Zealand Shipping Federation which is based on reciprocity and "level playing fields" principles is presented' (abstract). The costs and benefits of an open coast shipping policy are then examined.

595 Railway system in New Zealand: case study in strategic change.

R. Y. Cavana. Wellington: Graduate School of Business and Government Management, Victoria University of Wellington, 1992. 21p.

A working paper which 'examines the performance of the railway system in New Zealand from 1982 to 1992 during the period of considerable change in the regulatory and institutional environment in which it operated. It also discusses the issue of future public or private ownership of the railway system in New Zealand' (abstract). Further developments since this paper was written have seen the railway system privatized.

596 Railways of New Zealand: a journey through history.

G. Churchman. Auckland: Collins, 1990. 219p. bibliog. maps.

Railways exert a fascination over many people and this attractive publication looks at the many railway systems which developed in New Zealand from the bush tramways to the electrified systems of today. Many black-and-white photographs illustrate the text. Roy Sinclair's *Journeying with railways in New Zealand* (Auckland: Random House, 1997. 276p.) capitalizes on this fascination and combines a passion for transport with an ability to draw on interesting and unusual anecdotal interviews with people who are, or have been, involved with railways.

597 The history of New Zealand aviation.
Ross Ewing, Ross MacPherson.   Auckland: Heinemann, 1986. 287p. map.

Relates the history of aviation in New Zealand from the 1860s through to the deregulation of the airways in the 1980s. Sections on Maori kites, early balloons and parachuting, are matched by studies of the pioneers of aviation such as Richard Pearse, the Walsh Brothers and Joe Hammond and accounts of New Zealand's present-day air carriers. Whether for browsers or the more serious reader, there is much here to intrigue and interest.

598 On the road: the car in New Zealand.
Graham Hawkes.   Wellington: GP Books, 1990. 160p.

An enthusiast chronicles the history of the car in New Zealand. Lavishly illustrated, the book describes cars New Zealanders have loved, showing how much these cars have been a part of everyday lives from the beginning of the century. New Zealand culture through the years is inextricably linked with the narrative. Pam McLean and Brian Joyce's *The veteran years of New Zealand motoring* (Wellington: Reed, 1971. 230p.) describes the motoring experience as much as the cars, covering the years 1898 to 1919. Together these works show the importance of cars to the New Zealand way of life.

599 Issues for transport in the nineties: papers presented to the annual conference of the Chartered Institute of Transport in New Zealand, 21-22 November, 1990, Aotea Centre, Auckland.
Christchurch: The Institute, 1990. 2 vols.

A series of articles by experts in a variety of allied transport fields which consider problems relating to transport and the environment and how they might be resolved. Air, road, urban, railway and sea transport are covered. One chapter considers telecommunications, transport and tourism in the 1990s. Chiefly the problems relate to the need for greater energy efficiency, fuel efficiency and distance-travel reduction through better land-use planning.

600 New Zealand's maritime heritage.
David Johnson.   Auckland: Collins/David Bateman, 1987. 196p. bibliog.

Illustrated with contemporary works of art selected from the country's major galleries and museums and from private collections, this is a celebration of New Zealand's maritime heritage. From the first Polynesian canoes, through early European navigators in small sailing ships, to the whalers, sealers and trading adventurers in barques and brigs, to immigrants in larger sailing ships, all early contacts with New Zealand were via the sea. As the colony grew and changed so did the ships that serviced it. This story is told through text and illustration. Today the dependency on the sea for transport is not so great, but New Zealanders have continued their association by making themselves masters in the world of leisure sailing.

601 **Wellington Harbour.**
David Johnson. Wellington: Wellington Maritime Museum Trust, 1996. 556p. maps.

A big, beautiful book in all respects. The author traces the development of the capital's port, linking it with its surroundings and placing its trade in context as part of New Zealand's maritime history. The account spans from whaling to the export of frozen meat, from the fleet of small coastal schooners in the Cook Strait trade to the conveyor belt of the Interisland line, from wool clippers to the container ships of the Conference lines. With obvious variations, it is the development of New Zealand port and shipping services in microcosm.

602 **The southern octopus: the rise of a shipping empire.**
Gavin McLean. Wellington: New Zealand Ship and Marine Society/Wellington Harbour Board Maritime Trust, 1990. 239p.

Formed in 1875, the Union Steam Ship Company soon became an Australasian giant, New Zealand's first multinational. Backed by British capital and aided by skilful management, ruthless tactics and sheer good luck, the Company quickly monopolized the country's fuel and transport industries. Yet for all its antipodean supremacy, its leaders remained conscious of their geographical isolation and the need to build alliances. In 1917 their failure of nerve led to their absorption into a British combine. This book tells the story, as well as much more about the development of shipping, to the end of the First World War.

603 **Conquering isolation: the first 50 years of Air New Zealand.**
Neil Rennie. Auckland: Heinemann Reed, 1990. 200p. maps. bibliog.

From its early beginnings as TEAL (Tasman Empire Airways Ltd.) in 1940, to NAC (the National Airways Corporation) in 1946, through to 1990, this is the story of New Zealand's premier airline, Air New Zealand. The work is divided into sections which portray the development of air transport in New Zealand: 'The flying boat era, 1940-54'; 'Landplanes and turboprops, 1954-64'; 'The pure jets, 1965-80'; and 'The jumbo jet, 1981-90'. This is a story of people and events as much as it is about the airline itself – the many photographs will provide memories for those involved and a better understanding of life in New Zealand in the early years of aviation for others.

604 **Links: a history of transport and New Zealand society.**
James Watson. Wellington: GP Publications/Ministry of Transport, 1996. 315p. maps. bibliog.

'Travelling through the ages of the *waka* [canoe], sail, steam, motor and the jet, this book surveys the different forms of transport, the impact of each on society and the factors which shaped its development' (Introduction). The work has two central themes. The first argues that forms of transport technology available at different times did much to fashion New Zealand's economic, social and political life. The second maintains that the ways in which transport technology was deployed simultaneously reflected the nature of New Zealand society and not least its values. Running alongside and beneath is a subsidiary theme which considers the ways in which the physical environment has influenced the forms of transport New Zealanders have used. Well researched, attractively presented and copiously illustrated, this work contains plenty to entertain and instruct.

Tourism

605 Tourism investment in New Zealand: opportunities and constraints.

Ian Duncan. Wellington: New Zealand Institute of Economic Research, 1994. 133p.

Since the mid-1980s, in the wake of restructuring, considerable store has been placed on the tourism industry's potential for promoting employment growth. This report seeks to determine whether future industry growth should be facilitated through a co-ordinated investment strategy, or whether investment patterns should be determined by the market. Past experience of tourism investment in New Zealand is compared with theoretical models, the mix and nature of investment being analysed. The future constraints on, and opportunities for, tourism investment, as perceived by industry participants – in the transport, services and retail sectors – is assessed through interviews.

606 Leisure, recreation and tourism.

Edited by Harvey C. Perkins, Grant Cushman. Auckland: Longman Paul, 1993. 252p.

Designed as a source-book for New Zealand students studying leisure, recreation and tourism, this collection of essays is of far wider interest. Among the debates and issues discussed in New Zealand contexts are: the nature and meaning of leisure; the historical and contemporary experience of leisure, recreation and tourism; and policy issues associated with the planning and management of recreation and tourism services. The contributors are drawn from a range of disciplines, including geography, economics, sociology, psychology and landscape architecture.

607 **Developing eco-tourism in New Zealand.**
Julie A. N. Warren, C. Nicholas Taylor.   Wellington: New Zealand
Institute for Social Research and Development Ltd., 1994. 76p.
bibliog.

'Tourism is promoted as an essential part of our natural economy, particularly for its
potential to earn foreign exchange and generate employment. Projections are that the
industry will grow significantly in the next two decades, with tourists attracted to our
"clean green" environment. It is expected that eco-tourism – that is, tourism based on
sustainable resource use – will be an important part of this projected growth'
(Introduction). Using recently collected information, the report first presents an
overview identifying the major weaknesses in eco-tourism in New Zealand – both in
terms of its operating viability and its impact on local communities. In the second part
of the report, using a case-study approach from four areas, the planning and management strategies needed for sustainable tourism development in the future are
considered. The third part provides a more detailed analysis of the management issues
for each of the case-study areas.

608 **Billion dollar miracle: the authentic story of the birth and amazing
growth of the tourism industry in New Zealand.**
Leslie Watkins.   Auckland: Inhouse Publications, 1987. 224p.

A largely discursive account of the development of the New Zealand travel and
tourism industry from its 19th-century origins. The early role of government in promoting tourism is explored, as are the parts played by local and international travel
companies and transporters. Particular attention is paid to expansion from the 1960s
onwards. Failures, as well as triumphs, are identified. The book concludes with forecasts of the future from leading industry participants.

Human Resources and Employment

609 Incomes policy in New Zealand.

Jonathan Boston. Wellington: Victoria University Press, for Institute of Policy Studies, 1984. 344p.

This book is a comprehensive account of the attempts of successive New Zealand governments to regulate the growth of wages and salaries after the demise of the Arbitration Court in the late 1960s. It also describes the debate over long-term wage reform, and tentatively suggests policy options: '. . . the feasibility of any particular . . . strategy will be governed to a considerable extent by the political complexion of the Government in power and the policy stance adopted by the Federation of Labour' (p. 278).

610 The challenge of human resources management: directions and debates in New Zealand.

Edited by Peter Boxall. Auckland: Longman Paul, 1995. 315p.

'The most comprehensive assessment of management theory and practice in employment relations ever attempted in this country' (Preface) which seeks to provide an analytical framework, put forward an up-to-date review and critique of relevant theory, and to describe what is done in practice in New Zealand. Contributors are predominantly academic. They raise issues which they hope will be taken up for further study. A less theoretical and more practically based approach is Richard Rudman's *Human resources management in New Zealand: contexts and processes* (Auckland: Longman Paul, 1994. 2nd ed. 478p.).

611 Freedom at work: the case for reforming labour law in New Zealand.

Penelope Brook. Auckland: Oxford University Press, 1990. 193p.

The law surrounding New Zealand employment relations is examined, and a case for labour market deregulation is strongly advanced. Replacement of collective bargaining by a system of contractual relationships is advocated. 'It is economic competition, not coercive collective action, that minimizes opportunities for exploitation of workers, whether by employees or by unrepresentative unions' (p. 162). The author, an economist, was formerly a policy analyst with the New Zealand Business Roundtable.

612 **Full employment: whence it came and where it went.**
Simon Chapple. Wellington: New Zealand Institute of Economic Research, 1996. 125p. (New Zealand Institute of Economic Research. Research Monograph 66).

An analysis of employment history in New Zealand, broadly since the 1890s, but in more detail for recent decades. Explanations from a variety of sources for the current high unemployment levels are presented and assessed.

613 **Ordeal or opportunity: redundancy in the 'middle'.**
Judith A. Collins. Auckland: Department of Sociology, Auckland University, 1995. 77p. (Working Papers in Sociology no. 28).

The author identified and followed up a group of redundant 'middle' (-aged, -income, -management, -class) local government workers to try to understand their responses 'to the unforeseen threat to their previously secure employment tenure' (p. 3). The thesis of the report is that redundancy has resulted in downward mobility for this group and that too little is known about the economic, social and psychological costs of such redundancies. The research is an attempt to secure some hard data.

614 **Working free: the origins and impact of New Zealand's Employment Contracts Act.**
Ellen J. Dannin. Auckland: Auckland University Press, 1997. 327p.

A major contribution to the continuing debate about the New Zealand structural reforms. This book tells the story of the Employment Contracts Act 1991 – hailed by its proponents as a bold and radical measure, a key component of the reforms, and an international model for designing new labour laws. It reveals how the Act was passed, analyses its performance as labour law (a matter of wide disagreement), and explores its economic, social and legal impact. A strength is that the author recognizes that law is not just a matter of statute and interpretation, but operates in a context of economic, political and social factors, which in turn it shapes. Raymond Harbridge's *Employment contracts: New Zealand experiences* (Wellington: Victoria University Press, 1993. 253p.) also includes chapters on the making of the Act, together with an overview, an historical essay, state sector experiences, effects on employers and effects on workers.

615 **Women's labour force participation in New Zealand: the first 100 years.**
Lisa Davies, with Natalie Jackson. Wellington: Social Policy Agency, Department of Social Welfare, 1993. 167p.

This work is divided into seven sections: setting the scene; defining and measuring women's work; a literature review; an analysis of historical and contemporary trends; an examination of women in industry in terms of historical trends and current status; full- and part-time participation; and concluding comments. Overall, it 'presents a range of information on the patterns, trends and variation in women's patterns of labour force participation' over 100 years and offers 'a description of key demographic, social and economic developments which occurred over the period', linking and contrasting the two.

616 **False economy: New Zealanders face the conflict between paid and unpaid work.**
Anne Else.   North Shore City, New Zealand: Tandem Press, 1996. 170p.
Uses a combination of research, comments and interviews to examine the conflict between paid and unpaid work. The author considers the social effect and presents a belief that the problems and tensions will have to be resolved by society and not by individuals alone. Families and communities which are suffering are at the heart of social well-being.

617 **Labour market adjustment in New Zealand.**
Richard I. D. Harris, Bridget M. Daldy.   Aldershot, England: Avebury, 1994. 145p.
While there were strong reasons in favour of the government deregulating and opening up the New Zealand economy, the cost of the changes has primarily been borne by the labour market. The authors conclude that high levels of unemployment are largely attributable to 'downsizing' by firms and organizations, and that the levels will remain high. The contribution of technological change is also considered, as is the nature of organizational change. It is argued that 'flexibility' will be a feature of the future New Zealand workforce, with organizations opting to retain cores of full-time and skilled employees, other labour needs being met by part-time, casual or temporary workers.

618 **Labour adjustment in metropolitan regions.**
Philip S. Morrison.   Wellington: Victoria University Press, for Institute for Policy Studies, 1989. 254p.
'Systematically examines local labour markets and publicly discusses local context as a relevant policy variable in the development of labour market policy' (cover). The work considers four metropolitan regions: Auckland, Wellington, Christchurch and Dunedin. Only by knowing how the labour markets operate can the problem of unemployment be addressed.

619 **Reform at work: workplace change and the new industrial order.**
Martin Perry.   Auckland: Longman Paul, 1995. 304p.
'A comprehensive and up-to-date analysis of workplace change with a unique multidisciplinary focus and a blend of theory and case study' (Introduction). Using seven New Zealand-based companies, individual leading-edge workplace reform initiatives are assessed, with the dairy industry providing an example of industry-wide reform. The work concludes with some lessons that can be drawn from the case-studies.

620 **The vision and the reality: equal employment opportunities in the New Zealand workplace.**
Edited by Janet Sayers, Marianne Tremaine.   Palmerston North, New Zealand: Dunmore Press, 1994. 321p.
'Reviews Equal Employment Opportunities (EEO) progress from the viewpoints of key participants, bringing together the perspectives of academics, and practitioners on key issues for EEO and human resource management (HRM) practice and looks ahead at what the future holds in terms of making the vision a reality' (cover). This reference

work looks both backwards and forwards, taking stock and considering how the future might develop.

621 **Health and safety in New Zealand workplaces.**
Edited by Carol Slappendel.   Palmerston North, New Zealand:
Dunmore Press, 1995. 332p.

The intention of the book is to provide a text that introduces occupational health and safety questions in the New Zealand context. Written for students, industrial and business personnel, practitioners, teachers and researchers, the book covers a range of topics including patterns of injury and disease, legislation and compensation, the various professional groups and their perspectives, the theoretical bases of accident and hazard analysis and the management of occupational health and safety. The editor acknowledges that there is rapid progress in this area but considers the broad principles will be in place for some time.

New Zealand labour and employment research, 1859-1990: a bibliography of research and research materials.
See item no. 951.

Industrial Relations and Trade Unions

622 Against the wind: the story of the New Zealand Seamen's Union.
Conrad Bollinger. Wellington: New Zealand Seamen's Union, 1968.
260p. bibliog.

The Seamen's Union was one of the earliest of the militant unions. This history tells its story from the 1870s to the mid-1960s and includes accounts of the three great strikes in which it was involved: 1889-90, 1912-13, and 1951. Writing in a lively style, the author also has an ability to describe the personalities of the leaders. Although there appear to be the odd errors of detail, the work was based on comprehensive collections of union records held in Wellington and Dunedin. It is a classic of New Zealand trade union historiography.

623 The dynamics of New Zealand industrial relations.
Peter Brosnan, David F. Smith, Pat Walsh. Auckland: John Wiley & Sons, 1990. 230p.

The work focuses on the links between the industrial relations system and wider aspects of New Zealand society. The approach is analytical rather than descriptive, the authors wishing to avoid industrial details which would rapidly date. 'We believe that by considering the wider economic, social and political frameworks, we can explain contemporary industrial relations and the dynamics of their evolution' (Preface). Divisions include: economy and society, the organization of work, employer strategies, worker strategies, trade unions, employers' organizations, the state, collective bargaining and a summary entitled 'Dynamics of New Zealand industrial relations and their consequences'. John Deeks, Jane Parker and Rose Ryan's *Labour and employment relations in New Zealand* (Auckland: Longman Paul, 1994. 2nd ed. 622p.) also analyses the changes in employment relations in recent years in a perceptive and comprehensive manner.

624 **Industrial relations: a general introduction and the New Zealand system.**

A. J. Geare.   Dunedin: FIRRE(NZ), 1995. 3rd rev. ed. 538p.

This authoritative work is presented in two parts. The first is a general introduction to industrial relations, with an international focus. The second part concentrates on New Zealand. In this part a number of major eras are considered: 1895-1987, the arbitration era; 1987-91, the collective bargaining era; and 1991- , the laissez faire era.

625 **A sourcebook of New Zealand trade unions and employee organizations.**

Edited by Raymond Harbridge, Kevin Hince.   Wellington: Industrial Relations Centre, Victoria University of Wellington, 1994. 181p.

Legislative changes from the mid-1980s radically altered the status of many New Zealand trade unions. By 1993, several long-standing unions had folded or merged with other unions. The overall number of unions had fallen to around sixty, and membership had fallen accordingly. With the Office of the Registrar of Unions having been abolished by the Employment Contracts Act 1991, the task of keeping track of the organizations was voluntarily assumed by Victoria University's Industrial Relations Centre. This book both records the fate of individual unions in the ten years 1983-93, and provides detailed information on those still in existence as at 31 December 1993.

626 **Holding the balance: a history of New Zealand's Department of Labour, 1891-1995.**

John E. Martin.   Christchurch: Canterbury University Press, 1996. 478p. bibliog.

A multi-dimensional study of the Department of Labour from its beginnings in 1891 as the Bureau of Industries through to the 1990s. 'It attempts to integrate the full range of industrial relations, labour, workplace and employment policies that were the responsibility of the Department of Labour' (Preface). Government policy in the crucial areas of employment, industrial relations, immigration and workplace conditions are examined in depth. However, with many of the records having been destroyed by fire in 1952, the writing of this history has demanded much detective work. Scholarly yet readable, the volume is extensively illustrated with photographs and cartoons.

627 **The Red Feds: revolutionary industrial unionism and the New Zealand Federation of Labour, 1908-14.**

Erik Olssen.   Auckland: Oxford University Press, 1988. 296p. bibliog.

Beginning with the Blackball Strike of 1908 (an industrial dispute in the West Coast coal-mines) and finishing with the General Strike of 1913, this work details a turbulent period in New Zealand's industrial history: the period of the 'Red' Federation of Labour. This federation was of unskilled labourers, miners, wharfies, shearers and seamen. A scholarly work on the Federation, the book is humanized by the portraits of the leaders and the workers in their battle to achieve recognized status. It is 'a dramatic and thorough account of the decisive events in the making of New Zealand's working class' (cover).

628 **Coal, class and community: the United Mineworkers of New Zealand, 1880-1960.**
Len Richardson. Auckland: Auckland University Press, 1995. 344p. maps.

'This account of mining unionism in New Zealand . . . traces the attempts of migrant miners to establish a national organization appropriate to their new circumstances' (Preface). The author examines the role isolation played in the development of these unions, isolation both in terms of the workplace ('inaccessible and inhospitable environments') and the fact that many of the miners were migrants. That many of these migrants came with families provides an unexpected dimension to this work, the role of the women being also explored. Carefully researched, well written and illustrated, this is a compelling story.

629 **Remedy for present evils: a history of the New Zealand Public Service Association from 1890.**
H. Roth. Wellington: The Association, 1987. 320p.

From its early abortive beginnings, 1890-98, to its more solid establishment in 1913, and its growth as a union over the next seventy years, this is a history of the New Zealand Public Service Association (PSA) written by a sometime unionist/scholar well versed in the study of unions, New Zealand's foremost labour historian. This history may well be seen as recording the heyday of the PSA, as in the 1990s it has lost much of its strength and numbers following passage of the Employment Contracts Act 1991.

630 **Pioneering New Zealand labour history: essays in honour of Bert Roth.**
Edited by Pat Walsh. Palmerston North, New Zealand: Dunmore Press, 1994. 164p.

A collection of papers to celebrate the seventy-fifth birthday of Bert Roth, a well-known New Zealand labour historian. It includes discussion of Roth's early life 'and the process by which a bourgeois European came to take up the study of the labour movement in the distant country to which he fled to escape the Nazi regime' (cover). The essays cover West Coast mining unionism, the importance of theory to engendering New Zealand labour history, New Zealand and trade union internationalism in South Pacific Islands and the development of public sector unionism in New Zealand.

631 **Trade unions, work and society: the centenary of the arbitration system.**
Edited by Pat Walsh. Palmerston North, New Zealand: Dunmore Press, 1994. 244p.

The Industrial Conciliation and Arbitration Act 1894 gave New Zealand one of the most highly regulated systems of industrial relations in the capitalist world. This situation lasted until the passing of the Employment Contracts Act 1991. These essays document the experiences of trade unions and their members under the arbitration system. James Holt's *Compulsory arbitration in New Zealand: the first forty years* (Auckland: Auckland University Press, 1986. 247p.) provides another view of the subject.

New Zealand Journal of Industrial Relations.
See item no. 901.

Statistics

632 **New Zealand: a handbook of historical statistics.**
   G. T. Bloomfield.   Boston, Massachusetts: G. K. Hall, 1984. 429p.
   maps. (Reference Publications in International Historical Statistics).
Two main purposes are defined for the work: providing a convenient abstract of historical statistics on New Zealand as well as outlining the sources of more detailed material; and introducing researchers in other parts of the world to additional comparative data. Each of the chapters, variously dealing with the landbase, the population, social conditions, the labour force, production, transport, overseas trade, the state sector and finance, comprises a brief textual overview followed by the relevant statistical information. The work provides a good base for any statistical analysis of the development of New Zealand.

633 **Te hurihanga o te ao Maori: te ahua o te iwi Maori kua whakatatautia. A statistical profile of change in Maori society since the 1950s.**
   G. V. Butterworth, C. Mako.   Wellington: Department of Maori Affairs, 1989. 263p.
Compiled mainly from official statistics, the aim of the work is to provide statistical information to the Department of Maori Affairs and to Maoridom in general. The statistics collected are intended to be of use in the preparation of policy advice and therefore the net was cast as widely as possible. Key points which can be derived from the statistics are presented at the beginning of each section. The work brings together in one place statistics which would otherwise have to be drawn from diverse sources.

634 **Catalogue 1997.**
   Wellington: Statistics New Zealand, 1997. 69p.
Provides an up-to-date listing of publications available from Statistics New Zealand. These are becoming increasingly sophisticated with more and more information becoming available on databases and through the Internet. Information on how to

200

order and access the information is provided, together with an index to the publications listed. Areas covered include surveys, census information, agriculture, business, culture, demography, environment, health, income and expenditure, trade, the national economy, women and work.

635   Facts New Zealand.
Wellington: Statistics New Zealand, 1995. 2nd ed. 221p.

A potted collection of statistics about New Zealand, attractively packaged. Divided into land and people, social organization, work and leisure, Maori, primary production, industry, business, economics and international comparisons, its 'aim is to present material that is clear and easy to understand but does not lose its precise meaning' (Introduction).

636   New Zealand in profile.
Wellington: Statistics New Zealand, 1997. leaflet.

Produced annually, this is a compact selection of statistics used as a 'giveaway' for the general public. It provides basic information on the country, its geography, discovery, climate, economy and government, together with figures on population, production and trade.

637   Statistical publications 1840-1960 (mainly those produced by the Registrar-General 1853-1910 and the Government Statistician 1911-1960).
Wellington: Department of Statistics, 1961. 66p. bibliog.

'This publication has been prepared to present a historical record and a ready reference for users of statistics, librarians, etc . . . It should serve as a useful guide to the development of New Zealand since the proclamation of British Sovereignty and should have particular value to students and research workers' (Preface). The first third of the book includes a general description of early statistical reports, census reports, the *New Zealand Official Yearbook* (q.v.), and *Monthly Abstract of Statistics* (Wellington: Government Statistician, 1914-21; Census and Statistics Department, 1922-25; Department of Statistics, 1926-89. monthly – the latter publication has been replaced by *Key Statistics*, Wellington: Department of Statistics, 1989-May 1994; Statistics New Zealand, June 1994-). The remainder lists official and non-official publications (including early newspapers) which contain statistical information.

New Zealand Official Yearbook/Te Pukapuka Houanga Whaimana O Aotearoa.
See item no. 940.

Environment

General

638 Environmental policy in New Zealand: the politics of clean and green?

Tom Buhrs, Robert V. Bartlett.   Auckland: Auckland University Press, 1993. 192p.

Since the mid-1980s environmental policy has had a high profile in New Zealand politics, the country taking the initiative in promoting stronger measures to deal with international issues (e.g., ozone depletion, driftnet fishing, and the protection of Antarctica). Ironically, concern with domestic issues has not always been so evident. This book presents the first scholarly analysis of environmental policy in New Zealand. It assesses the strengths and weaknesses of New Zealand's policies in relation to four recurring themes: the need for anticipatory policy-making; the need to change our ways; the need for institutional reform; and the need for more integrated and comprehensive policy.

639 Working for Wildlife: a history of the New Zealand Wildlife Service.

R. A. Galbreath.   Wellington: Bridget Williams Books/Historical Branch, Department of Internal Affairs, 1993. 253p.

The Wildlife Service, formally created in 1945, was responsible both for game and fisheries management and for the conservation of native fauna. This book outlines the antecedents of the Service, its evolution, and its achievements during its forty years of existence. By the 1980s it had become widely known in New Zealand and internationally, especially for its efforts to save endangered species from extinction. The author also addresses the changing ideas and attitudes which led to the Service's disbandment in 1987, its functions being split between local fish and game councils and the newly formed Department of Conservation.

640 **Gamekeepers for the nation: the story of New Zealand's Acclimatisation Societies, 1861-1990.**
R. M. McDowall. Christchurch: Canterbury University Press, 1994. 508p. maps.

New Zealand's celebrated recreational hunting and freshwater fishing are based almost entirely on introduced fauna. The author, a scientist, recounts how these animals – from opossums and red deer, to brown trout and Canada geese, frogs and sparrows – were introduced, nurtured and managed. He describes the activities of acclimatization societies and fish and game councils, as well as probing their often unsteady relationships with government agencies. An assessment of the benefits, as well as the environmental costs, of the introductions is attempted.

641 **The greening of New Zealand: New Zealanders' visions of green alternatives.**
Scott McVarish. Auckland: Random Century, 1992. 194p.

'New Zealand conservationists in the 1970s were "green revolutionaries" battling with a reactionary forest service . . . However, the conservationists have now been joined by other individuals and groups with diverse interests to comprise an expanded green movement of the 1990s' (Introduction). The author interviewed seventy individuals with ranging perspectives on green issues, from conservation to economics, from resource management to business and trading practices, from lifestyle enhancement to politics. He finds there is no definitive New Zealand green ideology, rather a mix of viewpoints, critiques and solutions.

642 **Environmental planning in New Zealand.**
Edited by P. Ali Memon, Harvey C. Perkins. Palmerston North, New Zealand: Dunmore Press, 1993. 199p. maps.

The Environment Act 1986, the Conservation Act 1987 and the Resource Management Act 1991, together with related statutes, are perceived by many to signify the beginnings of a new approach to environmental planning in New Zealand. This book is designed to promote an in-depth understanding of a range of important environmental issues: the urban environment; transportation; the coastal environment; water resources; mineral and energy resources; indigenous forests; rural and mountain land use; and recreation and tourism. The contributors critically examine the issues from an historical perspective, within the contemporary context, and speculate on their possible future implications.

643 **Nga uruora = The groves of life: ecology and history in a New Zealand landscape.**
Geoff Park. Wellington: Victoria University Press, 1995. 376p. maps.

'Nga uruora – the groves of life takes the study of New Zealand's natural environment in radical new directions. Part ecology, part history, part personal odyssey, this book offers fresh perspectives on our landscapes and our relationships with them' (cover). Focusing on the fertile coastal plains, the author visits four particular places: Tauwhare on the Mokau River; Papaitonga in Horowhenua; Whanganui Inlet; and Punakaiki on the South Island's West Coast. In each of these locations small pockets of the plains forests' indigenous ecosystems of *kahikatea* (New Zealand white pine) and *harakeke* (New Zealand flax) survive. The meaning of these places to the Maori is explored. Ensuring the ongoing survival of such places of beauty and spiritual meaning is central to the work.

Parks and gardens

644 New Zealand forest parks.
G. R. Chavasse. Wellington: Government Printer, 1983. 287p. maps.

Each of the forest parks are portrayed, chiefly through photographs by well-known photographer, John Johns. The text is kept to a minimum allowing the photographs to speak for themselves, but for each park there are brief descriptions of location, size, access, development, physical details, vegetation, wildlife and other values. These values include protection, production, recreation, education and historical information.

645 Wild Fiordland: discovering the natural history of a world heritage area.
Neville Peat, Brian Patrick. Dunedin: University of Otago Press, 1996. 143p. maps. bibliog.

Beautifully illustrated with exceptionally clear colour photographs, this work describes a heritage area parts of which are still unexplored. Comprehensive descriptions are provided of the region and its many features. Chapters cover different geographical areas, mountains, forests, fiords, lakes and rivers; three general chapters describe the location and climate, geology and conservation issues.

646 Heritage: the parks of the people.
David Thom. Auckland: Lansdowne Press, 1987. 284p. maps.

Published to mark the centenary of the gifting by Maori of New Zealand's first National Park, Tongariro, in the central North Island, this sumptuous volume seeks to place the evolution of a National Parks system within the context of contemporary international thinking and the development of a distinctively New Zealand conservation movement. It also recounts the creation of a parks administration as uniquely New Zealand as the parks themselves. The author concludes, however, that in the creation of parks there has been a bias towards mountain and other unproductive land. 'In our cultural landscape – the landscapes of production – the losses have been already far too great' (p. 245). There are photo-essays covering the twelve National Parks in existence at the time of publication.

647 Botanic gardens and parks in New Zealand: an illustrated record.
Paul Trittenbach. Auckland: Excellence Press, 1987. 144p. maps.

Botanic gardens the length and breadth of New Zealand are described in photographs and text. For each of the gardens presented, a brief introduction setting the scene is followed by a chronological outline by eventful years, not always relating to the gardens but sometimes also to the city in which they were created. Plans for each garden are provided. A meticulously researched history of one garden, Winsome Shepherd and Walter Cook's The Botanic Garden, Wellington: a New Zealand history, 1840-

1987 (Wellington: Millwood Press, 1988. 396p.), tells the reader as much about the early days of settlement in Wellington as it does about the garden itself. 'Forged from a landscape that topographically presented unprecedented problems it has become a unique New Zealand feature and one of our best known gardens' (cover).

Water and soil conservation

648 **The land our future: essays on land use and conservation in New Zealand in honour of Kenneth Cumberland.**
Edited by A. Grant Anderson. Auckland: Longman Paul, 1980. 324p. maps. bibliog.

A series of essays to mark the retirement of Kenneth Cumberland, Professor of Geography at Auckland University. Generally academic in approach, the contributions cover the ecological and economic bases of land-use planning, the use and misuse of soil, forest and water resources, and the efficiency of systems and aspects of multiple resource use. Described as an 'interdisciplinary overview of wise resource management in New Zealand', the work includes a comprehensive bibliography of Cumberland's published work.

649 **Hold this land: a history of soil conservation in New Zealand.**
L. W. McCaskill. Wellington: Reed, 1973. 274p. maps. bibliog.

Within 100 years of European colonization it had become obvious to concerned observers that deforestation and current farming practices had created a national problem of extensive soil erosion. In this well-illustrated book, the author, who was personally involved in the campaign to awaken public and governmental awareness of soil erosion, tells of the measures, practical and political, which were taken to meet the problem.

650 **Steepland forests: a historical perspective of protection forestry in New Zealand.**
Peter McKelvey. Christchurch: Canterbury University Press, 1995. 295p. maps.

'The vast expanses of forest on the steep mountain lands of New Zealand are termed "protection forests" because they are essential to protect the soil, minimise flooding of lowlands, ensure quality water supplies and protect ecological values' (cover). The author, Emeritus Professor of Forestry, University of Canterbury, Christchurch, argues that these forests must continue to be managed and maintained, for they are a vital link in the conservation chain. This work looks at the threats that have been posed to the forests by man and wildlife, compares the New Zealand experience with those of Europe and North America, and describes the steps that have been taken to preserve the forests as their importance has been recognized. It also details the research that lies behind work to develop steepland forests.

651 **Land and water: water and soil conservation and central government in New Zealand, 1941-1988.**
Michael Roche.   Wellington: Historical Branch, Department of Internal Affairs, 1994. 219p. maps.

Soil and water conservation have become increasingly important in New Zealand, the side effects of land development through forest clearance, agriculture and mining taking their toll and resulting in erosion and flooding. Concentrating on a half-century of work by the central government agencies such as the National Water and Soil Conservation Authority, the author describes the attempts to control the problems. The present situation, where control has been devolved to regional authorities, is also examined.

Endangered species

652 **The black robin: saving the world's most endangered bird.**
David Butler, Don Merton.   Auckland: Oxford University Press, 1992. 294p. maps.

The inspiring story of how the black robin has been brought back from the brink of extinction using the technique of cross-fostering eggs and young to other species. The painstaking nature of this internationally recognized project, with its successes and failures, is outlined. Supported with black-and-white and colour photographs, this is an involving and readable story of the work of a committed team of conservationists.

653 **Little Barrier Island: New Zealand's foremost wildlife sanctuary.**
Ronald Cometti.   Auckland: Hodder & Stoughton, 1986. 144p. map.

Little Barrier Island lies 90 kilometres northwest of Auckland city at the mouth of the Hauraki Gulf. A reserve since 1894, 'cloaked with the country's largest areas of unmodified forest, unspoiled by browsing animals, and now after the complete eradication of feral cats, largely free of mammalian predators, [Little Barrier Island] has become New Zealand's safest wildlife refuge and one of international importance' (cover). An historical background essay leads into descriptions, supported by reproductions of colour paintings, of the endangered wildlife that has found a safe haven on the island.

654 **Immigrant killers: introduced predators and the conservation of birds in New Zealand.**
C. M. King.   Auckland: Oxford University Press, 1984. 234p. maps.

'The devastation of New Zealand's native fauna has become one of the world's best-known conservation horror stories. Over the last thousand years, since the arrival of the first people in these islands, about fifty-five species and subspecies of native birds have been made extinct or nearly so' (cover). In this book, published to mark the 100th anniversary of the introduction of stoats, the author tackles the problem of how the species that remain should be protected. Some cherished myths about predators and their prey are carefully examined, with provocative conclusions being reached.

655 **Threatened plants of New Zealand.**
Catherine M. Wilson, David R. Given.   Wellington: DSIR Publishing,
1989. 151p.

One in every ten New Zealand native plant species can be described as 'at risk'. The rarest plants may be restricted to a single lonely specimen growing on an offshore island. Other species – in danger from people, from commercial development, from introduced fauna and farm stock – may already exist only in collections. The authors comprehensively describe New Zealand's endangered plants and their habitats. They suggest ways of protecting such plants and propose a code of conduct for those coming into contact with them.

Environmental activism

656 **Birds, forests and natural features of New Zealand: including the growth of the Royal Forest and Bird Protection Society of New Zealand Inc.**
N. E. Dalmer.   Levin, New Zealand: Dalmer, 1983. 173p.

Founded in 1923, the Royal Forest and Bird Protection Society has in recent decades been a major player in the New Zealand environmental movement. This book outlines the origins of the Society, its formation, subsequent growth and changing preoccupations. Many of its past campaigns for habitat preservation and the elimination of environmental threats are reviewed.

657 **To save a forest: Whirinaki.**
John Morton.   Auckland: David Bateman, for the Whirinaki Forest Promotion Trust, 1984. 111p. maps.

'This book is a plea to preserve from logging all that is left of New Zealand's finest podocarp forest. It is an attack on political policies which insist on programmes which are ecologically damaging and economically questionable' (Introduction). To support their arguments, the authors have secured striking photographs of the forest in all seasons and the text provides evocative descriptions of the importance of the forest.

658 **Manapouri saved! New Zealand's first great conservation success story: integrating nature conservation with hydro-electric development of Lakes Manapouri and Te Anau . . .**
Neville Peat.   Dunedin: Longacre Press, for Guardians of Lake Manapouri, 1994. 106p. map.

Published to mark the twenty-first anniversary of the Guardians of Lakes Manapouri, Monowai and Te Anau, this book traces the history of the Save Manapouri Campaign and the ongoing efforts of the Lake Guardians. The Save Manapouri Campaign was one of the most successful environmental lobbying campaigns established in New Zealand. 'The campaign to save the lakes from being raised for the sake of a relatively small increase in hydro-electric power generation took on politicians and senior bureaucrats and won' (cover). This work draws out the lessons that can be learnt from the campaign.

659   **An abuse of power: the story of the Clyde Dam.**
Trevor Reeves, Judith Wolfe.   Dunedin: Square One Press, 1990.
144p.

A damning indictment of New Zealand's most recent major hydro-electric power project, 'which holds a warning for all who believe in the importance of informed, responsible decision-making' (Introduction). Despite doubts about the geological stability of the dam site, or indeed the need for the power to be produced, the scheme was pushed on by bureaucrats oblivious to public protest, with the support of politicians seeking short-term advantage. The price, beyond interminable delays and the fact that budgets were exceeded, included the drowning of scenic and historic areas.

660   **From Manapouri to Aramoana: the battle for New Zealand's environment.**
Roger Wilson.   Auckland: Earthworks Press, 1982. 192p. maps.

Environmental controversies for the period roughly between 1970 and 1980 are surveyed. This was a particularly important period, for it saw a raising of the environmental consciousness of New Zealanders – increasingly, people were becoming aware that there were aspects of the environment which were under siege and should be protected. Issues covered include nuclear power, the aluminium smelter at Aramoana, the protection of forests and many others. Each of the issues is presented with commentary and newspaper articles, chronologies and references.

The invasion of New Zealand by people, plants and animals: the South Island.
See item no. 19.

Landmarks.
See item no. 20.

Greenhouse New Zealand: our climate: past, present and future.
See item no. 48.

Walter Buller: the reluctant conservationist.
See item no. 235.

Richard Henry of Resolution Island.
See item no. 239.

A history of the garden in New Zealand.
See item no. 807.

Forest and Bird.
See item no. 878.

New Zealand Journal of Ecology.
See item no. 898.

Planning Quarterly.
See item no. 913.

Education

General

661 The biography of an idea: Beeby on education.
C. E. Beeby. Wellington: New Zealand Council for Educational Research, 1992. 326p.

A teacher, researcher, writer and educational administrator, Dr. Beeby is an authority figure in New Zealand education. He was particularly influential in the 1930s and 1940s when he introduced and planned the approach of greater equality of educational opportunity. In large part autobiographical, this work is, nevertheless, more than a life history, for it traverses the steps that took a young teacher from teaching in schools to being responsible for reconstructing the education system. Despite his retirement in 1960 Dr. Beeby remained influential through to the late 1980s. This is an important work for anyone interested in the development of the New Zealand educational environment and the ideas it deals with contrast strongly with the direction education is moving in today.

662 Education in change: twenty viewpoints.
Edited by Harvey McQueen. Wellington: Bridget Williams Books, 1994. 220p.

The editor talks to twenty leading educators about their views on the major educational issues of the 1990s. The interviewees 'were from all levels of the sector, representing a range of ages, viewpoints and geographical locations' (Introduction). The result is a picture of how education and educators have been coping with change. Pros and cons and different perspectives – international, Maori, female, male – are presented. The very personal nature of each of the chapters gives the work particular appeal.

663   **Revisiting the 'reforms' in education.**
        Edited by James D. Marshall.   Auckland: University of Auckland,
        1994. 99p. (Faculty of Education Annual Lectures).

In his Preface the editor of this series of lectures uses the word 'beleaguered' with respect to education and the education reforms carried out since the late 1980s. The lectures visit the reforms from the perspective of four educators who have been in key positions, from university posts to that of national secretary of the New Zealand Educational Institute. A 'Partially annotated bibliography' concludes the volume. Further comment on the 'costs' of the reforms can be gleaned from D. McKenzie, H. Lee and G. Lee's *Scholars or dollars?: selected historical case studies of opportunity costs in New Zealand education* (Palmerston North, New Zealand: Dunmore Press, 1996. 229p.), the stated purpose of which being 'to present a theoretical model of explanation which may both assist us to make sense of our past successes and failures to develop educational services in New Zealand and sharpen our judgements about the probity of future educational projects' (p. 11).

664   **Women and education in Aotearoa 2.**
        Sue Middleton, Alison Jones.   Auckland: Auckland University
        Press/Bridget Williams Books, 1997. 249p.

Volume one of this work, primarily historical in emphasis and based on studies carried out during the mid-1980s, was published in 1988. This successor volume considers women's and girls' contemporary educational experiences. 'Such a focus is particularly important in today's context of political ambivalence towards gender equity, or fairness in education' (Introduction). The research has been the almost exclusive domain of women and considers various aspects of education – gender equity and school charters, Maori women and their experiences, learning through play, and comparisons between male and female ability. All the contributors are professional educators and/or researchers who have worked in schools, pre-schools or tertiary institutions.

665   **Succeeding generations: family resources and access to education
        in New Zealand.**
        Roy Nash.   Auckland: Oxford University Press, 1993. 222p.

The author explores what causes some children to succeed at school and others to fail. 'This book asks and attempts to answer some fundamental questions about group differences in educational attainment and access to education by reporting the findings of a recent programme of research in New Zealand' (p. 1). It concludes that 'family resources of one kind or another are largely responsible for the differences in educational performance and access to education apparent between social groups in New Zealand' (p. 3). The work is probably of most interest to those with a professional concern with education although it is intended to be accessible to the general reader.

666   **Education policy in New Zealand: the 1990s and beyond.**
        Edited by Mark Olssen, Kay Morris Mathews.   Palmerston North,
        New Zealand: Dunmore Press, 1997. 442p.

This book focuses on critical developments in education policy during the 1990s: changes to the school curriculum; the emergence of a 'seamless education system', linking schools to industry; the development and implementation of the National Qualifications Framework; the appearance of new organizations, such as the ERO (Education Review Office) and the NZQA (New Zealand Qualifications Authority);

and the broader attempts to engender a culture based on 'enterprise' and 'self-reliance' as part of an overall strategy of dismantling the welfare state. Both the mechanics of the restructuring and the philosophies behind it are examined by nineteen contributors.

667 **Challenging the myths: rethinking New Zealand's educational history.**
Roger Openshaw, Greg Lee, Howard Lee. Palmerston North, New Zealand: Dunmore Press, 1993. 343p.

A history of education in New Zealand from 1858 to the 1990s. Following a chronological, rather than a thematic, ordering of the information, the authors cover issues such as: the nature of educational history; the relationship between educational policy and classroom practice and the correlation between classroom practice and student learning; the curriculum and Maori schooling; examinations; the education of girls; state and private schools; and the Picot Report on education. Above all, they have sought to place education in its political, social and economic contexts.

668 **Setting the standards: the assessment of competence in national qualifications.**
Edited by Roger Peddie, Bryan Tuck. Palmerston North, New Zealand: Dunmore Press, 1995. 209p.

The creation of the New Zealand Qualifications Authority (NZQA), arising from the Education Amendment Act 1990, has seen greater emphasis placed on the development of units of learning and standards-based assessment. This approach has not had unqualified support and the pros and cons are debated in this slim volume. The conclusion drawn is that there are areas which need further debate before 'we can accept that a national framework built on standards-based assessment is the only route to travel' (p. 203). For an even more critical view see Michael Irwin's *Curriculum, assessment and qualifications: an evaluation of current reforms* (Wellington: Education Forum, 1994. 179p.).

669 **He paepae korero: research perspectives in Maori education.**
Compiled by Bev Webber. Wellington: New Zealand Council for Educational Research, 1996. 162p.

'Using the context of past and present education policies and practices, the writers . . . tell research stories which offer insight, challenge and inspiration . . . In expressing the need for recognition of the cultural knowledge base which Maori students bring to their learning, issues of the future directions of Maori education are explored in the context of the widening networks in which individuals need to operate as part of the developmental process' (Foreword). The thoughts and experiences expressed will be of use in the development of policies in the critical area of Maori education. The immediacy of the essays, by virtue of the personal approach, ensures the involvement of the reader.

School system

670 Learners with special needs in Aotearoa/New Zealand.
Edited by Deborah Fraser, Roger Moltzen, Ken Ryba. Palmerston North, New Zealand: Dunmore Press, 1995. 444p.

Written by experts in the field of special education, this book takes an inclusive approach to education and the community. Information is provided both on the context of providing support for learners with special needs, as well as teaching methods and learning strategies. 'The book reflects the principle that students cannot truly be included in regular education until the teachers, resources and systems of "special" and "regular" education are viewed as one' (Preface). The book is presented in two parts: 'Special education policies and systems' and 'Partnership in special education'.

671 Myths and realities: schooling in New Zealand.
Edited by Alison Jones, James Marshall, Kay Morris Mathews, Graham Hingangaroa Smith, Linda Tuhiwai Smith. Palmerston North, New Zealand: Dunmore Press, 1995. 2nd ed. 240p. bibliog.

'Addresses issues in the area of relationships between education and other cultural-social-political features of society' (Introduction). The editors take up the theme that 'far from being a good in itself, as being liberating and promoting personal autonomy, attempts are being made to construe [education] as just another economic commodity which can be purchased, perhaps utilised and consumed, and if not discarded, traded for a later model' (Introduction). Changes in the academic study of education are also dealt with, as are the changes within particular academic studies and the realization that a combined academic approach to education is, perhaps, necessary. A major concern expressed is the need for social equity. The book concludes with an extensive bibliography.

672 The school curriculum in New Zealand: history, theory, policy and practice.
Edited by Gary McCulloch. Palmerston North, New Zealand: Dunmore Press, 1992. 278p.

'This collection brings together the work of scholars who have begun to think seriously about the historical dimensions of the school curriculum' (Introduction). The study urges that four key aspects be borne in mind: the need to develop the links between the past and present which are often assumed; the need to establish an adequate theoretical base for such a study; the need to see the curriculum as part of the wider society, culture and politics; and the need to recognize and explore the differences between policy and practice. The essays are academic in approach.

673 The discovery of early childhood: the development of services for the care and education of very young children, mid eighteenth century Europe to mid twentieth century New Zealand.
Helen May. Auckland: Auckland University Press/Bridget Williams Books/New Zealand Council for Educational Research, 1997. 244p.

An overview of the development of services for the care and education of very young children in New Zealand by the Professor of Early Childhood Teacher Education at

Victoria University of Wellington. Her book is divided into two parts: the first covers 18th- and 19th-century issues, such as industrialism and colonialism and the ideas of people such as Locke, Rousseau, Robert Owen and Mary Wollstonecraft; and the second moves into the 20th century. In this second part, the ideas of people such as Maria Montessori, Susan Isaacs, Mother Aubert, and Truby King are assessed together with their impact on childcare. The author also develops other themes, including the treatment of Maori, feminism, the impact of war and the involvement of the state. This well-referenced work concludes that over 200 years, 'society came to realise that early childhood education outside the home should be an integral part of every child's development and learning, and that this was a worthwhile investment by the community as a whole' (p. 213).

674 **Unresolved struggle: consensus and conflict in New Zealand state post-primary education.**
Roger Openshaw. Palmerston North, New Zealand: Dunmore Press, 1995. 173p.

The work considers post-primary education particularly in the light of the way it was shaped in the 1940s by reformers who sought educational equality. The author believes their goal has never been met, and that it is now crucial the style and presentation of post-primary education be re-examined. The book 'argues that many of the difficulties faced by New Zealand secondary schools today have their origin in the failure of the post-primary education settlement, constructed in the 1940s to retain sufficient support in the changing post-war political, social and economic environment' (p. 10). Roy Shuker's *The one best system?: a revisionist history of state schooling in New Zealand* (Palmerston North, New Zealand: Dunmore Press, 1987. 298p.) similarly challenges the accepted notion that state schooling provides equal opportunity in education. He argues that in fact it serves to 'reproduce existing social and economic divisions within society' (Introduction).

675 **Self-managing schools in New Zealand: the fifth year.**
Cathy Wylie. Wellington: New Zealand Council for Educational Research, 1994. 163p.

This report presents the results of a 1993 survey undertaken of principals, trustees and teachers at a national sample of 239 primary and intermediate schools, and of parents at a representative sub-sample of 26 of these schools. The aim of the study was to establish what changes had occurred in the management of schools since the reforms encompassed in the 1988 policy document, *Tomorrow's schools*. Those reforms had shifted substantial administrative and financial responsibility from the Department of Education and Education Boards to school staff and trustees at individual schools. The purpose of the survey was to find out the strengths, weaknesses and pressure points of the new system, the results being compared with those of three previous surveys (1989, 1990 and 1991).

Adult and higher education

676 The fourth sector: adult and community education in Aotearoa/New Zealand.
Edited by John Benseman, Brian Findsen, Mirama Scott. Palmerston North, New Zealand: Dunmore Press, 1996. 400p.

'The fourth sector which focuses on that learning beyond structured formalised learning combines [with early childhood education, primary and secondary education and higher education] to constitute lifelong learning' (Introduction). A bicultural approach is brought to this study of adult and community education, and the desire is to provide a comprehensive view while acknowledging this is not possible! The work divides into six parts: an initial overview; a Maori perspective; learning contexts; adult learning practices; educating adults and social justice; and a concluding international perspective.

677 The seed they sowed: centennial history of Lincoln College.
I. D. Blair. Christchurch: Lincoln College, University College of Agriculture, 1978. 360p.

A history of one of New Zealand's leading agricultural colleges (not then a full university), written by one of its former professors. The growth and development of the College is recounted, the account of the latter years reflecting the author's personal knowledge. A similar history of Massey Agricultural College is T. W. H. Brooking's *Massey: its early years* (Palmerston North, New Zealand: Massey Alumni Association, 1977. 171p.).

678 A shakeup anyway: government and the universities in New Zealand in a decade of reform.
Ruth Butterworth, Nicholas Tarling. Auckland: Auckland University Press, 1994. 268p.

Universities have not been immune from examination as to how they spend the money allocated to them. As a result, reforms have been forced upon them. 'The authors, both active participants in the events they describe, give a forthright analysis of the changing relationships between government and the universities and of the deeply disturbing implications for the future of university education in New Zealand' (cover). The work questions how universities are to be publicly accountable, how their activities might best be regulated, and how, if academic freedom is questioned, might they still continue to perform their tasks of teaching, research and community service.

679 The University Grants Committee, 1961-1986: a history.
John Gould. Wellington: University Grants Committee, 1988. 246p.

The University Grants Committee (UGC) was created following the disestablishment of the University of New Zealand at the end of 1961. After that date the UGC acted as an intermediary between the universities and government, negotiating funding, allocating funding allotted to the universities, and advising government on matters concerning universities. The Committee also supported the Universities Entrance Board and administered major public examinations. This history of its first twenty-five years (the Committee was disbanded in 1990) also expounds on policy formation in the university field including the changing role and attitude of the Treasury.

680   **Packed but not padded: Christchurch Polytechnic's first twenty-five years, 1965-89.**
Dick Hockley.   Christchurch: The Polytechnic, 1990. 163p.

Looks at the development of the Polytechnic in Christchurch from small beginnings to a thriving institution, at the mix of people who have worked and studied there, and at the obstacles that have had to be overcome. The way the institution has interpreted educational needs for its area is also examined. Other histories of these growing tertiary institutions include Greg Hurrell's *Our polytechnic: a 25 year history of Nelson Polytechnic* (Nelson, New Zealand: The Polytechnic, 1996. 144p.), Maryen Moss's *Coming of age: a history of the Hawke's Bay Polytechnic* (Waipukurau, New Zealand: CHB Print, 1996. 134p.) and David Bennett's *Shaping our futures: Taranaki Polytechnic's 25 years of educational service* (New Plymouth, New Zealand: The Polytechnic, 1996. 88p.).

681   **Between two worlds: the history of Palmerston North College of Education, 1956-1996.**
Roger Openshaw.   Palmerston North, New Zealand: Dunmore Press, 1996. 224p.

On 1 June 1996 the Palmerston North College of Education was officially disestablished and (together with the Faculty of Education at Massey University) became the Massey University College of Education. Written as the College of Education merged with Massey University in Palmerston North, this work reviews the development of the College. As both a regional and a national player in teacher education, it encompassed not only pre-service primary-teacher training, but also early childhood, secondary, bilingual, professional and community education. 'The main theme of this history is that throughout these forty years two models of teaching vied for supremacy as the focus of teacher education: teaching as a learned profession and teaching as a skilled craft . . . the tensions between the two models have still not been resolved' (Preface). While the author critically assesses the merger, he nevertheless presents an optimistic view of the future.

682   **Campus beyond the walls: the first 25 years of Massey University's extramural programme.**
J. M. R. Owens.   Palmerston North, New Zealand: Dunmore Press, 1985. 133p.

When elevated from agricultural college to full university status in 1963, Massey University pioneered extramural programmes in New Zealand. It is still the major player in this field. This history outlines the struggles to establish and develop the programme and the strengths of the programme today.

683   **The University of New Zealand.**
Hugh Parton.   Auckland: Auckland University Press; Wellington, London: Oxford University Press, for the University Grants Committee, 1979. 277p. bibliog.

The University of New Zealand existed from 1870 until 1961. With its administration based in Wellington, it covered all colleges on a quasi-federal basis. Its purpose was to prescribe courses, conduct examinations and award degrees for the university colleges which employed staff and taught students. As greater responsibility was given to the colleges, the University of New Zealand phased itself out of existence. This history gives emphasis to the years since 1937.

684 Players, protesters and politicians: a history of the University of Canterbury Students' Association.

Jean E. Sharfe. Christchurch: Clerestory Press/University of Canterbury Students' Association, 1995. 152p.

From its beginnings as a small group of students seeking a voice in dealing with the authorities of Canterbury College in 1894, to the large organization it is today, this is a lively history of the University of Canterbury Students' Association. Well illustrated, the work canvasses themes such as constitutional developments, matters of discipline, welfare provisions, capping and orientation. The speed with which the student body responds to signs of manipulation, even if on the surface students have appeared apathetic, is commented on. A similar history of the Otago University Students' Association is Sam Elworthy's *Ritual song of defiance* (Dunedin: Otago University Press, 1990. 171p.).

685 Educating the workers?: a history of the Workers' Education (i.e. Educational) Association in New Zealand.

Roy Shuker. Palmerston North, New Zealand: Dunmore Press, 1984. 190p.

The New Zealand Workers' Educational Association (WEA) has for many years been synonymous with adult education. Established in 1915, the WEA efforts have encompassed correspondence courses, educational broadcasting, prison lectures, education for the elderly and trade union education. This examination of the association does not sidestep the controversies which from time to time have surrounded the body. The culmination was a threat to remove government funding in 1982. A linked body has been the Council of Adult Education which was set up to provide an overview and promote adult education services. The history of this body, and its relationships with WEA, can be found in J. C. Dakin's *Focus for lifelong learning* (Wellington: New Zealand Council for Educational Research and National Council of Adult Education, 1988. 177p.).

686 A history of the University of Auckland, 1883-1983.

Keith Sinclair. Auckland: University of Auckland Press, 1983. 364p. maps.

The history of the University of Auckland from its establishment, 1883-93, through to the 1980s. 'What this history attempts to reveal are the ways in which people in a new university progressively adapted their institution to a new environment, and how the people at large reacted to the presence of a university in their midst' (Preface). Carefully researched and referenced, this is a detailed history of the University which is both well written and well illustrated. Histories of other New Zealand universities include: W. P. Morrell's *The University of Otago* (Dunedin: University of Otago Press, 1969. 261p.); W. J. Gardner, E. T. Beardsley and T. E. Carter's *A history of the University of Canterbury* (Christchurch: University of Canterbury, 1973. 530p.); J. C. Beaglehole's *Victoria University College: an essay towards a history* (Wellington: New Zealand University Press, 1949. 319p.); and Paul Day's *From the ground up: an informal chronicle of the genesis and development of the University of Waikato, 1964-1984* (Hamilton, New Zealand: The University, 1985. 322p.).

Sylvia!: the biography of Sylvia Ashton-Warner.
See item no. 241.

Childcare in New Zealand: people, programmes, politics.
See item no. 381.

New Zealand Journal of Educational Studies.
See item no. 899.

Science and Technology

687 **DSIR's first fifty years.**
J. D. Atkinson. Wellington: Department of Scientific and Industrial Research, 1976. 220p. bibliog. (New Zealand Department of Scientific and Industrial Research Information Series, 115).

An accurate but largely undocumented summary of the developments of organized scientific research during a period which saw changes and growth in agriculture and manufacturing. The author considers the foundations of the Department in 1926, the transfer of plant research from agriculture, the activities during the war years and the subsequent expansion. Throughout the study, the work of particular scientists is highlighted.

688 **Science and technology in New Zealand: opportunity for the future.**
E. G. Bollard. Wellington: National Research Advisory Council, 1986. 155p.

A report, by a senior New Zealand scientist, intended to lessen the distances between scientists, economists, policy makers and the general public in understanding the contribution science and technology could, and should, make to New Zealand's future. Part one generally reviews the place of science and technology in modern economics. Part two evaluates the situation in OECD (Organization for Economic Co-operation and Development) countries, the United States, the United Kingdom and Australia. Part three deals specifically with New Zealand. 'The purpose of the chapters that follow is to characterise more fully our present position with regard to industrial development and overseas trade, to describe the way scientific research has developed in New Zealand, to discuss the possibility of science playing a fuller role in national development, and finally to consider the role of Government in the development of science and technology' (p. 113).

689 **Sails to satellites: a history of meteorology in New Zealand.**
J. F. de Lisle.   Wellington: New Zealand Meteorological Service,
1986. 186p.

A pleasant book which 'describes some of the people, and the organizations, behind the search for understanding of weather and its vagaries and the application of this understanding for the benefit of New Zealanders and our Pacific neighbours' (Foreword). A predecessor of the 'Met Office' was set up in the Colonial Secretary's Office in 1861, the colonists having become aware very quickly of the enormous impact climatic conditions exert on New Zealand. As with other histories of organizations, so with the Meteorological Service, it is the contribution of the people that is important. The author allows this to come through, as well as describing the achievements of the service over the years to 1986.

690 **Science, settlers and scholars: the centennial history of the Royal
Society of New Zealand.**
C. A. Fleming.   Wellington: The Society, 1987. 353p. (Royal Society
of New Zealand Bulletin 25).

The Society's domestic affairs, including its library, the Common Seal and the search for accommodation, together with its national and its international responsibilities, are all described in this well-produced history. The Society has played a major role in the encouragement of research. The research grants it has funded and the awards it has given are detailed as is its extensive contribution to the international scene. Somewhat pedestrian in narration, this is nevertheless a worthy record of a society that has touched the lives of many New Zealanders.

691 **Science and technology: policy issues for the 1990s.**
Edited by R. Harker, P. Spoonley.   Wellington: Ministry of Research,
Science and Technology; Palmerston North, New Zealand: Educational
Research and Development Centre, Massey University, 1993. 77p.

The areas considered are 'Science, technology and culture', 'Conceptions of technology and the implications for education', 'Setting priorities for science and technology', 'The politics of the Information Society in New Zealand', and 'Knowledge needs for the Resource Management Act'. The papers are derived from a loose grouping of scientists with an interest in current changes in science policy. They provide a valuable contribution to the ongoing debate on the funding and organization of science in New Zealand.

692 **In search of New Zealand's scientific heritage.**
M. E. Hoare, L. G. Bell.   Wellington: Royal Society of New Zealand,
1984. 123p.

Comprises selected papers from the History of Science in New Zealand Conference, February 1983, held in Wellington. The primary objective of the Conference was 'to bring together researchers and others actively involved in preserving the sources of scientific research in New Zealand' (Introduction). Five major themes are explored: the sources and records of science; the physical sciences; the biological and life sciences; scientific biography and science; and society and institutions.

693 **The commonwealth of science: ANZAAS and the scientific enterprise in Australasia, 1888-1988.**
Edited by Roy MacLeod.   Melbourne; Auckland: Oxford University Press, 1988. 417p. bibliog.

An examination of a century of Australasian science, and an account of the activities of the Australian and New Zealand Association for the Advancement of Science (ANZAAS). Part one considers the circumstances surrounding the foundation and early development of the Association. Part two focuses on individual disciplines, including life sciences, earth sciences, physical sciences, chemistry, anthropology, education and social science. Part three examines the relationship between science and society, and looks towards the future. Perhaps significantly, all of the contributors are Australia-domiciled; the coverage of New Zealand is uneven.

694 **The reform of the public science system in New Zealand: a history of the background to and the implementation of the restructuring of the science system, 1988-1993.**
Chris M. Palmer.   Wellington: Ministry of Research, Science and Technology, 1994. 72p. bibliog. (Report 33).

'The period 1989-1992 has seen the completion of the most far-reaching reform of the science system in New Zealand for at least 50 years . . . [the reforms] have resulted in the disappearance of established organizations (notably the DSIR or Department of Scientific and Industrial Research) and the appearance of a whole range of new organizations – including a Ministry, a Foundation and ten Crown Research Institutes' (Preface). The role of this history is seen as describing the reform process for those interested nationally and internationally while it is still fresh in the minds of those who were involved, to provide a point of reference rather than an objective analysis. The result is an essentially descriptive work with those involved being too close and with the reforms being too recent to analyse whether the reforms have achieved their objectives.

695 **Manifest duty: the Polynesian Society over 100 years.**
M. P. K. Sorrenson.   Auckland: Polynesian Society/Department of Anthropology, Auckland University, 1992. 160p.

Founded in Wellington in January 1892 by S. Percy Smith and a small band of enthusiasts who saw it as their duty to record the lore and literature of Maori and other Polynesian peoples then thought to be headed for extinction, the Society and its journal have flourished beyond all expectations. The Journal is one of the oldest continuously published anthropological journals in the world. It is now well known for its authoritative articles while the Society has a well-earned reputation for having encouraged research that might not otherwise have been done.

Stars of the southern skies: an observer's guide for New Zealand.
See item no. 33.

The southern ark: zoological discovery in New Zealand, 1769-1900.
See item no. 59.

Early New Zealand botanical art.
See item no. 70.

An eye for country: the life and work of Leslie Adkin.
See item no. 232.

McMeekan: a biography.
See item no. 248.

The grasslands revolution in New Zealand.
See item no. 563.

Journal of the Royal Society of New Zealand.
See item no. 883.

New Zealand Science Review.
See item no. 909.

Literature

General

696 **The writing of New Zealand: inventions and identities.**
Edited by Alex Calder. Auckland: Reed, 1993. 289p.

Explores some of the ways non-fiction writers have represented and constructed themselves, others, and the country, as New Zealand. The result is a great variety of material from twenty-seven writers, male and female, Maori and Pakeha, from early contact (Cook, Banks and early colonists) to the present day. The criteria for inclusion included the authors' sense of belonging to New Zealand, sense of history and good writing, together with a desire for the selections to fit well together. The result is an absorbing collection of pieces which richly conjure up a picture of the country; 'a book of conjunctures and mismatching perspectives, a book of inventions and identities' (Introduction).

697 **A sea change: 145 years of New Zealand junior fiction.**
Betty Gilderdale. Auckland: Longman Paul, 1982. 300p.

Although a new edition is now needed, for much has been more recently published, this survey of New Zealand fiction for young people written between 1833 and 1978 remains useful. The quantity of material identified will probably surprise. The work is divided into themes, with each theme covering the entire span of years. Indexes by title and author and by illustrator give access when information is known; otherwise, much can be gained from browsing.

698 **Whole men: the masculine tradition in New Zealand literature.**
Kai Jensen. Auckland: Auckland University Press, 1996. 202p.

Arguing that 'New Zealand writing around the Second World War was shaped by excitement about masculinity as a way of challenging society' (cover), Kai Jensen examines masculinity in New Zealand literature. He suggests that the linking of national identity to the ordinary working man or soldier created a culture which discouraged women writers. Deliberately provocative, the author seeks to encourage debate. He concludes, 'it's my hope that this account of the masculine tradition will neither satisfy its admirers, who will resist seeing the tradition as characterized by masculine excitement, nor pro-feminist critics who need the tradition simply to reflect the larger society'.

699 Where did she come from? New Zealand women novelists 1862-1987.
Heather Roberts.   Wellington: Allen & Unwin/Port Nicholson Press, 1989. 177p. bibliog.

An antidote to Kai Jensen's work (q.v.) in some respects, this work brings women novelists to the fore. The author argues that 'the woman novelists in New Zealand belong to a strong female tradition in which the writers are linked across the generations by personal contact and friendship, by common themes and subject matters and by a universal commitment to describing and interpreting women's lives in New Zealand since European settlement' (Introduction). Writing is considered within periods (1862-1914, 1914-30, 1930-45, 1945-60 and 1960-87), and within each, particular themes are explored with a common thread of the power of the community. The work ends with a plea that the work of women, often unknown and difficult to locate, should be identified and preserved.

Literary history and criticism

700 Ending the silences: critical essays on the works of Maurice Shadbolt.
Edited by Ralph J. Crane.   Auckland: Hodder Moa Beckett, 1995. 170p.

Critical essays on the work of Maurice Shadbolt, including his fiction, his play *Once on Chunuk Bair* (Auckland: Hodder & Stoughton, 1982. 106p.), and his autobiography *One of Ben's* (Birkenhead, Auckland: David Ling, 1993. 313p.), are brought together in this work. All the essays were specifically commissioned for the book and provide a range of critical responses to the work of one of New Zealand's best-known authors. The book concludes with a selected checklist of Shadbolt's fiction.

701 The Penguin history of New Zealand literature.
Patrick Evans.   Auckland: Penguin, 1990. 287p.

'An attempt to show how New Zealand literature in English formed itself from the time European New Zealanders first began to think they were founding a national literature about a hundred years ago' (Introduction). The work deals with the period from 1890 through to the 1980s, providing commentary, criticism and information about the various eras identified. Groups that were formed, particularly among poets, influential publications and events that affected the writers are considered. Necessarily an overview, this nevertheless provides a valuable introduction to New Zealand literature.

702 **Barbed wire and mirrors: essays on New Zealand prose.**
Lawrence Jones. Dunedin: University of Otago Press, 1990. 2nd ed.
388p.

A number of articles and major reviews from a respected commentator on New Zealand literature (especially fiction) are collected together to provide an overview of New Zealand fiction and autobiography from the 1930s. Three themes are developed within the volume: critical realism, gathering together material dealing with the realist tradition; 'Mirrors and interiors', or the Impressionist tradition; and 'Man alone, the artist and literary history' which traces the theme of Man (and Woman) alone through writers of both traditions, through different genres and periods. Knowledgeably presented, this volume covers a wide range of New Zealand authors, throwing new light on their writing.

703 **Every kind of weather: selected writings on the arts, theatre, literature and current events in New Zealand, 1953-1981.**
Bruce Mason, edited by David Dowling. Auckland: Reed Methuen, 1986. 306p.

'A collection of Bruce Mason's essays, letters, and criticism selected from almost thirty years of outspoken and incisive comment on New Zealand's cultural life' (cover). Although the material represents just one man's view, it is that of a very involved person willing to comment on the life he saw around him and ways of presenting New Zealand life. The pieces reveal the person as well as being a commentary on the cultural life he describes.

704 **Introducing Denis Glover.**
Gordon Ogilvie. Auckland: Longman Paul, 1983. 60p.

A critical assessment of the work of the poet Denis Glover. The format is a brief biography followed by an examination of the poetry, providing a useful short introduction to the person and his work. The volume is one of a series which includes Peter Smart's *Introducing Sam Hunt* (Auckland: Longman Paul, 1981. 59p.), David Dowling's *Introducing Bruce Mason* (Auckland: Longman Paul, 1982. 50p.), Richard Corballis and Simon Garrett's *Introducing Witi Ihimaera* (Auckland: Longman Paul, 1984) and many others all by different, appropriately qualified authors.

705 **Ngaio Marsh: the woman and her work.**
Edited by B. J. Rahn. Metuchen, New Jersey: Scarecrow Press, 1995. 252p.

A collection of essays celebrating the multi-faceted talent of Ngaio Marsh – painter, playwright, director, and detective novelist – on the centennial of her birth (23 April 1995). The articles look at various aspects of her personality, life and work. Divided into themes (Biography – reminiscence, Theatre in life and fiction, Detective fiction, A mirror of social history, and Short fiction), these essays tell much about the woman. Marsh was made an Officer of the Order of the British Empire (OBE) in 1948 for services to literature and theatre, and became a Dame Commander (DBE) in 1967.

706 **In the glass case: essays on New Zealand literature.**
C. K. Stead. Auckland: Auckland University Press/Oxford University Press, 1981. 293p.

A selection of reviews, review articles and lectures published over more than twenty years, particularly examining fiction and poetry. The result is criticism as well as commentary on the various writers considered. Each section has an introductory essay which sets the following essays into context. The work is a useful precursor to a more detailed study of the particular authors.

707 **The Oxford history of New Zealand literature in English.**
Edited by Terry Sturm. Auckland: Oxford University Press, 1991. 748p.

Divided into broad sections on Maori literature, non-fiction, the novel, the short story, drama, poetry, children's literature, popular fiction and publishing, patronage, and literary magazines, each presented by specialists in the field, this work attempts to provide 'more comprehensive information about New Zealand literature than has ever appeared in a single volume before' (cover). As such it provides a useful commentary to be read in association with the anthologies giving extracts from the many works alluded to in this volume or alongside the works of the authors themselves.

708 **Leaving the highway: six contemporary New Zealand novelists.**
Mark Williams. Auckland: Auckland University Press, 1990. 232p.

A critical study of Janet Frame, C. K. Stead, Keri Hulme, Witi Ihimaera, Ian Wedde and Maurice Gee from the viewpoint of querying whether current arguments about race, culture and belonging have been reflected in fiction. 'The book consists of an introductory chapter sketching the literary context of the late 1970s and 1980s; six chapters on the individual novelists each focusing on one or two major novels; a conclusion which attempts some generalisations about the condition of and directions for New Zealand literature in terms of those particular novelists' (Preface).

709 **Opening the book: new essays on New Zealand writing.**
Mark Williams, Michele Leggott. Auckland: Auckland University Press, 1995. 335p.

Accepting that New Zealand literature has changed over time and become more diverse in the process, this book collects together new essays by writers and critics and shows how some well-known New Zealand authors – Katherine Mansfield, Frank Sargeson, Robin Hyde and Janet Frame – can be read and interpreted from a number of critical perspectives and how different types of writing can be freshly considered. Lively and challenging, these essays 're-examine our past, question long-held assumptions, analyse the contemporary scene and indicate new directions' (cover).

Maori writing

710 **Te whakahuatanga o te ao: reflections of reality.**
Selected and edited by Witi Ihimaera; contributing editors: Haare
Williams, Irihapeti Ramsden, D. S. Long. Auckland: Reed Books,
1992. 354p. (Ao Marama: Contemporary Maori Writing; vol. 1).

The first in a proposed six-volume set, this is a collection of fiction, poetry, song and
drama which expresses the anger, humour, passion and issues of the day as felt by
Maori writers. Not all the contributors are well known – for some these volumes have
provided a publishing opportunity. It is a timely publishing venture, as the outburst of
creative activity from Maori deserves to be recorded in this way. Using all the formats
available, these writers 'explore contemporary life on the streets of New Zealand cities,
with vibrant work that bursts beyond the expected to challenge both Maori and Pakeha
concepts of identity' (cover). Other volumes so far published are: *He whakaatanga o te
ao: the reality* (Auckland: Reed, 1993. 359p.); *Te puawaitanga o te korero: the flowering* (Auckland: Reed, 1993. 339p.); *Te ara o te hau: the path of the wind* (Auckland:
Reed, 1994. 350p.); and *Te torino: the spiral* (Auckland: Reed, 1996. 355p.).

711 **Maori poetry: an introductory anthology.**
Margaret Orbell. Auckland; London: Heinemann Educational, 1978.
104p. bibliog.

A small collection of traditional Maori poetry, particularly *waiata* (songs),with parallel texts in Maori and English. The selection gives a fair coverage of the poetry, and
the translations combine accuracy with feeling. Explanatory notes and a detailed introduction provide insights into a poetic tradition which embodies themes of love,
kinship, death and the invincibility of the human spirit.

712 **Traditional Maori stories: he korero Maori.**
Introduced and translated by Margaret Orbell. Auckland: Reed, 1992.
192p.

Presents the marvellous tales of legendary ancestors of the Maori, of heroes triumph-
ing over adversaries, and other tales of the supernatural in the original Maori and in
translation. The stories are prefaced with a brief introduction in each case. The work
offers a well-produced and authoritative introduction to these stories.

Anthologies

713 **The Picador book of contemporary New Zealand fiction.**
Edited by Fergus Barrowman. London: Picador, 1996. 470p.

Drawn from the period 1979 to 1994, this is a diverse and imaginative selection covering the work of thirty-one writers. The volume is arranged by the date of the first book
published by the writers and this divides them roughly into generational groups. An

introduction sets the writers into context within New Zealand society and considers the different emerging themes, styles and statements about life in New Zealand.

714 **An anthology of New Zealand poetry in English.**
Jenny Bornholdt, Gregory O'Brien, Mark Williams.   Auckland: Oxford University Press, 1997. 547p.

Spanning more than a century, the editors have compiled 'a collection of New Zealand poetry remarkable as much for its diversity of poetic forms as for its wealth of voices' (cover). Many well-known voices are here, such as Ursula Bethell, Allan Curnow, James K. Baxter and Hone Tuwhare. But there are also some lesser known poets represented, such as Eileen Duggan and Mary Stanley. A good selection of contemporary poets includes Vincent O'Sullivan, C. K. Stead and Bill Manhire.

715 **The Oxford book of New Zealand writing since 1945.**
Chosen by MacDonald P. Jackson, Vincent O'Sullivan.   Auckland: Oxford University Press, 1983. 679p. bibliog.

Divided simply into poetry and prose, this is an eclectic selection of New Zealand writing. The extensive introductory essay, with poetry covered by Jackson and prose by O'Sullivan, provides insights into the various writers, the period they were writing in, the influences upon them and those they influenced. This is a well-produced volume either for dipping into or reading at length.

716 **From the mainland: an anthology of South Island writing.**
Edited by Lawrence Jones, Heather Murray.   Auckland: Godwit, 1995. 248p. map.

'An anthology of recent writing that captures [a] strong sense of South Island places, people and history' (cover). It includes the work of authors born and bred in the South Island and strongly regionalistic in their writing and others who have come to identify with the South Island. Yet there are others again who are no longer living there, but whose association with the South Island shows in their writing. The writers Brian Turner, Ruth Dallas, Stevan Eldred-Grigg, Keri Hulme, Toss Wollaston, Dan Davin and Janet Frame are among those represented.

717 **Countless signs: the New Zealand landscape in literature: an anthology.**
Compiled by Trudie McNaughton.   Auckland: Reed Methuen, 1986. 389p.

'This anthology invites the reader to see New Zealand not through the lens of a camera but through the writer's imagination' (cover). Recognizing the extent to which the New Zealand landscape appears in both the oral traditions and the written literature of the country, Trudie McNaughton seeks to explain the fascination with the landscape through a wide selection of extracts which traverse all manner of emotional responses.

718 **The new place: the poetry of settlement in New Zealand, 1852-1914.**
Edited by Harvey McQueen. Wellington: Victoria University Press, 1993. 213p.

Taking an unusual theme, this book 'follows the changing preoccupation of New Zealand's early English speaking poets, from feelings of homesickness and alienation to planning for the future' (cover). The thirty-four poets included chronicle the founding of a colony, as well as expressing their reactions to the new environment in which they found themselves. Some of the poets are well-known figures such as Alfred Domett, others will be new to the reader.

719 **The Oxford book of New Zealand short stories.**
Selected by Vincent O'Sullivan. Auckland: Oxford University Press, 1994. 450p.

A selection of short stories by New Zealand authors which covers both the 19th and 20th centuries. The endeavour of the editor in collecting this group of stories is to dispel the myth that the only styles in this genre are those of Katherine Mansfield or Frank Sargeson. The collection provides an introduction not only to the writers but to New Zealand itself.

720 **Best mates: gay writing in Aotearoa New Zealand.**
Peter Wells, Rex Pilgrim. Auckland: Reed, 1997. 288p.

Using the definition of 'gay fiction' as 'fiction in which a homosexual presence is not consciously or subconsciously excluded . . . often . . . written from the point of view of a character who is homosexual' (Introduction), this is a collection of works which fall within this category. A lengthy introduction expounds on the themes suggested and provides a context for the writing which follows. The anthology covers a wide range of literary forms, including short fiction, poetry, autobiography, a song cycle and a film script. All illuminate the kinds of relationships men have with each other and the world.

Humour

721 **The Penguin book of New Zealand jokes.**
John Barnett, Lesley Kaiser, in association with Brian Schaab.
Auckland: Penguin Books, 1996. 261p.

'Includes mainly jokes, including jokes with specific New Zealand references, that have been adapted for local use from the global network of jokes, plus transnational jokes currently in circulation some of which gain an extra punch from location in this context' (Introduction).

722 **The unauthorized version: a cartoon history of New Zealand.**
Ian F. Grant.   Auckland: Cassell New Zealand, 1980. 234p.

'The cartoon is an act of protest, more effective than the placards of any police-baiting mob and more elegant, and certainly more biodegradable than any graffiti spray-painted on a concrete wall . . . The cartoons in this book have been selected because they more or less reflect the public's attitude towards happenings of historical importance' (Foreword). From 'The land grabbers 1840-1890' to 'Swings and roundabouts 1973-79', the skill of the cartoonist in summing up situations and events in a humorous and apposite manner is deftly and amply demonstrated.

723 **The acid test: an anthology of New Zealand humorous writing.**
Edited by Gordon McLauchlan.   Auckland: Methuen, 1981. 213p.

Sets out to disprove the notion that New Zealanders lack a sense of humour by collecting writings from a variety of authors from 1923 to 1980, selected on the basis of, 'does the piece make me smile – wryly, broadly, whimsically, grimly, thinly or happily? Does it amuse me?' (Introduction). The result is an anthology that will reward the reader with many a laugh. The range of authors and styles selected ensures that there is something here for everyone.

The life of Katherine Mansfield.
See item no. 222.

The life and times of a good keen man.
See item no. 228.

Autobiography.
See item no. 234.

Sylvia!: the biography of Sylvia Ashton-Warner.
See item no. 241.

Frank Sargeson: a life.
See item no. 243.

The life of James K. Baxter.
See item no. 247.

A fighting withdrawal: the life of Dan Davin, writer, soldier, publisher.
See item no. 254.

Fairburn.
See item no. 261.

Journal of New Zealand Literature.
See item no. 881.

Landfall.
See item no. 884.

Visual Arts

General

724 The arts in Aotearoa/New Zealand: themes and issues.
Peter Beatson, Dianne Beatson.   Palmerston North, New Zealand:
Sociology Department, Massey University, 1994. 270p.

'A comprehensive overview of the country's artistic culture, past and present, Maori
and Pakeha, male and female, high and popular, the main themes of the work are the
tension between art and commerce, the nationalist/internationalist debate and the contribution made by art to gender, ethnic, class and community identity' (Introduction).
Behind these are a number of other themes including the relationship between artist
and critic, the art/craft schism and the perennial quarrel between elitists and populists.
This is a work which brings the artistic scene and community, and the world of the
arts in New Zealand generally, to life. An interesting feature is the use of quotations
from writers to add emphasis to the themes.

Painting and printmaking

725 Colonial constructs: European images of Maori, 1840-1914.
Leonard Bell.   Auckland: Auckland University Press, 1992. 291p.

A serious and well-researched consideration of depictions of Maori by early settlers,
and an examination of what attitudes can be discerned from these portrayals. Artists
considered include G. F. Angas, J. T. Merrett, J. A. Gilfillan, W. Strutt, N. Chevalier,
H. G. Robley, G. F. von Tempsky, G. Lindauer and W. Dittmer. The author stresses
that this is not a study of social or political history but is about 'the processes of representations made *by* Europeans *for* Europeans' (Introduction). Particular pieces are

230

selected for study for what they represent and are not always the 'best' work of the artist concerned. Note also the same author's work, *The Maori in European art: a survey of the representation of the Maori by European artists from the time of Captain Cook to the present day* (Wellington: Reed, 1980. 138p.).

726 Colin McCahon, artist.

Gordon H. Brown.   Wellington: Reed, 1993. rev. ed. 246p.

Updates the 1984 edition to provide fresh insights following the death of this major New Zealand artist in 1987. The work discusses McCahon's major areas of interest (religious paintings and landscapes), but also covers his enthusiasm for Cubism, printmaking and portrait painting and his use of words and numbers in his works. Supported with many illustrations of the paintings discussed, this remains 'the definitive work on this important artist and an invaluable tool to understanding and appreciating his work' (cover). It includes two appendices, one of which discusses McCahon's interest in, and association with, Maori prophets, the second a chronology of his life. A more recent interpretation, albeit flawed through being a poor technical production, is Agnes Wood's *Colin McCahon: the man and the teacher* (Auckland: David Ling, 1997. 160p.).

727 Another 100 New Zealand artists.

Warwick Brown.   Auckland: Godwit, 1996. 223p.

A companion volume to Brown's *100 New Zealand paintings by 100 New Zealand artists* (Auckland: Godwit, 1995. 216p.), this work covers another 100 artists whose major focus is in an area other than painting. Included are sculptors, printmakers, photographers, assemblage and graphic artists. Well-known (such as Greer Twiss, Marilynn Webb, Rudolf Gopas and Megan Jenkinson) and emerging talent (such as Nichola Shanley, Terry Urbahn and Simon Endres) is included. Each artist is represented by one work, with a conscious endeavour to present the lesser-known rather than those generally known. The vibrancy and originality of contemporary art is evident.

728 Two hundred years of New Zealand painting.

Gil Docking.   Auckland: David Bateman, 1990. rev. ed. 248p.

To date, the major work on New Zealand painting. Arrangement is broadly chronological, in four main chapters: Exploration, covering the work of navigators and explorers; Settlement, running from 1840 to the 1870s; Transition, roughly from the 1870s to the 1920s; and New Impulses, bringing the coverage up to the present. Within each of these chapters discussion is by themes, with major artists being dealt with in detail. Profusely illustrated, with many full-page plates, the book has already been through several printings.

729 A concise history of New Zealand painting.

Michael Dunn.   Tortola, British Virgin Islands: Craftsman House, 1991. 188p.

'My aim in this concise history of New Zealand painting is to provide a short, accessible account of what I see as the main developments' (Introduction). Divided thematically rather than chronologically, the book describes important aspects of Colonial Landscape: 1840-70, Later Victorian Landscape: 1870-90, and Images of the Maori: 1840-1914, as well as featuring chapters on the Expatriates, the La Trobe scheme, Regionalism and Realism, Modernism, Neo-expressionism, Abstraction and Postmodernism. The focus is on painting rather than on painters; hence biographical data is minimal. The volume is in large format and handsomely illustrated.

730 **Early prints of New Zealand, 1642-1875.**
E. M. Ellis, D. G. Ellis.   Christchurch: Avon Fine Prints, 1978. 328p.
bibliog.

'A print . . . is defined as a commercially produced pictorial plate having no text . . . other than title and imprint on the face . . . The index is the key to the whole work . . . arrangement is basically chronological . . . it was decided to record the separately-issued print under the artist's name where known . . . Prints in books are fully described in the entry under author and title of the book. In all cases the index is the quick reference key' (Introduction). Twenty of the 1,782 items are reproduced in colour; others are reproduced in black-and-white. The book is the standard reference aid in its field.

731 **Portrait of a century: the history of the New Zealand Academy of Fine Arts, 1882-1982.**
Robin Kay, Tony Eden.   Wellington: Millwood, 1983. 219p.

The New Zealand Academy of Fine Arts was founded in 1882. Its first exhibition was held in the following year. This book celebrates both the Academy's 100 administrative years and the more than 4,000 artists who exhibited with it over those years. Both achievements, including the Academy's promotion of a National Art Gallery, and struggles, are recorded. Properly, in such a history, the many illustrations are a feature of the book.

732 **New Zealand women artists: a survey of 150 years.**
Anne Kirker.   Tortola, British Virgin Islands: Craftsman House, 1993. 255p.

Perceiving that women artists have been under-represented in standard New Zealand art histories, the author seeks to redress the imbalance. 'The present study aims to . . . produce an analysis of women who have been creative in the visual arts of this country, from the early colonial period to the present. My intention is not simply to assert that there have been women artists but also to show that their activities have been conditioned by a complex matrix which is social, political and psychological. The fact that an artist happens to be a woman rather than a man matters' (Introduction). The lives, careers and works of over seventy women are examined.

733 **Contemporary New Zealand prints.**
Edited by Jill McIntosh.   Wellington: Allen & Unwin/Port Nicholson Press/Wellington City Art Gallery, 1989. 104p.

The result of an exhibition at the Wellington City Art Gallery marking the twentieth anniversary of the establishment of the New Zealand Print Council, this collection brings together the work of more than thirty New Zealand printmakers. While the collection includes the work of some already well-known names (e.g., Kate Coolahan, John Drawbridge, Ralph Hotere and Stanley Palmer) much of the work represented has emerged from print workshops. Each of the contributors is profiled.

734 **Lands and deeds: profiles of contemporary New Zealand painters.**
Gregory O'Brien.   Auckland: Godwit, 1996. 214p. bibliog.
Presents the work of eighteen New Zealand artists through interview and illustration.
'The work gathered in this book reinterprets and reinvents notions of place and history, of lands and deeds' (cover). Generally, the recent work of artists is concentrated upon. Obviously, this is a selection according to the author's criteria, but a pleasing and involving work has resulted. Emerging, as well as established, artists are covered, providing a cross-section of 'figurative' painters.

735 **Frames on the land: early landscape painting in New Zealand.**
Francis Pound.   Auckland: Collins, 1983. 112p.
The author takes the long-held view that the clarity of the light in New Zealand inspired a unique approach to landscape painting and dismisses this as a myth, arguing that the immigrant artists brought to New Zealand 'European theories and practices and superimposed such "mental frames" on the New Zealand landscape' (cover). Looking in detail at the work of seventeen artists, he shows how the landscape has been modified to incorporate these 'mental frames'. This is an attractive work with an interesting theme.

Three-dimensional arts

736 **New art: some recent New Zealand sculpture and post-object art.**
Edited by Jim Allen, Wystan Curnow.   Auckland; London:
Heinemann Educational, 1976. 95p.
A book which describes the work and working methods of some New Zealand sculptors of the time and includes some biographical information. The editors state: 'Each was invited to submit a work or works . . . we did want full photographic documentation, details of dimensions, materials, method of construction, location, time place and date of performance . . . Essentially . . . each artist conceived and planned his own section of the book' (Introduction). Little else on sculpture has been published recently.

737 **Craft New Zealand: the art of the craftsman.**
Doreen Blumhardt, Brian Brake.   Wellington: Reed, 1981. 294p.
More than 250 photographs – over 200 in full colour – capture the essence of hundreds of innovative and exquisite handmade items, the work of 133 artists in all the major craft media. Each piece has been selected to display the variety of crafts practised and the diversity of materials used in New Zealand. There are nine broad categories: enamelware, ceramics, fibres of all kinds, jade, bone, stone, glass, wood and plastics. 'The intention in this book is to survey current developments and achievements of the crafts in New Zealand' (Introduction).

738 **A New Zealand potter's dictionary: techniques and materials for the South Pacific.**
Barry Brickell. Auckland: Reed Methuen, 1985. 164p. maps.

A comprehensive and practical A-Z handbook on the potter's craft, covering the geology, raw materials and economics of craft pottery in New Zealand and parts of the South Pacific, as well as providing detailed descriptions and explanations of the terms, techniques, materials and technology of the craft. The volume is illustrated with diagrams and photographs.

739 **Please touch: a survey of the three-dimensional arts in New Zealand.**
Peter Cape. Auckland: Collins, 1980. 160p.

A sequel to the author's earlier *Artists and craftsmen in New Zealand* (Auckland: Collins, 1969. 176p.), this book surveys the subsequent growth in the number of craftworkers and their patrons in New Zealand, also arguing that design has developed along new indigenous lines. Areas covered include the arts of sculpture, jewellery, ceramics, weaving and craftwork in leather, wood and base metals. In an Epilogue, the author presents forthright views on the relationship between the working artist and administrators. The title embodies Cape's concern for the tactile qualities of art: 'touch has a major part to play in all our experiences' (Introduction).

740 **Pottery in New Zealand: commercial and collectable.**
Gail Lambert. Auckland: Heinemann, 1985. 166p.

'This book aims to provide . . . information about New Zealand commercial ceramics – the factories, the craftsmen, and their wares' (Introduction). Not only does it identify a range of pottery made in New Zealand, but it also describes different techniques and processes involved in the making of pottery and provides an historical perspective to the growth of the ceramic industry in New Zealand. The author also explores the move from the secondhand shop to the antique outlets now being accorded this material, and the acknowledgement that New Zealand commercial pieces have a value in their own right.

741 **Profiles: 24 New Zealand potters.**
Cecilia Parkinson, John Parker. Auckland: David Bateman, 1988. 112p.

Coloured and black-and-white photographs of the products and the potters themselves provide an interesting picture of the evolution of pottery in New Zealand. The methods used by those profiled, in achieving their sometimes quite startling and unusual effects, are explored. The potters and the items speak for themselves, as the book takes a descriptive rather than analytical approach.

742 **Gold and silversmithing in nineteenth century and twentieth century New Zealand.**
Winsome Shepherd. Wellington: Museum of New Zealand, 1995. 239p.

An important reference work, accompanied by lavish illustrations, covering manufacturing and retailing goldsmiths, silversmiths and jewellers in New Zealand since the 1860s, when immigrants first began producing distinctive works incorporating local motifs, styles and influences. The extensive appendices contain biographies of many craftsmen and reports of exhibitions.

743   **All our own work: New Zealand folk art.**
Richard Wolfe.   Auckland: Viking, 1997. 152p. bibliog.

A 'fun' book which through its wealth of illustrations celebrates the folk art of New Zealand – the items which are handmade at home and mostly prepared for pleasure not profit. 'Beginning with the heritage of New Zealand's Polynesian and European founding culture [the work] traces the influences on our folk art of the New Zealand landscape, our natural history, agriculture, the sea, shipping, wartime and the Pacific' (cover). Photographs illustrate each type of art.

Photography

744   **New Zealand photographers: a selection.**
Hardwicke Knight.   Dunedin: Allied Press, 1981. 112p.

This book is made up of 23 selected biographies illustrated with 96 photographs, and a list of over 1,000 New Zealand photographers to 1900. It is particularly interesting for its depiction of the New Zealand of last century and the automatic comparison which the reader will make with the New Zealand of today.

745   **New Zealand photography from the 1840s to the present/Nga whakaahua o Aotearoa mai i 1840 ki nainei.**
William Main, John B. Turner, edited by Desmond Kelly.   Auckland: Photoforum Inc., 1993. 88p.

Drawing on the independent research of both authors, this book presents the history of New Zealand through the lens of a camera and the surviving work of the photographers represented. 'In over 100 striking images the authors trace the achievements of our best photographers from the time of the laborious daguerrotype and wet plate processes through to today's instant colour systems' (cover). The photographs are clearly and skilfully presented, and accompanied by biographical details of the photographers concerned and information about how they approached their profession.

746   **The Robin Morrison collection.**
Robin Morrison.   Auckland: Auckland Museum, 1997. 119p.

'The 100 images in this book are drawn from a pool of approximately 100,000 photographs which comprise the Robin Morrison Collection donated by Robin and his family to the Auckland Museum shortly before his death in 1993' (Introduction). Generally regarded as one of New Zealand's pre-eminent photographers, Morrison had an international reputation and produced work in Australia, Ireland, the United Kingdom and India. Morrison depicts a different, human and everyday picture of New Zealand, with a special insight which makes many of the images unforgettable.

Art New Zealand.
See item no. 876.

Performing Arts

Music

747 The mechanics of popular music: a New Zealand perspective.
Mike Chunn, Jeremy Chunn. Wellington: GP Publications, 1995.
132p.

Details much that anyone planning a career in any aspect of the music industry would need to know. The authors deal with making recordings, getting a manager, self-promotion, and ways of making money in the industry. Interviews with successful performers and administrators bring home the realities of the hard work needed to be successful in this field. This is a work which demystifies and deromanticizes.

748 The great New Zealand songbook.
Selected and edited by Les Cleveland. Auckland: Godwit Press,
1991. 130p. bibliog.

Provides the words and music to distinctively New Zealand popular songs. An introduction describes the intent of the work and sets this genre into the culture of the country. Contemporary illustrations and information on the song writers when known is included, together with an annotated bibliography.

749 Stranded in paradise: New Zealand rock 'n' roll, 1955-1988.
John Dix. Wellington: Paradise Publications, 1988. 352p.

A rumbustious evocation of Kiwi rock music, both the highs and the lows. The author, a journalist, reveals an encyclopaedic knowledge of the New Zealand popular music scene, as well as the passing parade of bands and performers. Now obscure artists are briefly restored to the spotlight, while the beginnings of groups who later achieved fame (in some cases notoriety) overseas are recorded. The book, split into forty profusely illustrated chapters, is clearly one fan's labour of love.

750   **When the Pakeha sings of home: a source guide to the folk and popular songs of New Zealand.**
Mike Harding.   Auckland: Godwit, 1992. 91p.
'This publication lists all those recorded and/or published songs I have been able to find in English that can be identified, perhaps by no more than a single local place-name or Maori word, as songs from New Zealand' (Preface). Maori songs have been excluded, as have those written in New Zealand or by New Zealanders that do not attempt to express something of the country. More than just a list of songs, this is also an attempt to show New Zealanders that they do have a unique culture. The work is presented in two parts: 'The sources', with a discography and bibliography; and 'The songs', divided into colonial folk and pop songs (1769-1945) and modern pop songs (1945-90). Each section contains a short contextual introduction.

751   **Opera's farthest frontier: a history of professional opera in New Zealand.**
Adrienne Simpson.   Auckland: Reed, 1996. 288p.
An entertaining and well-researched history of opera in New Zealand, from its beginnings in gold-rush Dunedin in 1862 to its ever-growing popularity with present-day audiences. Particularly evocative are the sections dealing with the vicissitudes of 19th-century touring companies from overseas, playing not only the major towns but also smaller provincial townships. The more recent past, however, with New Zealand becoming an exporter of international talent, is not neglected. The book addresses changing attitudes to opera over the years, and there are insights into the entertainment world as a whole.

752   **Southern voices: international opera singers of New Zealand.**
Adrienne Simpson, Peter Downes.   Auckland: Reed, 1992. 283p.
Throughout the 20th century, New Zealand has provided the world with some of its finest operatic talents. While a number – Kiri Te Kanawa, Donald McIntyre and Malvina Major – are household names in their home country, others are scarcely known. This book is a celebration of their achievements. The careers of nineteen international singers are described, with insights into their motivations, their views on other performers and their attitudes to their homeland. 'The nineteen singers chosen have pursued career paths that are fascinating in their diversity' (p. 5).

753   **Biographical dictionary of New Zealand composers.**
John M. Thomson.   Wellington: Victoria University Press, 1990. 168p.
Lists over 100 New Zealand composers from the 19th century to the present day. Select lists of works, writings and bibliographies are provided. The book is 'intended to convey knowledge of New Zealand composers, to show their qualities and to encourage performance and appreciation of their work' (Introduction). Major figures are treated at more length and in more depth. A small selection of photographs bring some of the composers to life.

754 **The Oxford history of New Zealand music.**
John M. Thomson. Auckland: Oxford University Press, 1991. 315p.

The first comprehensive account of music in New Zealand since the arrival of Europeans. 'I have seen my prime task as that of recovering as much of the buried history of music in New Zealand as possible' (Introduction). Outlining how the first settlers brought their music with them, the author demonstrates how the offshoot tradition was reinforced through choral and instrumental societies, bands, balls, and music in the home. Chapters on music in the 20th century cover the development of the tradition, and innovations such as music in the cinema, broadcasting, and in education. Two chapters focus on traditional Maori music and the influence of European music on Maori music.

755 **The New Zealand Symphony Orchestra: the first forty years.**
Joy Tonks. Auckland: Reed Methuen, 1986. 302p.

This comprehensive history examines the musical climate in which the New Zealand Symphony Orchestra (NZSO) first took root in 1946, under the aegis of the National Broadcasting Service, then traces its development from a diverse collection of musicians – many self-taught – to a fully grown, world-class orchestra. The conductors, players and composers who have been associated with the NZSO are discussed, as well as the musical milestones of the orchestra's career. Critics of the NZSO also have their say, and there is a balanced look at several controversies surrounding the orchestra. The same author's *Bravo!: the NZSO at fifty* (Auckland: Existe Publications, 1996. 232p.) updates the story.

Dance

756 **The New Zealand Ballet: the first twenty-five years.**
Beatrice Ashton, edited by John E. Watson. Wellington: Association of Ballet and Opera Trust Boards of New Zealand, 1978. 36p.

A brief, well-illustrated history of the company since it was founded in 1953 by Poul Knatt, when several experienced and talented New Zealand dancers returned from overseas. Much of the book revolves around the company's survival, due fundamentally to the dedication of the people involved.

757 **Dance New Zealand.**
Dawn Sanders. Auckland: Heinemann Reed, 1989. 77p.

Using young New Zealanders as models, this book takes the reader through various dance forms practised in New Zealand. Illustrative rather than textual, the many photographs show how the dances should be performed.

Theatre

758 Shadows on the stage: theatre in New Zealand – the first seventy years.

Peter Downes. Dunedin: McIndoe, 1975. 116p.

'This book is a modest attempt to recall from obscurity and place on record at least *some* of the story of professional theatre in early New Zealand, how it began and how it developed' (Introduction). The author recognizes that the quantity of material makes this an overview rather than a detailed history, but describes how the first twenty years was a pioneering period with local companies while the next thirty were dominated by touring companies from Australia. Reproductions of contemporary illustrations complement the text.

759 A centre of attraction: the story of Downstage Theatre.

Peter Harcourt. Wellington: Downstage Theatre, 1979. 32p.

An account of the development of New Zealand's most long-lived professional theatre, whose first home was a disused coffee bar. Notable productions and prominent personalities are described and illustrated. The book concludes with a list of Downstage productions. *Circa, 1976-1996*, edited by John Reid and Ruth Jeffrey (Wellington: Council of Circa Theatre, 1996. 120p.), provides the same kind of information for Wellington's Circa Theatre, including for each production a quote from a critic.

760 A dramatic appearance, New Zealand theatre 1920-1970.

Peter Harcourt. Wellington, London: Methuen, 1978. 177p. bibliog.

In the half-century to the 1970s New Zealand theatre came of age. This popular history by a much loved actor and dramatist traces the phases of this development. Through contemporary photographs, anecdotes, incidents and memories recalled for him by those who took part, the atmosphere of each phase is accurately recaptured. Harcourt also records the growth of the New Zealand Ballet and Opera Companies. For theatre buffs, this is a whimsical exercise in nostalgia.

761 New Zealand drama.

Howard McNaughton. Boston, Massachusetts: Twayne Publishers, 1981. 168p.

Although now dated, this is a scholarly assessment of drama in New Zealand from 1840 to 1979. Three introductory chapters provide an overview of the scene, followed by chapters on specific playwrights, such as Bruce Mason and James K. Baxter, and specific developments, such as the confrontational drama of the 1970s. There is much here of interest for those studying the evolution of drama in this country.

762 New Zealand drama, 1930-1980: an illustrated history.

J. E. P. Thomson. Auckland: Oxford University Press, 1984. 108p.

Until the 1930s few distinctively New Zealand plays were written, much less produced. This small book traces the development of an indigenous theatre tradition from its shaky beginnings to a coming of age in the 1970s. The role of the local branch of the British Drama League in promoting playwriting and amateur performance is assessed and the significance of Bruce Mason in carrying the tradition to adolescence is considered. The professionalization of New Zealand theatre is then outlined. The major plays, playwrights and theatre companies are all briefly noted.

Film

763 **Naming the other: images of the Maori in New Zealand film and television.**
Martin J. Blythe. Metuchen, New Jersey: Scarecrow Press, 1994. 335p.

As much an investigation of cultural relations in New Zealand as a study of film. The author studies film over four different periods (1910s-1920s, 1940s, 1950s-1980s and 1980s onwards) and assesses whether there is conflict between Maori and Pakeha cultures. This is a complex theme, which is interestingly developed.

764 **Shadows on the wall: a study of seven New Zealand feature films.**
Barbara Cairns, Helen Martin. Auckland: Longman Paul, 1994. 340p.

Intended for senior English and media studies students, this work provides an insight into how films are developed and made through examination of the structure of seven New Zealand feature films. Each of the films is analysed in detail, encouraging the reader to follow the process and think about the reasons behind the particular way the film has been constructed. Interviews with film-makers and publicity stills amplify the discussion.

765 **Film in Aotearoa New Zealand.**
Edited by Jonathan Dennis, Jan Bieringa. Wellington: Victoria University Press, 1996. 2nd ed. 244p.

The editors state that this work 'is not intended as a definitive statement on film in the country; rather it offers through the personal perspectives and histories of the filmmakers themselves, an opportunity to venture into the wealth and realm of film making here, and become aware of its cultural context' (Introduction). The second edition builds on the first and covers some of the significant work of the 1990s (*The Piano, Once were warriors, Heavenly creatures*). Copiously illustrated, this work provides a forum for those involved in the industry to express their hopes and achievements. It deals with feature films as well as documentaries and short and experimental films.

Every kind of weather: selected writings on the arts, theatre, literature and current events in New Zealand, 1953-1981.
See item no. 703.

The arts in Aotearoa/New Zealand: themes and issues.
See item no. 724.

Illusions.
See item no. 880.

Music in New Zealand.
See item no. 886.

A bibliography of writings about New Zealand music.
See item no. 954.

Maori Arts, Crafts, Music and Folklore

Art

766 Mataora: the living face: contemporary Maori art.
Sandy Adsett, Cliff Whiting, edited by Witi Ihimaera.   Auckland:
David Bateman/Creative New Zealand, 1996. 167p.

A very colourful compilation of the work of more than forty modern Maori artists and
writers. Examples of the works of art, paintings, sculpture and pottery are supported
by commentary and writings including poetry. The breadth of the coverage gives an
insight into Maori culture of today.

767 An illustrated guide to Maori art.
Terence Barrow.   Auckland: Reed, 1995. 104p.

Constantly being reprinted, this remains an accessible guide to the different facets of
Maori art. Following a general review, specific arts are looked at in detail, leading to
an understanding of the symbolic and spiritual significance of the works.

768 Maori art on the world scene: essays on Maori art.
S. M. (Sydney Moko) Mead.   Wellington: Ahua Design and
Illustration Ltd., Matau Associates, 1997. 241p.

Resulting from many years of research in the United States, Canada and New Zealand,
this is a collection of papers written over some thirty years on aspects of Maori art.
The author is trained in anthropology and is a specialist in this area of study.
Beautifully illustrated, the work provides insights into Maori art and raises issues
relating to how this art should be preserved. The author journeys widely through different kinds of art and personalizes it for the reader.

769 **Painted histories: early Maori figurative painting.**
Roger Neich. Auckland: Auckland University Press, 1993. 330p.
maps.

The decoration of Maori meeting houses with representational figurative painting was
a late 19th-century phenomenon, one unknown in traditional Maori culture, and one
that proved short-lived. Largely confined to the eastern districts of the North Island,
figurative painting reached its heights in the 1880s, the influence of the new Ringatu
religion being strong. This impressive study analyses the theory and practice of this
art and describes the paintings of more than eighty meeting houses, many of which
have now disappeared.

770 **Ta moko: the art of Maori tattoo.**
D. R. Simmons. Auckland: Reed, 1997. rev. ed. 183p. bibliog.

A well-researched study of male and female *moko* (face tattoo) which draws on the
observations of early explorers such as James Cook, Jean Francois Marie de Surville
and Marion du Fresne, and the work of artists such as Augustas Earle, George French
Angas, Major General Horatio Robley, Gottfried Lindauer and Charles Frederick
Goldie. A brief description of Maori tattooing is followed by a consideration of the
place of *moko* in Maori society, the different styles of *moko,* the decline of the male
moko and the development of the female *moko.* The work is lavishly illustrated in
black-and-white and colour.

771 **Maori: art and culture.**
Edited by D. C. Starzecka. Auckland: David Bateman, 1996. 168p.

Intended as an introduction to the Maori collections of the British Museum, this attractive publication is a result of collaboration between the Museum and New Zealand
colleagues. Authoritative essays discuss in detail wood-carving, cloak-making and
other fibre arts, tattoo, jewellery, musical instruments and weapons. Accompanying
contributions outline the history of the Maori from the arrival of the first Polynesian
settlers to the present, thus contextualizing the art. A concluding chapter offers a history of the Maori collections in the Museum, including artefacts collected during
Cook's voyages of exploration: 'probably the finest outside New Zealand' (p. 148).

772 **Prehistoric rock art of New Zealand.**
Michael Trotter, Beverley McCulloch. Auckland: Longman Paul,
1981. rev. ed. 88p. maps. (New Zealand Archaeological Association
Monograph no. 12).

Despite the wide occurrence of rock art in New Zealand, this is the first comprehensive book on the subject. The authors' approach is scientific rather than artistic. They
cover such aspects as the history of European investigations up to the present day,
and the methods employed by modern archaeologists. The distribution, subject matter, and techniques of execution to be found in the rock art of both the North and
South Islands are dealt with in separate chapters, and the place of rock art in Maori
culture is discussed.

Crafts

773 Treasured taonga: traditional and contemporary techniques and concepts in bone carving.
Ropata Davis.   Auckland: Random House, N.Z., 1994. 106p.

A study of Maori carving including the practicalities relating to carving, the materials, techniques, tools and designs. Desiring 'to further the knowledge of Maori art and craft and to offer inspirations', the author includes both contemporary and traditional designs, explaining how the former arise from the latter. *Taonga*, while generally interpreted as 'treasure', also has a broader meaning, 'covering the Maori language, customs, traditions and art' (Preface). Beautiful illustrations indicate why the author sees bone carving as a *taonga*.

774 Te toi whakairo = The art of Maori carving.
S. M. (Sydney Moko) Mead.   Auckland: Reed, 1995. rev. ed. 268p. maps.

A revised and greatly expanded version of a book first published in 1961, this is the most comprehensive book on Maori carving available. The author examines the historical and cultural tradition of carving, its origins and development, tribal variations and interpretation. He also explores the survival and vitality of the art, not only in the context of pre-European society, but also against the background of a resurgent Maori consciousness in modern New Zealand. In a concluding chapter he provides advice for the aspiring carver, discussing tools and timbers, styles, patterns and techniques.

775 Traditional Maori clothing: a study of technological and functional change.
S. M. (Sydney Moko) Mead.   Wellington: Reed, 1969. 238p.

Although published nearly thirty years ago, this remains the standard work on the subject. The study commences with an outline of the complete range of clothing used during the pre-European Classic Period, the technology of production, and functions. The author then proceeds to follow what has happened to Maori clothing technologically and functionally up to modern times. 'This study . . . is based on a corpus of material which includes ethnological accounts, museum collections, early pictorial records, photographic files, and some fieldwork' (p. 13).

776 Feathers and fibre: a survey of traditional and contemporary Maori craft.
Nick Prendergast.   Auckland: Penguin, 1986. 237p.

This publication arose from an exhibition mounted by the Rotorua Art Gallery, the intention being to highlight Maori fibre crafts, these, with the occasional exception of fine cloaks, having been previously largely ignored. Maori produced some very fine examples of woven flax cloaks. They used a twining form of weaving known as downward or finger weaving which resulted in 'magnificent ceremonial garments of exquisite workmanship' (Introduction). Although plaited articles make up the major part of the exhibition, examples of woven garments, fish traps and tackle, hunting apparatus and decorative wall panels, from a range of tribal backgrounds, were also included. The 280 plates are accompanied by a detailed catalogue.

777 **Maori weaving.**
Erenora Puketapu-Hetet. Auckland: Pitman, 1989. 88p.

An introduction to Maori weaving which, in addition to imparting manual skills, lays stress on the craft's inseparable spiritual dimension. The book includes a guide to the many plants that can be used for weaving and dyeing, and practical advice on how to prepare them for use. There are step-by-step instructions on how to make a variety of articles, including woven baskets and headbands.

Performance

778 **Games and dances of the Maori people.**
Alan Armstrong. Auckland: Viking Sevenseas, 1986. 92p.

'This book is an introduction to a selection of the games and dances of the Maori people. Some of the games are now seldom played but for the most part the book chronicles aspects of Maori culture which are still widely practised . . . and which will continue into the foreseeable future' (Foreword). Although somewhat slight, intended for the tourist market, the collection is nevertheless a useful introduction to, for example, string, stick and hand games, action songs, and the *haka* and *poi* dances. The emphasis is on performance, not context.

779 **Maori music.**
Mervyn McLean. Auckland: Auckland University Press, 1996. 418p. map.

An authoritative, detailed but very readable work by an ethnomusicologist with a special interest in traditional Maori song and dance forms. It is intended to be complementary to Mervyn McLean and Margaret Orbell's *Traditional songs of the Maori* (Auckland: Auckland University Press, 1990. rev. ed. 324p.) in which the authors explain traditional music and dance. In this work McLean examines the effects of European influences and looks at the development of modern genres.

780 **Waiata: Maori songs in history: an anthology.**
Margaret Orbell. Auckland: Reed, 1991. 116p.

The author, who has translated many ancient texts, in this volume looks at 19th-century *waiata*, and places them in their social and political setting. *Waiata* are a living form and new ones appear even today. They are generally laments or complaints sung publicly on a *marae* or elsewhere to express the poets' feelings, convey a message and sway the listener's emotions. The language is often elaborate, with specialized expressions and complex allusions. This work is not just a listing of *waiata* but a description and exploration to ensure understanding. Translations and a commentary are provided for each *waiata*.

781   The Maori action song: waiata a ringa, waiata kori, no whea tenei
      hou?
      Jennifer Shennan.   Wellington: New Zealand Council for Educational
      Research, 1984. 100p.
Maori action songs, involving both singing and dancing, are 'a vital, exhilarating, res-
onant, thriving and integral part of Maori life' (Foreword). The author, with dual
qualifications in anthropology and dance, explores how action songs came to occupy
so important a position in Maori culture, and looks at what they convey about current
Mao.i customs, values and aspirations. She prepares the ground by discussing the origins of the dance, then describing how it developed into what is now effectively the
national dance of New Zealand. The work is well illustrated.

Folklore

782   **Polynesian mythology and ancient traditional history of the Maori
      as told by their priests and chiefs.**
      George Grey.   Hamilton, New Zealand: University of Waikato
      Library, 1995. Reprint of 1956 ed. 1st English ed., 1855. 250p.
Many young New Zealanders have learned Maori myths and legends from the collection compiled by Grey for the purpose of helping him rule 'a numerous and turbulent
people'. A number of the classical tales are in the collection: they deal with the origin
of the human race, the doings of Maui the demi-god, and the legendary voyages etc.
The translations, however, were designed for Victorian reading, young as well as
adult; they therefore contain circumlocutions and lack some key passages. A more
recent rendition of these tales is presented by Antony Alpers' *Maori myths and tribal
legends* (Auckland: Longman, 1996. 256p.), attractively illustrated by Patrick Hanly.
This is a retelling which seeks to demonstrate the power and imagery of the stories to
a wider audience than the children for whom Grey's renderings were intended.

783   **The illustrated encyclopedia of Maori myth and legend.**
      Margaret Orbell.   Christchurch: Canterbury University Press, 1995.
      274p. map.
A beautifully illustrated, detailed guide to Maori myths and legends, religious beliefs,
folklore and history, containing more than 380 entries arranged alphabetically. The
introduction provides background information to set the entries in context, including
the Polynesian tradition behind the stories and sign posts to representations in the rituals and songs of gods and ancestors.

**Mana wahine Maori: selected writings on Maori women's art, culture
and politics.**
See item no. 303.

Landmarks, bridges and visions: aspects of Maori culture: essays.
See item no. 332.

Architecture

784 The bungalow in New Zealand.
Jeremy Ashford. Auckland: Viking, 1994. 96p.

Although found in many countries of the world, New Zealand developed its own variant style for houses which traditionally had low-slung roof-lines and imposing verandahs. The author investigates the origins of the style, and details the influences on it. He argues that changes to New Zealand society after the First World War made this style a particularly appropriate one for New Zealanders and this contention is explored. The houses will be familiar to all New Zealanders and anyone who has visited the country. Attractively presented, the work portrays both the interiors and the exteriors of the houses.

785 The big house: grand and opulent houses in colonial New Zealand.
Terence Hodgson. Auckland: Random Century, 1991. 126p.

'The idea and pursuit of wealth in colonial New Zealand was taken up by a number of settlers seemingly within minutes of landfall . . . Only a handful . . . attained what could be justifiably called fantastic wealth' (Introduction). One manifestation of wealth was the ostentatious house or homestead. Citing pastoralism and commerce as the predominant areas for acquiring wealth, the work considers this conspicuous manifestation through the portrayal and examination of some of the 'big houses' of the time and their owners. Many of the houses remain today, if often in modified form.

786 Historic buildings of New Zealand.
Edited by Frances Porter. Auckland: Methuen, 1983. 2 vols.

Covering not only European buildings but also those of the Maori, the editor has welded together contributions from a wide range of authors and illustrators. One volume is devoted to the North Island and the other to the South Island. Carefully researched information is presented with associated illustrations, black-and-white and coloured, and the whole has been produced with the support and assistance of the Historic Places Trust. The buildings described range from meeting houses to churches, private dwellings and commercial buildings. More than just an architectural survey of New Zealand, these volumes incorporate perceptive historical vignettes.

787 **Old New Zealand houses, 1800-1940.**

Jeremy Salmond. Auckland: Heinemann Reed, 1989. 2nd ed. 246p.

This book is both a history and a celebration of New Zealand's old houses and, unusually, as much attention is paid to methods of construction – the materials, the tools and technology, and the builders – as to architects and design. The scene shifts from traditional Maori dwellings and the earliest settler cottages of cob and adobe to the rise of the 'kitset' villa building industry in the late 19th century. Also recorded are early 20th-century trends: the Californian and Spanish bungalows; 'arts and crafts' cottages; and the quirky Modernes built just prior to the Second World War. Profusely illustrated with photographs and precise technical drawings, the book also contains information from contemporary trade literature.

788 **New Zealand architecture: from Polynesian beginnings to 1990.**

Peter Shaw. Auckland: Hodder & Stoughton, 1991. 216p.

A superbly illustrated introductory survey of 150 years of New Zealand architecture. 'The full diversity of architectural styles is examined: from early Maori functional simplicity, the elaborate Antipodean Gothic and Victorian domestic of the nineteenth century, the impressive Neo-classical and Edwardian Baroque and fashionable Arts and Crafts and neo-Georgian of the early twentieth century, to the Post-modernism of the 1980s' (cover). Also surveyed are the leading exponents of these styles and their philosophies. The author seeks to explore the way in which a country's architecture reflects the spirit and aspirations of its inhabitants.

789 **The New Zealand villa: past and present.**

Di Stewart. Auckland: Viking Pacific, 1992. 96p.

A unique style in New Zealand domestic architecture, the bay villa is found throughout the country. Built mainly in the late 19th and early 20th centuries, they occupy suburbs immediately adjacent to city centres, surround rural towns and are dotted throughout the countryside of both islands. Though neglected and abused for half a century, since the 1970s there has been wide enthusiasm to restore the structures as fashionable family homes. This book traces the origins and development of the villa, outlining both external construction and interior detail.

790 **Cast in concrete: concrete construction in New Zealand, 1850-1939.**

Geoffrey G. Thornton. Auckland: Reed, 1996. 240p.

'Beginning with the earliest known concrete structures from the 1850s *Cast in concrete* presents a comprehensive survey of its development and use in New Zealand up to the beginning of the Second World War' (cover). This type of construction was widely used for bridges, private homes, sheep dips, farm buildings, fence posts and municipal buildings. Its versatility encouraged inventiveness and experimentation. Many of the structures described are still standing. Well illustrated, this work describes some uses of concrete which will amaze the reader.

791 **The New Zealand heritage of farm buildings.**

Geoffrey G. Thornton. Auckland: Reed Methuen, 1986. 268p.

Homesteads of varying size, surrounded by woolsheds, barns, stables and other working buildings, stand at the centre of New Zealand's rural colonial heritage. More than 300 early farm buildings are depicted in this extended photographic essay, each with an accompanying text providing background details and explaining the farming process to which it relates. While a diversity of styles is apparent, within and between regions, the emergence of a distinctively New Zealand 'flavour' is no less clear.

792 **New Zealand's industrial heritage.**
Geoffrey G. Thornton. Wellington: Reed, 1982. 194p. maps.

The development of early New Zealand industry was inevitably on a small scale. Hence the housing structures were primitive; often little more than timber walls, corrugated iron roofs and earthen floors. As the 19th century progressed, however, more permanent buildings were erected. Some, architect-designed, were lavish in concept. The author charts in detail the progress of many early industries – flax, timber and flour milling, ship and bridge building, farm processing and mineral extraction – surveying the buildings that resulted. He draws attention to the importance of New Zealand's industrial archaeology, and the need to preserve that which has survived.

793 **Built in New Zealand: the houses we live in.**
William Toomath. Auckland: Harper Collins, 1996. 194p. bibliog.

A description of New Zealand through the houses found in the country, built for and lived in by the ordinary and not-so-ordinary New Zealander. From the earliest structures, the author looks for common forms, using these to comment also on the society and culture of the nation. This is an unusual and innovative approach to a study of architectural styles.

New Zealand Historic Places.
See item no. 894.

New Zealand Home and Building.
See item no. 895.

Domestic Lifestyles

General

794 New Zealand! New Zealand!: in praise of Kiwiana.
Stephen Barnett, Richard Wolfe.   Auckland: Hodder & Stoughton, 1989. 161p.

Described as a 'whimsical lucky-dip into New Zealand's popular culture', this colourful book is a fond remembrance of Kiwi icons, brands and customs, before the global-villagizing influences of travel, television and urbanization. 'If it tends to linger over the 1950s and 1960s then it is simply because this period spanned the authors' formative years, their earliest memories' (p. 9).

795 A guide to modern manners.
Helen Brown.   Auckland: Penguin Books, 1991. 187p.

In a frank and lively style, Helen Brown, a columnist, brings her own view of what is right and proper to an assessment of modern manners. In spite of the humorous approach, there is much common sense here, and fun is poked at just about every aspect of social intercourse.

796 Etiquette and elbow grease.
Miriam MacGregor.   Wellington: Reed, 1976. 77p.

A short, pictorial and textual account of the daily duties of the average Victorian New Zealand housewife. 'The principal aim of this brief survey is to give a general view of how they coped within the house and of the utensils at their disposal' (Introduction). The work discusses cooking, cleaning, sewing and making clothes, laundering, gardening and recreations. Changes to the daily round for later generations are addressed in relevant sections of Kurt Sanders' *The way we were* (Auckland: Hodder Moa Beckett, 1996. 205p.).

Food and drink

797 Colonial fare: in which we learn of the amazing fortune and fate of pioneering women who ventured from their kitchens at home to embark upon a new life in the unknown territory of New Zealand.
Jill Brewis.   Auckland: Methuen, 1982. 179p.

Incorporating anecdotes and recipes drawn from the letters, diaries and cookbooks of colonial women, this book shows how their lives were closely tied to the struggles to acquire food and to vary their diet, to improve their living conditions and to reconstruct a life in New Zealand better than that left behind. Dishes as varied as sheep's-head soup and pukeko (a swamp bird) pie are detailed, while there are handy recipes for home-made soap, folk medicines and cleansers.

798 Two hundred years of New Zealand food and cookery.
David Burton.   Auckland: Mural Books, 1987. new ed. 168p.

The author, a journalist and sociologist as well as a chef, argues that New Zealand has been fashioning its own distinctive culinary tradition for centuries. Alternating commentary and recipes, he points out how British cookery was soon modified by Maori methods and the availability of a new range of raw foodstuffs, and how newer arrivals such as the Greeks, Chinese and Samoans all brought something of their cultures to the New Zealand dinner table. 'Admittedly, the list of genuinely national dishes is limited . . . but there are literally hundreds which can be considered typical of New Zealand cooking' (Introduction).

799 Michael Cooper's buyer's guide to New Zealand wines.
Michael Cooper.   Auckland: Hodder Moa Beckett, 1996. 364p. map.

Listing 1,200 different wines, this has now become the definitive New Zealand wine buyer's guide. Not afraid to criticize some of the wines on the market, Cooper has also expanded his annual list of 'Classics' – those wines which are constantly in the forefront in terms of quality. Cooper also looks at the development of the same wine over several vintages and advises on those wines which will develop if kept for a period.

800 Wines and vineyards of New Zealand.
Michael Cooper.   Auckland: Hodder Moa Beckett, 1996. 5th ed. 191p. bibliog.

In text and colourful illustrations, this work presents information on vineyards throughout New Zealand. The introduction provides a list of wines produced in New Zealand, a region-by-region summary of the critical influences of climate and soil, a description of winemaking techniques and an in-depth look at the classic grape varieties of New Zealand 'varietal' wines. This is followed by a description of 135 wineries, covering their background and evaluating key labels. Richard Brimer, in *Boutique wineries of New Zealand* (Auckland: Random House NZ, 1993. 191p.), also provides commentary on many of the smaller vineyards of New Zealand.

801 **The story of beer: beer and brewing, a New Zealand history.**
Gordon McLauchlan.   Auckland: Viking Penguin, 1994. 168p.

Examines beer from every angle – how to brew it, how to taste and enjoy it, when to drink it, and historical and present-day brews. This is a rollicking approach to the subject which also passes comment on the social relationships surrounding this beverage (and, incidentally, says much about New Zealand and its licensing laws and social customs). A complementary volume is *Microbreweries of New Zealand* by Anne Russell (text) and Richard Brimer (photographs) (Auckland: Random House, 1995. 126p.), a celebration of 'the uniqueness and artistry in our beer industry' (Introduction).

802 **The New Zealand whisky book.**
Stuart Perry.   Auckland: Collins, 1980. 141p.

The name Hokonui conjures up illicit stills in the minds of most New Zealanders. This book traces the history of legitimate whisky making from the 1870s to the 1970s by which time two brands were well established in the country, Wilson's and 45 South. Such a story is not without incidents and the author makes the most of those he found in his research.

Clothing and furnishings

803 **A New Zealand guide to antique and modern furniture.**
Patricia M. de Lautour.   Wellington: Grantham House, 1993. 96p.

An introduction to the history of furniture both in New Zealand and overseas, pieces brought to this country being placed in historical contexts. Central to the book, however, is the account of New Zealand furniture makers, both colonial utilitarians and more recent craftsmen, who experimented with indigenous timbers and utilized them to advantage. There is a concluding chapter on New Zealand furniture today. This is a clearly written and accessible work by an antiques dealer.

804 **In the colonial fashion: a lively look at what New Zealanders wore.**
Eve Ebbett.   Wellington: Reed, 1977. 79p. bibliog.

An illustrated descriptive account of the clothing worn by people in the latter half of the 19th century. The attire of women, men, children, Maori people, sports groups and uniformed services is covered.

805 **Colonial furniture in New Zealand.**
S. Northcote-Bade.   Wellington: Reed, 1971. 164p. bibliog.

The research for this book was done in the 1920s to 1940s, but much of it is still relevant today. The work traces the colonial house, the colonial village, and the development of local furniture and furniture styles, describes the ingenious cabin furniture which the colonists brought with them and discusses the influence of European styles on the furniture of the Maori house. References at the end of each chapter lead the reader on to further information and research.

Leisure

806 **At the beach: the great New Zealand holiday.**
Stephen Barnett, Richard Wolfe. Auckland: Hodder & Stoughton, 1993. 115p.

Describes New Zealanders' relationships with the beach, the place where all mix together, no matter their status in life. Illustrations delightfully depict the tentative approaches of the early forays of the later 19th century to the exuberant attitudes of today. Other themes include the style of bathing costumes, the cars, sunbathing and the changing attitudes to exposure to the sun, food and many other social concerns. To gain an impression of the kind of accommodation New Zealanders enjoyed on their holidays at the beach, *The bach*, by Paul Thompson (Wellington: Government Printer, 1985. 89p.), is a photographic essay which shows the importance of these distinctive holiday houses to the New Zealand holiday lifestyle.

807 **A history of the garden in New Zealand.**
Edited by Matthew Bradbury. Auckland: Viking, 1995. 208p. map.

An illustrated history that traces the New Zealand garden from its first roots in traditional Maori horticulture and the early years of settlement through 150 years of fads and fancies to the present day. The work of botanists, horticulturalists, seedsmen and nursery men – all of whom influenced the colour, smell and form of gardens – is examined, while the role of the country's early town planners is also considered. The book is the work of nine contributors, specialists in the fields of archaeology, garden history and landscape design. For a more academic treatment of related topics see Helen Leach's *1000 years of New Zealand gardening* (Wellington: Reed, 1984. 157p.).

Sport and Recreation

General

808 Into the field of play.
Edited by Lloyd Jones.   Auckland: Tandem Press, 1992. 168p.

Despite the passion New Zealanders hold for sport, little has been written on the place of sport in the country's culture. In this book the editor brings together contributions from well-known New Zealand writers, some previously published and others specially commissioned for the collection, which explore particular aspects of sport in their neighbourhoods. The pieces clearly demonstrate that while high-performance sport tends to dominate the media, at a more modest level sport actively touches the lives of many.

809 The best of McLean.
Terry McLean.   Auckland: Hodder & Stoughton, 1984. 255p.

A varied collection from the doyen of New Zealand sports journalism (knighted in 1996), whose active career spans seven decades. While the emphasis is on his first sporting love, rugby football, the essays also encompass golf, tennis, boxing, cricket, lawn bowls, athletics, swimming, soccer, croquet, squash, polo, yachting and ski-racing. There are also essays on non-sporting subjects. McLean's trademark is the sensitivity of his profiles of people, whether in triumph or disappointment.

810 Guts, tears and glory: champion New Zealand sportswomen talk to Trish Stratford.
Trish Stratford.   Auckland: New Women's Press, 1988. 203p.

A number of New Zealand sportswomen who have excelled in their chosen sport talk to Trish Stratford of the difficulties they have encountered in striving for the top. It is clear that for all it has been an uphill battle, through lack of funds, unsympathetic sports administrators, the hard training and the loneliness. Their triumphs have been achieved through dedication and achievement.

Organized sport

811 **New Zealand's world cup: the inside story.**
John Adshead, Kevin Fallon. Auckland: Moa Publications/Country Wide Building Society, 1982. 231p.

The road to Spain, New Zealand's moment of glory in football (soccer) when it reached the finals of the 1982 World Cup, is here told to the journalist Armin Lindenberg by the manager and coach of the team. This was a time of inspiration for those involved in the sport and one that did much to establish an interest amongst young players which still continues today, although not to the same degree.

812 **Champions under sail: twenty five years of New Zealand yachting greats.**
Richard Becht. Auckland: Hodder Moa Beckett, 1995. 191p. bibliog.

When Chris Bouzaid and his crew sailed to victory in the World One Ton Cup in 1969, New Zealand established its name in offshore racing. This book looks at the twenty-five years since that event through chapters on the achievements of well-known sailors. The definition of sailing in this work is not simply confined to offshore racing, but also includes the windsurfing achievements of Barbara and Bruce Kendall and an evocation of the design genius of Bruce Farr. Becht provides an involving introduction to New Zealand's prowess on the water.

813 **Power league: rugby league in the 1990s.**
Richard Becht, Dean Bell. Auckland: David Bateman, 1995. 160p.

Combining the knowledge and skills of an international league player (Bell) and a rugby league writer (Becht), the authors have produced a fast-moving work which covers the essential elements of the game – the play-the-ball, the scrum, penalties, passing, etc. – with photographs showing top players in action. Each chapter is devoted to a particular aspect of the game and describes the rules and techniques required for a player to demonstrate this skill to the highest level. This is a good clear introduction to the game.

814 **Belliss on bowls.**
Peter Belliss. Auckland: Reed Methuen, 1987. 144p.

A champion bowler combines autobiography with commentary on tactics and techniques. His career spans almost thirty years and since 1984 Belliss has been at the top of his sport. He writes of the tournaments he has attended and the people, particularly other bowlers, he has met. This is a chatty and descriptive work, in which Belliss's enthusiasm for his sport shines through. For a work concentrating more on the techniques of the sport, see Mark de Lacy and Peter Belliss's *Think and play better bowls* (Christchurch: Reliance Sports/Mark de Lacy, 1992. 200p.).

815 **The encyclopaedia of New Zealand rugby.**
R. H. Chester, N. A. C. Macmillan, R. A. Palenski. Auckland: Moa Publications, 1987. 2nd ed. 359p.

First published in 1981, this is a revised edition in an expanded and larger format covering biographical profiles of every All Black player to July 1987 and full coverage of the first World Cup. Other features include profiles of leading referees, administrators and prominent provincial players, and histories of provincial unions. 'Essential for every rugby family' (cover).

816 Men in black, 1903-1993.
Rod Chester, Neville Macmillan.   Auckland: Moa Beckett, 1994.
5th ed. 588p.

First published in 1978, this edition includes information previously published in supplements. Aimed at aficionados, it brings together in one volume accounts of rugby tests up to 1993. A commentary on each international match is complemented by team lists, statistics and illustrations showing the skills of the men involved.

817 Sandra Edge: full circle: an autobiography.
Sandra Edge, with Joseph Romanos.   Auckland: Hodder Moa Beckett, 1995. 224p.

Relates the story of one of New Zealand's best-known and loved netball players who from 1985 to 1995 rose from 'a talented instinctive debutante to a thoughtful and caring captain' (p. 11). In the process the rise of New Zealand netball to major sport status is also detailed. Excerpts from her journals relate the highs and lows of involvement in this sport as she travelled around New Zealand and internationally. Included are profiles of many of her team mates and the coaches with whom she worked. Incidentally through the book are many tips for players and coaches. An attractive personality emerges.

818 Centrecourt: a century of New Zealand tennis, 1886-1986.
Paul Elenio.   Wellington: New Zealand Lawn Tennis Association, with the support of BP, 1986. 200p.

A history of 100 years of tennis in New Zealand. In spite of the dearth of material to draw on – the New Zealand Lawn Tennis Association possesses no official records for its first seventeen years, and other provincial associations have only sparse records – the author has employed photographs, newspaper reports and other information held in libraries to compile a record of people and achievements in a sport which is not as high profile as others in New Zealand.

819 Rhythm and swing: an autobiography.
Richard Hadlee, Richard Becht.   Auckland: Moa Publications, 1989. 303p.

One of the finest fast-medium bowlers in cricket history, Hadlee, New Zealand's only cricketing knight, recounts the highs and lows of a near twenty-year international career. No other cricketer has so stirred the imagination of New Zealand's sports-loving public. During the 1980s, the country's most successful era in international competition, he drew crowds through his performance and charisma. Beyond the standard fare of such autobiographies – matches, tours, contemporary players – this book contains thoughtful commentary on many facets of the game and its conduct.

820 Athletes of the century.

Peter Heidenstrom. Wellington: GP Publications, 1992. 224p.

The most comprehensive book on New Zealand athletics. Separate chapters cover men and women's track, field and long distance events, either individually or in groups. While the international stars – the Lovelocks, Snells and Walkers – receive appropriate attention, competitors of national significance are also duly recorded. Statistical sections document each event and individual performances in a way not previously available, while all-time ranking lists are also provided. From over 2,500 athletes, the author picks his 'dream New Zealand team'.

821 An association with soccer: the NZFA celebrates its first 100 years.

Tony Hilton, Barry Smith. Auckland: Sporting Press, 1991. 200p.

Divided into text plus statistics, this book presents a history of soccer (football) in New Zealand from 1891 to 1991. Tony Hilton comments, 'I have opted for a lighter tone and in many cases have sought to include those who have participated and ultimately shaped the modern day game' (Introduction), rather than opting for a detailed traversal of the records. The success of the 1982 World Cup obviously takes pride of place, but the contributions of many other people and teams are also recorded.

822 Golf in New Zealand: a centennial history.

G. M. Kelly. Wellington: New Zealand Golf Association, 1971. 262p.

Nostalgia, inspiration, a detailing of tradition, all are part of this centennial history of golf in New Zealand. People and courses are highlighted in this coverage of a sport in which New Zealand has had top players over many years. For a comprehensive guide to the many golf courses throughout the country see *New Zealand golf courses*, compiled by Robert Phillips (Auckland: Century Hutchinson, 1989. 390p.).

823 The Shell New Zealand cricket encyclopedia.

Lynn McConnell, Ian Smith. Auckland: Moa Beckett/Shell Group of Companies in New Zealand, 1993. 256p. bibliog.

A standard reference book on cricket in New Zealand produced by a sports journalist and a cricket statistician, this encyclopaedia covers the game in this country from its beginnings. It includes biographies of New Zealand representatives, statistics for matches, histories of all test matches, association histories and statistics, as well as many other facets of the game. This stands alongside *Men in white: the history of New Zealand international cricket, 1894-1895* (q.v.) which provides New Zealand's international record.

824 The game of our lives: the story of rugby and New Zealand and how they have shaped each other.

Finlay MacDonald. Auckland: Viking, 1996. 138p.

This is the accompanying book to a major four-part TVNZ documentary and the presentation reflects these origins to some extent. While the author disavows any claim to be writing 'definitive social history nor exhaustive rugby history', he nevertheless attempts to place the game's evolution in historical context. He provides an overview of rugby playing in New Zealand from the schoolboys' (and now girls') efforts to the achievements of the All Blacks.

825 **Polo: the Savile Cup: the first 100 years.**
T. P. McLean. Cambridge, New Zealand: New Zealand Polo
Association, 1990. 154p.

Written to commemorate the centenary of the game in New Zealand, this is a description of an elite sport in which New Zealand has gained an international reputation. Allied with New Zealand's ability to breed horses, in this instance, polo ponies, is the commitment of the men who ride them. As would be expected, men and horses dominate the illustrations.

826 **Men in white: the history of New Zealand international cricket, 1894-1985.**
Don Neely, Richard King. Auckland: Moa, 1986. 656p.

A definitive work covering every match played by New Zealand cricket teams between 1894 and May 1985. Full scoreboards are included for every test, first-class match and one-day international, while abbreviated details are set out for all games involving the national team. Authenticated statistics are fleshed out by an authoritative narrative, both being complemented by an impressive collection of illustrations. Attractively produced, and big in every way, this is a book against which all subsequent New Zealand cricket books must be judged. A complementary work is *The summer game: the illustrated history of New Zealand cricket* by D. O. Neely and P. W. Neely (Auckland: Moa Beckett/New Zealand Cricket Council, 1994. 256p.), produced to mark the centenary of the New Zealand Cricket Council. This depicts many special moments which would otherwise have gone unrecorded, the vicissitudes of early travelling teams, bush wickets, and the quaint and curious.

827 **Old heroes: the 1956 Springbok Tour and the lives beyond.**
Warwick Roger. Auckland: Hodder & Stoughton, 1991. 222p.

Writing as much a social as a sports history, the author sets out to discover what made the 1956 South African rugby tour of New Zealand a cultural landmark; why the country united in common cause to beat 'the Springboks'. Through his own recollections, aged eleven, and through the memories of contemporaries, older sports fans, sports commentators, and surviving players from both sides, he recreates a New Zealand long past. He then proceeds to investigate the subsequent life-histories of those most intimately involved. 'After 1956 nothing was ever to be the same again . . . The world was becoming a global village . . . The time of innocence was over' (Introduction).

828 **Arthur's boys: the golden era of New Zealand athletics.**
Joseph Romanos. Auckland: Moa Beckett, 1994. 215p.

Arthur Lydiard has acquired a considerable reputation for his skill in developing athletes to the point where they achieve world-rating results. This is the story of the man and the people he trained. 'He was an inspiring, innovative character, capable of being ruthless when he saw the need, but also with an obvious feeling for his athletes and his sport' (Introduction). Through interviews with athletes, each presented as a separate chapter, Romanos builds up a picture of the man and the regard in which 'his boys' held him.

829   **The golden era of New Zealand motor racing.**
      Graham Vercoe.   Auckland: Reed, 1993. 389p.

Acknowledging that motor racing in New Zealand reached a peak in the years 1946-76 (the great years of Formula Libre, Formula Tasman and Formula 5000), the author traces the development of the sport from the first road race in 1933 to 1977 which is seen as the end of an era. Each race is described in detail, covering drivers, cars, the tracks and running time of the race, together with lap times and weather and track conditions. Such bare details are embellished by human aspects, the dramas that lay behind the competitors, the disappointments as well as the triumphs. The book does not contain as many illustrations as might have been expected.

Outdoor recreation

830   **The New Zealand surfing guide.**
      Mike Bhana.   Auckland: Reed, 1996. rev. ed. 127p. maps.

Essential background information on all major surfing locations from Cape Reinga at the top of the North Island to Bluff at the bottom of the South Island. Details of the best, most consistent and accessible breaks are provided, as is information about optimum weather and tide conditions, problems of access, beach profiles, and the nature and idiosyncrasies of various waves.

831   **The New Zealand boating handbook.**
      Ian W. Butchart.   Auckland: Pacific Wave Publications, 1995. rev. ed. 146p. maps.

'With special emphasis on New Zealand charts, local regulations and boating conditions, the author presents a detailed but readable guide for all those who realise that safety is the key aspect to enjoyable boating everywhere' (cover). Good practical information is provided, including the gear required, the environment that needs to be considered, charts, seamanship, the art of handling a boat and the art of sailing.

832   **Great peaks of New Zealand.**
      Hugh Logan.   Dunedin: McIndoe, 1990. 176p. maps.

An attractively illustrated work, describing the origins, features, mythologies and human history relating to sixteen peaks selected because of their prominence and striking characteristics. A major focus is on mountaineering, but these peaks also attract anglers and hunters, climbers, skiers and walkers and are of course part of the farm for high country farmers.

833   **A guide to the ski areas of New Zealand.**
      Marty Sharpe.   Auckland: Random House, 1995. 336p. maps.

Lists twenty-five ski areas through the whole of New Zealand. The book covers such aspects as the beginnings and development of areas, the best way of getting to them, the facilities offered and a description of the slopes. In the centre of the book a series of coloured illustrations gives trail maps for each area.

834 **New Zealand: a wild place to play.**
Graeme Sinclair. Auckland: The Halcyon Press, 1993. 192p.
A celebration of the opportunities New Zealand offers for outdoor adventure of all
kinds. The author, formerly a professional hunter, guide, diving instructor and fisherman, is director of a company specializing in leisure event management. Beyond the
usual tales of hunting and fishing, adventures recounted include wilderness exploration, wreck-diving, rafting, jet-boating and heli-fishing.

Hunting and fishing

835 **New Zealand sea anglers' guide.**
Ray Doogue, John Moreland. Wellington: Reed, 1982. rev. ed. 320p.
map.
For those wanting to know how to catch fish, part one of this volume provides full
instructions, whether the prospective angler be a child casting a line off a wharf or a
more affluent adult hunting for marlin from a sea-going launch. Part two provides
detailed descriptions for over 100 fish species commonly caught off the New Zealand
coast. A feature is the more than 300 drawings, including explanatory diagrams of
tackle and sketches of all the fish described, by well-known illustrator, Eric Heath.

836 **Trout fishing in New Zealand.**
Rex Forrester. Wellington: Whitcoulls, 1987. rev. ed. 207p.
'From basic chapters on the types of fish and fishing available, the author goes on to
provide detailed advice on where to go, at what time of year, and how to fish your
chosen spot' (cover). Also included is information on tackle and lures, fishing guides
in New Zealand, tips for visiting anglers, and cooking and smoking fish. Although
dated in presentation, the information remains current and valuable. Bryn Hammond's
The New Zealand encyclopaedia of flyfishing (Auckland: Halcyon Press, 1988. 238p.)
provides additional flyfishing lore and history, fisheries science, streamside entomol-
ogy, artificial flies, sections on personalities, authors, and fishing books, as well as
general comment on the New Zealand angling scene.

837 **The golden years of fishing in New Zealand.**
Compiled by Philip Holden. Auckland: Hodder & Stoughton, 1984.
291p. maps.
The author has selected pieces from old books and popular magazines to present a picture of fishing in New Zealand from early settlement to the 1930s. Not just of interest
to fishermen, this book will also appeal to those who enjoy descriptions of the country
before civilization touched the wilds. Black-and-white photographs bring to life much
of the text.

838 **The golden years of hunting.**
Compiled by Philip Holden.   Auckland: Hodder & Stoughton, 1983.
345p.

Through the efforts of governments and acclimatization societies, New Zealand had
established a reputation as a shooters' paradise by 1900. By combing contemporary
books, magazines and reports, the compiler has assembled a history of 'the golden
years of hunting'. Every kind of hunting is covered, from the humble rabbiting which
provided a living for the poor, through to gentlemen's stalking expeditions in search
of prize stag heads. Eventually, rising hostility from farmers and foresters, objecting
to the damage done to pastures, crops and trees, caused protection to be lifted from
game animals. This opened up the way for commercial hunting, which decimated the
numbers of these animals, thus leading to the decline of hunting as a sport.

839 **The New Zealand hunters' companion.**
Roger Lentle, Frank Saxton.   Auckland: Bateman, 1996. 232p.

'Sets out to cover practical aspects of bushcraft which are essential for aspiring bushmen and hunters' (Introduction). There are sections on bushcraft, how to cope with
New Zealand's capricious weather, medical problems and first aid in the bush, the
quarry (general information on deer species, tahr, chamois, goats and pigs), hunting
techniques, and an introduction to wildlife photography. The book is of most interest
to the beginner as it has been written with the learner, rather than the expert, in mind.

Horse racing

840 **A salute to trotting: a history of harness racing in New Zealand.**
Ron Bisman.   Auckland: Moa Publications, 1983. 418p.

A sport that began in the early colonial days is documented here in text and photograph through to the 1980s. Much of the early material has been culled from
newspapers of the day, but the author has also had access to family scrapbooks and
photograph albums which have brought a more personal note to the record. As with
most such histories, people and horses are the real heroes.

841 **Tapestry of turf: the history of New Zealand racing, 1840-1987.**
John Costello, Pat Finnegan.   Auckland: Moa, 1988. 559p.

'The story of racehorses, great and good, and of the professional jockeys and trainers
who made their imprint on history, of the racing clubs up and down the country who
provided New Zealand with more racehorses per capita than any other country in the
world, of the owners who sustained the sport through boom times and depression, of
the administrators who shaped the course New Zealand racing has taken' (cover).
Painstakingly researched, this is probably the definitive book on New Zealand racing
and is supported by many illustrations, arranged by decade from 1840 to 1980.

842 **November gold: New Zealand's quest for the Melbourne Cup.**
Max Lambert. Auckland: Moa, 1986. 242p.

The Melbourne Cup has been a race often dominated by New Zealand-bred or trained horses. This is the story of New Zealand's involvement, successes and disappointments. Who will ever forget the magic words in 1983, 'Kiwi is flying'? The illustrations provide the feel of the day – the race, the men and the horses who participated, and the women in their finery.

New Zealand Sports Monthly.
See item no. 911.

Libraries, Art Galleries, Museums and Archives

843 The Turnbull: a library and its world.
Rachel Barrowman.   Auckland: Auckland University Press/Historical Branch, Department of Internal Affairs, 1995. 232p.

The history of the Alexander Turnbull Library on its seventy-fifth anniversary. Alexander Turnbull bequeathed his private library to the nation in 1918. The collection was for many years maintained in Turnbull's house. Now the collection is part of the National Library of New Zealand. The book describes the life of Turnbull as well as the subsequent fortunes of his collection. The collection (consisting of New Zealand books, other historical research materials, and international collections on John Milton, voyages and discovery, fine printing and 17th-century English literature) is amply described throughout the book. More information and detail on the donor can be found in E. H. McCormick's *Alexander Turnbull: his life, his circle, his collections* (Wellington: Alexander Turnbull Library, 1974. 324p.).

844 Changes in public libraries: New Zealand territorial authority library services, 1991-1994.
Anna Chalmers, Jo Lynch, Helen Slyfield.   Wellington: Research Unit, National Library of New Zealand, 1995. 115p.

The research reported in this work was designed 'to assist the National Library in policy development regarding its support for local authority libraries and the role of central and local government in access to and provision of information for all New Zealanders . . . [and] . . . to provide information for libraries and their local authorities to assist in policy development at the local government level' (p. iii). The work is essentially a technical report that analyses the responses to a survey and presents the results. These are collected under headings such as: the services offered by local authority libraries; the inputs provided, for example, expenditure, training and charging for services; the National Library services; networking and resource sharing; and planning and development. Further detail on services provided by the National Library and local authorities from an historical perspective can be gleaned from Mary Ronnie's *Books to the people* (Wellington: New Zealand Library and Information Association/Ancora Press, Graduate Department of Librarianship, Archives and Records, Monash University, 1993. 122p.).

845 **The Governor's gift: the Auckland Public Library, 1880-1980.**
Wynn Colgan. Auckland: Richards Publishing/Auckland City
Council, 1980. 235p.

The gift of the title was that of Sir George Grey (Governor Grey), 1812-98, which led
to the establishment of the Auckland Public Library in 1880. The generosity of the
Governor, in donating 14,000 manuscripts and books, led to gifts by others, personal
and business. This book recounts 'not only the story of a major public library and the
people who have guided it through its first century . . . but also in outline a lively
social history of a burgeoning city over the period of 140 years' (cover).

846 **Heritage management in New Zealand and Australia; visitor**
management, interpretation and marketing.
C. M. Hall, Simon McArthur. Auckland: Oxford University Press,
1996. 2nd ed. 314p. maps.

Confronts the issue of how to allow access to heritage and still ensure it is conserved.
'Heritage can only be preserved for future generations if appropriate management
policies and processes are developed and implemented' (Introduction). The problems
are considered from a number of perspectives: natural; senses of place (indigenous
and integrated perspectives); cultural; and a concluding section which looks at future
directions. As concern for, and interest in, heritage matters has increased in recent
years, this is a timely and thoughtful evaluation of the issues involved.

847 **The New Zealand Library Association, 1910-1960, and its part in**
New Zealand library development.
W. J. McEldowney. Wellington: New Zealand Library Association,
1962. 106p. bibliog.

During the first fifty years of its life, the New Zealand Library Association played a
leading role in the development of libraries in this country. 'The establishment of the
Country Library Service and later of the National Library Service [later to become the
National Library], the organization of interlibrary lending and many other noteworthy
features of the contemporary library scene can all be traced back to the work of the
Association' (cover). Now the New Zealand Library and Information Association, the
vicissitudes of the late 20th century makes it valuable and important to look back at
the dedication of the people involved and the magnitude of their achievements. This
work has been partially updated by 'The New Zealand Library Association: 1960-
1970', in *New Zealand Libraries*, vol. 33, no. 5 (Oct. 1970), p. 144-74.

848 **Bicultural developments in museums of Aotearoa: what is the**
current status?: Ki te whakamana i te kaupapa tikanga-a-rua ki
roto i nga whare taonga o te motu: kei hea e tu ana?
Gerard O'Regan. Wellington: Museum of New Zealand/TPT
National Services with Museums Association of Aotearoa/New
Zealand, 1997. 166p. maps.

'The primary goal of the research leading up to this report has been to identify the
issues and concerns of Maori already actively involved in staffed museums . . . The
project is intended to help develop strategies to achieve appropriate levels of participation, as determined by *iwi* Maori, in the management, care, interpretation,
presentation, and preservation of *taonga* Maori, by the year 2000' (Introduction). The

work includes: coverage of the legislative environment; a survey of museums; interviews with Maori working in museums; and suggestions for future developments to meet the challenge of ensuring Pakeha and Maori work together in this area.

849   **New Zealand archives futures: essays in honour of Michael Hoare.**
      Edited by Brad Patterson.   Wellington: Archives and Records
      Association of New Zealand, 1997. 242p.

Published as a special issue of *Archifacts: Journal of the Archives and Records Association of New Zealand* (q.v.), some nineteen essays look at aspects of the development of archives in New Zealand, at the same time celebrating the contribution of Michael Hoare (who died in 1996) to that work. The papers were originally presented at the twentieth conference of the Association. Guest speakers, Sarah Tyacke (Keeper of the Public Records, London), Bob Sharman (Western Australia) and Patricia Acton (British Columbia), bring an international perspective to the volume. The work offers a useful summary of the concerns and issues facing archivists and records keepers in New Zealand.

850   **Library service in New Zealand.**
      Edited by Alan D. Richardson.   Masterton, New Zealand: Wairarapa
      Education Resource Centre/Wellington College of Education, 1995.
      136p.

A basic text for a course in library training which nevertheless provides an overview of library services available in New Zealand. Each chapter is written by a head of the kind of library discussed. Background chapters on the Treaty of Waitangi and its implications for the library service and the development of library services in New Zealand provide a context for the following chapters. A new edition is currently in preparation.

851   **Archives New Zealand, 4, Directory of archives and manuscript repositories in New Zealand, the Cook Islands, Fiji, Niue, Tokelau, Tonga and Western Samoa.**
      Frank Rogers.   Plimmerton, New Zealand: Archives Press, 1992.
      2nd rev. ed. 73p.

'Designed to be complementary to . . . [the] *National register of archives and manuscripts in New Zealand* [q.v.]. The directory provides one descriptive entry for each repository whilst the register provides a separate description for each archives or manuscripts collection' (Introduction). The author has been as comprehensive as time, energy and the willingness of institutions to contribute information permitted. A most useful guide for the researcher, the book contains entries providing location information, opening hours, contacts and a brief description of the holdings. The work is indexed by repositories, by a classified index of repositories and by a general index to collections.

852   **Education for librarianship in New Zealand and the Pacific Islands.**
Mary A. Ronnie, with contributions from John Evans, Melvyn D. Rainey.   London: Mansell, 1996. 228p. bibliog.
A well-researched history of the development of education for librarianship, particularly in New Zealand but with chapters also covering the Pacific. The courses offered are examined critically and future ideas presented and assessed. At the time of writing, the author felt that there was a sense of buoyancy within the schools offering training and that there were positive plans for future expansion. Recent changes, however, have seen the New Zealand undergraduate course moving from the School of Library Studies at the Wellington College of Education to placement within a polytechnic, while the graduate course at the Victoria University of Wellington has become affiliated to the School of Communications and Information Management.

853   **Te ara tika: guiding voices: Maori opinion on libraries and information needs.**
Chris Szekely.   Wellington: New Zealand Library and Information Association/Te Rau Herenga o Aotearoa and Te Ropu Whakahau/Maori Library and Information Workers' Association, 1997. 69p. bibliog.
Follows up Tui MacDonald's *Te ara tika: Maori and libraries: a research report* (Wellington: NZLIA, 1993. 92p.), 'which documented the views of the profession in relation to biculturalism and services to Maori' (Introduction). This volume sought views directly from Maori: how Maori view libraries; and how libraries could better meet their needs. The findings are presented in the body of the work together with a literature review, conclusions and recommendations. This is a useful compilation of information for those institutions serious about presenting a bicultural approach.

854   **A guide to art galleries and museums of New Zealand.**
K. W. Thomson.   Auckland: Reed, 1991. 92p. maps.
This slim volume lists some 231 museums and art galleries throughout New Zealand. It is an updating and reworking of a 1981 work and is intended as a 'ready handbook rather than a volume for leisurely study' (Introduction). The entries are brief but informative. The institutions are grouped into four regions, each based on one of the four main cities. Illustrations throughout provide a glimpse of the treasures on display.

Archifacts: Journal of the Archives and Records Association of New Zealand.
See item no. 875.

New Zealand Historic Places.
See item no. 894.

New Zealand Libraries.
See item no. 903.

New Zealand Museums Journal.
See item no. 907.

Directory of New Zealand photograph collections.
See item no. 928.

Libraries, Art Galleries, Museums and Archives

Directory of museums and heritage institutions in Aotearoa-New Zealand.
See item no. 929.

Directory of information and library services in new Zealand.
See item no. 945.

Te hikoi marama: a directory of Maori information sources.
See item no. 948.

National register of archives and manuscripts in New Zealand.
See item no. 963.

Books and Printing

855 **Book and print in New Zealand: a guide to print culture in Aotearoa.**
Edited by Penny Griffith, Ross Harvey, Keith Maslen. Wellington: Victoria University Press, for the New Zealand Academy for the Humanities/Te Whainga Aronui, 1997. 370p.

With the traditional medium of print being challenged by new modes of communication, this work explores the past impact of books and print on New Zealand culture. Contributors first look at the impact of an imported print culture on Maori oral tradition and subsequent Maori uses of print. Later chapters deal with New Zealand printing, publishing, bookselling, libraries, book buying and collecting, readers and reading. The final chapter examines the print culture of other language groups in New Zealand. The chosen specialists deal authoritatively with a very large range of topics, summing up the present disjointed state of knowledge, and in many instances advancing it.

856 **New Zealand book values.**
Glenn Haszard. Christchurch: South Sea Books, 1996. 4th ed. unpaginated.

Lists prices for secondhand books published in, or about, New Zealand. The compiler urges caution in the use of the guide as prices can be variable, particularly when derived from auctions. Where possible, more than one price is given. Where obtainable, pseudonyms and the author's real name are given.

857 **The house of Reed, 1957-1967.**
A. W. Reed. Wellington: Reed, 1968. 115p. bibliog.

A sequel to *The house of Reed* (Wellington: Reed, 1957. 106p.), a brief history of New Zealand's most successful publishing firm to that date. Founded by A. H. Reed in 1907, who was later joined by nephew A. W. Reed, in 1925, the firm developed from a mail order business supplying literature and material for religious education to a publishing house with a significant body of titles to its name. The period described by this second volume saw the establishment of branches in Auckland and Sydney and an expansion in the range of publishing undertaken. The firm has been subjected to take-overs in recent decades and is now foreign owned.

858 Turning the pages: the story of bookselling in New Zealand.
Anna Rogers, Max Rogers. Auckland: Reed, for Booksellers NZ, 1993. 300p.

Disclaiming any attempt to provide a complete history of bookselling in New Zealand, the authors state they have tried instead 'to record something of the early days of bookselling in this country and to tell the stories of many of the long-standing businesses' (Authors' Note). In the process they also describe the growth of the Booksellers' Association (now Booksellers NZ) and consider issues such as wartime censorship and the introduction of a sales tax on books. Lively in style, the work includes many anecdotes. The interaction between people and books is a constant theme.

859 150 years of printing in New Zealand.
Compiled and edited by T. M. I. Williment. Wellington: Government Printing Office, 1985. 71p. bibliog.

A slight but informative history of printing in New Zealand, which begins with the missionary presses, considers the development of newspapers, and examines the general printing scene and the role of the Government Printing Office. It also briefly outlines union activities, the structure of the printing industry, the establishment of the New Zealand Press Association (1880) and the development of printing machinery. The work concludes with an assessment of the future and comments prophetically, 'the rate of change in printing technology whilst rapid over the past 60 years, will pale into insignificance compared with the changes that are likely to take place in the next 60 years' (p. 67).

New Zealand Books.
See item no. 887.

New Zealand Books In Print, Including Books Published In The Pacific Islands.
See item no. 964.

Media

General

860 **The making of the New Zealand press: a study of the organisational and political concerns of New Zealand newspaper controllers, 1840-1880.**
Patrick Day.   Wellington: Victoria University Press, 1990. 267p.

Who owned the first New Zealand newspapers? What were the logistics of these enterprises? What sort of readership did they attract? What exactly was the role of the newspaper in a colonial society? The author provides a comprehensive account of the evolving forms and functions of newspapers in the first four colonizing decades, charting their shift from being political discussion forums for high-profile politicians to profit-oriented businesses concerned with advertising and news-giving. The book contributes significantly to an understanding of the forces that shaped New Zealand journalism.

861 **Free press, free society.**
Karl du Fresne.   Wellington: Newspaper Publishers' Association of New Zealand, 1994. 41p.

Commissioned by the Newspaper Publishers' Association, experienced journalist Karl du Fresne presents a history of press freedom in New Zealand and overseas. The result is a very personal approach to the issues. The author considers the threats to freedom of the press, but also commends the commitment to the principle made by the media, politicians and people in general. Photographs and cartoons are used to good effect in discussing the issues. 'The booklet seeks to demonstrate that without a press enjoying comparative freedom – and we stress the word "comparative" – New Zealand would be an infinitely worse place' (Introduction).

269

862 **Dangerous democracy?: news media politics in New Zealand.**
Edited by Judy McGregor. Palmerston North, New Zealand:
Dunmore Press, 1996. 250p.

'A number of journalists, politicians, editors, journalism educators, political scientists and media commentators contribute to the discussion about whether or not democracy is endangered by political journalism' (Introduction). The chapters are written from a variety of viewpoints – based on personal experience, interviews and analytical discussions – with the intention to promote and stimulate debate. The result is a number of lively pieces on areas as diverse as the role of cartoons, the challenge of electoral reform, the constitutional role of the news media, the use of politicians as news sources, radio talk-backs and the coverage of female politicians and Maori politics. A companion volume, *Whose news?*, edited by Margie Comrie and Judy McGregor (Palmerston North, New Zealand: Dunmore Press, 1992. 237p.), features well-known New Zealanders discussing topical and controversial media subjects.

863 **Press, radio and TV guide: Australia-New Zealand-Pacific Islands, 1995/96.**
Edited by Jennifer Peden. Redfern, New South Wales: Media
Monitors Australia, 1995. 32nd ed.

Includes detailed listings of New Zealand media organizations, advertising agencies, public relations consultancies and media outlets. The latter incorporates entries for newspapers (national, metropolitan, regional and suburban), commercially produced magazines and journals, and radio and television stations. Full postal and street addresses are provided, in addition to circulation or audience figures, frequency of issue details and advertising rates.

864 **Dateline, NZPA: the New Zealand Press Association, 1880-1980.**
James Sanders. Auckland: Wilson & Horton, 1979. 216p.

Written to commemorate 100 years of the NZPA, which commenced with the establishment of the United Press Association in Christchurch in February 1880. The NZPA is a co-operative, non-profit-making organization which ensures a much wider distribution of news through its communication networks than would otherwise be possible. This work looks at how the Association has prospered in times of peace and war, through the advent of advanced technology, and through its news-breaking stories. As would be expected, there is an emphasis on the people involved.

865 **Newspapers in New Zealand.**
G. H. Scholefield. Wellington: Reed, 1958. 287p.

Although now showing its age, this book incorporates brief histories of every newspaper published in New Zealand between 1840 and the mid-1950s. Over 500 ventures are recorded, many short-lived, together with notes on owners and editors. The author, prior to his 1926 appointment as Parliamentary Librarian, had over thirty years' experience on New Zealand newspapers. In compiling the book he was able to study the vast collection of newspapers held by the General Assembly (now Parliamentary) Library, Wellington. It remains a good starting-point for enquirers.

Union list of New Zealand newspapers preserved in libraries, newspaper offices, local authority offices and museums in New Zealand.
See item no. 955.

INNZ: Index New Zealand.
See item no. 957.

Periodicals in print: Australia, New Zealand and South Pacific.
See item no. 965.

Newspapers

866 The Dominion.
Wellington: Wellington Newspapers Ltd., 1907- . daily.

The capital's (Wellington's) morning newspaper, and therefore understandably strong on political and business commentary, generally from a conservative perspective.

867 The Evening Post.
Wellington: Wellington Newspapers Ltd., 1865- . daily.

Although produced as the capital's (Wellington's) evening newspaper, the *Post* is perhaps New Zealand's nearest approach to a metropolitan daily, enjoying nation-wide distribution.

868 The Independent.
Auckland: Pauanui Publishing, 1992- . 48 issues per year.

A sometimes crusading approach to politics, business and current affairs.

869 National Business Review.
Wellington: National Business Review, 1975- . weekly.

Circulating widely within New Zealand's business and administrative communities, the *NBR* is a source of in-depth coverage on commercial and political matters. Its tone reflects the interests of the majority of subscribers.

870 The New Zealand Farmer.
Auckland: New Zealand Rural Press, 1885- . weekly.

Concentrates on issues of principal interest to rural dwellers.

871 New Zealand Herald.
Auckland: Wilson & Horton, 1863- . daily.

Almost certainly New Zealand's largest daily newspaper by size, the *Herald's* focus is unashamedly parochial, its preoccupation being Auckland and the city's immediate environs.

872   **Otago Daily Times.**
        Dunedin: Otago Daily Times, 1861- . daily.
While maintaining its regional emphasis, this major daily also frequently publishes features of national interest.

873   **The Press.**
        Christchurch: Christchurch Press, 1861- . daily.
The principal daily of the northern half of the South Island.

874   **Sunday Star Times.**
        Auckland: Independent News, 1994- . weekly.
New Zealand's 'quality' Sunday newspaper, published in six sections: news, sport, magazine, money, lifestyles and entertainment.

Periodicals

875   **Archifacts: Journal of the Archives and Records Association of New Zealand.**
        Wellington: Archives and Records Association of New Zealand,
        1977- . 2 issues per year.
Carries articles on: archives and manuscripts curatorship; records management; and history.

876   **Art New Zealand.**
        Auckland: The Art Magazine Press Ltd., 1976- . quarterly.
Contains coverage of contemporary art and art history and reviews of exhibitions.

877   **Consumer.**
        Wellington: Consumers' Institute, 1974- . monthly.
Assesses products and services from the consumer's point of view.

878   **Forest and Bird.**
        Wellington: Royal Forest and Bird Society of New Zealand, 1923- .
        quarterly.
The oldest environmental protection periodical in New Zealand, this deals with the protection of the indigenous fauna and flora, and the landscape.

879 **He Pukenga Korero: A Journal of Maori Studies.**
Palmerston North, New Zealand: Department of Maori Studies, Massey
University, 1995- . 2 issues per year.
Contains original articles in Maori or English relevant to Maori language, or Maori
cultural, social, scientific, technological and economic development.

880 **Illusions.**
Wellington: Illusions Press, 1986- . 3 issues per year.
A publication containing New Zealand moving image and performing arts criticism.

881 **Journal of New Zealand Literature.**
Dunedin: University of Otago Press, for the Department of English,
1983- . annual.
Carries criticism and commentary on all aspects of New Zealand writing.

882 **Journal of the Polynesian Society.**
Auckland: University of Auckland, for the Polynesian Society,
1892- . quarterly.
Comprising anthropological and prehistorical studies relating to New Zealand and the
Pacific, this journal pays particular attention to the Maori and other Polynesian peoples.

883 **Journal of the Royal Society of New Zealand.**
Wellington: Royal Society of New Zealand, 1971- . quarterly.
This journal contains reports and findings of Fellows and members of New Zealand's
leading scientific society. First published in 1868 as *Transactions of the New Zealand
Institute*, it is the country's oldest periodical. There have been several changes in its
title and form since.

884 **Landfall.**
Dunedin: University of Otago Press, 1947- . 2 issues per year.
Landfall is New Zealand's oldest surviving literary journal. Mainly covering prose,
poetry and literary criticism, it also contains some articles on art and music.

885 **Management.**
Auckland: Profile Publishing, 1955- . 11 issues per year.
A publication dealing with business and finance.

886 **Music in New Zealand.**
Auckland: Music in New Zealand, 1988-96. quarterly.
Carries wide-ranging articles by, for, and about, music and musicians particularly
relating to New Zealand.

887 **New Zealand Books.**
Wellington: Peppercorn Press, 1990- . 5 issues per year.
New Zealand's foremost general reviewing journal, this publication covers fiction and non-fiction, with occasional related articles.

888 **New Zealand Defence Quarterly.**
Wellington: Ministry of Defence, 1993- . quarterly.
Carries popular articles on defence policy and military history.

889 **New Zealand Economic Papers.**
Wellington: New Zealand Association of Economists, 1966- . annual.
A journal, containing research in economics and reviews of economics publications.

890 **New Zealand Forestry.**
Wellington: C. R. Monigatti, for New Zealand Institute of Foresters, 1985- . quarterly.
Reports scientific research into silviculture and wood processing matters.

891 **New Zealand Genealogist.**
Auckland: New Zealand Society of Genealogists, 1965- . 6 issues per year.
Prints articles and reviews relating to family history and research.

892 **New Zealand Geographer.**
Christchurch: New Zealand Geographical Society, 1945- . 2 issues per year.
Publishes researched articles covering the full range of geographical topics.

893 **New Zealand Geographic.**
Auckland: New Zealand Geographic Publications Ltd., 1989- . quarterly.
Contains superbly illustrated articles on aspects of the New Zealand natural and human environments.

894 **New Zealand Historic Places.**
Wellington: New Zealand Historic Places Trust, 1989- . 5 issues per year.
Concerned with historic sites, this journal typically contains some general historical articles and contributions on current heritage issues.

895 **New Zealand Home and Building.**
Auckland: Australian Consolidated Press (New Zealand) Ltd., 1936- .
bimonthly.
A well-illustrated periodical on current architecture in New Zealand.

896 **New Zealand International Review.**
Wellington: New Zealand Institute of International Affairs, 1975- .
bimonthly.
A review of foreign affairs, generally from an establishment point of view.

897 **New Zealand Journal of Archaeology.**
Dunedin: New Zealand Archaeological Association, 1979- . annual.
Carries research articles relating to New Zealand archaeology and prehistory.

898 **New Zealand Journal of Ecology.**
Wellington: New Zealand Ecological Society, 1978- . 2 issues
per year.
Includes papers on original research, critical reviews, short communications for matters of debate or brief results of research of general interest, book reviews and the Society's annual report.

899 **New Zealand Journal of Educational Studies.**
Wellington: New Zealand Council for Educational Research/New
Zealand Association for Research in Education, 1966- . 2 issues
per year.
Publishes the results of educational research, with emphasis on New Zealand and the Pacific.

900 **New Zealand Journal of History.**
Auckland: University of Auckland, 1967- . 2 issues per year.
Offers scholarly articles on New Zealand history, some articles on foreign history, and informed reviews of historical publications.

901 **New Zealand Journal of Industrial Relations.**
Kaikohe, New Zealand: The News Ltd., 1976- . quarterly.
Contains articles, research notes and reviews, principally relating to New Zealand.

902 **New Zealand Law Journal.**
Wellington: Butterworths of New Zealand Ltd., 1925- . monthly.
Includes articles and reviews on law in New Zealand.

903 **New Zealand Libraries.**
Wellington: New Zealand Library and Information Association,
1937- . quarterly.
A publication concerned with librarianship and information management.

904 **New Zealand Listener.**
Auckland: New Zealand Magazines Ltd., 1939- . weekly.
A magazine containing: television and radio programmes listings; political, social and sporting comment; and book reviews.

905 **New Zealand Local Government.**
Auckland: Trade Publications Ltd., 1965- . monthly.
Concerns local government issues in New Zealand.

906 **New Zealand Medical Journal.**
Wellington: New Zealand Medical Association, 1900- . bimonthly.
Presents the results of research and other matters concerning medical practitioners.

907 **New Zealand Museums Journal.**
Wellington: Museums Association of New Zealand, 1991- . 2 issues
per year.
Carries articles relating to art galleries and museums.

908 **New Zealand Population Review.**
Wellington: New Zealand Demographic Society, 1980- . 2 issues
per year.
A forum for the discussion and study of population issues in New Zealand.

909 **New Zealand Science Review.**
Wellington: New Zealand Association of Scientists, 1942- .
bimonthly.
Presents scientific articles written for the intelligent layperson.

910 **New Zealand Sociology.**
Palmerston North, New Zealand: Department of Sociology, Massey
University, 1986- . 2 issues per year.
This is a scholarly journal, disseminating research and thought in New Zealand sociology and related disciplines.

911 **New Zealand Sports Monthly.**
Auckland: Sport Magazines Ltd., 1992- . 11 issues per year.
Includes general articles on a range of sports, with particular emphasis on individuals.

912 **North and South.**
Auckland: Australian Consolidated Press (New Zealand) Ltd.,
1986- . monthly.
A periodical concerned with New Zealanders' lifestyles, carrying well-researched articles of general interest.

913 **Planning Quarterly.**
Auckland: Associated Group Media/New Zealand Planning Institute,
1982- . quarterly.
Prints articles on town and environmental planning, and related issues.

914 **Political Science.**
Wellington: Department of Politics, Victoria University of
Wellington/New Zealand Political Studies Association, 1948- .
2 issues per year.
Contains researched articles relating to political studies, principally in New Zealand.

915 **Public Sector.**
Wellington: New Zealand Institute of Public Administration, 1979- .
quarterly.
Mainly includes articles by senior civil servants and academics on administration in national and local government.

916 **Sites: Journal for South Pacific Cultural Studies.**
Palmerston North, New Zealand: Department of Social Anthropology,
Massey University, 1980- . 2 issues per year.
A publication presenting articles on a wide range of New Zealand cultural questions, predominantly within the broad tradition of leftwing scholarship.

917 **Straight Furrow.**
Wellington: Federated Farmers, 1933- . 22 issues per year.
Concerns farming issues.

918 **Women's Studies Journal.**
Auckland: Women's Studies Association New Zealand, 1984- .
biannual.
Publishes articles on issues relating to women's studies.

Radio, television and telecommunications

919 Shaping the news: Waitangi Day on television.

Sue Abel. Auckland: Auckland University Press, 1997. 230p. bibliog.

Using Waitangi Day (New Zealand's national day, which celebrates the signing of the Treaty of Waitangi) as a case-study, the author critically examines the make-up of local television news. The conclusion reached is, 'the challenge for the future is to find methods of news reporting that reflect and acknowledge both Pakeha and Maori styles, views and perspectives . . . that find favour with enough of the audience to satisfy the commercial imperatives under which both broadcasters currently operate' (p. 196).

920 New Zealand television: the first 25 years.

Robert Boyd-Bell. Auckland: Reed Methuen, 1985. 207p.

'This is not a detailed history of New Zealand television. It is an attempt to record some of the successes and failures, recall some of the memories, and chronicle the sometimes erratic course that television has followed here' (Introduction). Introduced into New Zealand in the 1960s, television rapidly grew in popularity. Using anecdote and records, the author has compiled a popular history of this form of media, its effect on the people of New Zealand, and the effect people had on its development. Commencing with a summary, year by year, from 1960 to 1984, the work brings back memories and provides explanations and information.

921 The radio years: a history of broadcasting in New Zealand.

Patrick Day. Auckland: Auckland University Press/Broadcasting History Trust, 1994. 344p. map.

The authoritative first volume of a proposed two-volume history of broadcasting in New Zealand begins with the early experiments into wireless telegraphy conducted by Ernest Rutherford and ends with the New Zealand Broadcasting Service in the 1950s. During this period, broadcasting grew from an eccentric fad to a powerful and enduring social institution with a daily presence in the life of most New Zealanders. The development and spread of transmission and reception facilities, the creation and content of many different types of radio programmes, political debates about the role of the state in broadcasting, the changes to its organization and administration, and the radical social and cultural consequences of the new medium are covered.

922 Voices in the air: radio broadcasting in New Zealand: a documentary.

Peter Downes, Peter Harcourt. Wellington: Methuen/Radio New Zealand, 1976. 176p.

For many New Zealanders even today, the radio is a constant friend, always at their side. Deriving in part from a series of Golden Jubilee radio programmes broadcast in 1975, this work describes the founding and growth of broadcasting, with particular emphasis on commercial broadcasting in New Zealand. Illustrated with many black-and-white photographs of personalities, this popular presentation amply demonstrates the importance of radio to a country where many are far from centres of population and where the geography sometimes precludes reception of a television signal.

923 Internet: a New Zealand user's guide.

David Merritt, Paul Reynolds. Auckland: Penguin, 1995. 172p.

Written specifically for the New Zealand Internet user, this booklet presumes the reader has a basic knowledge only. The first part covers the issues relating to computer connectivity via a modem to the Internet; the second lists by subject resources that might be of interest. Written by an on-line consultant in collaboration with a freelance writer, this will lead the beginner into new highways. A more extended treatment is *Wired Kiwis: every New Zealander's guide to the Internet*, by Peter Wiggin (Christchurch: Shoal Bay Press, 1996. 215p.).

924 Revolution in the air!

Paul Smith. Auckland: Longman, 1996. 170p.

Chapter titles such as 'Smoke and mirrors', 'The privateers', 'Stunned mullets', 'The market and monopoly', 'Granny gets frisky' and 'For sale: Kiwi broadcasting – Martians allowed', draw the reader into this discussion of the structural changes in New Zealand television following deregulation. The author has worked within television and brings a personal insight to his examination of the issues. He concludes, 'the reform offered no genuine choice between commercial and non-commercial or even semi-commercial television. The result is an increasingly bland medium, whose potential to satisfy viewers has yet to be fulfilled' (p. 166). Barry Spicer, Michael Powell and David Emmanuel's *The remaking of Television New Zealand, 1984-1992* (Auckland: Auckland University Press/Broadcasting History Trust, 1996. 207p.) covers roughly the same period, but this work details the transformation of 'a conservative public television broadcaster into a market-oriented and entrepreneurial business' (cover). The work will not have the popular appeal of Smith's but together they produce a more balanced view of the current state of television in New Zealand.

925 Wire and wireless: a history of telecommunications in New Zealand, 1860-1987.

A. C. Wilson. Palmerston North, New Zealand: Dunmore Press, 1994. 263p.

A detailed and well-researched history of telecommunications in New Zealand from its beginnings as part of the Post Office through to 1987. The author argues that 'the management of this country's telecommunications under the Post Office deserves credit. However, its faults '. . . overcentralised, slow administration, limited marketing capacity and so on – would have made the Post Office an inadequate vehicle for meeting the country's needs in the 1990s' (p. 185).

926 Broadcasting in New Zealand: waves of change.

John Yeabsley, Ian Duncan, Doug James. Wellington: New Zealand Institute of Economic Research, 1994. 152p. bibliog.

Examines the impact of the reforms to broadcasting in 1988/89 from the points of view of the efficiency of the broadcasting industry and the effectiveness of social policy mechanisms. An empirical study presented as a report, the work concentrates on providing information on the effectiveness of the reforms in these two areas. The results are probably of no great surprise to those involved or even the listening public: some positive, some negative, and some areas in which there has been little change. However, the documenting of the information is useful.

Media. Radio, television and telecommunications

Gadfly: the life and times of James Shelley.
See item no. 226.

Encyclopaedias and Directories

927 **A'Courts business handbook: products, brands, trades, companies.**
Auckland: A'Court Publications Ltd., 1997. 22nd ed. 1,421p.

The information is divided into a products index (under product headings), brands (alphabetical with suppliers), companies (under trade headings) and companies (alphabetical with details). A similar work is *Kompass New Zealand: register of industry and commerce of New Zealand* (Auckland: Kompass, 1996. 1,306p.).

928 **Directory of New Zealand photograph collections.**
Alexander Turnbull Library (Pictorial Reference Services).
Wellington: Alexander Turnbull Library/National Library of New Zealand, 1992. 64p.

A new and enlarged edition of a typescript work published in 1986, this work was compiled by sending out a questionnaire to 350 institutions and selecting from the responses. The introduction sets out the scope of the guide and lists the information included in each entry. Entries vary from institution to institution, but most contain sufficient information to direct the researcher.

929 **Directory of museums and heritage institutions in Aotearoa-New Zealand.**
Wanganui, New Zealand: Museums Association of New Zealand, 1995. 70p. bibliog.

Moving geographically from north to south, this directory aims to provide as complete a list as possible of museums and heritage-related institutions. 'In publishing the Directory, the Museums Association hopes to improve and facilitate communication and co-operation among individuals and institutions whose primary concern is the preservation, in one form or another, of our cultural heritage' (Introduction). Information provided is brief – name, address, telephone, fax and at least one contact name.

930 **Directory of official information = Te rangi whakaatu whakahaere kawanatanga 1995-97.**
Wellington: Ministry of Justice, 1995. 611p.

Published pursuant to Part III, Section 20 of the Official Information Act 1982, and updated every two years, the purpose of the book is to assist citizens to exercise their rights under the Act by providing detailed information on the structure of central government departments and organizations, and by providing sign posts to the types of information held and to probable location. Where appropriate, details of statutory or advisory committees are included. Entries are arranged alphabetically, by agency, and there is a comprehensive index. General subject areas are also indexed and cross-referenced. Procedures for requests are set out, and the grounds upon which requests might be refused stated clearly.

931 **A directory of philanthropic trusts in New Zealand.**
Wellington: New Zealand Council for Educational Research/Funding Information Service Inc., 1994. 4th ed. 64p.

'Earlier editions included only trusts and foundations whose funds came from non-profit sources. A number of trusts funded through Government departments are included in this edition. Also included are a number of community trusts associated with the New Zealand Trust Bank Group' (Foreword). The information has been obtained for this work by using the database of the Funding Information Service (FIS), a recently established service initiated by the Roy McKenzie Foundation under the auspices of the New Zealand Association of Philanthropic Trusts. The directory provides a list of philanthropic trusts with sufficient information for those seeking funds to make an application. The database expands on the information which is provided in the directory and is accessible to enquirers.

932 **Directory of women's organisations and groups = Te rereangi ingoa o nga ropu wahine kei Aotearoa nei.**
Wellington: Ministry of Women's Affairs, 1994. 39p.

The listing of national women's organizations claims to be a complete and comprehensive coverage of those groups operating on a country-wide basis. Maori women's organizations are listed in a separate section. Information on groups and organizations in geographic regions is more selective. The work also contains information on government agencies, women's studies, courses and women's bookshops.

933 **The directory directory: the family, local and social historian's guide to contents and holdings of New Zealand almanacs, business, postal and telephone directories, 1842-1960.**
Donald I. Hansen. Wellington: D. Hansen, 1994. 107p.

Contains sections on 'About directories and how to use this guide', 'Details of directories and holdings', and 'Finding a directory', by province, type and decade and addresses of repositories. This is a most useful compilation, especially for those undertaking historical research.

934   **Who's who in New Zealand.**
      Edited by Max Lambert.   Wellington: Reed, 1991. 12th ed. 731p.

The twelfth edition of this essential reference work includes supplied details on the background and achievements of nearly 3,000 New Zealanders in every conceivable field of activity, including business, politics, education, medicine, law, science, the arts and sport. The information is set out in standard form: academic achievements, professional qualifications, positions held, published works, awards and honours, recreations, family details and addresses. Inevitably, a number of people declined invitations to be included, and others failed to respond, but the long pedigree of the publication ensures that it is probably more comprehensive than any comparable work.

935   **Bateman New Zealand encylopedia.**
      Editor in chief, Gordon McLauchlan.   Auckland: David Bateman, 1995. 4th ed. 664p. maps.

Updated and expanded since the first edition was published in 1984, 'the editorial aim is to keep the fact-count high within a succinct text' (Introduction). The work is not an almanac of contemporary events nor a who's who of contemporary people. It does present information clearly and, within the limits of a one-volume encyclopaedia, provides basic coverage of a wide variety of topics. The work commences with a selective chronology of important events in the history of New Zealand.

936   **Encylopaedia of New Zealand.**
      Edited by A. H. McLintock.   Wellington: Government Printer, 1966. 3 vols. maps. bibliog.

Much of value can still be gleaned from this thirty-year-old work. Produced with limited resources, the coverage of topics is uneven. Some entries are accurate, balanced and well written; others are inaccurate and cliché-ridden. A number of important facets of New Zealand life are hardly touched on. Nevertheless, no other work matches its scope. All entries are signed and the index is comprehensive.

937   **The New Zealand business who's who.**
      Wellington; Auckland: New Zealand Financial Press, 1997. 38th ed. 1,104p.

A most useful compendium of information, including corporate, personnel, function, product service, agency and brand information for more than 21,000 New Zealand businesses. The layout includes a New Zealand profile, international markets, nominal index, the main listings, a classified business index, 150 approved firms, facsimile numbers, addresses, index of directors, company ownership index and buyer's guide.

938   **New Zealand company register, 1996-97.**
      Christchurch: Mercantile Gazette of New Zealand Ltd., 1997. 35th ed.

An introductory essay, reviewing the past year, leads into information about New Zealand companies listed alphabetically. Details for each company include directors, share register, principal results, balance-sheet summary and comment on performance.

939 **New Zealand government directory.**
Sydney; Auckland; Wellington: Network Communications Ltd., 1997.
516p.

Produced annually, this directory covers the New Zealand system of government, the New Zealand electoral system, the 1996 election and coalition agreement, sections on contacting Members of Parliament and presenting submissions to Select Committees, a who's who in Parliament, addresses of government departments and ministries, crown-owned companies and state-owned enterprises, overseas trade representatives, and the diplomatic corps in New Zealand. The work concludes with the Crown financial statements. This is a succinct compendium of information relating to contacting the government in a range of ways.

940 **New Zealand Official Yearbook/Te Pukapuka Houanga Whaimana O Aotearoa.**
Wellington: Statistics New Zealand, 1892- . annual. maps. bibliog.

Now produced in an attractive large-size format, this annual publication is an indispensable reference work on all matters relating to New Zealand. Following upon the 1990 sesquicentennial edition, historically based yearbooks are produced every five years, while interim editions emphasize contemporary issues. Through text, tables and graphs, an authoritative overview of the social, economic and cultural life and institutions of New Zealand is provided. Each edition contains special articles. 'The *Yearbook* monitors our place in the world and records objectively the comparative position of New Zealand' (Introduction).

941 **Newzindex: The Monthly Index of New Zealand Business and Commercial Publications.**
Auckland: Factfinders, 1979- . monthly.

'Newzindex is a monthly index of current New Zealand business and commercial publications. It indexes selected items of specific interest to business and industry in New Zealand from more than 130 magazines, newsletters, house journals and the business section of the Auckland newspapers. There is a combined December/January issue and an annual accumulation on microfiche. Newzindex has three sections: "Subjects", "Companies", and "Products"' (Introduction).

942 **Dictionary of New Zealand biography.**
Edited by W. H. Oliver, Claudia Orange.   Vol. I, Wellington: Allen & Unwin/Department of Internal Affairs, 1990. 674p. Vol. II,
Wellington: Bridget Williams Books/Department of Internal Affairs, 1993. 664p. Vol. III, Auckland: Auckland University Press/Bridget Williams Books and the Department of Education, 1996. 649p.

This is probably the most ambitious historical publishing project yet to be undertaken in New Zealand, the editors being determined to redress perceived imbalances in previous works. 'Readers will be introduced not only to a roll-call of the famous: they will also gain an insight into the scope and variety of . . . New Zealand . . . Between a quarter and a third of the biographies are of Maori people; around a fifth explore the lives of women. A considerable number were chosen for their standing, not on a national scale, but within a locality, a tribe, an institution or an activity. Others were chosen because their lives, as well as being interesting stories, represent significant aspects of their times' (cover, Volume I). Volume I covers the period 1769-1869; Volume II, 1870-1900; and Volume III, 1901-20. Two further volumes, plus ancillary volumes, are planned. The work is comprehensively indexed and the generally author-itative articles together constitute a social history as much as a reference work.

943 **Playmarket directory of New Zealand plays and playwrights.**
Wellington: Playmarket, 1992. 228p.

An updating of a 1978 version, but now also dated, this work does provide a compila-tion of material not readily available elsewhere. It includes information on where to obtain scripts and on performing rights. Both plays and playwrights are indexed. Further information is provided under 'Full length plays', 'One act plays', 'Plays for children', 'Young people and theatre in education' and 'Musicals and operas'.

944 **A dictionary of New Zealand biography.**
Edited by G. H. Scholefield. Wellington: Department of Internal Affairs, 1940. 2 vols.

Around 2,600 leading New Zealand personalities, mainly of the 19th century, are listed with biographies, brief for the less well known and longer for the more famous. However, the paucity of information available to the editor, often little more than newspaper obituaries, ensures inaccuracies. Negative aspects of behaviour and charac-ter tend to be overlooked. Nevertheless, the work is by no means superseded by the more recent *Dictionary of New Zealand biography* (q.v.), the efforts of the latter's edi-tors to ensure 'representativeness' in their entries occasioning some surprising omissions.

945 **Directory of information and library services in New Zealand.**
Edited by Paul Szentirmay, Thiam Ch'ng Szentirmay. Wellington: New Zealand Library Association, 1988. 145p.

'An inventory of those information resources and services in New Zealand which make essential and critical information accessible to knowledge workers' (Preface). The editors acknowledge that such a work cannot be comprehensive and that new ways of accessing information will obviously affect use of this directory. However, it still provides an entry point. Information in each entry is quite detailed, providing contact numbers and names, hours of opening, a brief description of the resources offered in each place, and the services provided.

946 **Takoa 1996: te aka kumara o Aotearoa = Directory of Maori organisations & resource people.**
Auckland: Tuhi Tuhi Communications, 1996. 2nd ed. 168p. map.

Designed as 'a networking resource for whanau, community groups, iwi and govern-ment agencies' (Introduction), the directory is compiled from information gathered from around the country through sending out forms, contacting organizations or research. The listings have been organized into regional groupings.

947 New Zealand who's who in Aotearoa.

Edited by Alister Taylor, Deborah Coddington. Auckland: New Zealand Who's Who in Aotearoa, 1992- . annual.

Published annually and 'intended as a useful and accessible information resource about leading New Zealanders and about New Zealanders who gave evidence of becoming future leaders of their professions, their crafts, their country or their community' (Preface). The guide also lists deaths of prominent New Zealanders. Entrants are given an opportunity to update their entry with each new edition. This vies with *Who's who in New Zealand* (q.v.), but the latter remains the more comprehensive work.

948 Te hikoi marama: a directory of Maori information sources.

Auckland: Auckland Public Library; Wellington: Bridget Williams Books/Te Ropu Whakahau, 1993. 2nd ed. 144p.

'The first edition sought to present an overview of Maori resources held by institutions throughout New Zealand. The second edition builds significantly on this foundation' (Preface). Entries have been amended to include changes to contact details and descriptions of collections, and the net has been cast more widely. Arrangement is geographical, north to south, and within each city entries are organized alphabetically. Three indexes – general, subject and organizations – are provided. Entries are clearly set out to assist enquirers – they include descriptions of the collections and access details as well as contact details.

The encyclopaedia of New Zealand rugby.

See item no. 815.

The Shell New Zealand cricket encyclopedia.

See item no. 823.

Bibliographies

949 New Zealand national bibliography to the year 1960.
Edited by A. G. Bagnall.   Wellington: Government Printer, 1969-85.
5 vols.

The major work in New Zealand historical bibliography, retrospectively compiled by the country's best-known bibliographer. The scope of the *Bibliography* covers all books and pamphlets first published in New Zealand or which contain significant reference to it. Maori publications are listed only if they fall within this scope. Background to the project is provided in the introduction to volume two. Volume one (1980) covers the years to 1889 in two parts; volume two (1969) contains entries from A to H, 1890-1960; volume three (1972), entries I to O, 1890 to 1960; volume four (1976), entries P to Z, 1890-1960. Volume five (1985) is a cumulated index to the earlier published volumes. Arrangement is alphabetically by author, and some entries carry brief annotations.

950 Bennett's government publications: a tool to help you identify the source of government and related reports, publications and discussion documents.
Wellington: Bennett's Government Bookshops, with the support of GP Legislation Services, 1996- .

'This catalogue has been designed to help . . . answer questions about current and older reports. It covers government departments, ministries, agencies and related interest groups such as the Business Roundtable and the Employers Federation' (Introduction). For each item the author and title, publisher, place and date of publication and availability are listed. Amendments are produced to keep the publication current.

951 **New Zealand labour and employment research, 1859-1990: a bibliography of research and research materials.**
Peter Brosnan.   Wellington: New Zealand Institute of Industrial Relations Research, 1991. 324p.

An expanded version of a bibliography published in 1984 as part of the proceedings of a conference. New entries have been added and all entries are now indexed by key words. Scholastic sections include an abstract for every entry. This is an extremely detailed and thorough work (4,775 entries) which will be invaluable to those working in the field. The coverage includes official publications, statistical sources, reports of Royal Commissions and Commissions of Inquiry, monographs, articles and theses.

952 **Guide to New Zealand information sources: official publications.**
Compiled by C. L. Carpenter, second edition edited by Jill Best.
Palmerston North, New Zealand: Massey University, 1994. 2nd ed. 28p. (Massey University Library Series: no. 16).

Sections one and two of this guide deal with official publications of New Zealand; section three is a brief guide to some lists which indicate the whereabouts of papers in Australia and England relating wholly or in part to early New Zealand history; section four considers statistics and statistical publications and it is this section that has been almost entirely rewritten for the second edition. This is a useful work for the researcher as all the listings are annotated.

953 **Annotated bibliography for the history of medicine and health in New Zealand.**
Compiled by Derek A. Dow.   Dunedin: Hocken Library/University of Otago, 1994. 322p.

The compiler has 'attempted to incorporate all published works relating to medicine and health care in New Zealand . . . Therefore the entries embrace areas such as anthropology, demography and social welfare where these have a bearing on the provision of health care' (Introduction). Also included are research essays and theses, which make up around ten per cent of the bibliography. This is a well-presented, carefully researched work which will be invaluable to researchers in this field. Short annotations indicate the content of each item.

954 **A bibliography of writings about New Zealand music.**
D. R. Harvey.   Wellington: Victoria University Press, 1985. 222p.

Presented in typescript format, 'this bibliography attempts to list all material published as monographs, periodical articles or dissertations accepted for university degrees relating to New Zealand music and musicians published to the end of 1983. The whole field of music and music-making in New Zealand is covered, with the main exceptions of recent popular music, Maori music, material published in newspapers and reviews and notices of performances' (Introduction). The entries are arranged in subject groupings such as histories and surveys, compositions and composers, performance and performing groups. See also *Bibliography of New Zealand compositions* (Christchurch: Nota Bene Music, 1991. 3rd ed. 176p.), compiled by Philip Norman.

955   **Union list of New Zealand newspapers preserved in libraries, newspaper offices, local authority offices and museums in New Zealand.**
D. R. Harvey.   Wellington: National Library of New Zealand, 1987. 326p.

Updates the *Union list of New Zealand newspapers before 1940 preserved in libraries, newspaper offices, local authority offices and museums in New Zealand* (Wellington: National Library of New Zealand, 1985. 158 columns). The work provides a most useful research tool for those seeking to use New Zealand newspapers, particularly for historical information where there may be few other sources.

956   **A bibliography of the literature relating to New Zealand.**
Edited by T. H. Hocken.   Wellington: Newrick Associates, 1973. Reprint of 1909 ed. 619p. bibliog.

The original 1909 edition was for over seventy years the standard bibliography of 19th-century publications relating to New Zealand. It is as comprehensive as could be achieved by one man working alone: '. . . frequently the author has strayed from the ordinary track of bibliography. He has introduced many little sidelights, biographical references, dates . . . and an attempt has been made to run throughout a thread of historical interest' (Introduction). Many entries include descriptive annotations. Arrangement is by year of publication and alphabetically within each year. The index lists authors and subjects, and titles are listed under author and subject headings.

957   **INNZ: Index New Zealand.**
Wellington: National Library of New Zealand, 1989- .
4 cumulative issues per year.

INNZ: Index New Zealand replaces *Index to New Zealand Periodicals* which was produced in printed form from 1941-86. Issued in two parts, General and Research, it is produced in microfiche with four cumulative issues of fiche per year. It is also available on CD-ROM and on the New Zealand *Kiwinet information retrieval system,* an on-line database, as *INNZ.*

958   **Religious history of New Zealand: a bibliography.**
Peter J. Lineham.   Palmerston North, New Zealand: Department of History, Massey University, 1993. 4th ed. 260p.

First published in 1984, the work was 'conceived as a way to identify the secondary resources about the phenomena of religion in New Zealand, although a few primary works with a significant historical content, notably memoirs, have been included and there has been some attempt to list the periodical sources available to the student' (Preface). Containing some 2,400 annotated entries, listed by author, this publication does not claim to be complete. It suggests researchers should also consult *INNZ: Index New Zealand* and the *New Zealand National Bibliography* (qq.v.).

959 **Bibliographical work in New Zealand: work in progress and work published.**
Edited by A. P. U. Millett. Hamilton, New Zealand: University of Waikato, 1980- . annual.

Presented in two sections, the first listing bibliographical work in progress compiled from questionnaires sent to all those listed in issues of the previous two years who have not yet published, and to educational, government, medical, special and large public libraries in New Zealand. The second section lists bibliographies published since the last issue, compiled from library accession lists and from bibliographies received by the University of Waikato library. The entries in both sections are arranged under broad subject headings. Indexes are by author and subject.

960 **He pukaki Maori – Te Whare Tohu Tuhituhinga o Aotearoa: a guide to Maori sources at National Archives.**
National Archives of New Zealand. Wellington: National Archives/Te Puni Kokiri, 1995. 100p.

Produced with assistance from Te Puni Kokiri, the Ministry of Maori Development, this volume details sources held at the National Archives 'which contain significant amounts of Maori material or are seen to be useful sources of information when researching topics of Maori interest' (Introduction). Information is also provided on what to do before visiting National Archives in order to make the visit as productive as possible together with a brief description of the holdings of the National Archives and how these are accessed.

961 **National Archives of New Zealand: a cumulative list of holdings, 1976.**
Wellington: National Archives, 1977. 60p.

Although now grossly out of date, this small volume provides guidance to the major 19th-century holdings of the National Archives of New Zealand, and also to some 20th-century holdings. The primary entries are archives groups, arranged alphabetically, with major series listed under each group. Some of the substantial post-1976 accessions are listed irregularly in *Archifacts: Journal of the Archives and Records Association of New Zealand* (q.v.). Also of ongoing value are the *Preliminary inventories* produced by National Archives between 1953 and 1961. They describe in detail the following archival groups: Governor General (no. 1); New Zealand Company (no. 2); Army Department (no. 3); New Ulster, New Munster and the Civil Secretary's Office (no. 4); Provinces of Otago and Southland (no. 5); Provinces of Wellington and Hawke's Bay (no. 6); Provinces of Auckland and Taranaki (no. 7); Provinces of Nelson and Marlborough (no. 8); and Old Land Claims Commission (no. 9).

962 **New Zealand National Bibliography.**
National Library of New Zealand. Wellington: National Library of New Zealand, 1967- . monthly.

Issued monthly with annual cumulations, this is a comprehensive current listing of books, pamphlets, art prints, music scores, sound recordings, maps and new periodicals published in New Zealand or overseas dealing with New Zealand or written by New Zealand authors. It also includes a list of addresses for the publishers of the items. Since 1983 the annual cumulations have been produced on microfiche. On-line access is also available.

963 **National register of archives and manuscripts in New Zealand.**
Wellington: Alexander Turnbull Library; National Archives, 1977-93.
An essential aid for historical research, this work is compiled in a loose-leaf format from sheets prepared by repositories throughout New Zealand: all manuscript and archival collections were eligible for inclusion. Names, types of records, dates, quantity, location, description, access conditions, subjects and places mentioned in the collections are given. Publication was suspended in 1993, but in 1997 a project was set up to investigate the creation of an electronic database.

964 **New Zealand Books In Print, Including Books Published In The Pacific Islands.**
Wellington; Melbourne: D. W. Thorpe, 1979- . annual.
Includes New Zealand book trade information, listings of books by author and title, series of books, overseas publications with New Zealand agents and distributors and representatives for New Zealand publications.

965 **Periodicals in print: Australia, New Zealand and South Pacific.**
Toowong, Queensland: ISA Australia, 1997. 14th ed. 844p.
The entries are derived from the database of the subscription agent ISA Australia which is regarded as holding the most comprehensive and up-to-date information on regional periodicals available in Australia. The volume contains over 14,000 entries, of which 16 per cent are based in New Zealand. It is divided into five sections: an alphabetical listing of titles; ceased titles; publishers' names and addresses, and titles for each publisher; subject classification; and ISSN listing.

966 **Victoria's furthest daughters: a bibliography of published sources for the study of women in New Zealand, 1830-1914.**
Patricia A. Sargison.   Wellington: Alexander Turnbull Library Endowment Trust/New Zealand Founders Society, 1984. 107p.
'The bibliography lists printed works (other than newspaper articles) and theses concerning women and their activities in New Zealand during the pioneer period of European settlement, published up to the end of 1982' (Introduction). While the author has tried to be comprehensive for sections dealing with the earlier periods ('The voyage out', 'The new land: diaries, journals and reminiscences', 'Secondary accounts of pioneer women'), in other sections only a general indication of the available material is provided. Indexes are arranged by subject, author, and title.

967 **A bibliography of publications on the New Zealand Maori and the Moriori of the Chatham Islands.**
Edited by C. R. H. Taylor.   Oxford: Clarendon Press, 1972. 161p. bibliog.
The standard bibliography of books, pamphlets, periodical articles and selected government papers relating to the New Zealand Maori up to the late 1960s. Items are listed in sections under the forty subject headings, twenty-six of which were first used in *A Pacific bibliography* (Oxford: Clarendon Press, 1965. 2nd ed. 692p. First published, Wellington: Polynesian Society, 1951). Additional subject headings include: 'Race relations', 'Modified Maori life', 'Sports controversy', 'Economic and social aspects' and 'Rock carvings and paintings'.

968 **Ethnic groups in New Zealand: a bibliography. An annotated bibliography of New Zealand material of particular interest to the ethnic sector.**
Barbara Thomson. Wellington: Policy and Planning Unit, Department of Internal Affairs, 1993. 73p. (Research Series no. 19 Policy Research Section, Policy and Planning Unit, Department of Internal Affairs).

'Provides information about books, research reports, theses and journal articles published or available in New Zealand and dealing with ethnic heritage, ethnic communities, ethnic services and policy issues that are important for these minority ethnic groups' (Introduction). Notes on the 260 books and reports and 80 journal articles included give some idea of the type of publication and the content. The author does not claim to provide a comprehensive listing and has concentrated on material from the 1980s and 1990s.

969 **New Zealand studies: a guide to bibliographic resources.**
J. E. Traue. Wellington: Victoria University Press, for Stout Research Centre, 1985. 26p.

Recognizing that the published sources of information are not always enough in New Zealand, the author seeks to 'travel the private roads – the unpublished catalogues in card indexes in the major research collections – and make substantial use of the byways, the cart tracks, bush roads and walking tracks of bibliography' (Introduction). In this essay he suggests avenues to the intending researcher which will take them beyond the obvious, into sometimes uncharted, territory. Thirteen chapters approach the adventure by themes: printed matter, theses, general guides, manuscripts, music, film, maps and visual images. The conclusion sounds a note of caution to those who come from a book-based research culture.

970 **Union list of theses of the University of New Zealand, 1910-1954.**
Wellington: New Zealand Library Association, 1956. bibliog.

This original work has been regularly supplemented by the *Union list of higher degree theses of the universities of New Zealand*, published by the New Zealand Library Association until 1993. The latest supplement is to be published by the University of Otago, Dunedin. Each supplement lists successful doctoral and master's theses presented to New Zealand universities in the years since the last supplement as reported by co-operating libraries up to September of the year of publication. They also include any reportings of earlier theses not previously listed and New Zealand holdings of higher degree theses relating to New Zealand and the Pacific presented to overseas universities. All volumes indicate the location of theses when known.

971 **A select bibliography of the business history of New Zealand.**
Simon Ville. Auckland: Centre for Business History, Department of Economics, University of Auckland, 1993. 43p.

Published books, journal articles, pamphlets and graduate theses are included in the 1,000 entries. Many of the listings are slight works, reflecting the underdeveloped state of the discipline in New Zealand. The bibliography is thematically subdivided into: general works and source material; the primary, secondary and tertiary sectors; and state involvement, industrial groups and business biographies. 'The aim has been to provide a valuable resource for those studying or researching into the business history of New Zealand' (Introduction).

972 **Studying New Zealand history.**
G. A. Wood, revised by G. A. Wood, Simon Cauchi.   Dunedin:
University of Otago Press, 1992. 2nd ed. 145p.
A guide to how to find and use primary and secondary reference sources for the study of New Zealand political, social and cultural history. It does not describe the sources but explains how to find them. The information is presented thematically, divided into: libraries and archives; preliminary reading; bibliographies; printed reference works; periodicals; theses and research in progress; and primary sources.

Indexes

There follow three separate indexes: authors (personal and corporate); titles; and subjects. The numbers refer to bibliographic entry rather than page number. Title entries are italicized.

Index of Authors

A

Abel, S. 919
Acland, L. G. D. 171
Adkin, G. L. 203
Adsett, S. 766
Adshead, J. 811
Aimer, P. 434
Akenson, D. H. 271
Akoorie, M. 525
Aldridge, G. F. 565
Allan, H. H. 65
Allan, J. 345
Allan, R. M. 162
Allen, J. 736
Allison, K. W. 66
Alpers, A. 222, 782
Anderson, A. 85, 195
Anderson, A. G. 648
Andrews, J. R. H. 59
Angus, J. H. 176, 546
Archie, C. 333
Armstrong, A. 778
Arnold, R. 112, 122
Ashford, J. 784
Ashton, B. 756
Ashton, T. 380
Atkinson, J. D. 687
Ayling, T. 74

B

Bagnall, A. G. 152, 949
Baker, J. V. T. 130

Ballara, A. 351
Ballard, K. 375
Barber, L. H. 137-38
Barlow, C. 327
Barnett, J. 721
Barnett, S. 794, 806
Barrow, T. 767
Barrowman, F. 713
Barrowman, R. 843
Barry, J. M. 585-86
Bartlett, R. V. 638
Barton, R. A. 547
Bassett, M. 223-24
Bates, A. P. 153
Bauer, W. 410
Baxt, R. 526
Beaglehole, A. 272
Beaglehole, J. C. 93-94, 686
Beardsley, E. T. 686
Beatson, David 47
Beatson, Dianne 724
Beatson, P. 724
Beattie, J. H. 195
Becht, R. 812-13, 819
Beeby, C. E. 661
Beever, J. 66
Begg, A. C. 181
Begg, N. C. 181
Belgrave, M. 366
Belich, J. 97, 113
Bell, A. 415
Bell, B. 558
Bell, D. 813

Bell, L. G. 692
Bell, Leonard 725
Bellamy, A. C. 140
Belliss, P. 814
Bender, H. 273
Bennett, D. 680
Benseman, J. 676
Bercovitch, J. 488
Berg, P. 575
Best, E. 196, 204
Best, J. 952
Bhana, M. 830
Bieringa, J. 765
Biggs, B. 197, 207, 404
Binney, J. 213-14
Birchfield, R. 572
Birks, S. 498
Bisman, R. 840
Blair, I. D. 677
Blank, R. H. 382
Bloomfield, G. T. 632
Blumhardt, D. 737
Blythe, M. J. 763
Boast, R. 459
Bohan, E. 225
Bollard, A. 311, 472, 499-500, 508, 522, 524, 540, 543
Bollard, E. G. 688
Bollinger, C. 622
Bornholdt, J. 714
Boston, J. 338, 390, 425, 430, 469-70, 609
Bowden, R. J. 510

Index of Titles

318

322

Index of Subjects

Maps of New Zealand

ALSO FROM CLIO PRESS

INTERNATIONAL ORGANIZATIONS SERIES

Each volume in the International Organizations Series is either devoted to one specific organization, or to a number of different organizations operating in a particular region, or engaged in a specific field of activity. The scope of the series is wide-ranging and includes intergovernmental organizations, international non-governmental organizations, and national bodies dealing with international issues. The series is aimed mainly at the English-speaker and each volume provides a selective, annotated, critical bibliography of the organization, or organizations, concerned. The bibliographies cover books, articles, pamphlets, directories, databases and theses and, wherever possible, attention is focused on material about the organizations rather than on the organizations' own publications. Notwithstanding this, the most important official publications, and guides to those publications, will be included. The views expressed in individual volumes, however, are not necessarily those of the publishers.

VOLUMES IN THE SERIES